Imitation as Resistance

Imitation as Resistance

Appropriations of English Literature in Nineteenth-Century America

Raoul Granqvist

Madison ● Teaneck
Fairleigh Dickinson University Press
London: Associated University Presses

Associated University Presses
440 Forsgate Drive
Cranbury, NJ 08512

Associated University Presses
25 Sicilian Avenue
London WC1A 2QH, England

Associated University Presses
P.O. Box 338, Port Credit
Mississauga, Ontario
Canada L5G 4L8

The paper used in this publication meets the requirements
of the American National Standard for Permanence of Paper
for Printed Library Materials Z39.48-1984.

Library of Congress Cataloging-in-Publication Data

Granqvist, Raoul, 1940–
    Imitation as resistance : appropriations of English literature in
nineteenth-century America / Raoul Granqvist.
        p.   cm.
    Includes bibliographical references and index.
    ISBN 0-8386-3639-X
    1. English literature—Appreciation—United States.   2. United
States—Civilization—British influences.   3. United States—
Civilization—19th century.   4. American literature—English
influences.   5. Imitation in literature.   I. Title.
PR129.U5G68   1995
820.9—dc20
                                                                    95-2618
                                                                    CIP

To my mother
the memory of my father
and
Johanna and Tina

Contents

Preface

The material I examine in this book is admittedly heterogeneous, including as it does poems, prose satires, novels, elocutionary handbooks, and theater performances. Some readers may call the treatment of these genres desultory, since admittedly each of these genres deserves its own unique treatment, its own book; but as my focus is on an examination of nineteenth-century cultural changes and acculturalization processes, on their periodization and regionalization, and the mode and nature of the expressions they adopted, I have found it extremely challenging to move across, not only a broad range of time (the whole of the nineteenth century) and place (East, South, and West), but also a broad spectrum of literary-rhetorical discourses.

My approach to the research subject can best be described as triangular. One of the bases is the particular matter that is being appropriated, the "sum" of the British writer and her/his work; I use the word *code* to denote this complexity. The code is understood, then, as an extended formula that incorporates many tangential factors, including the work's production history, the literary norms attached to it, and the connotations containing the writer. Thus, an American imitation of Byron's *Don Juan* may incorporate a multiplicity of strands, some of which are only peripheral in the actual poem. It is the codified system inherent in *Don Juan* that is transformed and acculturalized in an American imitation for an American audience, rather than the verbatim poem.

Another base of the triangle consists of the American reciprocal work. Again, I will be using the totality of the referential system suggested by the individual work, such as prefaces, commentaries, and other circumstantial details. The motives of the American writer for his/her imitation is an additional useful factor that conforms to the existing cultural and readerly expectations. It is through an understanding of the expectations of the literary culture on its immediate or local level that the full implications of the text's resistance or cooperation can be discerned.

The third base of the triangle is the American reader. It is alleged that no appropriation or imitation can be successful without the negotiation of a reader who can interpret the literary langue that defines the context of the lateral texts. This third base presupposes an interpretation of the readerly cultural and colonial ramifications, of which the literary langue and its realizations (allusions, references) are subordinated expressions. As decolonization was slow and moved across the continent at varying pace, the reactions of the recipients to the values and impacts of the literary projects were both ambiguous and hesitant. These ambiguities are inherent in the transferred works. They reflect a society uncertain about its inner values and morals, yet triumphantly clear about its future place in the world community as the first republic governed by true democratic principles.

This ambiguity underlies the imitations of the British writers. These writers and the sombre worldview they were seen to uphold represented an antipode against which the New World stood out in a clearer and healthier light. This contrast thus produced largely governs the perceptions of American literary culture in the nineteenth century.

A limited number of British writers—Shakespeare, Byron, Scott, Dickens, and to a lesser degree Milton,Tennyson, and a few others—form the inner circle whose transatlantic "popular" pilgrimage I trace and follow with some consistency. The book then offers American perspectives on the individual reputation of a number of British writers and their specific works, often down to the particular lines in plays and poems. Although tangential and adducive to the main theses of the book I have refrained from using all the references gathered in the footnotes, the bibliographies, the appendices, and so on—and not only for very obvious practical reasons. I have retained them in this undigested form partly in protest against the stream-lining and reductionism of much academic reasoning, partly to provoke and stimulate the reader to discover additional and alternative ways to use the book. And if this information provides sustenance to question, extend, and contradict even this writer's own assumptions, so much the better! Also, the reader whose interest is limited, say, to the singular reputation of a Dickens novel, or a Byron poem, may find the book functional for its bibliographical qualities.

In Chapter 1 I present the theoretical frame of my work, premising that imitation—viewed historically—involved acts of creative resistance and inversion; I give an outline the reputations of the most important British writers in the country, and survey the reseach in this field. In Chapter 2, I study the mechanisms of imitation (I call them integration, emulation, and documentary) mainly as they have come down in lesser-known American poetry and prose (the term "lesser-known" would in fact apply to all of my material!). In Chapter 3, I deal with elocutionary handbooks, a genre that in its nineteenth-century formula was highly inclusive, spanning literature, theater, music, and of course the disciplines of rhetoric and phonetics, and thus extremely appropriate for this kind of study. A corresponding bibliographical listing of sources, titles, and genres is appended. The Appendix also includes Dion Boucicault's adaptation of Walter Scott's *The Heart of Midlothian,* called "Jeanie Deans; or, The Heart of Midlothian"—published for the first time. Chapter 4 is devoted to theater, a subject that has been treated with little respect by many generations of literary historians. Naturally, nineteenth-century theater, still very much anchored—happily I would say—in an oral-popular phase, is a rewarding arena for a cross-cultural study such as this one; in it meet and compete the local (regional) and the universal (Old World) in endless improvisations and dramatizations—of the novels Dickens and Scott, of poems and closet plays of Byron. The book will then demonstrate the complexity of cultural appropriation, as well as its vector of resistance and harmonization. Thus, the theme of cultural resistance, in the sense of advocating and practicing alternative and deviating expression, runs through my discussion from beginning to end.

It needs to be emphasized that the American works I have chosen for treatment are laid in an American literature tradition that a majority of Americanists would qualify as "popular," "secondary," or even "redundant" (for this reason I do not discuss, say, Thomas Carlyle). In the sense of being broadly read, appreciated, and widely diffused, the texts that I will consider were, indeed, "popular" throughout the nineteenth century. They are works immersed in and characterized by a rich flow of cultural transformations, and, hence, most appropriate for the kind of study I am undertaking. The unconventional, genre-disparaging, and eclectic approach that I have adopted for the book is in fact necessary, I suggest, if one wants to do justice to and appreciate a culture as volatile and expansive as that of nineteenth-century America, as well as to understand its struggle for cultural independence.

Acknowledgments

It all started—as it should have—in New England in 1983. While preparing a chapter on the reputation of John Donne in Boston in the 1890s, Joel Porte, then professor of English at Harvard University, suggested to me that I should consider extending my inquiries into a few other American nineteenth-century "reputations" of individual British writers to see whether there were "linkages" between them that could explain the overall importance of English literature in this century. This challenging idea stayed with me for some time, and by 1987, thanks to very generous funding by the Swedish Council for Research in the Humanities and Social Sciences, I could embark on the project that by this time had moved from the category of a writer-oriented analysis to the larger domain of a cross-cultural and postcolonial study of the American appropriations. A number of very good people have been instrumental in the progress of my research and the completion of my book, and I would herewith like to thank them all for their support and encouragement: Joel Porte (Cornell University) for directing me in the first place to the research field; Sacvan Berkovitch (Harvard University) for pointing out to me the potentialities inherent in American theater for this kind of examination, and for his general interest in my work; Jerome McGann (University of Virginia) for his progressive ideas about the value of the "footnote" and the multiple reference in scholarly and methodological presentation; Lawrence W. Levine (University of California, Berkeley) for his contributions to the postcolonial positioning of my work; and to a number of other scholars, including Carl F. Hovde (Columbia University) and Hugh Egan (Ithaca College), who took time to discuss, and also read early chapters of my work. Many thanks go to the faculties of the English departments of both Harvard University and the University of California, Berkeley, who generously assisted me both collectively and as individual members (and not only with scholarly matters!) during my two research visits to the United States, as well as the staffs of the university library of Harvard and that of the University of California, Berkeley. I am particularly thankful for the assistance provided me by the Harvard Theatre Collection. Without the expert help of these individuals and organizations the work for this book could never have been contemplated, still less completed.

13

I also wish to thank Nancy Richey (Austin) for reading and correcting the work and Deborah Homsher (Ithaca College) for transcribing the play by Dion Boucicault. Finally, I wish to thank all my American friends who in one way or another have supported me—from offering me a place to sleep to advising me on style and lexicon; they include Eugene Green (Brookline), Bruce Lowen (Cambridge), Susanna Kaysen (Cambridge), and Lars Nylander (Berkeley).

The publication of this volume has been supported by the Swedish Council for Research in the Humanities and Social Sciences.

Imitation as Resistance

1

Imitation as Resistance

Imitation and Nineteenth-Century American Culture

In its endeavor to establish its own cultural boundaries, its own space, nineteenth-century America sought frantically to free itself from dependence on Old World value systems and worldviews and from its historical bonds with England. At the same time—and here lies the paradox—it sought and found fresh nourishment in the same Old World gardens it supposedly despised. It is fascinating to follow this drama. It involves all the familiar antithetical elements of the decolonizing process, such as self-denial and self-aggrandizement. It involves class struggle and tensions between popular culture and elitist culture. It tells the story of a world power in formation, but it also provides insight into the process of change that cultural attitudes and institutions were undergoing. This last aspect will be the main focus of this book.

The United States was a heterogeneous country, despite the balancing and leveling factor of the flow of immigrants, all of whom came from backgrounds equally poverty-stricken and barren of opportunity. The cultural differences established over the years between New England, the South, and the West, were not much as much altered as one would have thought by the immigration movement. What it did create was a society susceptible to change and vulnerable to influence, a society easily persuaded, for better and worse, because it lacked permanence and stability.

An emergent culture such as that of nineteenth-century America adopts and adapts. The outside and the inside, the alien and the domestic, interact, not always without agony and strife. This can be a neutralizing or a leveling process; it normally presupposes and requires different forms of appropriation. In other words, cultures, however antithetical, appropriate and incorporate basically what they need and leave the rest. Without this neutralizing factor cultures would stagnate, collapse, or be annihilated by a stronger and more receptive candidate. However, this seldom happens. Cultures merge, even if they are politically unequal or alien to each other's values.

The centripetal forces that contain this cultural competition as a rule impel it toward a centrality of significance, while a centrifugal countermovement seeks to dilute and dissolve the unifying force, splitting it into eddies and side currents. This image can be applied to the cultural map of nineteenth-century America. It helps to point out some of the paradoxes and contradictions that are characteristic of the period.

One of the most complex issues in any colonial or postcolonial structure is, then, the question of imitation. It defines the very fiber of the relationship of the dominant culture and the Other. Traditionally, the concept of imitation in a colonial context refers to a situation where a culture in formation seeks to formulate a competitive discourse based on principles inherited from the dominant one. It is a term that underpins such qualities as servility, dependence, and self-negation. It is often believed to underscore the alleged discrepancies of development (civilization) and progress that inhere in the two systems, suggesting that the "inferior" should continuously be trying to "catch up." The negative concept of course still prevails. Imitation in this sense falls short, however, of explaining the elements of appropriation and revolt that inform cultural transactions. It is this aspect of imitation as a counterdiscourse that is the main subject of this book.

Nineteenth-century America was deeply engaged in, as well as embarrassed and stimulated by, imitation. It was far from unique in this respect. Most colonial and neocolonial societies are engrossed with it. However, imitation is an activity that no society can avoid. On the basis of imitation of artifacts and ideas we sustain our memory, enliven our traditions, embody our history. In most cases it also has formidable effects. Imitation fosters hierarchies: the weak and the strong are in unequal communication. Imitation is a cultural operation often derided and ridiculed; it can be compared to stealing; it is often seen to be the near-synonym of plagiarism.

While societies that take recourse to imitation are seen by implication as culturally dependent, underdeveloped, primitive, and uncivilized, only that, we need to remember, absent imitations and works like James Joyce's *Ulysses* and Shakespeare's dramas would hardly have seen the light of the day. Nineteenth-century America held strong, if not clear, opinions about this phenomenon, and sought in no way to escape its often allegedly embarrassing delimitations and provocative demands. "The transmission of Old World culture to America (or of Eastern culture to the West) involves a marked attenuation of style," is Albert J. von Frank's dismissive judgment; "the relative flatness or thinness of the transmitted culture becomes, in turn, a source of vague shame, a hint, often only perceived, of an encroaching grossness, and a verification, certainly, of the radical separateness of provincial life."[1] A statement like this, blind to the complexities of the American public/popular culture, does not heed the energy, creativity, and consciousness that went into its expressions and its various subspecies of literary activity, the parody, the burlesque, the satire, and so on—and above all to the resistance it was formulating by its manner of speaking.

Imitation as cultural dialectics, and in the manner I will be using the term in this book, lies, then, at the heart of every colonial or postcolonial society that seeks to find a way out of years of dependence and raise its own national monuments. It permeates cultural conflicts, particularly those in the parts of the world where local cultures are repressed or rejected. Yet, I believe, that nineteenth-century colonial and postcolonial America, in contrast to other similar emergent societies, constitutes a special case, mainly because the historical parallels and linguistic uniformities that connect the "two" transatlantic cultures formed a basis for the mistrust or the admiration that reciprocity can create.

It follows, then, that my understanding of "imitation" is hardly shared by a majority of American literary scholars who define the literary activities of this kind as "redundant" or at best "popular" (a negative term). A representative outlook is offered by Bernard Smith in *Forces in American Criticism: A Study in the History of American Literary Thought*. He writes about the interaction of American writing and English in the following derogatory manner:

> Not only were the ancient classics and the recent English classicists adored for their own sake, revered with an almost religious fanaticism, but they were also upheld as irreproachable and imperishable models of literary eloquence, which no sane person should want, let alone try, to amend or modify, and writers were commended to go only to them for advice on style, philosophy, and the propriety of emotions. . . . It put a premium on fear and cautiousness, legitimated imitation, and discouraged those qualities—imagination, adventurousness, and a sense of freedom— which were necessary to the rise of an original art.[2]

This point of view is both untenable and erroneous. The American writers, playwrights, and essayists who transliterated the English "classicists" or used them to satisfy the local needs and the social requirements of their time were far from cowardly and servile. They knew extremely well what they were doing: they were reflecting on these issues on a daily basis. They may be said to have listened to the advice of Patrick A. Halpin who told his readers and students: "Make what you take, your own; remember the jay in the peacock's feathers, the ass in the lion's skin; the deceit will always be discovered, the long ears will always peep through."[3] And, as we will see in the following, "the long ears" without any perceivable cover or ornamentation were always laughed at.

An equally misdirected assumption is that the American writers either reacted against the alien "influence" or gravitated toward it.[4] Of course, they did both. Imitation, despite common belief, does not function as the antithesis of originality; it does not materialize without permitting and stimulating reciprocity on many levels. Thus, like an African mask, it makes sense only within the framework of "local" action or performance, which engages simultaneously the observer and the mask itself. The American "imitation" of Lord Byron's *Childe Harold* was a multifaceted artifact that embedded both the "local" and the "faraway." As an imitation it was original.

Russell Blaine Nye's comment on the interdependence of American literary activity up to the 1830s is another culturally hostile description, worth noting in this context. He states that it is "in large part derivative," "moralistic," "increasingly nationalistic," "consciously committed to the use of native materials and the expression of native attributes," and "ridden by a colonial prejudice." He gives reasons for the American propensity to look eastward for inspiration. I would like to quote the whole passage as it is central in our discussion of the American cultural scene of the early nineteenth century:

> Few American artists attempted to create a literature for its own values. In effect, they were trying to create a new, native, independent literature within the framework of an older, colonial, British, basically neo-classic tradition. What Americans wanted was their own Augustan age, built out of American materials and attitudes comfortably couched in the approved, time-tested literary forms that could be accepted with confidence and safety.[5]

It is only that the forms and structures that were imitated or borrowed quite often clashed, or were made to clash, with the themes and forms Nye believes they were supposed to carry forth. He, and many with him, refuse to consider the interconnections of the larger cultural spectrum in which an "imitation" was to operate. The dominant viewpoints varied, then, from accusing England of a colonial oppression that suffocated all domestic initiatives in the literary scene, to derogating all American cultural productions as imitative and base. The two viewpoints were seen to be diametrical and complementary. Solyman Brown's diatribes against the influence of the Old World on American writing have the ring of the anxiety and frustration all first-generation colonial writers have felt (and still feel). England, he proposes, has launched America into "literary thraldom,"[6] and he continues:

It is thus [England] has subjugated Scotland and Ireland, and used all her efforts to smother, in its cradle, the rising genius of both these countries. It has ever been the policy and practice of England, to decry Scotch and Irish intellect, and affects a sovereign contempt for all that are born on . . . the Liffey . . . excite in the minds of the people of this country a prejudice against the literary works of their compatriots. (8–9)

Another garrulous view, but from an altogether different perspective, is provided by one of the many correspondents of William Gilmore Simms. The letter was written in 1841. The writer makes the same point about American servility toward their "masters" that Nye was to echo over a hundred years later:

Among our thousand poets and our hundred romancers, there is not one upon whose performances you may not place your hand with ease, and say,—"This is after Milton;" "this, after Scott;" . . . You will look in vain for any thing half so daring as "The Ancient Mariner" of Coleridge. . . . All is imitative—coldly correct, baldly imitative! Yet this servility is scarcely the fault of the poets themselves;—it may be in part: . . . but who will pretend to say that it is not in the people:—in the base habit in which we have begun, which make us turn our eyes as with an inevitable instinct to a foreign land, to know at what moment to applaud, and where! This servility is chiefly maintained by our journalists. Their criticism, the most sorry, slavish and inconclusive of all kinds of criticism—is generally comparative.[7]

However, the full implications of this "comparative" criticism so much practiced was not really understood; consequently, the interpretation of the statement "This is after Milton" is one-sided and contradictory. But one must add: it is this "blindness" that keeps discussions about American culture alive and active.

The impact of English writing on the American cultural scene was, then, discussed right from the beginning of the century. The questions asked were, Was the emergent New World writing—labeled imitative—an inherent part of English literature, a variant outgrowth in the same garden, or an outside and strange weed to be cleansed to create room for the real, native genius to blossom? (We saw how this question pained Simms's correspondent.) Could English writing be integrated with American without impeding the American (democratic!) (r)evolution? What did imitation of Old World writers and genres really lead to, could it be pursued and developed without harming the native expression, if there was such? To what extent could, or should, more oblique forms of imitation (such as parody, satire) be encouraged? Similar questions, it is true, are asked by most generations of critics and writers in colonial or postcolonial societies.

What is at stake is the probing search of an epistemology for a new culture and a new nation.

The alliance that nineteenth-century America entertained with Great Britain, diachronically and synchronically, was a problematic one that seemed to encourage double standards among the many who spoke on the issue. The full critical range of an assessment such as "This is after Milton" was hard to stomach. William Crafts, for example, exclaimed:

> Milton is ours. Shakespeare is ours. Everything English is and shall be ours—except their political government and their agricultural distresses. . . . Our rights in the English literature and English arts cannot be taken from us, unless you cut our tongues. It is not a voyage across the Atlantic that is to disinherit us.[8]

But before touching the new soil, before being acknowledged, the British writers, it was proposed, had to be purged or cleansed of qualities that did not meet American standards. "We will not cavil," Crafts continued, "for Byron, who stains his soul with sin, and mingles blasphemy with genius, . . . nor Wordsworth, the poet of the nursery, . . . [nor] will we complain of . . . the interstices of Scotch in the Waverley Novels, which . . . is very much as if a gentleman should cut ditches in his garden walk to try the agility of his company" (276–77). This may seem a contradictory approach, but it was not seen or treated as one. In fact, it represents the very complexity of the matter under investigation in this book. The appropriation of the Old World artifact was not a simple technical matter of receiving or rejecting; its operational rationale was as complex as its formulations were manifold.

It was often said that a nation like America could not produce literary work since, in the Englishman John Bristed's words, "nearly all the active talent in the nation is employed in prosecuting some commercial, or agricultural, or professional pursuit, instead of being devoted to the quieter and less lucrative labours of literature."[9] The implication from this quarter was that the American writers stood no real chance in competing, and therefore Scott, Byron, and, later on, Dickens could flood the country with their products, without little disrepute. The English writing consequently "depresses the spirit of the native literature, by creating a fastidious rage for foreign publications, and an affectation of contempt for the productions of our own press."[10] So if "Byron could no more be kept at bay, than the cholera,"[11] what else was there to do with him, the Americans seemed to think, but make use of him, imitate him, emulate him, transculturalize him. The other approach toward cultural self-determination was to try to erect monuments with little or no association with the Old World. In his illustrious article "On National Literature" (1830) William Ellery Channing said:

> The more we receive from other countries, the greater the need of an original literature. A people into whose minds the thoughts are poured perpetually, need an energy within itself to resist, to modify this mighty influence, and without it will inevitably sink under the worst bondage, will become intellectually tame and enslaved.[12]

Channing was miscalculating the resourcefulness of his people. Their energy did "modify the mighty influence," although perhaps not in the way Channing had envisioned. The foreign influx of books, plays, and other cultural materials and ideas, it was true, went on throughout the century without intermission. But the recipients of these books, the readers of British novels, the spectators in the theaters, and the listeners in the lyceums, were not "enslaved" by the imported goods; they turned the artifacts to good usage.

The American writer qualified as "American"—and Channing would have agreed—only if his subjects could be demarcated as native. This is the way John G. C. Brainard was introduced:

> Brainard has recommended himself to his countrymen, as a truly *American* poet. His topics, his imagery, his illustrations are mostly of native growth. There is a raciness about them which cannot be mistaken. . . . Most of the commonplace of poetry is avoided. The mountains, lakes, trees, animals,—the characters, pursuits, pastimes, and superstitions, which are touched by the pen of the bard are American. . . . He is more truly American, than some English bards are English. . . . Our native bard has made his mother tongue a better vehicle of American peculiarities, than the Englishman has of the characteristics of Old England.[13]

This passage may represent hundreds of similar bold declarations that harped on the same subject: the pressing need to produce American artifacts along these normative lines. Romances, plays, satirical poems, novels were also written that were seen as meeting such standards. It is only that they were also in one way or another prefigured and inscribed by other persuasions and traditions.

The prefaces to such works are revelatory of the nature of relationship the writer wished to project between his/her supposed model and his/her work. Often they come out as simply apologetic. "[I had] a desire," writes William Gilmore Simms in his preface to *Donna Florida,* an imitation of Byron's *Don Juan,* "to echo the strain which he [Simms as a young poet] hears, and emulate the sweet notes which have fastened themselves upon his senses. He fancied, with a boyish presumption, that he might imitate the grace and exceeding felicity of expression in that unhappy performance,—its playfulness, and, possibly, its wit,—without falling into its licentiousness of utterance, and malignity of mood."[14] It is a typical apology in several respects. Simms acknowledges frankly the origin of his imitation (almost boasts of it), but characterizes it as a *Lehrjahre* experience. Then he alienates himself from it (note his usage of the neutral pronoun "he") after having accounted for what his objectives were at the time and what he wanted to eschew. It is obvious that for Simms his work *Donna Florida* was supposed to stand clear of *Don Juan's* precedence by cooperating and competing with it through adhering to American values and morals. The reader was intended to recognize the simultaneous presence of the two poems. Byron is both his tool and his model. When I. S. Clason named Fitz-Greene Halleck an American "Byron" and dedicated to him the following lines, it is done with the hope that "the block you work on is your own":

> You've found the silver nib of Byron's pen,
> Prove that its iron stem can plough again.
> The last touch of the chisel you have shown;
> Prove that the block you work on is your own.[15]

One should be very suspicious of any commentator who claims, à propos the literary situation in antebellum America, that "Byron is scarcely heard of. Wordsworth lies at the heart of the people,"[16] as both observations are false—in fact it was the reverse. Yet Harriet Martineau's other comment that "America has yet no creation, either in literature or the arts, and cannot even distinguish a creation from a combination, imitation, or delineation" (208) sums up very well the metropolitan and British view of American cultural production in the nineteenth century. Unfortunately, the view has persisted to our own day.

On the rhetorical and semantic level, imitation, as an overall generic term, can be described as either an act of emulation or an allusion. Gian Biago Conté, to whom I am largely indebted for the gist of the following discussion, defines these two activities as one depending on the degrees of "visibility." Emulation stands in direct contrastive or competitive relationship with the original; allusion, on the other hand, creates a poetic dimension out of the two, involving "the simultaneous presence of two different realities whose competition with one another produces a single more complex reality."[17] The latter phenomenon would produce a text whose inherited components are rendered invisible to the eye of the reader (but still, for the erudite reader, tangible), whereas in the former the two components stand out for readers to compare and "see." Allusion and emulation are not identical: emulation cannot exist without allusion, allusion can do without emulation.

Contë also clarifies another important point, however self-evident. "Allusion must be recognized not only in its relation to culture but also as an integral part of a literary system."[18] Since every literary system, convention, or tradition is already inscribed by the culture in which it has developed, his observation is not of much help. Yet, it points out the vital relationship—and pointing out this is quite necessary—between the literary system and the cultural structure, or to use the term of the cultural anthropologist Victor V. Turner, *cultural drama*.[19]

Imitation, I suggest, must also be seen in this broad perspective, as a paradox that seeks, simultaneously, to harmonize values and standpoints *and* to create a gap between them. It is a social and cultural drama where the protagonists involved provoke each other, tear each other apart, seek solutions, alienate themselves from each other, and occasionally adjust themselves and accept solutions and compromises. It is drama of appropriation where the recipient culture is the active one, but often compelled to operate by rules set by the "donor" culture. The usage of the concept of imitation in this book reflects, then, both a narrow rhetorical aspect of the correspondences between two literary texts and systems, and a broader view of one (the American) culture seeking to adjust and re-form itself via another. Through its rendering of the dialogical mode of imitation, the book treats then the problematic issues of the American decolonizing process—or, in fact, any decolonizing process where the powerful has to be eaten before new food can be found.

The Popularity of British Writers in North America

Like all colonial encounters, the one between North America and England was aggressive, far-reaching, and overwhelmingly complex. The new residents of North America were from the start, and continued to be so throughout the period of my investigation, not a homogenous group of people. They ranged from the extremely poor to the incredibly wealthy (with the first group in a clear majority), from illiterates to literates, from English speakers to non-English speakers. To a large extent the cultural landscape we are surveying was lacking in unity and compatibility. However, its people—from the self-conscious and highly "cultural" *literati* of New England, to the gruff New York theatergoers, and the young, mostly male, students of elocutionary handbooks—had at least one thing in common: they were proud of the society they were building and anxious to raise its monuments and sing its praises.

In this they show remarkable similarities with other aspiring ex-colonial societies. The West African nations that were liberated from direct colonial rule in the early 1960s, for example, took great pains in giving culture and education a prominent role in nation building. Writers and politicians (often in the same person) formed belligerent cultural fronts, and within a few years hundreds of books, novels, dramas, and anthologies, poured out of the region. Despite the fact that they were written in the former colonial languages and in most cases were published in the metropolitan centers, situating themselves, then, in a double way, outside the reach of the same people whose stories they were narrating, these texts must be seen as important decolonizing props.

The similarities to the situation in nineteenth-century America should perhaps not be overemphasized, yet they are there. Like the West African writers of the sixties, the American writers, a Hawthorne, a Melville, a Bryant, were fighting uneven struggles against the domination of English culture that denied them easy access to popularity. And like the West African writers, their American counterparts have always been accused of servility toward the literary models of the Old World.

Constance Rourke has this to say about the depreciation of nineteenth-century American culture arising from the assumption of its servile dependence on England:

> The result has been that the main approach to our culture has been the segmented literary approach with major efforts going toward the attempt to trace relationships between American literature and English literature, and in a minor fashion between the other arts in America and the British or European arts. Our historical studies are ridden by such efforts . . . which prove nothing at all as to the underlying forces. No civilisation has sprung full-blown into existence without ancestry. No society has been free from alien or antecedent influences. . . .[20]

To imitate Old World artifacts became a legitimate manner of recapturing structures that were needed to fall back upon. To imitate a poem by Byron was one way of reintroducing the known into the unknown, of reasserting oneself in an alien surrounding. But the imitation, that is, the transformation of the well-known item A into a new recognizable, or nonrecognizable, item B, would go hand in hand with the manifestation of change, and preferably, with harsh notions of defiance and protest.

The evidence is overwhelming. The popularity of the British writers in nineteenth-century America is unquestionable: it by far stripped that of their American counterparts. No contemporary American writer (to make another generalization) could match the single reputation of Byron, Scott, Dickens—not even Cooper and Irving. Byron, Scott, and Dickens were, indeed, the luminaries of the American readership for more than two generations. They were in fact more popular on the other side of the Atlantic than at home. Their productions and those of many other nineteenth-century British writers, such as Thomas Campbell, Thomas Moore, and later in the century, Alfred Tennyson, were American best-sellers in their day.

There were many reasons for their popularity. One was their accessibility. Novels by Scott and later Dickens were relatively cheap, due to the ubiquitous marketing of them. They could be found everywhere—in miners' huts and on scholars' tables, on the eastern seaboard, as well as in the West. They were reviewed, pirated, and parodied. They provided a background of common allusion, were variously dramatized on the Western stage, and lent their names to steamers plying the rivers: "Lady of the Lake," "Ellen Douglas," "Marmion," "Corsair," "Mazeppa," "Medona."[21] Dickens's novels were made into melodramas or burlesques, of which there were as many variants as there were regional theaters that produced them. The murder of Nancy Sykes in *Oliver Twist* (to give an example) became one of the most familiar scenes on the nineteenth-century American stage. Obviously it responded to specific needs then latent in the society (of which more later).[22] Scott's and Byron's novels and poems were received with an enthusiasm that is difficult to understand today.

The South especially adored Byron and Scott. "*Marmion, Ivanhoe* and the *Heart of Midlothian* [were] common intellectual property in all parts of the South," as they, William E. Dodd believed, "stirred Southern men to think of themselves as proud knights ready to do or die for some romantic ideal."[23] The dream world of feudalism and the pageantry of chivalry fascinated the plantation owners; and in Scott and Byron there were plenty of reminiscences and parallels to evoke this sensibility. Furthermore, Byron's literary conservatism grounded his reputation in the South. No public library, no private bookshelf was devoid of his books, no daily newspaper gossiper, no single well-informed citizen did not boast familiarity with some of his poems and aspects of his life.[24] Scott and Byron had also admirers in other parts of the United States, but their influence lasted much longer in the South.

We are told that publishers literally raced to procure the early copies of the British writers. All kinds of tricks were used, even to bribing the compositors in London printing offices to steal uncorrected galleys and smuggle them across the Atlantic or to hiring American spies or shorthand writers to go to the first nights of important plays in order to copy them.[25] And having procured them, they were printed with amazingly speed. James C. Derby tells how Carey & Lee in 1823 procured an advance copy of Byron's *Don Juan,* and wasting no time by cutting the leaves, sent it to the various printing houses in Philadelphia, where thirty or forty compositors worked on it. Within thirty-six hours an American edition was on sale in the bookstores.[26] *Manfred* was received, printed and published all in one single day.[27] No wonder that between 1811 and 1830 forty-eight editions of Byron's works were printed in the United States.[28]

The publishers turned out Scott's novels at the same feverish speed. His *Quentin Durward,* for instance, was printed in twenty-eight hours.[29] In 1830 there were at least ten printing offices in Philadelphia which did little more than reprint his novels and there were perhaps as many in New York.[30] Other statistics demonstrate that five million copies of his novels came out of the American presses between 1813 and 1823.[31] Commenting on the stealing and disseminating of the bard's texts, Frank Luther Mott states: "Ironically enough, this piratical publishing did much, through its wide and cheap distribution of the Waverly novels, to make Scott beloved in the new world by robbing him of proper American returns for his genius."[32] The same could be said for Dickens. His *American Notes,* despite its disparaging remarks on the South, sold 50,000–60,000 copies by the end of the week of its publication in 1842. It long remained one of the most popular books with the American readers.[33]

Dickens, well known as a champion for an international acceptance of rules regulating the ownership of literary texts, was at the beginning of his career quite generous about the ownership of his books in the United States. In a famous letter to his American publisher Carey & Co., in 1837, he claimed that he was quite content with receiving a *copy* of the American edition of *The Pickwick Papers,* as a "sufficient acknowledgement of the American sale."[34] His attitude and tone were to change dramatically toward the end of his career, but his early view can be said to be the prevailing one throughout the century at least with the publishers, and of course with the reading public, the great winners. Hellmut Lehmann-Haupt states that "the free reprinting of English books in this century was a tremendous service to a people craving cultural enlightenment."[35] It is important to remember this aspect of the American book production in the nineteenth century.

More or less the same stories could be told about the other British writers. It is understandable then that the libraries and the booksellers' shops were filled with English or foreign works. For anyone

browsing through bookstores and libraries in Africa, this sight is even
today all too familiar: the bulk of the available books are British- or
French-made or in English or French.

Books and plays by European writers were then handled as com-
modities which, on arriving in the New World, automatically became
every man's possessions. Curtailing, cutting, revising, piracy in all
its forms, the free price setting—as well as all the modes of appropriation that form the main subject of this book—were integral parts of
the acculturational process. The copyright rule debate in the United
States in the midcentury centered not only on the ownership questions, but also on the prerogatives of imitation. The licence to "imitate" the well-established model, the Byronic sentiment or Scott's
verse form, also extended to reproducing their texts for an avid
American marketplace. The two were part of the same cultural
contract.

When cultural or literary historians—such as Frank Luther Mott,
James D. Hart, and Carl Bode—account for these circumstances they
place undue attention on the lack of copyright rules that permitted
the Americans to print and copy the English texts and disseminate
them without paying royalties to their makers. No doubt, this factor
created a competitive market that favored the sales of English books
and disfavored and discouraged domestic writing. But it does not
explain the full thrust of the popularity of the British writers. The
real reason for Scott's popularity with, say, the men and women on
the frontier is that they needed, and thus appropriated, him. They
were upholding the ties with the Old World, says Ray Charles Billington, in their attempts "to recognize the lusty young civilization
they were helping to create." But, he adds in a significant aside:
"[their] new culture [was] based on tradition, but significantly altered.
This transformation was predestined by the nature of the migration
process and by the demands of frontiering."[36]

As we have seen, one of the most cited statements about the impact
of English writing is that it fatally diminished the popularity of American writers. "From *Waverly* in 1814, to *The Mystery of Edwin Drood,*
1870, the year that did not produce one highly popular British novel
was a barren period. Against this continuous stream the American
novelist was compelled to wage a bitter struggle."[37] This statement,
by Earl L. Bradsher, does not hold. This "struggle" was not "against,"
it was "with." American literary culture, of which the writers were
only one part, must be seen as a complex composition of producers,
actors, and consumers. There is no simple formula linking the "alien"
text with its local recipient. Scott's novels were popular in both the
North and the South for a variety of reasons; his popularity was

not merely due to favorable publishing conditions or to any single component inherent in his text.

A Survey of Scholarship

Much has been written about the American reputation of the British writers in the nineteenth century. Strikingly, most of the articles, monographs, and sections in literary histories on this extremely important stage in the development of American literature were written during the early part of this century.[38] American nineteenth-century appropriations of the British writers are hardly mentioned by Americanists and American literary historians in their assessments of the cultural and literary scene of this century. Instead, it has become a subject for cultural historians and writers on popular culture, which is of course satisfactory.[39] However, to the extent that cultural history should receive more attention from the literary historians, it is even more imperative that the chroniclers of nineteenth-century American literature pay more attention to both the circumstances and the artifacts that the colonial encounters have yielded.

The following survey of the research done on this subject is not exhaustive. It suggests, however, the direction of the arguments put forward in this book, and demonstrates, by indirection, the vitality of the American appropriation of English literature. There are several works on Shakespeare's and Milton's reputations in nineteenth-century America; some of those on Shakespeare are recent ones.[40] Milton was a formidable presence in the first part of the century, mainly through the political and religious compatibility that were seen to exist between his views and those of liberal Americans.[41] Of the eighteenth-century writers, Alexander Pope alone had a secure place with the Americans, mainly due to his reputation as a rhetorician. Agnes Marie Sibley's work on Alexander Pope should be mentioned.[42]

On Byron's reception in the nineteenth-century America there is one full monograph and a number of articles, all of some date by now; what is more interesting is that all of them are condescendingly dismissive of the subject they profess to examine: the effect of Byron on American society. William Ellery Leonard's *Byron and Byronism in America* is the most thoroughgoing of these studies. It is detailed, humorous, and bombastic.[43] He retrieves echoes and parallels, he finds "similarities" in verse technique and rhythm between more than thirty American poets and their alleged mentor, and he identifies common grounds and common themes. He presents these discoveries with a lofty pose of irony and dismay. Samuel C. Chew's article,

"Byron in America," describes a smaller circle of American "epigones," but notes, interestingly, that American fascination with the wild and self-willed hero in the posture of the Indian chief had its counterpart in Byron's corsair and bandit and Scott's border outlaw. Like Leonard, he admits the difficulty of separating these links, but ends, typically, in accusing the "American Byronists" of delaying the advent of a true and original American literature.[44] Two other works on Byron's reputation add little to the foregoing texts: G. Werner Krug's *Lord Byron als Dichterische Gestalt in England, Frankreich, Deutchland, und Amerika* and Frank Lentrichhia's "Byron in America: The Later Nineteenth Century."[45] Apart from these more specialized works Byron's popularity in the South has been discussed by a number of literary historians. I will only mention a few: William E. Dodd, M. F. Heiser, and Jay B. Hubbell. The best of these is Hubbell who has written extensively on the American craze for Byron's personality and lifestyle among Southern literati, plantation owners, and general readers and on his status as a literary icon for boundless recklessness and intrepidity.[46]

No other Romantic poet approaches Byron in fame and popular appreciation. Coleridge was almost unknown, except among the small group of New England essayists and poets surrounding Emerson. Keats began to gain ground only during the very last decade of the century, and Wordsworth and Shelley, although better known than Coleridge and Keats, were still relatively unknown. Of critical works on these writers I would like to mention Annabel Newton's *Wordsworth in Early American Criticism,* Hyder Edward Rollins's *Keats' Reputation in America to 1848* and Julia Power's *Shelley in America in the Nineteenth Century.*[47]

Scott's reputation in the United States has been extensively and minutely charted by George Harrison Orians. He has shown that Southern readers in particular turned to Scott (and Byron) in the pursuit of romance, chivalry, nationalism, and a kind of commonsense moralism, all peculiar American attachments.[48] Apart from his works, other writers who have studied Scott, with special reference to the South, include: Hamilton James Eckenrode, Grace Warren Landrum, M. F. Heiser, William E. Dodd, Francis Pendleton Gaines, Rollin G. Osterweis, and Edd Winfield Parks (with emphasis on the interest of William Gilmore Simms in Scott and Byron).[49] Supplementary information on the Waverley novels can be found in articles by David A. Randall, on Scott in New Orleans in Harold F. Bogner, and on Scott as a Western hero in Ralph Leslie Rusk's *The Literature of the Middle Western Frontier.*[50] For my chapter on Scott and the theater, Henry Adelbert White's *Walter Scott's Novels on the Stage* has been indispensable.[51]

While the position of Dickens in nineteenth-century American culture and literature, like that of Byron and Scott, has been dealt with in a desultory fashion, the nineteenth-century veneration and admiration of Dickens in America was responded to with a vengeance. Again, the works that have treated different aspects of his reputation in the United States belong to the early part of this century. As Dickens was Boston's favorite son throughout this period, his visits there and the repercussions of them on Boston's cultural life, have been the subjects of separate treatments. Edward F. Payne's *Dickens Days in Boston* approaches a hagiography, but is a useful source of information through its detailed account of Dickens's visits in 1842 and 1876.[52] *Charles Dickens in America* and *Dickens in Cartoon and Caricature,* both compiled by William Clyde Wilkins, give further evidence of the strong and varied reactions Dickens provoked in the United States.[53] Other works that I have found useful are by Herman Leroy Edgar and R. W. G. Vail, who have assessed the American editions of his works, and the compilation of *Dickensiana* by Fred G. Kitton that contains significant bibliographical information.[54] On Dickens on the American stage there exist two very informative works by George Edgar Montgomery and Paul Wilstach.[55]

None of the other Victorian novelists reached the same level of reputation and recognition as Dickens. William Thackeray, who also traveled in the United States, came closest. He was particularly popular—in contrast to Dickens—in the South, because of his conservative leanings.[56]

Among the Victorian poets Tennyson was without rivals, although toward the end of the century Robert Browning became something of a cult poet in Boston. There are two major works on Tennyson.[57]

2

Appropriations in Literature

In this chapter I will deal with three types of appropriations. The first consists of American texts that attempt to secure their own reading system and defy and resist what Gian Biago Contë calls the "double reading." The "double reading" installs in the reader (and by "reader" I indicate the "generic reader" who also may represent my own prejudices) the presence of two or several writing conventions, or two or several cultural codes. In this first group, the British (let's call it) A-text (by Byron, Scott, etc.) is *integrated* with a new American artifact, the B-text. In my second categorization and section, A and B stand apart; B loosely corresponds or cooperates with A. B *emulates* A. The third includes texts where B constitutes an extension, a critique of, or a commentary on, A. A and B *comment* on each other.

The whetting stone, then, is the degree or level of activity that the British text, or code, perform in its Americanized form. A text in which the model is being incorporated and harmonized to create a new text persuades the reader to participate in accepting and extending the "new" voice; whereas a text where the two hold each other at an arm's length invites the reader to endorse and admire the gap or the tension. The two are not supposed to synchronize, as in the first group; they compete and debate.

In the third category the gap is even wider. Here the B-text is used to comment on itself, and on A, and via itself on matters outside it. This means, for instance, that a commentary on Byron (a eulogy or a satire) can perform several functions within the imitative formula: praising and criticizing the Byron code, while also castigating contemporary American writers and epigones. The American reader, as it were, steps outside it and attempts to assess it critically, without, however, violating or breaking the recognized syntagmas.

It is along these broad lines of integration, emulation, and commentary that I have organized my material in this chapter, knowing very well that many of my options and categories could have been constructed differently, depending on the nature of the arbitrary liaison

of A and B. In most cases it is a fairly straightforward business to
identify an emulation; the presence of, say, the Byron code in a B-
text is all too obvious. But in many other cases it is extremely difficult
to be certain of who or what is being imitated or emulated, because
"sources" coalesce. In these cases I have not thought it essential to
try to distinguish them, as my objective is not to trace, say, Byron's
influence on American writing, but to illustrate various aspects of a
decolonization process via the American reception of the poet. I
deem it more to the point to describe the forms of displacement
that Byron's works were subjected to, than his overall influence on
American writing.

Integration as Imitation

Publishing, particularly of poetry, in the antebellum United States
and continuing through the next two decades was seen as an overt
act of intervention. The book was a manifestation of cultural independence, a veto of some kind against Old World dominance across the
whole field of literature. Most prefaces elaborate the same, often
contradictory, declarations: the nationalistic objective to produce poetry that emerges out of American realities, as an antidote to foreign
ideas, the exhortation that the example be followed by others, and
the self-deprecating, and paradoxical, appeal to the readership that
the project be accepted for whatever it is. So, the briskness and
confidence of voice is often undermined by a lingering uncertainty
about the *real* value of the particular book.

An even bigger problem for the American writers and collectors
of poetry, whether the site of publication was to be the magazine, the
gift book, or the anthology, touched on the literary preferences they
were expected to project. There was no way around the implication,
it was felt, that it was the English literary tradition and the English
canon that gave these poems their raison d'être. In one way or another, the writers were simply "compelled" to acknowledge and comment on their "conditional freedom." Without such a stand the
literary project, paradoxically, would have seemed unauthoritative,
lacking in the cultural perception it purported to present. So there
is much inconsistent double-talk in the prefatorial assessments of
the day.

The writers who sought to integrate their expression with the literary tradition they had adopted chose different ways of stating this.
The most common way was to pinpoint the genre they had adopted:
simply evoking such literary terms as "minstrelsy," "romance," or
"epic" seemed to be enough. Another way was to stoically refrain

from any normative comments about genre, style, and diction, and instead emphasize the very abscence of them in the development and discussion of a national literature; the implication was then that there was a need to be filled. A third and a less common way to achieve critical authority was to rank and define the British model by a direct or indirect reference or quote from it and thus establish a referential norm according to which the present text could be judged.

An example that incorporates all of these prefatorial options is offered by Samuel B. Beach in the "Advertisement" to his *Escalala: An American Tale* (1824). This poem, he explains,

> aims at no higher rank, and aspires to no greater dignity, than such as belong to a tale of fancy; and in which—without stopping to inquire which school of poetry is the best, I have indulged that frequent change of measure which forms one of the most prominent characteristics of modern minstrelsy.[1]

The poem is self-depreciatingly labeled a "tale of fancy," an epithet that seems curiously at odds with the lofty aspirations contained in the book's subtitle "An American Tale." Beach, furthermore, links it with the contemporary ballad traditions which he has reduced to one simply consisting of measures and prosody. The reader of the poem would no doubt be led to recognize the romance tradition that Walter Scott's ballads were part of. By foregrounding Scott in this indirect way Beach achieves at least two things. Adopting the Scott frame of reference, the Scott code, he accords his poem the credibility that it otherwise would lack. Subsuming a literary authority has the double effect of enabling him to counter, challenge, or defy the very authority his poem leans on. The title "An American Tale," provides proof of this. So do also the scholarly apparatus, annotations, introductions, notes, explanations of archaic terms and customs, and geographical and historical references that the poem is laid in—and that a poem of this stature was expected to include.

Escalala: An American Tale is one of the hundreds of poems that were written during the century that prefigured parts of American history where the "Red Indian" is the hero. Today, we would more likely name this literary prototype a "victim." Like the Scott of border legend "Lay of the Last Minstrel," Beach employs the metonymy of orality to sustain the patriotism of his poem. Beach passes over two racial memories (Scott also employs two time shifts to signal ideological shifts: the minstrel, displaced by events taking place in 1689, sings of events that occurred a century and a half earlier). Beach concocts a fable, founded nevertheless, he claims, on historical material, about a "nation more civilised than the wandering tribes

in whose possessions it was found by the English and French." This
is a twelfth-century colony of pagan Scandinavians who have settled
down near the "junction of the Ohio and the Mississippi," descend-
ants of Norwegians migrating the seas after the colonization of Green-
land. Ruric, shipwrecked son of the Norwegian king, carries off
Escalala who is, of course, the daughter of an Indian chief. A war
ensues and, due to the ingenuity and callousness of the Indian princess, the colonists are exterminated. Only the "ruins" remain. This
is the plot line of the story told in predictably dull, rhyming couplets.

Beach employs two narrative hierarchies in his story: one ideological, the other racial. The first transforms the English/Scottish
privilege to tell the patriotic tale to an American. Right in the "Introduction" he sets the tone. "Land of the brave, the generous and the
free, / Hope of the world and nurse of Liberty! / Thy sons, when
Bute conceived th' ignoble plan / To crush fair Freedom's rights—
the rights of man; / Prompt, at their country's call, to vengeance
woke, / Burst th' oppressor's chain and spurned the tyrant's yoke"
(vii). In addition, in the fashion of Scott and Byron, he employs the
exegesis of the "Notes" to bolster the patriotic function of his poem.
He lists various honorable Americans who "have become the orna-
ments, or the benefactors of the human race through the medium of
ingenious or useful invention, [in] the United States" (35). This boast
links, then, directly with an attack on the prerogatives and priorities
of English books and English literature in present-day America. "It
is true," he complains, "that our libraries, public and private, have
been too much lumbered with the mere sickly trash of European
scribblers" (96). But he is sure that "the day is at hand, when the
American public will be . . . ready to hail . . . the literary merit which
is the growth of either hemisphere." By subtly outmanoeuvring and
appropriating its continental genesis, Beach launches the poem as a
contemporary American role model.

The racial transformation on the other hand goes a much longer
way, in narrative terms, to attain its goal. Beach rehearses the dicta
and stereotypes about the Native American, as "savage," "dull,
phlegmatic, silent and inert" (99). He also adopts the well-known
sexual cliché of attributing the worst characteristics of this race to
the female gender. Escalala personifies revenge, which "sparkles in
every eye, and gives activity to every limb" (101) of its carrier. She
seeks revenge and is instrumental in destroying "the seat of a people,
numerous, warlike and civilised, far beyond what can be predicated
of either the present aborigines, or their ancestors" (v).

In a summary, then, Beach's strange Arcadian vision establishes
various hierarchies. The projection of an American literary text presupposes first of all a continental or English literary code which can

be appropriated and then rejected. It advances cultural prejudice through racial and sexual reduction. The reciprocating hierarchies embedded in his cultural program are of this order: (a) the English literary code is imitated by being integrated; (b) English literature, in which the same code is inscribed, is reclassified and devalued to give room for American expressions; (c) in this endeavor the Native American is exoticized, ritualized, and declared a nonbeing, useful only as a literary metaphor; and, finally, (d) the romance about the lost Scandinavian colony perpetuates the notions about the racial hegemony of the Caucasians.

The example suggested by Beach may be unique: most of the metric romances dealing with Indian lore cannot be deconstructed in the above manner, yet his poem is relevant for my purposes because its parameters are typical of those of the whole genre—if not of single poems.

"INDIAN" POEMS: POLITICAL ALLEGORIES

The "Indian" poems that integrated the Scott and Byron codes can be divided into three main groups.[2] A number of them read best as *political allegories* where the weak and helpless are sentimentalized, pitied, and privileged with resistance; and the abuse of the mighty is castigated and condemned. The texts thus evolve around the antithesis of power and powerlessness. In Scott's border landscape with its moss-troopers and thieves, the prototype of the solitary Byron outlaw moves around with ease. In its American version, on one level, the outlaw and rebel disguised as a "Red Indian" is a helpless uncivilized victim of the White Man's greed; on another, the same allegory subsumes a larger network of political and cultural oppositions and tensions between the Old World and the New World. The "Red Indian"— and Beech's *Escalala* is one example of such use—is here instrumentalized to illustrate the emergence of a new cultural politics. In the final analysis, it is, however, the other end of the antithesis, the one containing and defining Power and White America, that is being projected and eulogized in this dialectical manner. There was to be no mistake about the racial-cultural priorities of the cultural program.

Charles Fenno Hoffman's *Greyslaer: A Romance of the Mohawk* that appeared anonymously in 1840 falls into this category of allegorical "Indian" poems. It is organized into three "Books," forming a narrative cycle of epic nationalistic drama; the first is symptomatically called "The Border Rising," the second "Days of Darkness," and the third "Invasion and Retribution."[3] A number of epigraphs, including many from English Renaissance writers (Ford, Tourneur, Massinger, Suckling, Marston, Marlowe, and Shakespeare), are attached to the title pages, providing a frame of authority and also suggesting, as we saw with Beach, points of interchange. The following caption from Ford is placed at the beginning of Book First: "Why, peers of England, / We'll lead 'em courageously. I read / A triumph over tyranny upon / Their several foreheads," and one of the fours mottoes prefacing Book Third projects the following lines from *Henry V,* "Thus come the English with full power upon us; / And more than carefully it us concerns / To answer royally in our defences, / To line and new-repair our towns of war; / For England his approaches makes as fierce / As waters to the sucking of a gulf" (2.4.4–10). The function of the allusions to England is pretty clear. Via English Renaissance dramatists and the Scott "romance" code, the poem, as it were, projects an American ideal history that both legitimates and advocates acts of retribution against "tyranny" and disorder. Out of this evolves the revenge theme which, as we will see shortly, is one of the most cherished subjects of these poems—of all categories.

In a letter to John B. Van Schaick, 16 September 1828, Hoffman writes about his poem "The Ambuscade" (cf. Byron's *The Corsair*), which appeared two years later in *New-York American:* "I have a fragment à la Walter Scott a poem of an Indian fray partly written which I'd send except fear it would be recognised here as miner."[4] Obviously, he was afraid that the poem would be deemed too encroaching on its acknowledged model, Scott's *Lady of the Lake.* He included, however, the twenty-one-stanza-long poem, later on in his *Wild Scenes in the Forest and Prairie* (1843), where he integrated it between the war reminiscences (1812–13) told by a retired major and a fable, "The Origin of Indian Corn," narrated by an "old chief." This mediating position is symbolic of the cultural pacification scheme Hoffman's poem gropes after, but fails to achieve.[5]

The poem describes the serenity of the landscape, its organic unity of animal and plant life where moose on "rushy brinks," screech owls in tulip trees and tamaracks, and copperhead snakes in the black abysses encircle and contain the "natural" man, "the men of bronze," lying in silence waiting for their "prey." The motive for the slaughter of the white soldiers, who, it seems, unwittingly and in "gallant ranks in close array," walk into the trap—the ambush—is, Hoffman explains, the Native American's "gathered agony of years" and "griefs untold by tears." But the "revenge" inflicted upon the intruders also seem to have another rationale: it is "nature" violated against and striking back. The lines "Why cannot that loon's wild shriek / To them a feeble warning speak" are repeated twice as if Hoffman wanted to underline that nature was conspiring by not being cooperative with "civilization." Nature protected its "native" cohabiters. Hoffman is employing the well-known romantic category of the "primitive man," epitome of purity and innocence, who possesses the unalienable "right" to express fury, even irrational fury, at the injustices committed against him. Yet Hoffman's poem does not condemn the white intrusion of the "wilderness," nor does it provide a wider frame of explanation of the colonial enterprise. It could not. It was entrenched in the mythology of the day where the "Indian" served as one partner in the antithesis between "good" and "evil," between "unspoilt nature" and "encroaching civilization."

In other poems of the same category the Indian chief is credited with qualities such as leader, warrior, and head of a family. The idealization also includes such virtues as entrepreneurship, pride, and perseverance. The image of the savage has been reverted from the one we saw earlier, it seems. However the "positive" markers that fill these delineations of brave and virtuous Indian princes and princesses only indicate a shift in the metaphorical field. The image of the Other has always acted as a self-reflexive mirror. Outside the narratives, the alienation and oppression of the Red Indians continued.

Seba Smith's Indian chief, in *Powhatan, a Metrical Romance, in Seven Cantos* (1841), may serve to illustrate similar qualities ascribed to the Red Indian in American literature. His Scott-Milton-inspired romance is dedicated to the "young people of the United States," as an act of "rational enjoyment and mental culture." The rhetoric of the hero Powhatan, the Indian chief, seems to be closely drafted on Milton's Satan, who was one the most cited literary protagonists in American elocutionary handbooks, as well as in contemporary polemics on political issues. Scott had provided the classroom meter and the precedent of the historicized topography, Milton the pathos and the political nerve. But, the cultural landscape of the poem is definitely nineteenth-century American.

> To Powhatan now every chief
> Turn'd his dark eye, while slow and brief,
> As monarch speaketh to a man,
> The council-talk he thus began.
> "Chiefs and warriors! let your ears
> Be open to the word we say:
> The cloud, that rests upon our land,
> Portends a troubled day."[6]

The romantic appropriation of the Native Indian chief warrior as an emblem of the political leader could be seen as an expression of the idealization of the underdog and the repressed, in confrontation with the strong. The American self-image contained this paradox of projecting both the oppressor (the Old World *and* its American alliances) and the oppressed (the Old World *against* its American alliances). The myths about the "Red Indians" were endlessly employed to talk about these things.

A far less conciliatory picture of the "Indian" than Sheba's *Powhatan* emerges out of Andrew Coffinberry's rhymed tale of seven cantos, *The Forest Rangers* (1842), which is based on factual incidents such as the "Battle of General Wayne's Army (1794)." The narrative delineates a military operation against "the deluded aborigines," with captures of hostages, marches, combat scenes, rescues, and negotiations, quite like stereotyped scenes in an early Western movie.[7] The "Indian" represents an evil power that needs to be circumscribed to give room for the expansionism of the white man. The energy of Byron's humanistic pilgrimage has been deployed to motivate images of a colonial intrusion; Scott's antiquarian passion and ballad form act as narrative mediators. In this way the whole spectrum of convergence with the "Indian" myths could be used to forward a program of abstract nationalism. Robert C. Sands, who himself produced a number of "Indian" poems, wrote, self-reproachingly, on the subject in *Atlantic Magazine* that

> we have surely a better acquaintance here with our own Highlands, than with Skiddaw, Schehrahn [?], or any other hill in Scotland. But we read and relish the descriptive poetry of Scott, solely for its own excellence. Can we not admire a beautiful landscape, without knowing from what country it is copied? . . . What associations have we with the Cumberland lakes? What kind of a name for a romantic river is Duddon, which has, nevertheless, been taught to meander through many new pleasing sonnets?[8]

American literature must discover its own place nomenclature, it was endlessly repeated; it must dwell and move in its own landscape. Few writers on the necessity to stimulate and advance "American subjects" would fail to mention the importance of the role of the American landscape, whether it was the "sublimity" of Niagara Falls or the buzz of a Manhattan street. The notion also prevailed that the place was an organic part of human life. The Scott and Byron codes were influential in advocating the rich potentialities of time and place.[9] To this must be added the teachings of the evolutionary grammar of the day that registered the "Indian" not only a part of the American landscape, but placed him at the bottom of the scale with the buffalo and the snake.

"INDIAN" LORE: TRAVELOGUE

With the second grouping of Indian lore, then, the North American "Indian" romance had turned into a rambling *travelogue,* interspersed with elements of romantic landscape descriptions and illustrations, as it were, from nineteenth-century tourist brochures.

One of the most ardent followers and original imitators of Byron in the midcentury was Frederick W. Thomas, whom we will meet on a number of occasions in the pages that follow. His versified travelogue with "Indian" lore-based motives, *Emigrant; or, Reflections while Descending the Ohio* (1833), uses the Spenserian stanza form of *Childe Harold* to take the traveler down the river. He acknowledges openly the literary source from which he had derived the form.[10] The fascination with "Indian" lore permeates most of these American travel accounts; there was no wilderness, it seems, where the Indian was not present. Further, the American traveler of the first half of the century would hardly conceptualize wilderness without resorting to the company of either Byron and Scott. One third of the forty-odd chapters of Edmund Flagg's *The Far West; or, A Tour beyond the Mountains* (1838) are headed with captions from Byron; a majority of them are from *Childe Harold* (6) (the rest from *Manfred* [4], *Corsair* [1] and "Mazeppa" [1]). The American traveler wandering through his pristine land has adopted the gaze of an epic hero. He is the American incarnation *Childe Harold*. The reader is allowed to fuse the two. Edmund Flagg upholds no distance: he takes his bearings, and, self-consciously, ponders:

No wandering Harold has roamed on a pilgrimage of poetry over the sublime and romantic scenery of our land, to hymn its praise in breathing thoughts and glowing words; . . .[11]

Flagg avails himself of the whole canon of English literature to illustrate and, as it were, authenticate his landscape observations. Poetry—English (and marginally American) poetry—subsumes the function of a secondary referential discourse with both magic and universal bearings within which the narrativization of the American landscape is executed. Flagg—as we saw Hoffman had done—antithetically calls on writers such as Davenant, Ben Jonson, Herbert ("Sweet day, so cool, so calm, so bright. . . ."), Sterne, Burns, Coleridge, Hemans, Halleck, and Bryant, in his cultural enterprise to give his American reader a more acute sense of belonging. So, inevitably, Scott's Highlands come to his mind when surveying the Mississippi from his imperial height:

Seldom have I gazed upon a scene more eminently imposing than that of these hoary old cliffs, when the mid-summer-sun, rushing upwards from the eastern horizon, bathed their splintered pinnacles and spires and the rifled tree-tops in a flood of golden effulgence. The scene was not unwor-

thy of Walter Scott's graphic description of the view from the Trosachs
of Loch Katrine, in the "Lady of the Lake."[12]

Then follows a quote from the poem. Flagg's touristic Mississippi
River view has, as if unwillingly and unconsciously, transformed itself
into a "graphic" piece of Gothic stage scenery. Flagg's juxtaposition
of "his" text (the B-text) (although it is only a "reported scene") with
Scott's, functions as a deliberate eye-opener. The range of the Scott
code is extended and encroached upon to project another mode of
narration, another national discourse, the potentials of another yet
"lesser" writer, and to meet the expectations of a new and fresh
readership.

There is a clear note of urban arrogance in the following Scott-
inspired couplets, taken from Charles Fenno Hoffman's song "The
Vigil of Faith: A Legend of the Adirondach Mountains," where the
leisured poet-observer, down from the boisterous eastern city, is encapsulated by the wilderness of the river landscape and confronted
with the mysterious haunt of the "Indians." The antithesis of civilization and nature is presented for us to marvel at and be intimidated by:

> 'T'was in the mellow autumn time,
> When I, an idle from the town,
> With gun and rod was lured to climb
> Those peaks where fresh the Hudson takes
> His tribute from an hundred lakes;
>
> .   .   .   .
>
> Gleaming from out the dusky wood;
> And in that moment on the shore,
> Just when I brush'd with my oar,
> An aged INDIAN stood![13]

"Nay! Shrink not, lady, from my tale," he appeals to his readership,
mimicking the slack urbanity of the Byron protagonist-traveler. He
also promises that the readers should not expect "images . . . dire
and gory." On the contrary, his travelogue, he explains, is the result
of a peaceful mission-journey, motivated by curiosity and balanced
by the reporter's ambition to know. In this, he claims, he embodies
an alternative voice:

> We talk'd that night—I love to talk
> With these grown children of the wild,
> When in their native forest walk,
> Confiding, simple as a child,
> They lose at times that sullen mood
> Which marks the wanderer of the woods[14]

Like most of his generation of American writers Charles Fenno Hoffman was very concerned about the problematic issues of imitation. In a review article in *The American Monthly* as early as 1835, he comments on the contradictions he found hindering the American literary community from competing with the English:

> We are indeed, in one respect, an inconsistent people! We rail at our writers, if they follow in the footsteps of the English novelists, and we desert them if they quit the beaten track! We make a great clamour about the patronage due to native genius, and we suffer it to die of exhaustion and poverty! We complain the want of an original school of literature, and when, by chance, a strong and daring mind bursts through the trammels . . . we frown into silence, or smile into contempt. . . .[15]

And, in another review, from the same time, he said:

> As for our domestic poetry, what shall we say of the incipient Byrons, and L. E. L.'s [Letitia E. Landon], which the daily prints let loose upon the community. (ibid.)

Quite unjustly, he himself would become a victim of these "inconsistencies." In 1844, he was accused by a reviewer of Rufus W. Griswold's *The Poets and Poetry of America* (in which he, by the way, was more abundantly represented than any other American writer) of having freely copied from Moore.[16] He objected, of course, and strongly disclaimed that he was conscious of any such overt act, while admitting that there were similarities between the two. This is a telling case of how delicate the situation was for the American writer who was anxious to contribute to the building of a native literature, but who considered, rightly or wrongly, that in this construction "foreign help" was needed. The process of appropriation the American writers were involved in was like walking on an eggshell. If the shell broke you were out in the cold with the wolves howling.

"INDIAN" POEMS: MELODRAMA

The largest group of "Indian"-lore-based poems impregnated with the Byron and Scott codes are melodramas, often drenched—as they should be—in melancholy and gloom. Like all good melodramas they play on the taboos of the day, on illegitimate passions between members of antagonistic races, on acts of revenge and compassion, on violence, cruelty, death (or preferably "dying"), and pity. They thrive on prejudices and racial stereotypes. A large number of them are sentimental showpieces absorbing and activating popular myths about relationships between "paleface" and "red face." Scott and

Byron provided the poems with their narrative framework and some-times even lent them their rhythm, diction, and syntax. The American writers transformed them, in their turn, into texts that the readers would respond to and recognize as chronicles sprung out of their own history. "Scott's northern clan chieftains . . . were not so very distantly related to Byron's Levantine pirates; the Celtic Ossian and the oriental Giaour were but two phases of the same romantic move-ment; and a third . . . is to be found in the American Indian, whether in Cooper, on the stage, or in such tales as these after Scott and Byron."[17]

An astonishing number of poems dwell on the theme of Puritan captivity; their narrative structure invariably involves a white woman or a white man captured in the enemy's camp, pining, threatened to death, but saved by the heartrending appeals of her/his lover. Lucre-tia Maria Davidson tells the story, "founded on actual occurrences," about "the tender-hearted daughter of Hillis-ad-jo [who] threw herself between the prisoner [Duncan M. Rimmon] and his executioners, and interceded with her father for his release."[18]

> She threw back the mantle which shaded her face,
> She spoke not, but looked the pale spirit of woe!
> The angel of mercy, the herald of grace,
> Knelt the sorrowful daughter of Hillis-ad-joe!
> "My father! my father!" the maiden exclaims,
> "O doom not the white man to die 'midst the flames!
> 'Tis thy daughter who kneels, 'tis Chicomico sues,
> Can my father, the friend of my childhood, refuse?
> This heart is the white man's, with him will I die,
> With him to the Great Spirit's mansion I'll fly;
> The flames which to heaven will waft his pure soul,
> Round the form of *thy* daughter encircling shall roll;
> *My* life is *his* life—*his* fate shall be *mine;*
> For *his* image around *thy child's* heart will entwine!"[19]
>
>   [italics Davidson's]

The pattern of the first four lines suggest the Spenserian stanza used by Byron in *Childe Harold* and the five couplets in iambic pentame-ters have their immediate origin in either Scott or Byron. The stiff-ness and archaisms of her diction and syntax draw on Scott rather than Byron, but it is Byron who has staged the tableau for her and helped her transform it into vivid drama (the scene is also illus-trated!). This zigzag manner of utilizing and integrating the British sources is typical of the American imitations. Yet Davidson is pro-fessing to write an American epic poem (whatever its worth), basing it on conventional American material (history and legend), and premising in her readers shared fantasies and biases. She was confidently employing the popular truisms of the day, the oral stories and the common storage of tall tales about the "Indians" and the "Whites."

Many other storytellers and writers of rhymed fiction used more or less the same story plot, the same pathetic rhetoric, and the same English codes.[20] P. Hamilton Myers explains prefatorially that although his poem "Ensenore" attempts to "elucidate the character and customs of the aborigines" and thus give "more of a national feature to American poetry," it is still only a romance in the style of Scott.[21] The poem features the captivity of the white woman Kathleen, with "flowing hair, / And curled in untaught beauty" (39), and the fatal passions she evokes in Ensenore, with "the scowling brow, that bood-red plume, / That bracelet and brawny arm" (50–51). It is crude in tone, sentimental in plot, cliché-ridden, and full of environmental and literary loans from Scott. But, as we saw, Myers's project was not to spare Scott, but to expand on him and, via him, enhance national writing.

Of a different order are the melodramas where the Indian element has been naturalized. George Hooker Colton's long Scott-echoing requiem "Tecumseh" is a graveyard poem in the best gothic traditions of the midcentury, featuring a defeated member of a lost race, lamenting the death of his father, which also, we are to believe, signifies the subjugation of a whole people. The poet, however, often intervenes, as if to reconsider the historical question: whose fault was it?

> Stranger—there are who think and write
> The Indian's soul untouched with light,
> And that to him belongs the guilt
> For all the blood his hand hath spilt:
> But surely, if their feet had strayed,
> Like mine, his friendly homes among,
> They would have known, god never made
> A heart all darkness, and—how long
> The savage bore aggressive wrong.[22]

The reconciliatory cultural note is even stronger in Carlos D. Stuart's poem "Wa-con-tam-ee," which, entrenched in Byronic moods and diction, tells the hortative story about the compassion of a white woman over a dying young Indian woman.

> Ah, there was one, a pale-faced good;
> Who loves the red-race of the wood;
> A woman, with noble heart,
> Who watched the fading rose at morn
> . . . .

> Long shall the pale-face' love be kept
> A talisman in woods afar. . . .[23]

OTHER MODES OF INTEGRATION

It would seem from above that a majority of the American imitative poems written during the first half of the century dealt with aspects of "Indian" life and legend, of the warfare against them, and of the pacification processes. The Byron and Scott codes were particularly applicable, we must recognize, in portraying the ineffable pathos and stoic suffering that made up some of the myths about the "Indian" and they were equally adaptable and applicable for the representations of the environment (place and time), of which the Native American was believed to be an integral and Arcadian part. But, of course, the codes were also influential outside the "Indian" domains, too. A few examples of this appropriation might suffice.

The "intellectual wonder," the deaf and dumb poet James Nack, wrote "The Minstrel Boy" at the age of sixteen, imitating the ottava rima of *Don Juan* and filling it with the indignation and the ruefulness of *Childe Harold;* adding his own—and Byron's—agony of being alienated by a physical, and, therefore, social handicap.

> Unheard, unheeded are the lips by *me,*
> To others that unfold some heav'n-born art;—
> And melody—Oh dearest melody![24]

His contemporaries were quick to pick up the resemblances between the two. An early memoir writer, P. M. Wetmore, quotes this assessment of him in *New England Magazine:*

> It is not too much to say of this gifted young American, that when matured by time and finished by labour, some of his future efforts in song may equal the happiest of those that have immortalised the author of *Childe Harold.*[25]

There were many American writers, actors, and artists in the nineteenth century who competed for the label "American Byron" (outside the rank of such obvious candidates as Felicia Heman and Lydia H. Sigourney) and many did the most bizarre things to become worthy of this label. In the appropriation of Byron there were no restrictions or limits—as we will see many times in this book.

Two women writers will be considered next, Emma Catherina Embury and Anna Cora Ritchie. Each of them was literally imbued with Byron and could hardly compose a single phrase without setting in motion some kind of allusion of or reference to their master. Throughout their lives, however, they were—and this is why they merit to be discussed in this context—carving out for themselves independent careers as writers (and, in Ritchie's case, also as actress and lecturer). They were, indeed, read and listened to.

Embury, under the Byronic pen name "Ianthe," prefaced her early poem "Guido, a Tale" with four lines from *Childe Harold,* applying to it one of Byron's most significant poetic formulas on literary creation: "'T'is to create, and in creating live / a being more intense, that we endow / With form our fancy, gaining as we give / The life we image, even as I do now" (3.47–50). This was far too advanced a poetics to be of any help for most of the Byron imitators. But if Byronic immediacy and intensity could not capture their poems, it was still there, in the almost rapturous rapport they were establishing with the poet, with his life and his works. Embury, we saw, prefaced many of her poems with mottoes, mostly from Canto III of *Childe Harold,* all chosen to bolster the vacuity of her timid lines, such as "And, now he stood apart from all, a smile / Of cold contempt curled his pale lip. . . ."[26] Yet it must be understood that it was imitations (paraphrases and parodies) of Byron such as these that swelled the poetry sections of local newspapers and national or regional magazines. To recite or quote Byron, or to imitate him, had far more significance than following a fad; it was to enter into an established mode of cultural discourse and take a place as a competent participant.

Timid is not the word one could use about the other woman "Byronist," Anna Cora Ritchie, a progressive and audacious advocate for more liberal attitudes toward women artists, an able actress and one of the first American women elocutionists.[27] Ritchie knew her Byron by heart and sprinkled him across her conversations and her writings, like a fundamentalist sprouting Bible quotations. And she was deadly serious. The Byron she adopted is only delimited by her creative instincts and factual literary enterprises. In 1837 she published *Pelayo; or, The Cavern of Covadonga,* like Embury using a pseudonym, "Isabel." Her Preface offers more interesting reading than her "romance," which is about a medieval Spanish heroic king and his sister. She anticipates and, in fact, debates, imagined points of averse criticism that her poem was likely to invite: she clarifies *why* she has departed from Poet Laureate Robert Southey's rendering of the legend by making the hero of her work a woman; *why* she "wants in rhyme" and as an apology cites examples from a number of British writers, among them some lines from Byron's "English Bards and Scotch Reviewers" (97–102, with the famous quote "Better to err with Pope than shine with Pye").[28] All these swaggering precautions reflect not only the uncertainty of a young aspiring writer and the cultural prejudices attached to her gender, but ultimately—pride. Entrance into literary culture, uninvited and unsought for, meant challenging a number of traditions, among them the male dominance through an established order of literary figureheads and a canon of English literary texts. In this early work Ritchie is challenging this dominance in her naïve way by aligning herself with such luminaries as Southey and Byron. Resistance and independence can be coupled in many ways.

Ritchie's choice of Spain as the locale for her romance probably originates in the interest in Spain and the Orient that Byron's poems and tales created among his American readers. At the same time that American writers were exploring their own Western borders and the cultures of the indigenous population they were also looking outside their continent for mood and scene. So, we had a deluge of poems in various modifications of the Spenserian stanza or the ottava rima, harping on oriental themes, on luxury, sensuality, determinism, vengeful stars, and ivory towers. Occasionally the Scott code intrudes, providing these poems glimpses of medieval castles and loading them with the monotony of the ballad form. George H. Boker's "The Podesta's Daughter," "The Ivory Carver," "The Song of the East," "A Ballad of Sir John Franklin" are representative of this genre.[29]

The most fascinating of all the writers of this category is without comparison Bayard Taylor, who has been called the "America's Marco Polo." One of the first to report from the gold rush, he traveled widely in America in Africa, and in Scandinavia. And, he wrote books about his travels that were appreciated on both sides of the Atlantic.[30] The best one could say about his *Poems from the Orient* and such lines as "From the Desert I come to thee / On a stallion shrod with fire; / And the winds are left behind / In the speed of my desire" is that he must have validated the trumped-up language and the tinsel plot of his poems only under the compulsion and propulsion of a literary standard.[31] His reporting eyes surely would not have accepted them. For him the exigencies of a convention and a tradition were stronger than the urgencies of reality.

Mary E. Brooks and James E. Brooks imitated Byron with as much gusto. Lines from Byron poems serve as epigraphs for many of the poems in their joint anthology *The Rivals of Este* (1829). Mary E. Brooks's "Tasso" meditates on the loss of youth and the evanescence of time, a theme that underpins Byron's "Lament of Tasso," whose line "The wretched are the faithful" (60) she quotes.[32] The writers authenticate their texts by such prefaces. But the allusive network is laid in an integration of the A-text and the B-text.

Hoffman's "Song—Rosalie Clare," a poem very popular in his time, is of particular interest for us. Like the poem "The Ambuscade" (see above) it was printed in *Wild Scenes in the Forest and Prairie* with an introductory prose text. Hoffman's prose narrative about a legal fraud, involving a mother and a daughter masquerading as a handsome and enticing young man who becomes the fantasy object of her/his teenage cousin Rosalie Clare, includes many ingredients from the Byron code: sexual transgression, love as obsession, a fatally handsome Byronic hero and a young innocent belle, and the deleterious lust for power and money. This code transcends and instructs the tale. However, technically speaking, the accompanying poem is a close imitation of Scott, in observing the rhythm and diction of his border songs.

> Who owns not she's peerless? who calls not her fair?
> Who questions the beauty of Rosalie Clare?
> Let him saddle his courser and spur to the field,
> And, though harnessed in proof, he must perish or yield;
> For no gallant can splinter—no charger cab dare
> The lance that is couched for young Rosalie Clare.[33]

This is a good instance, not only of Hoffman's admiration of the two British writers, but also of the way the two English discourses or codes could merge or cooperate within a single work. Fitz-Greene Halleck's works provide many examples of these transactions. His poem "Alnwick Castle" imitates Scott's *Marmion* in its employment of a medieval theme and—as does another of his poems "Marco Bozzaris"—in its use of his meter.[34] Byron's presence is also felt throughout. The initial lines of "Marco Bozzaris" invite the reader to study the corruption of liberty and the struggle for political independence. The young idealist fighting for republicanism and liberty in Greece was the supreme American political hero. Halleck chose to write poems that were echoic of Byron's life and work.

> At midnight, in his guarded tent,
> The Turk was dreaming of the hour
> When Greece, her knee in supplicance bent,
> Should tremble at his power: . . . .[35]

The Southerner St. Leger L. Carter's imitation "The Discarded" is a self-acknowledged imitation of Byron's "Ode to Napoleon." Carter has transformed the poem into a pitiless sarcastic account of an aging man dreaming about a young lover. However, by the way of inversion, the poem could be seen as an indirect glorification of another, but different, man of war, George Washington. In another of his poems, "Washington and Napoleon," Carter had drawn out the differences between the two: Washington "the Friend of Mankind" and Napoleon

"the Corsican despot in dust."[36] Another poem in the same category
is James Gates Percival's "Prometheus," in which his contemporary
biographer Julius H. Ward had detected clear parallels; the poem, he
said, was "a just and discriminating examination of the dangers to be
apprehended by us from somewhat similar causes."[37]

John Milton, naturally, provided the American writers with material, ideas, and models. Micah P. Flint began by writing highly romantic poems that blended Byron's melancholy with Scott's pathos. His
poem "In Contento," however, had a different background. He introduced it in the following circumscribed and subtle manner:

> The form of the stanza, and the structure of the verse in the following
> piece, may, perhaps, incline the reader, to think, that I have been making
> too free with the *L'Allegro* of Milton.
>   I will hope, that such prepossession will not prevent my being read.
> There is no farther imitation, than that of the measure and structure. It
> was as little my intention to copy, as it was my presumption to hope, to
> rival that imitable [*sic*] production.[38]

An "invocation," such as this passage of Flint's, was one of the rhetorical devices that the American writers bent on producing lofty verse
epics adapted from Milton. Another American poet who imitated this
epic verse formula, and in so doing, comes close to producing an
involuntary parody of it, is Richard M. D. Emmons. Moreover, who
could be a more useful model—for several reasons—than the English
and Puritan Milton when singing the heroism of the 1812 war against
the English! This is the project inspiring Emmons's *The Freedoniad;
or, Independence Preserved. An Epic Poem on the Late War of 1812.*
The lines "Thou spirit—breathing power—celestial Muse! / With
thoughts sublime my weary mind infuse—" initiate Canto XXI which
is called "Invocation."[39]

An American writer sensitive to the cultural climate of his time
thus faced a delicate dilemma: how to respond intelligently to the
popular interest in Scott and Byron and simultaneously, be in the
national vanguard advocating an independent American literary production? This dilemma, we have shown, had an obvious solution.
The American writer, like Hoffman or Halleck, tried to *combine*
these two apparently antithetical projects. It is, then, through imitation that American cultural resistance was uphold. In an arcticle in
the *New-York American* in 1831 on the reputation of Scott and Byron
in his country, Hoffman made the following observation:

> Memorials of him [Scott] in the shape of his works are to be met in almost
> every tavern and canal boat on the Erie line. Byron, in several of his
> letters to Moore, expresses himself delighted with the idea of being read

upon the banks of the Hudson. Sir Walter, if he attaches half the value to his cis-atlantic reputation, could not but be gratified to learn that his writings are only equalled in familiar popularity here by those of Burns in his own country.[40]

"Imitation" in the sense I have used the term was the reason for this "cisatlantic" recognition of Byron and Scott and all the other British writers.

Emulation as Imitation

We have defined emulation as an aspect of imitation that defies synthesis, that insists on maintaining a defining gap between the A-text (English) and the B-text (American). In the following discussion I will consider poetry and prose adaptations that perform this feat of sustaining two communicating or rivaling systems. Byron's presence is unique in the poetry section: no other British writer could compete with him here. In the prose section Dickens is outstanding. Byron and Dickens are unrecognized forces in the American process toward greater cultural independence. Paradoxically, the preoccupation with British writers, so much ridiculed by American *literati* during the century, was helpful in this process.

VERSE EMULATIONS OF BYRON

The emulations of Byron served a multiplicity of purposes in the American intellectual climate of the second and the third quarters of the century: ideological, religious, and social. The variety of expressions was immense. We have straightforward emulations of the Spenserian stanza of *Childe Harold* and the ottava rima of *Don Juan*, of his travel diary reporting technique, of the blurring of the narrator and the poet, of the vacillation between the serious and the buffoonery, between guilt and melancholy, and of a number of other aspects.

My intention here is to annotate a number of American emulations—eight "Childe Harolds" and eight "Don Juans"—which incorporate the Byron code and thereby lay bare a discourse of resistance with clear anticolonial directives. These expressions, I argue, involve the ideological beginnings of what today is called "American literature(s)" and "American culture(s)."

AMERICAN CHILDE HAROLDS

Byron's *Childe Harold* was bound to attract followers: its characteristics—the voyage of liberation, the boisterous, male melodrama; the

resolute, action-packed language; and the free-bounding imagery—
seemed so much a part of the progressively alternative American
myth or mentality that rewriting or Americanizing it proved to be a
profound act of cultural mediation.

The earliest specimen I have been able to trace is most likely to
have been written by a preacher. *Childe Harold's Pilgrimage to the
Dead Sea* (1818) is a Christian parable. The poem contains two antagonistic voices: that of the dissolute, restless Harold, who

> many a day of sin,
> And night of blasphemy and din:
> For I well knew the riot train
> Whom virtue looks on with disdain;
>
> . . . .
>
> The flowers of my fancy remain'd
> As bright—yea, brighter than ever;
> But sin had my bosom stain'd,
> And tainted its blossoms for ever[41]

and that of the condemning, edifying preacher. The story line follows
ruefully the melancholic itinerary of Childe Harold through Greece,
among whose tombs of heroes, ruins of squandered wealth, "hapless
clime," and lost freedom, the poet-sinner is expected to "lose the
image of the past"; but here is no solace to be found, "even Echo
heard me not" (17). The poem recollects and refashions material from
Byron's life, his unhappy marriage, his plaintive lines about his
daughter Ada, a scene from his mother's deathbed, and rumors about
his suicide attempts. All in all, the writer creates the cautionary image of a man in deep distress who faces the only remaining alternative: to go to the Holy Land to seek repentence. So, the second part
of the the 572-line-long poem is formulated as an intensively eloquent
sermon with a direct address to the poet Byron himself:

> Oh thou, whose untam'd heart
> Questions the truth divine—prostrate thee low,
> And hear—nor plunge into the deep abyss
> Where guilt remains, till the last hour be come,
> And all is finished. (29)

The second American "Childe Harold" poem, *The Pilgrimage of
Ormond, or Childe Harold in The New World,* is an attempt to
"Americanize" the poem by actually transferring Harold, or Ormond,
as he is called, to America.[42] The poem imitates Byron's Spenserian
verse scheme closely and consists of two long-winded cantos of 111
and 131 stanzas. The narrator, who nervously shifts from the Ameri-

can "Harold" to his own persona, thereby emulating the narrative structure of the model itself, dwells on the complex public image of Byron as "deadly sins" incarnate and scornful damner of Old World hypocrisy and petty conventions. To escape being suffocated, the English hero of the poem takes off to the "new world," of which he had "such wonders read / That I resolv'd, I e'en would cross the sea, / To know if man is so much better off when free, / From Kings, and Princes, Lords, and all the rest, / And wise connection 'twixt the Church and the State; / Or if, as I suspected, 'twas a jest, / The tales of trav'lers. . . ." (14). Discovering that here is, indeed, much likeness between the two worlds, Harold/Ormond is disturbed. Madness, the narrator explains, is the ultimate urge behind the outbreak of the French and American revolutions and death, its ultimate consequence. These two themes inform the poem from beginning to end. It is therefore appropriate, but somewhat cynical, that the poem's hero, the "mad" and "dying" poet, poses as a wanderer-observer-commentator of the American landscape and a few of its famous inhabitants. What is juxtaposed or paralleled is Old World lethargy-in-death and New World obsession with foolhardy action-that-invites-death. The poem also projects some typical American cultural icons, such as typographical exaltations of the historic rocks in Rock Bridge county in Virginia, encomiums to the American "Patriot Sage" George Washington, and a lively account of John of Roanoke, a Kentucky actor, elocutionist, and freedom fighter. Its aspirations are highly patriotic and idealistic.

A less sophisticated American "Childe Harold" is enlisted by William D. Gallagher's *Erato, Number I* and *Erato, Number II* (1835), a Scott-Southey-Byron concoction that features another "weary wanderer" from a distant shore who stops outside a wigwam door—the American icon par excellence—one evening and unfolds a dark story of pentitence and guilt. Byron/*Childe Harold* has provided the main impetus of this confessional lament; Scott has been helpful in providing the metric system and the diction. "I cannot wear this galling chain, / And will not longer bear this load," cries the poet missing the company of women and "savage men," with whom he would feel at ease, and perhaps "free."[43] The association of woman and "savage" performs a mythic/racist rite that has been extremely persistent in the Western world. Gallagher also quotes from Byron's conversation with Captain Parry: "I had too much of my mother about me to be dictated to." "Freedom" is, indeed, a relative term (which the next poem also demonstrates).[44]

William R. Wallace's six-stanza-long poem "Childe Harold," in *The Battle of Tippecanoe, Triumphs of Science, and Other Poems* (1837), rehearses like a catalogue most of the events, sentiments, and scenes of *Childe Harold:* the turbulence of sea and passion, the qualms of exile, the melancholy of travel, the Alps and Italy, the volcanoes of the South, the mosques of the Orient, the Byron mother-son relationship, Byron's death. In addition to these crude paraphrases there are direct addresses to Byron (that we also saw as a feature of the 1818 *Childe Harold* emulation) and eulogies or apostrophes that employ the icons of the ship and the sea to commemorate the poet.[45] The book was dedicated to General William H. Harrison, "The Gallant [War] Hero," to "embalm in immortal verse the deeds of those, who, for us and ours, bared their bosoms to the iron bold of battle . . ." that bespeaks of the colonialist message he wished his poem to convey. Wallace's collection of poems is also prefaced by an elegy singing the disastrous efficacy of "the iron bold of battle," that is, the holocaust directed against the "Red Indian" "shattered is our band. / Closed is the combat's weary eye; / Oh! whither shall the Indian fly?" The apotheosis of freedom, and the fighting for freedom which Byron's *Childe Harold* was normally associated with could, as in Wallace's case, be turned against itself and serve as the apparatus of oppression.

    Cabiro (1840 and 1864), by George H. Calvert is similar to *Ormond* in its portrayal of an unruly outsider—a Childe Harold or a Don Juan—traveling from the Old World to the New, a courier of foreign notions and a keen observer of and commentator on the new and unexpected.[46] Byron's perspective has been "brought home." Cabiro represents the nineteenth-century emigrant to the continent, an American Everyman. "To say of him / he promises t'unfold / High qualitites; and that, whether he's Dutch, / Swede, Englishman or Greek, is information / Kept wisely back, as also shape and station" (I, 16). Cabiro describes his arrival in New York City. The buzz and the commerce of the city are overwhelming. In Whitman-like lines he describes the city as "a huge giant," "couched in its sea-girt bed / As it were asleep" (II, 29). The mighty "ocean appetite" has spread upland and lent its energy to the management of well-furnished, clean hotels and spiced their customers' robust appetite. Cabiro, the newcomer, eats, and we are reminded of—and are expected to experience the contrast with—the neurotic, high-class eating seances in *Don Juan*. Then Cabiro buys a guide book and strolls on Broadway in the best tourist fashion, looking into newsmagazine shops, banks, and libraries, and marveling at the wealth and variety displayed. Eventually, he meets Diana and redeemed, marries. Don Juan, we remember, would or could not; and Byron the English poet had failed. Interspersed with the main plot are the customary homages to George Washington and orotund commentaries about British writers (Chaucer, Spenser, and Milton) and their place in the American literary tradition. They are headed by Shakespeare, "a second Adam on the earth, / Repeopling it, the one unparallel'd, / Th'absolute lord of pathos and of mirth . . . him too we claim" (II, 34). Shakespeare, like Cabiro, epitomizes universal man with natural and historical rights to an American citizenship, which was a widespread credo in nineteenth-century America.

That *Childe Harold* also should be parodied was to be expected: few, if any, nineteenth-century literary reputations were not subjected to parodic treatment. Phæbe Carey, for instance, supplied a "Canto the Seventh" of the poem, a doleful meditation of Byron and futility of life. The last stanza runs like this:

> Roll on, thou shallow stream of Pleasure!—roll!
> Ten thousand skiffs float over thee in vain,
> Prows prone to rapids, helms beyond control;
> Awhile they dance upon thy watery plain,
> Then fleet to wreck, and nothing doth remain
> Save a sad memory of the bitter groan
> When one more struggler, slackening the fierce strain,
> Sinks wave-choked, weed-encumbered, stark, alone,
> Gone to the dogs, unstayed, unfriended, and unknown.[47]

In 1848 a peculiar work appeared in Boston called *The Baby and the Bards. Childe Harvard. A Romance of Cambridge By Senor Alguno.*[48] The work is attributed to Nathan Ames. It is a whimsical long-winded (172 pages and four cantos) piece of gibberish that only a young student with hysterical literary pretensions could execute. It provides some individual ironic glimpses of contemporary Harvard life, with its "Exhibition Day," academic rivalries, and student life of work and leisure. Its irony is self-reflective—it laughs at the demagogy and style of rhetoric that Harvard was promoting. Doing this, the poem turns upon itself.

The poem describes an academic teacher who is modeled on an accumulated image collected from the Byron legends or code of the day. The audience listening to the speaker in the poem is enthralled, which is meant to reflect and scoff at the totalizing impact of Byron on the American public. But the writer of the poem continuously points out that it is this very recognition and admiration he wants to achieve by his own efforts at simulating Byron and moulding a fantastic dreamlike medieval saga out of Byron's poem. This is the Byronic speaker at an Harvard meeting; his coquetry is the author's (Byron's), but he is also an object for derision and American self-reflection:

> the gallery hummeth
> Loud thunders of applause; and, like a bee to

A flower, the maidens' eyes are turned on him,
That lordly Senior of the lofty limb.

Strong was his manly voice, deep, loud, sonorous,
As is the wave-lashed caves of the sounding ocean;
Far swept his gestures, and, like shadows o'er us,
Waved his long arms in terrible commotion!
Full were his periods rolling, like waters
Swollen by the mood; his thoughts, whales, sharks, and otters! (29)

AMERICAN DON JUANS

The production and reproduction story of Fitz-Greene Halleck's
"Fanny" is one of the best examples of the way reduplicative imitation worked within the codification process of Byron in America.
Halleck's poem, which first appeared on 27 December 1819, was an
instant hit and the edition sold out immediately. Adopting the fashion
for the seriocomic form and a modified form (six lines) of the ottava
rima of Byron's *Beppo,* Halleck tells the story of the rise into fortune
and society of a poor New York merchant and his beautiful daughter.
The burlesque is full of referential comments on the talk of the day,
on local politics, on local scandals, on literature, and so on.[49] The
following stanzas describe Fanny's affection for literature:

> And though by no means a bas bleu, she had
> For literature a most becoming passion;
> Had skimm'd the latest novels, good and bad,
> And read the Croakers, when they were in fashion;
> And Doctor Chalmer's sermons, of a Sunday;
> And Wordsworth's Cabinet, and the new Salmagundi.
>
> She was among the first and warmest patrons
> Of Griscom's concersaziónes, where
> In rainbow groups, our bright-eyed maids and matrons,
> On science bent, assemble; to prepare
> Themselves for acting well, in life, their part
> As wives and mothers. . . .[50]

From the very beginning this successful poem (it had gone through
four editions by 1839) was understood by most critics as an imitation
of Byron's *Don Juan* and *Beppo.* Halleck claimed that he had written
the poem without any reference to Byron's *Don Juan.* But textual
similarities and echoes suggest that he was familiar with the first two
cantos. Throughout his life he expressed bewilderment at the poem's
popularity with the readers. In a letter to his sister, dated 7 February
1820, he noted that "the popularity of 'Fanny' is far above my expec-

tations, and certainly far above its merits, . . . it is fashionable to
admire it." And in another letter to her he said he thought that the
poem's "localities will render it almost entirely uninteresting to
you."[51] However, it was the presence of these very "localities" in the
poem that made the poem attractive. Halleck's "Fanny" decentred
Byron's *Don Juan/Beppo* and placed itself in a dialectical or related
position vis-à-vis its models. It is not the operation of, as Nelson
Frederick Adkins believes,[52] Byron's "universals" and Halleck's "localities" which differentiates the two poets, it is the dialogical pattern
that their works are inscribed in. William H. Prescott, a Boston editor,
writing to Halleck in 1820, commending him for his poem, confirms
this view: "Fanny," he says, "for its easy conversational wit, and
poetry of descriptions, must go alongside of Lord Byron's . . . productions. . . ."[53] "Go alongside" means that he is able and willing to
recognize both the differences and similarities of the two—and admire them. Interestingly, the emulative area containing the Byron
Don Juan code was extended to include, cumulatively, other imitations and parodies. Gulian C. Verplanck published in 1819 a nine-
stanza-long bogus version of the nonexistent "The Fourth Canto of
Don Juan," featuring Pindar Puff as his Harold-like hero-castigator
of New York politics and society.[54] Isaac Starr Clason published a
pamphlet called "Fanny Continued" at the end of 1820, before Halleck's second enlarged edition (1821) (the publisher had given Halleck
$500 to add fifty stanzas to the the new edition)[55] had even appeared.
It wittily parodied its target, Halleck's "Fanny," but also—by indirection—Byron's *Don Juan*.[56] Clason's text then contains a substrata of
imitations, each performing a unique act of appropriation.

"Fanny" was the voice of agitated New York, *Sukey* that of cool and
intellectual Boston. This rambling seriocomic treatise, which quite
remarkably went through three editions within one single year, 1821,
was written by a certain William Barker Walter. Using Halleck's
stanza form and verse scheme, but without his elegance and adroit-
ness, he seems to have been determined to write a poem that first of
all demonstrated his beliefs in the "Doctrine of Association of
Ideas."[57] He thought Byron's narrative technique was a most suitable
model for this purpose. But despite the 171 stanzas available to him
Walter has, perhaps also as a consequence of his adoption of the
Byron format, very little to say, as he swings from one cluster of
associations to another. The plot structure, the orphan girl Sukey's
upbringing by her scholastic aunt and Sukey's falling in love with "a
wild hunter of the stormy north, / The deepening valley, and the
mountain high, / Were still his favourite haunts! He loved the cry, /
Of eagles in their solitudes;—the roar / Of cataracts!—the darkness
of that hour, / When spectres are abroad!" (23) paraphrase and echo

the Byron code in a most rudimentary and simplistic manner. However, the specifics of the setting of the poem—winter scenes, rides in "stage sleighs," "blue smoke, slowly curling / From cottage roofs" lends it a special New England flavor that distinguishes it from its other American counterparts. In addition, its bookish mannerisms reflect the self-confidence of a dignified university town, in a way that Halleck's "Fanny" reverbated with New York urban cockiness and vigor.

These two poems then reflect upon each other, as much as they reflected upon the first two cantos of Byron's *Don Juan*. They are mutually inscribed with the code, hybridized and acculturalized. An additional example of this is the function they ascribe to the illustrious, fatal party in *Don Juan*. Halleck uses it as a parable to sneer at capitalistic greed and banter about arrivistic pretensions; in *Sukey,* true to its nature as a poem of meditation and scholasticism, it functions as a mildly ironic exposure of human frivolity and indulgence. The closures of the poems are also very different and indicate the range of appropriations that the Byron *Don Juan* could be subjected to. The party naturally ruins Fanny's father and the couple is literally thrown out into the street and publicly disgraced. Halleck has written a moral tale of social comedy. At the end of the party in Boston's *Sukey* an African messager rushes in to deliver a letter that announces the sensational arrival of Sukey's forlorn lover who has heroically fought and killed a pirate chief with "tiger eyeballs." The martial end reads as a mock-heroic piece of American bravado and a sardonic hymn to freedom from overseas tyranny.

There was regional competition over the model forces of Byron's women, captains, and pirates. "In New-York, they have FANNY, in Boston, SUKEY, and why should not we have KITTY, in Charleston?," asks William Crafts and proceeds to rectify the situation.[58] His "Extract from Kitty. An unpublished Manuscript" portrays a Charleston belle, "the hapless maiden," Kitty, who parades her elegance *cum* nationalism during a long Fourth of July celebration, in the midst of soldiers, orators, and simple republicans.

> The night was dark, but Kitty must be seen,
> So to the Fireworks trippingly she went;
> Such as they kindle, on the Inspection Green,
> To show the crowd, and then the firmament.
> For when the *Fourth of July's* in the socket
> They send to its relief a blazing rocket.[59]

Kitty is a bleak Southern variant of such Byron women protagonists as Laura (*Beppo*) or Julia (*Don Juan*), but she is astonishly vivid seen in comparison with Fanny and Sukey who hardly materialize as persons of flesh and blood. Crafts's "Kitty" poem attempts to attach to the locality of the poem the grander design of canon formation, adopting the distancing of Byron's *Beppo* and *Don Juan,* while at the same time contravening the "base licentiousness" and "slandering pool of corruption and pestilence" that he believed characterized Byron's poems.[60] His contemporaries, however, only saw the obvious characteristics of this poem: its awkwardness and mimicry. Hugh Swinton Legaré's comments on the poem are typical:

> It is bad thing badly imitated—the exaggeration of a caricature. Lord Byron with his Beppos' and Juans' has done infinite mischief in the rhyming world. . . . Nothing is so easy as to rival the noble poet in his slipshod, zig-zag, desultory style, and doggrel versification—but nothing is more difficicult than to pour out, with such perfect *nonchalance,* strains of the most beautiful poetry, and sallies of incomparable wit.[61]

The urge to emulate Byron's *Don Juan,* but to abjure the alleged immoral allures of the poem, was seemingly part of any aspiring young contemporary poet's cultural conditioning. William Gilmore Simms composed his *Donna Florida* in the 1830, in what he later in the Preface to the issue of 1843, called "a boyish presumption . . . to imitate the grace and exceeding felicity of expression in that unhappy performance,—its playfulness, and possibly, its wit, without falling into its licentiousness of utterance, and malignity of mood" (see above, p. 23–24) Simms must have had qualms about publishing it; fearing that its closeness to the original might be too transparent. In a letter to George Frederick Holmes, preceding the publication, Simms anticipated—and rebuked—the criticism that was to follow. He explains that

> the verse is not that of Byron. It is an independent verse,—having an original construction. There is nothing lavish in the structure, and I am very certain that it is quite as easy in its flow, as that of its prototype. The last canto (the 4th) is quite original, and I suppose was the one which convinced you of my disposition to break away from my model.[62]

The rhyme scheme is a conventional reworking of the ottava rima, abababcc, and the verse is monotonous and dull, definitely "easy in its flow." Leonora (the Donna Florida of the poem) is an unintimidating mixture of Julia, Haidée, and Catherine, borrowing Julia and Haidée's sensuousness and Catherine's callousness: her self-indulgent father is modeled on the unreliable male figures that swarm *Don Juan.*

> She had but one old relative, a sire,
> A thick, short, gouty, drowsy, frowsy knight;
> Whose only care, beside his kitchen fire,
> Was how to boil his eggs and boil them right;
> His omelet served, he had no more desire,
> And slept, not waiting the approach of night;—
> Not profitless his faith, as it appears,
> In eating,—he had kept it sixty years. (16)

The Canto 4, then, from which Simms wanted Rufus W. Griswold to print an extract for his *Prose Writers of America* (1847) because in it "the Muse of the Nation is invoked, and the country specified,"[63] does offer a new slant to Byron's story. It describes two moonstruck lovers, Don Ferdinand de Laye and Ponce de Leon, who fall prey to the evil charms of the heroine. However, the bitch-witch Leonora refuses to yield to their persuasions before she has received the ultimate gifts of long life and abundant wealth. She dispatches them off to the "Isle of Youth's Desire" to help them procure these coveted qualities. Not surprisingly, the location of the sparkling fountain of life and the glittering treasure house is—America. The two erring knights are overcome by "savages" in a fight that Simms furnishes with the paraphernalia of the medieval tournament à la Scott. His message is that the old decrepit and immoral world of Leonora (Spain = Europe) cannot be rejuvenated by contacts with the New World. They are separate entities and should so remain. So Byron's *Don Juan* has been appropriated with a vengeance. The emulative impulse of the Southern writers Crafts and Simms was strongly reformative and nationalistic; the Byron code is employed to produce sagas that have the potential to reproduce authentic American works. However, Griswold, one of the century's most influential American canon builders, had refused, we saw, to include Simms's Byron construct in his anthologies.

But the bulk of the *Don Juan* emulations that poured out of the presses in mid-nineteenth century America were far less presumptuous documents and more in tune with Halleck's social comedy, *Fanny*. We will look at three such texts, all firmly planted in the period and the locale of their production, Rufus Dawes's "Geraldine" (1839), N. Parker Willis's "The Lady Jane. A Novel in Rhyme" (1849), and George Lunt's *Julia. A Poem* (1855).[64]

Rufus Dawes's "Geraldine" is another hybridized melodrama with cultural pretensions far beyond the limits of its genre. First of all, it incorporates the Byron code in a way that no other emulation we have discussed this far has done: paraphrasing Byron's letters, echoing, citing, alluding to popular passages across his whole œuvre, robbing them of their qualities in the process. The poem's sentimental hero Waldron, an English pirate, lascivious and mysterious, falls in love with Geraldine of New England. Naturally, the lovers die in the midst of the war between their countries. But this plot is secondary to the poem's larger frame of ambitions where the Byron code is made extravagant use of. "Where are thy bards, AMERICA!" (22) is its leitmotiv and Dawes sings of the rugged beauty of America's coastline, its rivers and mountains, and lauds the heroic past of New England and the emblems of liberty attached to it. Byron's individual and decaying world of free enterprise is repopulated by another, bolder and more imaginative, race of men and women.

N. Parker Willis's conversational, light-hearted "Lady Jane" is a social comedy, for "Broadway demoiselles," ridiculing the stylish fashions and puppet mannerisms of the British leisure class. We move into ladies' boudoirs redolent of perfume and attend Friday night soirées among countesses, earls, and their slick varlets. The "novel" lacks a narrative; it is preoccupied with creating the claustrophobic "atmosphere" surrounding the couple Lady Jane and Jules. Again, there are many threads of the Byron code woven into the text: facts from Byron's married life, the ensnaring orientalism of Byron's "tales," and above all the intimacies of Julia and Juan and the medieval setting of Norman Abbey. The latter part of Willis's text has an Italian setting reminiscent of similar passages in *Childe Harold*.[65]

Yet, it is the mélange of "fact" and "fiction" that forms the poem's most effective critical locus. In the following two stanzas the two "Byrons" seem to have the same function. There is no reciprocation between the two. It is the persona of the writer (Willis) that mediates and lays bare the connections:

> Jules was at perfect liberty *in fact*
> To love again, and still be true *in fancy;*
> Else were this story at its closing act.
> Nay, he *in fact* might wed, and *in romance* he
> Might find the qualities his *sposa* lack'd—
> (A truth that I could easier make a man see,)
> And woman's great mistake, if I may tell it, is
> The calling such stray fancies "infidelities."

> Byron was man and bard, and Lady B.,
> In wishing to monopolise him wholly,
> Committed bigamy, you plainly see.
> She, being *very* single, Guiccioli
> Took off the odd one of the wedded three—
> A change, 'twould seem, quite natural and holy.
> The *after* sin, which still his fame environs,
> Was giving Guiccioli *both* the Byrons. (856)

And the next line carves out the consequence: "The stern wife drove him from her." But not so in Willis's poem; Jules holds his paternal "harem" intact. Willis's poem interacts with the legends spinning around the Byron scandal; it becomes a defense of Byron's right, as a poet, to "sin," commit adultery, and divorce. Jules, his alter ego, dramatizes the unperturbed, hedonistic Byron, a physical male prototype who could be used to satirize attitudes and social norms. Willis's poem is double-edged: it supports Byron the poet on the issue of his private morality *and* it employs the Byron code to point out the well-known concepts of England as corrupt and degenerate.

The Byron character occupying the American emulations was in most cases a hybrid configuration, often embodying contradictory qualities. The writers could choose among quite a number of characterizations; their choice was actuated by the kind of comment they wanted to make about matters that were essential to them. Willis, we saw, depicted the "oriental" sensualist, the superego and the womanizer. Another protoype was the tempestuous and wild Byron figure, tempered only by womanly adulation. He is a key figure in countless poems throughout the century. In Carlos Stuart's "Ianthe" we meet a hero possessed by "an Italian fire," looking upon "the world as a dark den," and trying to quell "the tempest of [his] wrath."[66] But in vain. By mistake he kills his lover, the faithful Ianthe, "so fair, so gentle, innocent, and good" (15) and ends up in prison bitterly lamenting his cruel fate:

> And here am I, in this bleak world alone,
> Struck from the roll of virtuous and the blest,
> Sad as the soul whose solitary moan
> Is o'er the grave of all it loved the best; (25)

In each case the writers employed the modality of the Byron code that best suited their literary project: Willis's "Don Juan" projects his view of the poet's private life but also serves as an ironical and twisted commentary on domestic urban mores and on the superfluity of British aristocratic mores; the persona of Stuart's "Ianthe," who compounds traits from *Childe Harold, Don Juan,* and Byron the poet, is a vehicle for his romantic and idealized notion of love's consummation.

The lines "Her father was a merchant-prince of Boston, / Famed chiefly for a fortune made in tea" (8) bear witness to another *Don Juan* poem, George Lunt's *Julia,* presented with a strong local accent. Her father, "a hard, good, upright, steady, pious man" (9), in every respect a good Boston Brahmin, impersonates the successful and scrupulous business man, a representative of the emerging class of nouveau riche that Halleck had ridiculed. The sentimental plot describes the harsh father's favoring of the rich suitor and the pathetic disaster of Julia's choice of the poor feminine Arden. The poem is firmly anchored in Boston, in its mundane social life of and picturesque environs. Perhaps the most interesting aspect of the poem, at least from the point of view of my analysis, is Lunt's endeavor to raise his emulation to a higher category of productions than what constituted the domestic melodrama.

As in so many other Byron imitations with a New England sea setting, the topography of the rocky cliffs of Nahant are evoked to call forth their "primal grandeur" and "Indian legendary story" (cf. Dawes's "Geraldine" and Ballou's *Fanny Campbell*). The present pictorial situation with sad Julia is looking out over the ocean languishing for her bosom friend Arden (N.B. his name) is linked with a general situation represented by the cliff's historical and mythological content.

> But, stern in primal grandeur, when it threw
> Its broad, bare shoulder to the mad wave's lash,-
> And the red savage, poised in light canoe,
> Lit the sea-sparkles, to his paddle's flash,-
> Or, but wild sea-bird whistled as he flew,
> To the wild sea-wind and the billowy dash,-
> Good were it there, mid wrecks primeval strown,
> To look on Nature's sacred face alone! (52)

Here nature in its pristine and primitive form, contained by images as seemingly disparate as "the red savage," the wild sea-bird," and "wrecks primeval strown," is summoned up to lend a time frame to the poem, beyong its immediate context. The references to the "red savage" and the "wreck," one evoking a "legendary" all-American past and the other a more recent and local New England locale, serve to historicize and generalize the poem. The metonymic projection they constitute provides the Boston *Don Juan* emulation with an aspect of sadness and grimness; a grimness that is deepened by the modern reader's recognition of the artistic functionalism that Lunt had ascribed to the "red savage" trope. The ruins of *Childe Harold* had been transposed into wrecks. But the function is the same: to strike a balance and form a bond between the past and the present.

There were also mock-humorous skits constructing an end to the *Don Juan* epic. One such piece was by Isaac Starr Clason who also wrote a continuation of Halleck's *Fanny*. His *Don Juan. Cantos XVII–XVII* (1825) is a rambling parody of Don Juan's women and his final marriage to a widow. "Beware of sending Juan to the devil," is his appeal to the readers.[67] Another much highly elaborated poem

continuing Byron's was Henry Morford's *The Rest of Don Juan;
Inscribed to the Shade of Byron* (1846).[68] It is the most boring of all
the emulations I have studied. In five cantos, each spouting about
seventy to eighty stanzas in ottava rima, the poem starts by com-
memorating Byron's death by a visit to his grave, investing and ex-
panding on various bits and pieces from his life, and then turning to
sketch a mocking aftermath to Don Juan's life in England. The satire
is aimed at the whims and follies of British aristocracy. The following
verses are typical of Morford's verbiosity, but also, on a thematic
level, characteristic of one of the American obsessions with Byron:

> They have few quarrels, very little hatred,
> And not a spark of love. Oh riches, riches,
> Oh rank, of fortune, noble blood and title!
> The dull plebeians whom your sound bewitches,
> Would judg'd difference if they judge aright all,
> They might see some aristocratic hitches,
> And aristocracy with no requital,
> They might see, could they read the whole page through,
> Some things that would not make them envy you. (II, xci–xcii)

It is on this social stage that Don Juan carries out his amorous
escapades among the nobility in England, in France and later on in
Spain, where in the end he meets a mysterious death. Morford's
winding poem intersects on occasions with Willis' *Lady Jane* (II,
lxxxviii–xc, IV, lv–lx). It highlights Willis's ideal of American womanhood with middle class values and juxtaposes it with the degenerate
norm system of an effeminate British aristocracy. The Byron code
in its American mould refused to serve neutral ends.

Fusions of Scott and Byron

The fusion of the Scott and the Byron codes, we saw in the first
section of this chapter, was a significant phenomenon in nineteenth-
century appropriation of English literature. The two frequently inter-
acted to the point of becoming indistinguishable, although, in fact,
most writers tried hard to separate them. However, what is more
relevant for our purposes is the identification of the separation between these codes *and* their American operators. Insofar as such a
separation can be validated, imitation changes character and integration turns into emulation.

Robert C. Sands explains that his *The Bridal of Vaumond* (1817)
was a

> metrical romance, in the irregular measure of Scott's Lay of the Last
> Minstrel, and founded on the same legend of the transformation of a

decrepit and miserable wretch into a youthful hero, by compact with the infernal powers, which forms the groundwork of Byron's Deformed-Transformed.[69]

The performative pattern of the poem includes, then, two operators, two codes of influence; Walter Scott, Sands claims, who provides the poem its mechanics, and Lord Byron, its thematics. Sands does not seem to be able to uphold and carry out this distinction, as the following quote from the poem illustrates. The Scott code (mode, tone, and theme) is here an integral part of the overall narrative pattern of the poem. Perhaps this is the reason he was compelled to explain that he was "yet a youth" when he wrote the poem.[70] In any case Sands is trying to write, as it were, against the codes, against the "rotten dynasties" and "fungus hierarchy" of Europe.[71]

> It was the morn of a summer's day,
> And brightly did its radiance play
> Or armour burnish'd fair,
> The breeze that blythely swept the grave
> A nodding field of plumes did hove
> All stately waving there:[72]

Jonathan M. Scott, in *Blue Lights, or The Convention* (1817), also appeals to Scott and his authority in publishing his book. But there is a sardonic undertone of dismissal in his Preface, as if he is challenging the very Scott code he is adhering to, which was not an altogether unusual procedure in the appropriation history of English literature in the nineteenth century. Walter Scott's "Lady of the Lake" was allegedly his source of inspiration. But this is the way he goes about defending his project:

> For surely they who can commend and read with delight, an account of a Scottish girl becoming miraculously pregnant merely by having a quantity of ashes blown under her petticoats by a puff of a wind, may surely pass without censure the peccadillos committed in this book.[73]

A third example of an emulation of the Scott code—with a vengeance—can be found in *The Frontier Maid; or, A Tale of Wyoming* (1819). The writer dedicated his book to the "police magistrates in the world of Letters, devoting themselves peculiarly to the detection of Literary crimes, and the punishment of the culprits."[74] Having said this, he launches into a lenghty announcement that he has adapted "the form of Walter Scott's stanza, and the mechanical characteristics of his verse," but patterned them on "American scenes and incidents."[75]

PROSE EMULATIONS

In this section we will deal with emulations in prose, with stories, novels and drama, a much thinner area, despite the fact that among the British writers most prominent in my material only Byron was primarily a poet. There was little stimulus for performing wholesale appropriations in prose: it was probably seen as both cumbersome and unimaginative. Yet, as we will see, Byron and Dickens scored pretty well in this sphere which is further proof of the latitude of their applicability.[76]

BYRON

That Byron's *Don Juan* would find its way also to the American stage is no wonder, as this happened virtually to most of his works—prose and poetry. Second, that it was the Haidée episode that would be chosen for dramatization comes neither as a surprise. It offered the imitators of Byron, in poetry, prose, and now also in drama, a tantalizing, "oriental" material to elaborate on. The play *The Sultana; or a Trip to Turkey* (1822), ascribed to John Bailey, offers such an example.

It is a three-act teenage melodrama revolving around the elopement of Haidée on a slave ship dressed as a boy, and her reunion with Juan at the court of a loveable Turkish sultan, who by his benevolent and liberating act stands in a sharp contrast to Haidée's mercantile Greek father. The irony is that it is the Turk, not the Greek, who sets the couple free. The simple plot is interspersed with casual ruminations on the abomination of slavery. Orloff, Juan's friend, who is the pragmatic thinker, advises the intemperate, but fast-learning Juan, while they are still on board the slave ship, that they "travel in pursuit of knowledge. [And] we get it *here*. For instance, now, we learn what slavery is, and how to behave ourselves, when we get to the masters." On seeing four blacks being sold sold Juan comments: "Tis too shocking, humanity should *blush* at it—all men were born to be free, and the curse of Heaven light on the wretch who would enslave them" (18).[77] Juan rebels in front of Sultana (a faint representation of Byron's seductive women-bitches) who insists on having him kiss her foot. "Love is for the free," he exclaims and the audiences could not miss the message (26). Lord Byron's *Don Juan* had been transformed into a New York political pamphlet.

To build a story around the setting of the sea, including piracy, shipwrecks, and seaside caves, and mingle with it sensational escapes to freedom or their opposites, sensational events of kidnapping, and the like, was, as we have seen, a definite American way of responding to the Byron code. Byron's Tales and both *Childe Harold* and *Don Juan* provided scripts and concepts to similar constructs. One of the most elaborate texts of this category is Maturin Murrey Ballou's *Fanny Campbell, The Female Pirate Captain. A Tale of the Revolution* (1844).[78]

The New England seascape with the obligatory homage to the beauty of "rock-bound Nahant" and the political climate of the 1770s, witnessing the "thousand petty acts of tyranny practised by the soldiers of the crown" (11), form the background for this melodramatic prose narrative of one hundred pages. On a rough stone "hewn from the solid rock by the hand of the red man" (11), Fanny, the fisherman's daughter, and her childhood lover William, in the best manner of the Byronic hero, gaze upon the distant sea, form a revolutionary bond to fight the English oppressors, and demonstrate that among the "lower classes of society, there is more of the germ of true intellect and courage, nobleness of purpose, and strength of will then may be found among the pampered and wealthy children of fortune" (99). William is captured by pirates and, amid mutinies and breaches of loyalties, Fanny disguised as a sea captain, rescues him from being imprisoned in a Cuban prison. Together they launch a private war against British vessels, for American resurgence.

The narrative includes two subplots, one politico-sentimental, the other purely ideological. The first involves the Captain Burnet, a British officer of one of the Royal Cutters lying in Boston harbor. He falls in love with Fanny who, of course, true to her commitment to William and the colonial pine-tree flag, resists him; the second debates the abolition of the capital punishment that is part of the derelict British penal system and its inhuman values.

This political allegory then includes several strands of the Byron code, ranging from historicizing the physical setting to politicizing the time frame. These aspects are strongly imbued with American notions of the indigenous landscape and with American concepts of liberalism and nationalism. But the text also sums up the American taste for muscular romance and outdoor action.

The formula John Neal uses for his crude "novel" *Randolph* (1823), an exchange of letters between the American Edward Molton and the Englishman George Stafford, establishes a colonial disparity even on the structural level of the book's discourse system. In discursive bombast, Molton answers the critique, imagined or real, that Stafford, or the colonializing Other, is made to voice.[79] Most of Molton's litanies concern the well-known problematic issues of the American projects, the concerns of the American writers to promote a national literature, the ignorant condescension that the Old World heaped on those Americans that do write, and the familiar rant about Scott and Byron. Molton's main vituperations seem to be directed against "the licentiousness and imbecility of Don Juan," whose popularity he thinks stems from "a conspiracy between the reviewers and the publishers, and perhaps Lord Byron himself" (I, 163). Yet, it is the same Molton that another of the novel's correspondents, Sarah Ramsay, describes as a man of "the most depraved inclinations" (I, 202). It is uncertain whether this seeming contradiction in Neal's characterization of Morton was a deliberate "literary" gesture of discomfort or a "technical" flaw. Whatever the reason, it underscores the ambiguity that structures the overall American appreciation of Byron. The rejection of him was frequently—although seldom overtly expressed by the same writer—informed by its opposite. It is a distancing mechanism that characterizes the American decolonizing process.

In John Neal's other work, his play *Otho* (1819), the Byron code the play encapsulates is of a different nature.[80] He wrote the play, he explains in the Preface, for Thomas Abthorpe Cooper, who never played it (and nobody else did, for that matter). The reason was probably Neal's admission that he had paraphrased scenes and employed ideas stolen from a whole range of English works, including Maturin's *Bertram,* Byron's *Corsair* and *Manfred,* and Shakespeare's *Macbeth* (and *King Lear,* which he does not mention). His ultimate motive was to construct "an American Tragedy, and I was on fire," he confessed," with the ambition of letting off the first—good, bad, or indifferent" (v). "About this time MANFRED appeared, and his farewell to the sun, the night before *his* death—so commanding—so alone in its supernatural uplifting—. . . left an impression upon my mind that I fear has been communicated to a scene in OTHO. I did not intend to profit by that great picture—but I fear that—involuntarily I have done it" (v). He goes on explaining that despite the obvious parallels he has no intention to change the scene, or strike it out, because, he believes that "though it is not altogether original . . . there is still enough originality in it to redeem it" (vi). And, he claims, even without the inference of a "Corsair" and a "Manfred," he would in any case have come upon the idea of having Otho, his rebel-bastard hero face a death sentence and take farewell from life in more or less the same magniloquent style.

What is noteworthy here is not only the arrogance of Neal's self-righteous act of committing a literary fraud, but also his belief that he could, indeed, create an "American tragedy" through an act of concocting and paraphrasing. It can only be understood as prejudiced by the colonial context. *Otho* is a literary expression of rebellion and resistance. This is why the B-text confronts the A-text in the latter's terms, by its tropes and grammar and not by the creation of a new scheme of presentation.

Molton in Neal's epistolary novel *Randolph* had, we saw, projected antagonistic aspects of the American Byron code, thus, problematizing the colonial distance. Frederick W. Thomas's novel *Thomas Pinckney* (1841) shows many similarities with *Randolph*.[81] The hero of the novel, Thomas Pinckney, is another melancholic, slightly cynical Byronic hero, but imbued with fewer of the "contradictions" of Neal's Molton. He has traveled in Italy, fallen in love, been severely bruised by the affair, and is now returning to his native country to rest from the turmoil of the world. On the boat he meditates in the best manner of the ultraliterary characters of the American midcentury popular story.

Often as I have looked out upon the waves I found myself repeating Byron's lines, as though they were my own spontaneous thoughts:—

> "Once more upon the waters—yet once more;
> And the waves bound beneath me as a steed
> That knows his rider." [CH, III, 9–11]

I have trod the deck beneath a bright and holy moon, and felt as if the sensation of drowsiness would never weigh my eyelids down again. Those three lines . . . pleased me more than all Byron's address to the ocean, in the conclusion of *Childe Harold*. There is too much effect in the address—too much theatrical effect—it seems studied for the occasion, like a player's dignified exit in the last scene; . . . (11–12)

He is invited to spend time at the house of a Southern plantation family where he meets their daughter Fanny whom he seduces by the same twofold strategy that the previous quote postulated, by advocating and projecting Byron critically and simultaneously attempting to personify him; he embodies the Byron myth. In a whole chapter of the book (XIII) Pinckney lectures on Byron. Fanny is impressed, especially as he is able to sprinkle his performance with lines from his own Byronisms.[82]

In another novel by Thomas, *Clinton Bradshaw; or, the Adventures of a Lawyer* (1835), the protagonist visits the monument of Colonel William Glover, "a flower in the cap of liberty." He cuts out a bullet from a tree and with "a quickening pulse" he ruminates: "It is a remarkable fact, notwithstanding these heart wounds, the tree, as you see, is green and flourishing." Then he recalls the pathos of the Waterloo scenery in Byron's *Childe Harold* and quotes from it the comparison of man's inhumanity with Nature's passionate serenity (III, xxx–xxxi).[83] In addition to winning the heart of a Southern belle and her cotton fortune, the Byronic hero of *Clinton Bradshaw* also becomes a celebrant of the national cause. Thomas's protagonists Pinckney and Bradshaw, Southern gentlemen, well-traveled, eloquent, versed, good-looking, and successful as both lovers and family men, then derive their personal attraction and social success from the chauvinistic potentialities provided by the Byron code. The cult of Byron could be transformed into a novelistic male ideal that not only pointed to, but also could guarantee, commercial success.

My third prose writer of some reputation is the most devoted Byronist of them all, Anna Cora Ritchie, whose poetry we have already discussed. As we also saw she was both actress, elocutionist, lecturer, and prose writer or novelist.[84] She wrote a few books in the epistolary and discursive style of Neal and Thomas. And like these writers she sprinkled her text with literary allusions and quotations, either as chapter headings or interspersed in the narration.[85] This indicates that the social context in which these books is laid is urban and intellectual. Ritchie's *Evelyn; or, A Heart Unmasked. A Tale of Domestic Life* (1845), which I will discuss in some detail, is situated in a midcentury artistic milieu in New York.[86] One of the pastimes of Evelyn and her friends is to organize highly elaborate costumed tableaux that illustrate scenes from various works of art *à la mode*. On one such evening the company produces Byron's *Corsair* with some of the novel's protagonists as the main characters. Each scene—and there are nine of them—is preceded by a recitation of the appropriate passage and then follows the "Oriental" dumb-show with dervishes, seyds, silken couches, heavy turbans of gold, and the whole rhetorical mechanism of gestures and postures.[87] The narrator invites us to understand that the melodrama is a covert representation of Evelyn's (who performs Gulnare in *Corsair*) teeming love for the stylish Colonel Danoreau.[88] The obvious title for the chapter is "A Heart Unmasked." Through glosses, rich in sexual connotations and implications, the narrator interpretes the impact of the scene for us. It is as if she were watching an illegitimate pornographic maneuver through a peephole:

> Her features [Gulnare's] expressed the most feminine helplessness of grief, and her very position bespoke the approach of despair. The guitar which she had touched in his absence was lying neglected at her feet. Her long, fair hair, wholly unbound, stole in loose and waving ringlets from beneath a small Greek cap of blue velvet and silver, fitting closely to her head, and secured by a string of pearls that bound her pure brow. . . . Conrad was standing at the foot of her couch, in the act of retreating, but with his face turned back to take the last, longing look of pitying and admiring affection. (90–91)

Then followed other tableaux illustrative of scenes from *The Pickwick Papers* and *Nicholas Nickleby,* but the narrator's interest was gone. She could not rouse herself, she admits. Ritchie's Conrad tableau includes a number of representational icons, all illustrative of the utility of the Byron code. Apart from the obvious genre tranformations of Byron's oriental tale into a mid-nineteenth century New York tableau, a tranformation which has traveled from graphic art to stage art (voice, body, costume, music), it extends and elaborates it further by forming the dramatic locus in an epistolary novel. That the Dickens's *Pickwick* figures could not "rouse" our mediator after such a performance is understandable. She is exhausted; particularly, she says, by watching Evelyn's shifting gestures and loosening robes. It is as if she (and the audience) had participated in an intense sexual act that has consumed all their energy. The "illegitimacy" stigma connoted with the Byron code has definitely prejudiced her gaze. This is the oblique way she formulates her approach to Byron and his influence on her:

> I do not admire the works of Byron—I admire them for their power, their sublimity, their earnestness, and the intenseness of the passions they portray, and yet I do not rise from their perusal better, and happier, and more elevated in spirit. There is a touch of mildew on every leaf—he weaves the poisonous nightshade into a garland of beauty—and while the hues of the flowers dazzle the eye, their breath contaminates the soul. (86)

So it is not the "reading" of the text that consumes her; its performance does. The outcome is not happiness or spiritual elevation, but a "truth" that she cannot avail herself of. Only the reader may. Ritchie's narration reflects the gender-based ambiguities of the cultural resistance to Byron and the Byron code. The female protagonists of her novels, whether they are outside "observers" or inside "actors," are victimized, which is a process leading to their unmasking. The Byron code Ritchie so skillfully employed for novelistic purposes could have a liberating influence on women, as it had had on her. But, she was fully aware of its alluringly reductive influence on gender formation. These two aspects of women are present in Ritchie's tableaux.

FUSIONS OF BYRON, SCOTT, AND SHAKESPEARE

Another playwright attempting to devise a model that could fuse an English base and an American form was James W. Simmons from whom we have at least two plays that deserve to be mentioned here: *Manfredi* and *Valdemar*. The first is an oratorical showpiece, with ingredients from Shakespeare's *Hamlet* (personal revenge theme) and

Romeo and Juliet (romantic passion); but above all it is modeled on the heroic stance of Byron's *Manfred*.[89] The setting is America. Instead of the Alps, the action takes place near the rapids of the Metaurus [?]. The other play, Simmons explains in the Preface, is based on Scott's *The Bride of Lammermoor.* But

> we hope, however, that it may be conceded to us, as it was to Otway in his Orphan, that while we have been indebted to a foreign source for the outline of our fable, the sentiments and characters are yet are own. Few know perhaps, that the Orphan, one of the most pathetic of dramas, was founded upon a novel entitled, English Adventures, said to be written by Robert Boyle, Earl of Orrery.[90]

Like his other play *Manfredi* this one not only echoes Shakespeare, it quotes and paraphrases from his works extensively. None of these plays seems to have been acted, apparently for this very reason. The prefatorial reference to a literary tradition did not help him.

Another imitator who failed to attract an actor to perform his plays was Gilmore Simms who also had a professional interest in the drama. Apart from writing and reviewing plays, he revised plays by Shakespeare and edited a work on the Shakespeare apocrypha and imputations. And throughout his life he kept on approaching actors and publishers to have them produce his plays, but without success.[91] In 1845 he wrote to James Lawson and asked when Edwin Forrest, the famous American actor, would be back. He obviously wanted to introduce him to his adaptation of "Locrine" (a text he had imputed to Shakespeare) and had published as "The Death of the British Brutus. A Dramatic Sketch." Seven years later he was making another attempt to persuade Forrest to accept another of his adaptations, this one of *Timon of Athens.* In another letter to James Lawson he explained his motives. "I have long ago concieved [sic] the propriety of altering Timon, so as to show his wrongs to have been such as to justify his subsequent career of passionate cynicism; and the story, as I designed to change it, will be singularly appropriate to F's fortunes."[92] But Forrest did not think so.[93] The play was neither produced nor published. Nor was produced another of his sketches, "The Death of Cleopatra," which gives a macabre, almost lascivious, account of Cleopatra's half-naked corpse on her deathbed.[94] Simms, in all these attempts, moved dangerously close to parody.

DICKENS

With the craze for the stage production of Dickens's novels culminating in the midcentury, his novels, their printed stage adaptations, and above all his two visits to the country and the books, comments, and slander that accompanied these well-publicized events, spun off new adaptations, burlesques, and parodies that met a variety of interests and needs outside the purely professional theaters.

Two such venues were the home theater and the school. The mooted objective of the adaptations for these institutions was either simply to "entertain" or to "exhibit" a domestic moral for a young audience. Understandably, these objectives were hardly separable. George Melville Baker, for instance, rewrote Dickens all his life. His adaptation of *A Christmas Carol* is included in his *Amateur Dramas for Parlor Theatricals, Evening Entertainments, and School Exhibitions.*[95] Through a series of educational tableaux that are organized at an inner recess of Scrooge's office to confront Scrooge with his selfish past and teach him the hard lessons of charity and humbleness that is, "to think of people below them as if they really were fellow-travelers to the grave, and not another race of creatures, bound on other journeys" (230). Variations of this republican credo lay behind most of the American Dickens adaptations in prose. George B. Bartlett introduced his *The Grand Dickens Cosmorama* (1885) as "a novel method of raising funds for charitable purposes" and suggested further that on such a public occasion the fund-raising team should perform to achieve their goals: Pickwick could be president, Samuel Weller, business manager, Alfred Jingle, treasurer, and Mrs. Leo Hunter and Mrs. Jellyby, secretaries.[96] He then goes on to suggest themes for the enactment of the most popular scenes from Dickens's novels, in all fifty-one tableax, such as "Smike at Rehearsal," "Oliver Twist and Fagin," "Caleb Plummer's Toy shop," and "Little Nell." They have all been dramatized with a strong emphasis on socialization: costume and language serve as ironic markers of a social class, which in many of the scenes gradually withers under the pressure of the instincts for a more equal world order. The message of Dickens is supposed to lie here. "Buoyant" and "Dotage" are two such charades, with similar social programs, each consisting of three scenes from different Dickens novels; the former was written by Lucia Chase Bell, the latter by Fannie M. Johnson.[97] Like *The Grand Dickens Cosmorama,* their function is partly burlesque, partly moral.[98] The humor of the pieces is almost proverbial: it captures the well-known Dickens comedy of the day. Surprisingly little of Dickens's settings and language have been altered or transformed; it is as if the producers of these tableaux and dramatic sketches made a point of retaining their "Englishness," even to the point of absurdity. Perhaps this deliberate rigidity was in itself an act of cultural inversion and a trope for irony. "Sam Weller's Visit to His Mother-In-Law" and "Bumble's Courtship: A Comic Interlude, in One Act" by Frank E.

Emson, intended for "The Home Circle, Private Theatricals, and the American Stage," were no doubt played on the New York stage. The humor of situation and language is Dickensian in the broad manner of the contemporary stage, but the jibes each play directs against religious hypocrisy and Christian relief work seem to derive from experiences gained on New York streets.[99]

There were also other adaptations of Dickens's works. The most spectacular one to my mind is by Robert Henry Newall or Orpheus C. Kerr, whose *The Cloven Foot* is a burlesque adaptation of Dickens's unfinished novel "The Mystery of Edwin Drood."[100] In his Preface, called an "Apology," Newall explains wryly that the reason he has undertaken the adaptation is first that Dickens's work is artistically infelicitous in its characterization of Mr. Jasper, second that American literature, being crude as the country itself, deserves no contributions other than ludicrous ones such as the one by the present writer. This is why he has "deliberately reduc[ed] the current work of some great foreign novelist to American equivalents" (15). The "reduction" he aimed at involves "imitating . . . the style and idiosyncrasies of the English author," while Americanizing the plot, transforming John Jasper, the English opium-smoker into John Bumstead, the American clove-eater, turning the city of Cloisterham, with its "venerable Cathedral and Nun's House" into the suburban Bumsteadville, with its "Ritualistic Church and Alms-House," and Edwin Drood, the brilliant Londoner into a "mere boy" in New York (15–16). Newall's ironic resituation of Dickens's narration is superbly skillful, its wit simultaneously directed in many directions, whipping the unseemly and unhealthy American veneration of Dickens, the American lack of self-understanding, and the very quandary of American letters. Through this irony it also ventured to pull an ironic film over the Dickens text itself and over the values and concepts it incorporated.

Commentary as Imitation

In the following I will mainly examine two modes of nineteenth-century American commentaries on British writers: the eulogy and the satire. These commentaries include elements of both commendatory praise and derogatory scoff; they laud and rail. They are often self-reflective: their form and content collaborate. This means that, like Thomas Carew's "Elegy of John Donne," while singing a laudatory hymn they simultaneously recapture or simulate the tenor and grammar of their object. They also occasionally orient themselves away from their origin of inspiration and produce B-texts whose "independence" is established only with inscriptions of the other. So, we have many Byron-inspired satires that target American conventions and American hypocrisy. The texts discussed in this section differ from those in the previous ones, first, in their direct and open confrontation with the semantics of the cultural codes we are dealing with (Byron, Scott, Dickens) and, second, through their expository/rhetorical form of presentation.

EULOGIES

The deaths of Byron in 1824 and of Scott in 1832 launched a string of commendatory and obituary verse and prose that continued to issue for decades. Most of it is highly idealistic and utterly ephemeral. The poet shrouded, as it were, in the poetic garb of the Elysian hinterworld is elevated to the position of Genius Laureate. Upon the death of Scott, a committee was founded in New York to raise funds to erect a monument, as "it may be doubted whether so prolific and so magnetic a brain had existed since that of Shakespeare. . . ."[101] On 20 December 1832 the Park produced a pageant with tableaux from four of his novels and his two most famous poems, *Marmion* and *The Lady of the Lake.*[102] P. Hamilton Myers, admirer and imitator of Scott and writer of *Ensenore,* expressed his veneration for the dead poet in a rhymed poem of twenty-two stanzas that had its inspirational origin in a talismanic grey lock of Walter Scott's hair that Colonel William L. Stone had given him.[103] The poem unrolls a funereal dramatization of various Scott characters from his poems and novels that, in a dreamlike procession, resembling the Park pageant, confront the reader. The poem is drenched in a sentimental fake-medieval atmosphere of nostalgia and ritual; we are in "land of chivalry and song / Of fairy green and haunted well." Myers derives from Scott's poetry something that could even be seen as a poetic credo: "Thank heaven, the charms are unconfined / With which the ideal world is fraught! / No mountains bar the human mind: / No seas divide the world of thought" (172). Scott's poetry, in other words, is universal, all-encompassing. The Park performance in 1832 also staged such abstractions as the "genii of Europe, America, Asia & Africa." The same universal lament is expressed by William Walter in his valediction to Scott, called "Ogilvie."[104] Only it is even more highfalutin and pathetic in its lavish use of bird images and imperial connotations.[105]

That Byron's death became larger than all the accumulated famous deaths of the century is a truism worth rehearsing. Here only a few samples may suffice to indicate what thematics it upheld. Grenville Mellen's "Ode on Byron" ("written soon after his death") was a windy elegy, strung with catcalling epithets such as "self-exil'd prince of song," "imperial monarch of the Nile," and "a homeless King."[106]

As in the two elegies on Scott, cosmic and imperial imagery has been used abundantly. The following lines suggest, however, that—unlike Scott—Byron was always a thorn in the flesh, for himself and for his American admirers and readers:

> Who sent, to jewel earth, that starry mind?
> Thou has't but dimm'd its ray,
> Or flung its splendor on the wind-
> Or lavish'd half its beams away,
> And left a deadly light behind! (201)

Rufus W. Griswold included *three* dedicatory poems to Byron in his anthology *The Poets and Poetry of America* (1842), which is more than anything else a pungent manifestation of Byron's position in nineteenth-century American literary culture. "To Lord Byron" by Richard Henry Wilde, is very traditional, rehearsing the cosmic imagery already familiar to us, and pointing to his status as an outcast and a rebel. But his co-option by American culture is also noted; he is the "TACITUS of song," whose "echoes, thronging / O'er the Atlantic, fill the mountains hoary / And forests with the name my name is wronging."[107] The second by Charles Fenno Hoffman, Griswold's favorite American poet, adds little to the general image of Byron in predicating his wandering instincts; he is "A TANTALUS," and "an Arab on life's waste."[108]

With the third poem in Griswold's collection of American poems, Walter Colton's "Byron," we enter a somewhat different category of eulogistic poems. These poems cast wider ring of doubt and ambiguity over the popular reputation of Byron than we have seen before. In contrast to the former group of obituary verse these poems are also argumentative and apologetic. The idealistic assertion has withered; instead, we are to experience insecurity about Byron's real worth as a poet and a model. In Colton's view, Byron, instead of "soaring," "betray'd his trust, and lent his gift / Of glorious faculties to blight and mar / The moral universe."[109] Young Lucretia Maria Davidson, not surprisingly, had detected a "demon" in Byron who thwarted the "sweet chords" of his harp to the exposure of "Sin and Fear."[110] But Byron was still an exemplary poet, at least for other poets, if not for readers in general.

The apology par excellence James W. Simmons's prose treatise *An Inquiry into the Moral Character of Lord Byron* (1826), which seeks to explain, in the Romantic jargon of the day, the moral flaws of the poet resulting from his passionate, unruly nature. The sublimity that inheres in his poetry—and Simmons quotes passages from *Childe Harold* to corroborate this—its grandeur and awfulness, must be endorsed, he urges, because they exemplify the "sympathetic" link that connects the moral and the natural world.[111] James G. Brooks approached the problem of Byron's "immorality" in a different way. In 450 lines of highly formulaic, pentametric couplets, delivered before the "Connecticut Alpha of The Phi Beta Kappa" on 12 September 1826, Brooks commemorates Byron as the poet of wild waterfalls and silent mountains, a romantic genius, a demon man, a proud and ambitious sinner, and an unhealthy sceptic.[112] In the presence of the mythic corpse of the poet, Brooks penitentially asks where "haughty Byron" is now.

> On his high front such majesty before?
> Where is the passion of that noble brow,
> Where is its wild and lofty beauty now?
> Wan, pale, he lies, while fate's uplifted dart
> Flames fearfully above that generous heart!
> Away—away! avert the anxious eye,
> In silent solitude let genius die: (19)

"Death hath broke rudely into beauty's bower" (25) and the only way to dispute Death's "melancholy pall" is through a humble, religious surrender. Byron rejected such a surrender and in necroscopic glosses Brooks gloats over his mistake. Brooks has translated Byron's death into a Christian homily, into an exemplary of the need to redeem and repent. No doubt, it was the specific audience to whom this poem was addressed that shaped its content and the formulæ he couched them in, because in another obituary poem he wrote about Byron the tone is much more subdued and sincerely grieveous.

> Thy manhood met upon the earth
> With joys, while mine did meet with none
> to thee life was a thing of worth
> Yet I am left, and thou art gone![113]

Two poems that fall outside these categories are James Nack's "Dedicatory Lines to Charles Dickens, Esq." (1850) and "Byron. To His Accusers" (1869). Nack's tribute to Dickens stands as frontispiece to his book, *The Immortal; A Dramatic Romance; and Other Poems* (1850); the other is included in *Strange Visitors* (1869), an anonymous collection of disparate essays and poems.[114] Nack's dedication of his book to Dickens is paradigmatic. Dickens is hailed as the generous "friend of the human race," of sundry and all, of poor and rich. Nack evokes the descriptions of the deaths of Little Paul and Little Nell, as markers of Dickens's good heart and compassion. "[Greatness] rests not in externals, nor its worth / Derives from gorgeous pomp, or glittering pelf, / Or chance of arms, or accident of birth; / It lays its deep foundations in the soul." In his Byron poem, "To His Accusers," "Byron" is given the chance to voice his bitterness at the way an insensitive society (English) has punished him for his temperament and insurgant withdrawal from mainstream thinking. The two poems can be seen as reflections of the nineteenth-century American "freedom" agenda, a solicitation for greater tolerance and generosity.

SATIRES

To write "against" the code, to parody, satirize, or laugh at it, can also be seen as a vehicle for co-option or distancing; however, whatever critical operation of this kind was employed, the two texts (A and B) remained undisturbed. But, if you like, the readerly enterprise originated a third "text," a new attitude.

One of the earliest American travesties and appropriations we have of the Scott code is by James Kirke Paulding, *The Lay of the Scottish Fiddle: A Tale of Havre de Grace. Supposed to be Written by Walter Scott, Esq.* (1813).[115] Paulding's sarcasms are skillfully contrived. The *Lay* extends its narration to include America, and Scott's usual "extraordinary acquaintance with local scenery and traditions" (Preface) fails him now when "making a poor blind fiddler and his little dog, walk from New-York to Princeton in one day; a thing altogether beyond the bounds of probability to which all civilised poets are restricted by the rules of criticism" (5). The author also shows "a singular sort of perverseness dubbing a tavern keeper a lord." Scott seems "to labour under a species of madness similar to that of Don Quixote," and what is even a worse crime, in Paulding's mind, is that Scott gives voice in his Notes to "political opinions, which we think might as well have been let alone" (6). Yet, what Paulding is sardonically accusing Scott of, that is, taking a political stand, he himself does, although in a rather oblique way. His ridiculing of Scott's passionate interest in "tracing genealogies of illustrious families to their sources" (Preface) and ironic comparison of the Scottish border warfare with the Anglo-American skirmishes are undercut by manifest political motives that no one reading the satire would have missed. And it was not! The *Lay,* it seems, was reproduced in London the next year with a new condemnatory—English—preface. The reason was that Paulding

> for the purpose of his burlesque, describes the unhappy war then raging between Great Britain and his own country, as predatory, and treats of the British officers as border chieftains and freebooters. Such poetical

license, especially on the part of an avowed foe, seems quite excusable, yet the Editor of the English Edition, in his preface, is very severe both on the poem and the notes that accompany it.[116]

Two major transactions have taken place. The formulas of a Scott minstrel song have been tranferred to an American setting and motivated with American concerns. Simultaneously, the same formulas (but not their content) have been subjected to distortion through the operations of travesty. So we have the paradoxical situation of Scott being employed allusively to project a political agenda, as well as being ridiculed. There is additional irony of a self-reflective kind in the following vituperation of Scott's "originality." Paulding, unwittingly perhaps, is laughing at himself and all the other imitators of English writing.

> Another conspicuous excellence of the Lay of the Scottish Fiddle is its orginality. . . . We will venture to say that Mr. Scott has borrowed from no poet ancient or modern, except himself; and that is a species of plagiarism, which deserves to to be pardoned on account of its novelty. (100)

"The proudest freedom to which a nation can aspire, not excepting even political independence, is found in complete emancipation of literary thraldom," says one of the most belligerent American advocates of American letters, Solyman Brown in the Preface to his famous *An Essay on American Poetry* (1818).[117] It is quite logical then that he would castigate, using the mood and form of Byron's *English Bards* (which choice is equally logical), the main representatives of this "tyranny," Milton, Byron, and Scott. "And Milton! Prince of Poets! didst thou sour, / By royal aid, to fields until before? / A faithless Byron, or a swaggering Scott / A knave, a sot, a dunce, no matter what" (22, 26), he rhymes. He includes Byron's poem "Fare thee well" as an example of Byron's fickleness as lover and husband, "for the amusement of the reader" (87, 188) and Scott's "Waterloo," "in which the great Reviewer of the North, has succeeded in writing a poem, without conveying one solitary idea" (181).

McDonald Clarke could be as ascerbic in his account of Byron as Brown, but he recognized, even if reluctantly, his own debt to and fascination with his models. Like so many other imitators, he attempted to establish distance and voice his resistance to the British poets by his use of irony and mockery. He is writing his poem, "The Gossip," in a "flowery style," he admits, "cause Byron wrote with it his Juan." Yet—and within this poetic formula—he launches an unmerciful attack on his mentor and idol.

> Oh, Byron, Byron, thou'rt wretch indeed!
> And fame hath curs'd thee with a balmy breath;

> Posterity's sad hiss shall steal upon
> The dying echo of the present's praise;
> And all the lowering laurels thou hast won;
> That his shall blast in time's less blinded days;
> Thou poet Laureat to the court of Hell![118]

It is, he wants us to believe, immoral Byron (son, father, and husband) he rejects, Byron who "danced upon a mother's grave,"[119] Byron the "sentimental devil" with "his face from heaven and his heart from hell." This is hard to believe. What is at stake is quite simply an imitator's aggressive jealousy. In actual fact, as Leonard has pointed out, he copied Byron to the extreme: his verse, his costume, his locks—and his misfortunes. He was a Byron bravado and idolizer and in this capacity he was compelled to smear him.[120]

George Lunt's two poems *The Grave of Byron* (1826) and *The Lay of the Last Pilgrim* (1832), can be discussed together because each tries to rewrite or "co-write" Byron, and in this writing project they encompass and circumscribe tenets of his life and philosophy with paraphrases and suggestions from his poetry.[121] Occasionally the text moves outside this perspective and Lunt comments on and criticizes the very discourse he has been simulating. In the texts of this kind there is an ongoing dialogue between two antagonistic operations of imitation: whether and/or how to seek identification and integration and whether and/or how to strike the necessary notes of dissonance and resistance.

Next I will review American satires whose form, and often pitch and tone, derive from Byron's satires, and in particular from his *English Bards, and Scotch Reviewers*. The targets for their bashing are contemporary writers (in most cases it is colleagues attacking each other) and the circumstances of their emergence are current literary debates and conflicts. In his *Horace in New-York* (1826), Isaac Starr Clason advises Halleck, once he has learnt to imitate Byron, that the next step he has to take is to write independently: "You've found the silver mill in Byron's pen; / Prove that its iron stem can plunge again. / The last touch if the chissel you have shown; / Prove that the block you work on is your own."[122] Self-ironically, or only naïvely, it would seem, he can make such an assessment, as in the previous year Clason had himself written a "continuation of Don Juan" (see above, p. 63) that had definitely not sprung out of his own "block." Grenville Mellen's commentaries in his *Our Chronicle of '26. A Satirical Poem* (1827) are more sweeping and cover, as a yearly chronicle should do, the broad spectrum of cultural events, with specific ironies aimed at literary quacks and their all too supportive readers.[123] But this work too is congenially Byronic.

This broad theme of satire as a kind of editorial commentary also occupied J. L. Martin, who wrote the most exciting satire on imitation and emulation that we have from this period. He made Pope and Dennis the instigators of his *Native Bards* (1831)[124]—"Spirit of Pope! Oh! might I catch a spark / Of thine immortal flame, amid the dark/ In which I dwell" (12)—yet it is Byron that is is his mentor. Byron constitutes both subject and object of the poem. Apart from echoing Byron's *English Bards* in the verse form and *Don Juan* in tone, *Native Bards* sneers contemptuously at the endeavors of the time to imitate Byron, or as himself says, to "Byronise" (a gloss which he claims to have invented [40]) his verse.

> And first, ye Yankee Byrons, take your part,
> Ye mimic Harolds, feel the well earn'd smart,
> Ye, whose wild strains, and dark, defying air,
> Would ape the thrilling songster of despair;
> Ye merchant Corsairs, legal Laras, lend
> An ear attentive, to a candid friend
>
> . . . .
> Why will ye seek, aspiring, to attain
> The lordly poet's dark, Promethean strain?
> Why emulate by your low, grovelling flight
> The monarch eagle's proud career of light
> And seek to track his journey toward the sun,
> Whose blaze your feeble glance must ever shun?
>
> . . . .
> Go, plough your fields, teach hopeful youth, engross,
> Plant onions, notions vend, for gold sell dross,
> Vote, muster, edit journals, import tea,
> Make Goshen cheeses, wretched rum for sea,
>
> . . . .
> But sport no antics on the awful grave. . . . (17–19)

In the remainder of the poem he addresses Byron the man and poet in terms that recall the heightened nerve of the obituaries that we have already discussed: "Thy course was short, thy flight though proud and high, / Glanced like a meteor through the frighted sky," . . . "martyr to freedom" (19). Martin's multiform satire is an eloquent paradigm of the intertextuality that was involved in the Byron code.

Grenville Mellen in *Our Chronicle of '26* had poked fun at the "feminization" and "triviliazation" of American romance writing, where "Fair ladies write our novels—and alas! / They should have pensions for their desperation— / Where love is little and romance a farce" (cxlii). In the poem *The Quacks of Helicon* (1841), which employed the same verse structure and meter, the satiric target is another popular American art form, the burlesque theatre and its convention of engulfing foreign materials and repossessing them with American notions. In particular, Lambert A. Wilmer asked:

> But say, what need of Shakspeare's pilfered scenes,
> When all the art on noise and tinsel leans,
> And guns and drums and littering jackets boast
> That praise which wit and intellect have lost?[125]

Parnassus in Pillory (1851) takes as its objective not only the circumstances of American literature, its alleged dependence and incompetence, but above all its actual practitioners, calling on them to stand up to a merciless inquiry about their artistic honesty. It calls them tattlers and hacks; there is Tuckerman who "reads Milton listlessly, with half-closed lips, / And wonders if the devil wore white kids," "Byron-BOKER, with a slight mustache," and "DAWES's poems [that] sound like Taylor's sermons."[126] "I will candidly admit," says the anonymous writer of *The Mongrelites; or, The Radicals— So Called, a Satiric Poem* (1866), "that it is an imitation of Byron's celebrated Satire entitled 'English Bards and Scotch Reviewers'. . . . But while I have adopted the same *measure, sound,* and *style* of 'English Bards,' the reader will plainly perceive that I have in but few instances *borrowed* the thoughts and words of the great poet."[127] This satire, by a "Southerner," comes close to a political pamphlet, sneering at the assumptions and arrogance associated with New England cultural life.

The "rewriting" of British authors also encompassed Charles Dickens, one of nineteenth-century America's hate-and love-objects. *Dolby and Father by "Buz"* (1868) is a testimonial of such an approach. It is a prose narrative in twelve chapters that does everything that literature can to reduce, and mimic, and "rewrite," him.[128] It paraphrases and quotes well-known passages from his novels in order to expose them to some scathing comment; it travesties them by distorting their values or factuality; it makes use of irony, understatement, and inversion. It translates the "Englishness" of Dickens's characters into an "Americanness" that itself becomes absurd and comical; this operation is intended to ridicule the antiquated and fabulous world that Dickens was understood to represent. One of the indexes of the narrative is Dickens's *American Notes;* the other is his recent lecture tour in the country (1867–68). Many of the chapters can be read as subtle transpositions and convolutions of these events, to the point that almost each sentence runs parallel with a sentence or an idea despatched from the "orginal."

Apart from the intertextual sarcasms and the ridiculing of the idiosyncracies of Dickens as a public lecturer, the book attempts to project two very antithetical world views—an old one replete with aging customs and institutions, and a new one teeming with invention and respect for the individual. Yet the real motive force is the one that lies behind any decolonizing campaign: the search of popular and national identity and the summons to resistance.

> It is a little over fifty years since the impressment of our seamen, and their imprisonement in Dartmouth Prison. In a few years we forgot that, and now in this last conflict, when our free institutions were assailed, and destruction was well nigh upon us, England, who for long years has denounced African slavery as iniquitous and unjust, renders assistance to a party who openly declared it the corner-stone of their new Constitution. Three years have passed, and we have almost forgotten that. We have been denounced by her editors, her essayists and her novelists, and still we receive them again and again in our arms. Truly, is not this national forgiveness a marvel. . . . Only twenty-five years ago one of England's finest writers visited us, or rather our insane asylums and canal boats, and went away to revile our institutions. . . . (43)

The bitterness of the these lines becomes even more acute when it is measured against the enormous popularity that Dickens enjoyed in midcentury America, which made, for instance, his lectures in the sixties the events of the decade.[129] That the writer of *Dolby and Father* preferred to publish his satire under a pseudonym is understandable.

3

British Writers in American Elocutionary/Literary Textbooks

The data that has provided me with the basis for another exploration of Anglo-American cultural mediation, and its decolonizing constituent, are nineteenth-century literary handbooks. I have examined sixty of what I call elocutionary handbooks, all published in America mainly during the first half of the century. These handbooks constitute, of course, no simple category. Basically, their function was to teach students at all levels of education the art of oratory, which inferred several things. It presupposed skills in articulation, in memorizing, in declamation, in public speaking, and therefore in dramatic delivery or posturing. It taught what we today call phonetics, it taught rhetorics, and it provided as a rule some literary information about the passages that were used as samples. During the latter part of the century the literary annotations increased and many of these books developed into full-fledged literary textbooks. These constitute the second group of my material. The whole corpus includes about 120 titles that could be classified in this manner.

In the nineteenth century, speaking, and speaking well, was considered an essential attribute of every man's material and moral wealth. This view was intensified by the social and political situation the country was experiencing with thousands of poor emigrants pouring daily into the country from all parts of the world. Literacy was far from common, and literacy in English was even less so. Oral communication was naturally the main form of cultural exchange. Lines or passages from Shakespeare's plays, for example, were communicated orally in most cases, rather than via the liberal arts institutions of theater and library.[1] Moreover, the ability to voice opinions—if possible, elegantly and impressively—was recognized to be every man's fundamental and, indeed, civic right. In this way oratory was ultimately linked with the aspirations and the ideals of the new democratic republic. It is thus easy to understand the great importance attached to the formal training of the voice and the body.

The elocution books had to be useful. No writer of such a manual

failed to point out its practical and utilitarian value. The author of
The American Orator's Own Book (1836), for instance, advertizes his
book in this way:

> The situations in this free country in which eloquence is particularly
> valuable, are the halls of legislation, the pulpit, and the bar: and in each
> of these stations, it is rewarded always with fame, and generally with
> wealth. . . . Town meetings, and other local assemblies, are frequently
> convened, to decide on subjects materially affecting general interests.
> On these occasions, artifice can be exposed, or prejudice successfully
> encountered, only by the aid of ready elucidation.[2]

Eloquence must pay off, it was argued; it must also be of help to
everyone. John Hanbury Dwyer has this to say in the Preface to one
of the most widely published books of this type in the country:

> In this [oral eloquence], the freest country that *now* exists, or ever *did*
> exist, although elocutive knowledge will not make us orators, yet it will
> cause us to be fearless and correct speakers in a land like ours, where
> the humblest of persons has continually occasion to address his fellow-
> citizens.[3]

Although the formal aspect of the elocutionary handbook was quite
prominent in its endless listing of rhetorical devices and voice modu-
lations adapted to different gestures and moods, one must understand
that its overall function, in consonance with the educational preferences of the time, was moralistic, nationalistic, or both.[4] The following
passage from Samuel Kirkham's *An Essay on Elocution, Designed
for the Use of Schools and Private Learners* (1836) illustrates, both
in terms of style and content, what this teaching ideally purported to
achieve on a broad scale. His address is provocatively nationalistic
and antagonistic.[5] The self-reflective bombast that informs his lines
is logical and pedagogical; it is an end in itself. Only by adopting this
style of delivery, he implies, can Americans make a difference in the
world. We are also to note that, like most educationalists of the day,
he chose writers, teachers, and politicians as his target groups, because, he said, they "preside over the destinies of a free people" (6).
Through their instruction, then,

> our publick institutions will extend their civilizing, and humanizing, and
> christianizing influence over every island, sea, and mountain, and pene-
> trate the remotest corners of the earth—a day in which Europe, Asia,
> and Africa, will thankfully look up to her for light and direction, and be
> proud to imitate her noble example—an era of literary redemption, and
> the advent of science, in which national prejudices will be overthrown,

national animosities, trampled down, national restrictions, rescinded, and
the sons of science rise up in every republick, and kingdom, and country,
and hold communion at the fountain of Apollo—in short, a literary millen-
nium, in which the Alps will salute the Alleganies, the Himalayas will
make obeisance to the Andes, the Niger, the Volga, the Ganges, and
the Nile, will claim kindred with the Columbia, the Mississippi, and the
Colorado, and the waters of the Caspian and of the Superiour, will rise
up and embrace each other. (7)

One wonders whether any other culture at any other time has placed
this kind of elated faith in the encompassing power of the word. Thus
it is all the more appropriate that we also try to deconstruct the
cultural implications that these textbooks contain. By what means of
persuasion do they try impress their information upon the ears of
their listeners and the minds of their readers? How do they appropriate the material they have adopted? How do they attempt to stay
away from mediating the Other? How do the centrifugal and the
centripetal forces of power and attraction operate?

An obvious step is to gauge the relative importance and measure
the sheer volume of the samples of these handbooks. However, such
an inquiry would not yield an answer to my questions about their
roles as cultural catalysts or mediators. It is more pertinent to find
out what the American educators did with Byron, with Dickens, with
Scott, with Shakespeare and so on. How are these writers treated in
the material?

First of all one will observe that the compilers or authors of the
literary textbooks are extremely conservative in their selection of
extracts from the British writers. There is literally no deviation from
a tradition once it has been established. In Shakespeare the most-
quoted sequence by any measurement adopted is Antony's oration
over Caesar's body in *Julius Caesar*. This passage is included in most
nineteenth-century literary handbooks from the beginning of the century to its end. For Scott the favorite quotations were certain passages from the poem *Marmion* and for Dickens it was the deathbed
scenes in *David Copperfield* and *Dombey and Son*. There seem to be
two reasons for the consensus about the textbook canon. One is the
obvious one that always has been a compelling factor in the transmis-
sive history of any literary production: the conjunctive and authori-
tarian power of the literary institution. The literary textbook was an
institution in itself, associated with the personal and political ambitions of well-known educators and professors of arts and literature.
The prestige attached to a particular textbook was linked with its
enrollment in the national campaign for an improved all-American
school system. The textbook (despite the fact that it had a solid
grounding in English literature) was defined as an instructive and

ethical component in the project to instill into the young citizens of the country a sense of the binding value of traditions. Thus it must not deviate from or question the raison-d'être of the inherited assemblage of texts. Its adherence to continuity and permanence postulated visions and ideals of what Walt Whitman characterized as the great American project, the birth of a national literature that "will prove grander than its material wealth and trade."[6]

The other reason for the conservatism of literary textbooks of the period is of a different but related nature. It eagerly absorbed the genteel and "literary" aspects of the reputation of the British writers. They were explicitly seen to reject or counter other less sophisticated or "literary" elements governing their reputation in America. It comes therefore as no surprise that Byron's *Don Juan* and *Mazeppa*, both extensively appropriated (imitated, satirized, dramatized) in the nineteenth century, were hardly recognized by the educationalists. These works were associated with other class interests and other "popular" aspirations and consequently employed differently.

It would, however, be a mistake to claim that the literary textbooks, although seemingly mechanically rehearsing tradition-bound lines and passages from the British writers, were only stultified and imitative cultural denominators. Though they were this, they were more than this. Their rich diversity will not emerge until we have examined in more detail the nature of the *employment* of the texts.[7]

Shakespeare: Rhetoric and Morality

Shakespeare's position in nineteenth-century elocutionary and literary handbooks was so solid that quotations from his plays often went unacknowledged, as a concrete reference to the actual play would probably have seemed superfluous. The reason for the omission of such a reference could also be that the place the quotation came from was ignored. The point is that knowledge about Shakespeare was transmitted in much the same way as folklore; his plays were shared cultural property and therefore did not seem to require to be cited formally.

Shakespearean works were conveyed via two major intersecting channels: one oral, the other literary. Orality transferred Shakespeare through various popular means: stagecraft, public declamations, and political and commercial negotiations; the literary channel disseminated the book of plays, the school anthology, the newspaper review, the academic article, and so on. It is impossible to distinguish in any clearcut way between the two as they propelled Shakespeare through American nineteenth-century culture. Thus, the passage from *Julius*

Casear that eventually found its way to the elocution manual had had to negotiate between a number of interlinking, cooperative stations, oral as well as written. Shakespeare passed from mouth to mouth, and occasionally print intervened, changing the direction and the emphasis of the production. Shakespeare fitted, marvellously well, an emergent society like the American, in which the word was vital not only as an instrument to advance ideas but also as an arena for broad social interplay. His role diminished toward the end of the century when this binary communicative model (oral and print) had expanded into two separate cultural domains, the popular and the elitist.[8]

Shakespeare, it would seem, then, provided images that Americans adopted to structure their own worldview. Thus the collective sharing of Shakespeare went hand in hand with the promotion of a philosophy of thinking that rated trust in individual freedom, moral responsibility, and the dichotomies of good and bad extremely high. These concepts were promoted, we will see, with a distinct degree of masculine aggressiveness: individual freedom that conditioned national freedom could only be achieved through struggle against, either your "immoral" self or—by a stretch of metonymy—your equally "immoral" neighbor, or both. These are the underlying strata of thinking that cut right through nineteenth-century appropriations of Shakespeare and the other British writers considered here; whether these appropriations were intended for the stage or the elocutionary handbook, the culturally motivated project and its mediating audience were principally the same.

Nor was there any greater difference between the earlier (1820–1860) elocutionary manuals and the later (1850–1900) literary textbooks in their principles of selection from Shakespeare. The educators are equally original and orthodox: they mediate the well-known passage, subscribe to its popularity, but "transform" it to make it serve their project. Lawrence W. Levine is of course right in his characterization of the role Shakespeare played in the American school system:

> For many youngsters Shakespeare was first encountered in schoolbook as texts to be recited aloud and memorized. Through this impressive panoply of means, Shakespearean phrases, aporisms, ideas, and language helped shape American speech and became so integral a part of nineteenth centiry imagination that it is a futile exercise to separate Americans' love of Shakespearean oratory from their appreciation for his subtle use of language.[9]

But I do not agree when he states that "Shakespeare was taught in nineteenth century schools as declamation or rhetoric, *not literature* [italics mine]."[10] The teaching of rhetoric was, as will see, a many-sided practice that encompassed several areas. "Literature" was one of them, another was drama, and a third was elocution. It is within these broad cultural parameters that Shakespeare's works were employed. Any elocutionary handbook could be said to reproduce each of them in a differing order. Thus, in the following chapter, the differences between the manuals and the textbooks will be noted—but not enlisted as organizing factors in the characterization of the appropriations.

Instead, the focus will be on the nature of the sample itself, the range of its applicability, and its quality as a cultural differentiator. How does it embed and reflect the "resistance" we are concerned about? The inquiry will cut right through the Shakespeare canon. But as a preliminary comment, one could note that on the basis of a sheer quantitative analysis a few of the plays stood out as more or less popular with the educators. Among the tragedies it is *Julius Caesar* and *Hamlet* and—stepping further into the these plays—in each case, Act 3. *King Lear* is not annotated or quoted at all, which corresponds naturally with its neglect by nineteenth-century American theater. The history plays were far more appreciated than the comedies, and even, taken as a group, the tragedies. Here it is particularly *Henry IV* (I and II), *Henry V, Henry VIII,* and *Richard III* that the educators selected their material from. Of the comedies only *The Merchant of Venice* could compete with the four tragedies. As was the case with Shakespeare on the stage, only particular scenes, individual acts, or set passages were highlighted; these constitute the chief resource for the writers of the pedagogical textbooks, not the plays themselves, although familiarity with particular plays is anticipated and implied by use of the quote. In the case of *The Merchant* it is Act 4 or a combination of the "trial scene" and Portia's speech about mercy. All the other comedies were only peripherally cited.

This sketch of the occurrences of Shakespeare indicates the nature of the preferences of the time. The popularity of the history plays is probably due to the correlation that in these plays of public speech and private meditation. This is also the likely reason behind the acclaim of the third act of *Hamlet* where both Hamlet's famous soliloquy and his advice to the players were much appreciated: an exchange between two modes of verbal delivery.

Thus, in the following, we will proceed along a communicative line that combines the two extremes suggested by the soliloquy one on side and the multiloquence on the other. In between these we will encounter various rhetorical forms such as the interlocution (one speaker and one or several [silent] listeners), the address (the uninterrupted public speech), and the dialogue (several intercommunicating speakers).

THE SOLILOQUY

Again, it comes as little surprise that some of the most famous soliloquys in the Shakespeare canon and celebrated stage pieces also appear extensively in the elocutionary and literary handbooks. In order of their competetive presence in this material they form two distinct groups: one represented well, the other sparsely. To the first group belong Antonio's oration over Caesar's body (*Julius Caesar* 3.1.254–75), Hamlet's soliloquy on death (*Hamlet* 3.1.55–89), Cardinal Wolsey's farewell to Cromwell (*Henry VIII* 3.3.350–72), the dagger scene in *Macbeth* (*Macbeth* 2.1.49–64), and the meditation of Jacques on "the seven ages" (*As You Like It* 2.7.139–66); to the second group belong passages from *Romeo* on the truth of sleep (*Romeo and Juliet* 5.1.1–5), Timon's apostrophe to his town (*Timon of Athens* 4.1.32–33), the King's monologue on sleep (*II Henry IV* 3.1.5–31), Shylock's vituperations (*The Merchant of Venice* 1.3.41–54), and Brutus's and King of Denmark's monologues (*Julius Caesar* 2.1.61–69, 76–85; *Hamlet* 3.3.38–72).

Whether the primary objective was to practise intonation, recitation, or public speaking, these passages were as rule retailored to suit the context in which they were to operate; they were "interpreted." In this way literary judgments and close textual readings coexisted and collaborated with often minute observations on voice and gesture. James Rush, quoting the two lines from Antony's oration, "*Par*don me thou *bleed*ing piece of earth, / That I am meek and gentle with these butchers!" (Rush's emphases) (3.1.254–55), to illustrate "the time of the voice," integrated this "phonetic" observation with a "literary" one in the following manner:

> The syllable "Par" . . . has a natural quantity, which, without impropriety, may be doubled or more in expressive utterance; and the same may be said of "bleed. . . ."
> The circumstances of the scene . . . inform us that Mark Antony's sentiments, as first expresssed in this passage, are those of love, grief and contrition; his feeling of revenge does not appear until the second line.[11]

William Russell recommended the reading of the same passage to practise "explosive orotund" syllables. Only delivered in this way could Antony's feelings of anger and excitement be conveyed. He also taught that the horror and fear that Macbeth sensed should be expressed through an aspiration that was "nearly a whisper" and that the utterance shaping Shylock's hatred was best produced in a "guttural and pectorial" voice.[12] Rush thought that the "guttural emphasis" was appropriate for the sentiments of disgust and aversion that Timon of Athens expressed in his anathema of his city: "Nothing I'll bear from thee / But nakedness, thou de*test*able town!" (4.1.33). "I am disposed to think it [the guttural emphasis] might be used," Rush explains, "on the word 'destestable'. . . . When this element is compounded with the highest powers of stress and aspiration, it produces the most impulsive blast of speech."[13] The educators on elocution and literature often laid out schemas of correspondences where a certain modulation of the voice encapsulated or projected a particular feeling. The "guttural emphasis" was obviously thought to evoke feelings of horror and disgust, levels of pitch, for instance, served other functions. "The buoyant, joyous feeling" of Romeo's apostrophe to sleep "is best expressed by the light and sparkling tones of high pitch," thought George Vandenhoff, as this is a vocal mode, he continued, that is the best "representative of elevated feeling."[14]

The correlation between strategies of elocution and posturing and patterns of sentiments was allied with a loose rule system that seemed to prevent too liberal an attitude from developing. The mannerisms of gesticulation and speaking that characterized nineteenth-century American theater had their parallels in the teaching of elocution.

THE SPEECH

The passages which I have named "speech" contain either one single and solitary speaker, or one speaker and one or several listeners. Normally, in these exemplaries the "listeners" are not given rhetorical space or control. So, from the point of view of the evolving "story/ drama," they remain silent. In relation to their degree of activity as "listeners," their presence clearly modulates the speech patterns of the protagonist. Obviously, the level of this interaction would have an effect on the elocutionary didactic strategy a particular passage was subjected to.

Of the performances with one speaker and explicit or implicit participation from another speaker or listener there are several instances. Many of these samples look like soliloquys, but they are not. One can assume that both the writers and the users of these handbooks fully recognized the wider context from where the extract had been pulled. Rush uses a two-liner from *Othello,* "Yield up, O love, thy crown, and hearted throne / To tyrannous *hate!* swell, bosom, with thy fraught" (3.3.447–48; his emphasis) to illustrate the "emphatic vocule,"[15] and McGuffey's *Fifth Reader* includes Hamlet's meditations on seeing the skull of Yorick, with Horatio as the silent witness and listener (5.1.202–6). McGuffey provides the short extract, intended for reading practice, with marks for rising and falling intonation and stress.[16] In each case the presence of the interlocutor, Desdemona or Horatio respectively, is conducive to the elocutionary application of the passage. In the reading of "Prospero's Invocation" or Prospero's speech to the "Elves of hills, brooks, standing lakes, and groves" (5.1.32–57), George Vandenhoff suggests a transition toward the end of the passage from a deep tone to a softer one. The absence of an active "listener" fashioned the reading and the presentation of it, making it less dramatic, more recitative or vocal.[17]

Many of these modified solos were well known and scarcely needed any referential commentary. Such much-used passages were "Clarence's Dream" in *Richard III* (1.4.1–34), a couple of Richard II's speeches on loyalty and vanity of power (3.2.37–62; 3.2.143–85), Theseus's speech on love in *A Midsummer Night's Dream* (5.1.4–8), Mercutio on Queen Mab in *Romeo and Juliet* (1.4.54–94), and Leonato's grief at the loss of his daughter in *Much Ado about Nothing* (4.1.119–43). As can be seen the extracts also function as exemplaries of moral conduct and emendable human qualities.

F. Taverner Graham taught her students to uphold a distinction in their "body language" between "curve-lines" and "straight body lines." The former express feelings of the "graceful order"—tenderness, affection, beauty of thought; the latter underline sentiments that express "energy" of pride, anger, and excessive joy. One of the most cited passages in *The Merchant of Venice,* Portia's famous speech on mercy, serves as her textual and dramatic illustration of these things (4.1.180–214). "In Shylock's reply, gestures of the second order are employed, and in Bassanio *eagerness* in tendering the ducats; the same straight lines are necessary; in the concluding lines from Portia 'negative' gestures are predominant." The "negative" is expressed, she continues, "by the hand prone (or palm downward); if the negative be regretfully given, or the reproof be gentle, the negative gestures will partake more or less of the curved line, . . . if the thought, which prompt negative gestures, be awe-inspiring, the result of horror, or of shame, etc., straight lines given in rather faster time are necessary." She takes her example of this from Claudio's speech on dying in *Measure for Measure* (3.1.117–31), where, she suggests, the first lines should be more gracefully executed and as action grows more and more energetic and negative the "elevation of hands is required."[18]

It is a complicated interrelated system of voice and gesture, on one hand, and of literary intrepretation and of moral exemplification, on the other, that these elocutionists are advocating. George Vandenhoff gave the following explanation of this professional orientation:

> The Mimicry of Passion, by the simultaneous expression of voice, gesture, face, and attitude, is the *Actor's* study. It is not my design to form a theatrical style; but it is desirable that the student should make himself master of certain tones and variations of expression, a judicious use of which will add much to the beauty and power of his declamation, and is, in fact, absolutely nesessary to be attained before he can aspire to the high character of a *perfect* ORATOR.[19] [his emphases]

Addresses and advice

The "perfect" orator was the public speaker who could address a gathering and move them to take a stand, change their minds, or simply affect their receptivity in one way or another. The elocutionists had a clear understanding of the demand for a competence among such groups of people such as businessmen, politicians, priests and teachers. They also knew that to improve these skills they had to capitalize on the canonized texts, whether they represented classical rhetoric or English literature. So, a number of set pieces became received tools in demonstrating the fluency and vigor that characterized public or private address.

Several of the most cherished exemplaries of the public address were taken from Shakespeare. Three came from *Julius Casear:* Marullus to the mob (1.1.35–59), Antony's speech to the Romans (3.2.12–35), and—the most illustrious of them all—Brutus on the death of Caesar (3.2.12–34); one from *Othello,* that is, his address to the senate (1.3.76–93); and three from *Henry V* (3.1.1–34; 3.3.1–58; 4.3.19–67).

Jonathan Barber included in his *A Practical Treatise on Gesture* (1831) a detailed mapping, down to the slightest movement of the hand, of how Brutus's speech in Act 3 how should be executed. His glossary (within the parentheses) to one and a half lines from the speech is extremely laborius.

> *Romans, countrymen, and lovers,* (Feet advance to Right 2nd. Both hands supine, horizontal, forwards, pushing—oblique—vertical, elevated, extended, springing. Feet retire, to Right 1st) *hear me for my cause,* (Both hands natural, elevated, forwards—both supine, horizontal, forwards, striking) *and be silent,* (Right hand prone, elevated, forward; left prone, horizontal, extended).[20]

Vandenhoff used the same passage to practise intonation and taught his student to commence on "a low tone—inspiring on the pauses (so as to keep his lungs filled with breath)—and increasing the volume of his voice on the <crescendo."[21] J. C. Zackos also employed the speech to train intonation, or more precisely what he called "Diatonic Melody," an "unimpassioned use of the voice" that "proceeds from one tone to another adjacent to it on the scale, without any skips." He appended a musical scale to the text (indicating the register of the voice, intonation curves, beats, etc.) in order to guide the voice of the student till "he learns to associate thought and sentiment with the conditions of his voice in all respects, and has disciplined it into obedience to the demands of the *soul*."[22]

The Franklin Sixth Reader chose the piece from *Henry V* in which the king so eloquently urges his men to follow him into the Battle of Agincourt (4.3.19–67). It is an appeal for patriotism and loyalty, two extremely strong motive forces in American nineteenth-century teaching, for both rhetoric and literature.[23] Shakespeare's life and writings, added the compilers of the Franklin textbook, teach two extraneous lessons: opposition to "Byronism" and the compatability of the genius of Shakespeare with the American businessman; Shakespeare was "an excellent man of business, for he accumulated an ample fortune within a few years, and by occupations in which punctuality, economy, and method are particularly important" (148).

The straightforward projecting of Shakespeare and a Shakespearean text as moral guides is inherent in most specimens used by the literary handbooks, only it tends to be more overt in a handbook of literature for young people. The public address prototype carried, as we saw, overtones of nationalism and chauvinism, the private address was less belligerent and grandiose, but equally hortatory and energizing.

Familiarity of tone and authoritative counseling informed the many instances where superior and inferior, father or son, lady and servant, relate. Polonius's admonishing of his son Laertes (*Hamlet* 1.3.56–81), King Henry's rebuke of his son (*2 Henry IV* 4.5.92–137), and Portia's advice to Nerissa (*The Merchant of Venice* 1.1.1–131) are some examples of this. But the most popular of these "private address" speeches was Hamlet's talk with the players (3.2.1–39). Few elocutionary or literary handbooks omitted this scene. This choice passage had most of the qualities that were required to instruct nineteenth-century students in colloquial ease, explanatory and expository skill, and preceptive moralizing.

THE DIALOGUE AND THE "SCENE"

The dialogue as a forum for dramatic interaction and rhetorical variety naturally had many propagators. Its applicability was first and foremost felt by teachers at schools and academies. But a repartee or a conversation could also be a useful source in training voice and gesture. James Rush employed a couple of passages from the quarrel of Brutus and Cassius (*Julius Caesar* 1.2.78–81 and 5.3.15–17) to illustrate the use of "aspiration" which "combined with the vanishing stress on a simple concrete communicates an expression of sneer, contempt, or scorn" (288), and the exchange between Hamlet and Laertes (*Hamlet* 5.1.266–67) to exemplify "the time of the voice" (130) undercutting Hamlet's rage or madness.[24] Rush understood that any comment on articulation must be integrated with an analysis of the dramatic context. Barber also availed himself of the dialogue to teach clarity and vividness of expression in declamation and recitation. He chose in all several scenes from Shakespeare for his *Elocutionist:* from the "tent scene" (or the "quarrel scene") from *Julius Caesar* (4.3.1–37), from the early exchange between Hamlet and Horatio (*Hamlet* 1.2.159–212), from the conversation of Corolianus and Aufidius (*Coriolanus* 4.5.50–153), Prince Henry and Falstaff (*1 Henry IV* 2.4.310–404) and Prince Arthur and Hubert (*King John* 4.1.1–134).[25] *The Franklin Sixth Reader* also included the macabre and pathetic "Heat me these irons" scene from *King John.*[26] Its exciting dialogue was bound to appeal to readers of a school anthology. It promoted the myth about the premature child as both sufferer and hero, object and subject. Joshua Leavitt, Russell, and B. W. Atwell chose the dialogues of Shylock and Antonio (*The Merchant of Venice* 1.3.106–82), Miranda and Ferdinand (*The Tempest* 3.1.16–91), and Jaques and the Clown (*As You Like It* 5.4.39–106), to discuss shifts in style, language, and dramatic context.[27]

When studied across this larger temporal space the application of Shakespeare's dialogue by the educationalist appears extremely diverse. The picture is somewhat less variegated when seen through the perspective of one writer, however creative. McGuffey took a lively interest in Shakespearean dialogue and chose excerpts for his different *Readers* that were sanctioned by convenience. In no way was McGuffey an original composer of literary textbooks; his taste was conservative and protectionist. As a rule he curtailed, bowdlerized, and rewrote Shakespeare as he did most of his other quotations from English and American literature.

The Fifth Reader (1857) included the conversation of Hamlet and Horatio (1.2.160–252) and a glossy picture of the ghost in armor. In contrast to the passage from *The Merchant* called "Shylock, or the Pound of Flesh" (4.1) it was unaltered. As Stanley W. Lindberg has shown, McGuffey's Shylock, which first appeared in the *1844 Fourth Reader* (but was transferred to the *Fifth* for the 1857 and 1866 editions), was drastically reduced for reasons of propriety and concentration.[28] McGuffey's four selections from Shakespeare in the *Sixth*

Edition—two from tragedies, one from a comedy, and one from a history—are all treated differently depending on their degree of compliance with the prejudices of their editor. The simple and straightforward quarrel scene between Brutus and Cassius in *Julius Caesar* (4.3.1–121) is of course not tampered with at all, whereas Cassio's and Iago's conversation about their drinking habits (*Othello* 2.3.259–335) is slightly cut and changed to project the moral: "The folly of intoxication." So, for instance, the terms "God forbid" and "pleasance" were replaced by "heaven forbid," respectively, "gayety."[29] A much more radical operation was performed on a few scenes in *All's Well That Ends Well* where McGuffey compressed five scenes into three, omitting scenes 3.1 and 3.6 and 4.2. The objective was to highlight the unmasking and the demobilizing of the knave Parolles (who is called Delgrado in the *Reader*) through the deletion of four, as it were, superfluous characters, Helen and the Widow, Bertam and the Maid. In addition, the language is pruned, simplified, and shortened. Much of the vitality of the stage drama has, in fact, been lost. But a much worse problem confronted the careful editor of the Falstaff section from *1 Henry IV* (2.4.113–283). McGuffey deformed a number of Falstaff 's lines, to some extent by Americanizing and modernizing the language, but above all cleansing it of all disturbing sexual and religious connotations. In this vein he included in his *Sixth Reader* innovations or emendations, if you like (the original terms occur within the parentheses), of the following kind: "base-born dog" ("whoreson round man"), "ye fat braggart" ("ye fat paunch"), "gibbeted" ("damn'd"), "Pray heaven" ("Pray God"), "But three knaves, in Kendal green" ("But, as the devil would have it, three misbegotten knaves in Kendal green"), "These lies are like the father of them" ("These lies are like their father that begets them"). He omitted consequently the following expressions: "God help the while," "by the Lord," "whoreson, obscene," "this bed-presser," "you bull's pizzle," and "you vile standing tuck." One could say that McGuffey's Falstaff text (like his Shylock) was acculturalized through distortion and contraction.

The dialogue, as we have seen, was often part of a larger network of stage communication, with many characters interacting. Thus one can assume that the attraction of such scenes—apart from offering the compiler of an elocutionary or a literary handbook a distinct rhetorical form—was also motivated by the sheer delight in the scene itself, in its local and dramatical particularity that were enhanced by their popularity in the theater. Such scenes (some of which we have already discussed) offering both verbal or rhetorical variability and intense dramatic contextualization were, for instance, the tent scene in *Julius Caesar,* the sequence with the ghost and Yorick's skull in

Hamlet, the trial scene in *The Merchant of Venice,* and the garden scene in *Romeo and Juliet.* To learn by heart Portia's speech on mercy, to retrieve its "correct" pronunciation and diction, and execute the "correct" parallel body language required, by necessity, an overall assessment of the play. In this the complexity of a whole and the unity of a part were implicated. Thus a brief sample from Shakespeare in an elocutionary handbook conveyed far more than its actual contents: it both recalled a familiar passage and anticipated a new one. It was much larger than itself, in the same way as Shakespeare proved larger than life for his American audiences.

Milton and Rebellion

More than any other English writer John Milton occupied an extremely clear-cut position in nineteenth-century American textbooks. Of his works it is basically only *Paradise Lost* that is employed (his other poems only peripherally).[30] The overall message that the appropriations of it convey is heavily weighted toward rebellion, with submission, its ideological handmaid, projected as a necessary complement. The central theme of *Paradise Lost* as a poem of resurrection of faith and homage to Christ is, then, undermined by a strong antiauthoritarian credo that finds its main propagators in Satan and his band. The emphasis of the American educators is "Satanic." In other words the malevolent forces of *Paradise Lost* were recruited boldly to advance the notions of American republicanism and nationalism. Of course no educator would have conceded the accuracy of such a statement. The centripetal direction of the poem is clear: the elocutionists, for instance, did not select the passage containing Moloch's address simply to demonstrate heresy and anarchy. While they did expect the reader to imbue it with the traditional Christian meaning, they also expected the reader to provide it with a symbolic narrative function. This intellectual exercise was "required" of any student of a literary manual. However, even if the mostly young students that were exposed to *Paradise Lost* admittedly knew the whole poem and were thus able to conceptualize the individual passage they were studying, its centrifugal movement suggesting resistance and rebellion was overpowering. This is evidenced by the fact that the textbook samples involving a paternalistic God, a submissive Adam, and a reforming Eve, quantitively and comparatively, are in such a definite minority.

It follows then that Books I and II together represent more than all the rest of the samples from the poem: passages from Satan's debates with his crew are triumphantly prominent in the literary textbooks. Again—as we saw in the account of Shakespeare—the process of standardization was very successful. The same sample keeps being repeated. But what is even more interesting is that the adaptation of it may vary: the same passage can illustrate a sequence of vocal changes, it can represent a certain emotional impact, it can project a thematic or a dramatic issue, and so on. In my material Satan's rallying of the fallen angels (315–30) in Book I occurs several times and the description of Moloch (392–96) once; in Book II there are three conspicuous passages: Moloch's address (51–105), Belial's address (119–225), and Satan's meeting with Death (681–703); they occur seven, three, and six times, respectively.

In Andrew Comstock's *A System of Elocution, with Special Reference to Gesture, to the Treatment of Stammering and Defective Articulation* (1843), "The Speech of Satan to His Legions" has literally been turned into melodramatics. Each phrase (sometimes each word) is accompanied by a graphic illustration that depicts in extreme detail the curves and movements of the body language and gives instruction about pronunciation and intonation. So for the lines "Princes, Potentates, / Warriers, the Flowr of Heav'n, once yours, now lost, / If such astonishment as this can seise / Eternal Spirits" (315–18) there are eight correlating mimetic drawings of this kind. Comstock's purpose is to teach declamation, an interdisciplinary art form with a high status at the time. This is the way Comstock described his pedagogy:

> Before the student attempts to declaim, he should learn to stand *erect;* to hold his book in a *proper manner,* and to read *correctly.* He should then select some short piece, and learn a set of gestures for its illustration by practising them in pantomime, after the teacher. Lastly, he should learn to combine the words and gestures, by repeating them together, after the teacher.[31] [Comstock's emphases]

Stilted mimicry and gesticulation combined with an equally mannered form of enunciation and pronunciation must have formed speakers lacking in both personal style and immediacy. This mode of acting was in fact associated with an English tradition and was often ridiculed by American actors. For instance, one of its main practitioners, Charles Macready, suffered greatly, when touring the country in the 1840s, from having to face, as he interpreted it, American extravagance of dramatic style and ignorance of the "rules." It is likely that Comstock's manual, although intended for a different audience, would have pleased him. On the other hand, it is also doubtful whether the regimen Comstock is advocating had any impact. The reasons for this are at least two: first, there was a welter of competing systems of elocution in operation that were far less rigid than Comstock's[32] and, consequently, the effect of any individual program such as Comstock's would be reduced; second, it is the principles in Comstock's coaching program that were convincing and influential, as they were in consonance with an accepted formula, but the particularities of his training were ludicrous.

The three specimens from Book II, on Moloch, Belial, and Satan and Death, fall all within the category of the angry protest speech. They are analytic, scornful, and rambunctious and, because of the energy they contain, they were resorted to for a number of elocutionary purposes. In many cases, they were selected to illustrate and practise different levels of agitation and frenzy, in others, such as in Rush's *The Philosophy of the Human Voice,* to demonstrate the effect of pauses on the meaning of speech. "Milton and Shakspeare can not be read well," he explained, "without strict attention to the apparent collision between the purposes of the pause and of the sense, and to the reconciling power of the phrases of melody."[33] He takes a couple of lines out of Death's answer to Satan (689–91), "Art thou that Traitor Angel, art thou hee, / Who first broke peace in Heav'n and Faith, till then / Unbrok'n," and gives the following advice how to read the passage:

> In this passage the phrase "in Heav'n" is interposed between peace and faith, the two objectives of broke. Now in order that the syntactic connexion between these words may be impressively shown, the slightest pause only is admissable after "Heav'n"; and a more conspicuous one must be placed after "Faith." But the further expletive "till then/Unbrok'n" is immediately connected with "Faith"; and the only means by which this close relationship can be represented in contravention to the delay of the pause after "Faith," . . . is by using the phrase of the rising ditone or the monotone on "Faith."[34]

This example in analytic reading would have satisfied any 1960 practitioner of "close reading." However, Rush's interpretation is based more on a "dramatic" understanding of the passage than on a "readerly" one. He is in fact teaching his students how to achieve dramatic suspension by the balancing of silence and pause and by discrete applications of phraseology, stress, and intonation. His selection of this particular section from *Paradise Lost* was not accidental. The passages (II, 674–76, 689–91, 706–10) describe the nightmarish encounter between two of the most terrifying characters in English literature and Christian mythology. It is the diverse ideological implications of Milton's text that imbricate Rush's analysis and challenge its myopia.

The elocutionists' preference was definitely for the satanic world of *Paradise Lost*—no doubt also because the language of the angels was monotonous, as well as, from the point of view of the rhetoricians, uninspiring. God, for instance, is altogether absent from the elocutionary and literary handbooks. The lesser heroic and ebullient Satan, the Satan of second part of the poem, crops up only sporadically. His envy of the Sun (IV, 33–41), his meeting with Abdiel (VI, 189–93), and the tête-à-tête of Sin and Death at the Gates of Hell (X, 235–64) do meet with the appproval of the elocutionists. The accomplished reader of Gabriel's answer to Satan's apology for his flight from the Hell (IV, 950–54) must convey "a degree of admiration at the well marked fellowship between a ringleader and his crew," explains James Rush. The six syllables of "fit body to fit head," although short, must therefore be modulated to make them ring with admiration, mingled with scorn at the wickedness of the outcast.

> With an accomplished speaker, the management of this phrase would be like the efforts of a musician of feeling and skill, on a defective instrument: and the different success of his voice, on the above short syllables, and on indefinite quantities would be like the inexpressive chattering of the harp or piano-forte, compared with the rich resources of the violoncello.[35]

Thus Gabriel, an archangel, is projected as another agent in Satan's project, which is condemned mechanically but admired for its frenzy. Satan the outcast and rebel was never conceptualized as a loser by the Americans. They appropriated his energy and his activism and recognized in it similarities with their own attempts to bolster the causes of republicanism.

God's presence in this material is oblique and mediated by his two domesticated servants, Adam and Eve. Acceptable conformist passages were Eve's address to the morning (IV, 641–58), Adam and Eve's Morning Hymn (V, 153–208), and the Astrophe to Light (VII, 243–60). Each sample evokes the cosmic expansionism and value system of the Christian faith. More explicitly, these passages were found to be useful for their intense poetic tenor, their pantheism, and the majesty of their images and quoted to illustrate, among other things, "impassioned expressions" and "poetic invocations."[36]

The conjugal bliss of Adam and Eve had few proponents. Eve's love for Adam (IV, 440–91), but, in particular, her pathetic supplication at his feet (X, 914–36), were annotated with some regularity. Rush, in his continued application of *Paradise Lost,* suggested that Eve's crying in front of her mate should be represented by a fair distribution of the "tremulous" voice on "judiciously selected emphatic words," such as "bereave," "only," and "forlorn."[37]

Byron: Devil and Freedom Fighter

Byron was often associated, as we have already seen, with sensuality, adultery, indecency, and low morals, but also with courage, nonconformity and democracy; he was projected as the prototype for the free roaming agent, the writer of immense individual energy, and the depictor of crude, romantic outdoor nature. All these qualities were capitalized upon in a multitude of ways, each appropriated in keeping with the usage the American recipient could make of it.

In fact it is for these very reasons that Byron is such an interesting case. The diverse spectrum of interests and usages he was subjected to illustrates one of the main theses of my exposition: that is, the commonplace (but often ignored) fact that all reception and mediation of cultural artifacts is relational and dialectical, and both nonauthorized and authorized. Its intensity and multivocality further complicate the picture. One strand could be sketched as conservative, another as subversive and uncompromising.

At the outset Byron's contributions to nineteenth-century American textbooks looks very neat and uncomplicated. And in a sense it is. Number one with the educationalists was *Childe Harold's Pilgrimage*. In fact, any handbook, whatever its chief bias, would print extracts from this poem as examples for emulation or illustrations of some elucidative principle. The other texts by Byron that appealed to the educationalists were, in terms of rank and popularity, *The Giaour*, "Darkness," and "The Destruction of Semnacherib." These texts form a class of their own. Other texts by Byron were employed and inserted only sporadically. They are in order of most-numerous appearances *Manfred, Marino Faliero, Don Juan, The Corsair, The Prisoner of Chillon, The Bride of Abydos,* and *Mazeppa*.

With the exception of the two poems "Darkness" and "The Destruction of Semnacherib," which normally were quoted *in extenso,* the other poems were not recognized as whole poems. The sections or passages that were printed were often unspecified; their exemplary or illustrative function, it seems, superseded any bibliographical comment. This omission could also be taken as a sign of their popularity; household phrases or well-known poems need no corroborative support. The rationale for their employment must then be sought in a synthesis involving the current preconceptions about Byron and the serviceability associated with aspects of his works. A closer look at this area of hybridization will highlight some of the mediating principles that were at work.

CHILDE HAROLD'S PILGRIMAGE

Childe Harold, as Jerome McGann has pointed out, was not initially regarded as a single composition.[38] In a sense the disparity infiltrating the work's conception history is represented by the Americans who were greatly attracted to Cantos III and IV, and rarely commented upon the first. As we have already pointed out, the makers of the elocutionary and literary handbooks selected their material with extreme caution; only the passages that earlier publications had endorsed and legitimized met with their approval. Deviations were extremely rare. There were five passages from *Childe Harold* that became stock ingredients in the handbook canon of English poetry. These are, in the order of their popularity, a section from Canto IV often called "The ocean" (mostly linked with lines 1585–656), a passage often named "The battle of Waterloo" from Canto III (181–89), the others were frequently called "The night before the battle of Waterloo" from Canto II (181–89), "Alpine scenery" from Canto III (variably 590–98, 796–832, 860–77, 914–22), and "The dying gladiator" from Canto IV (1251–60). The relative popularity of these set pieces from Byron's poem is evidenced by the fact that out of the thirty-six handbooks I have examined that contain passages from *Childe Harold*, "The ocean" was included in 20, "The battle of Waterloo" in 16, "Alpine scenery" in 8, "The dying gladiator" in 8 and "The night before the battle of Waterloo" in 7. Other extracts, often with topographical references, like "Greece," "Rome," and "Venice" were also popular.

This selection and the internal order of preferences testify to the interest among Byron's "readers" in topographical romance, history, heroic death, and traveling—subject areas that were dear to readers on both sides of the Atlantic. Yet, when surveying the whole corpus of Byron extracts in the American textbooks, or, indeed, only the pieces chosen from *Childe Harold*, it is evident that they were inscribed with significances that must be understood in relation to various sociological and cultural circumstances that adhere to the American scene. The fascination with set pieces such as the ones on heroism in war, or its contrast, the brutality of war, and on holy dying and sacrifice, on one hand, and with representations illuminating the corruption of the Old World in the image of Greece and the (Byron's) struggle for (its) freedom, on the other, can be interpreted as allegorical submissions to the dictates and aspirations that prepossessed Americans in the nineteenth century.[39]

It is necessary, I suggest, to bear these considerations in mind when examining the textbooks; they are not one-eye witnesses to the historical process, they are participants. The anonymous writer of *The American Orator's Own Book,* we saw, linked skill in oral delivery with the emergence and development of a "free state." It is no coincidence that the same writer included the two passages "Speech of Macbriar to the Scotch Insurgents" from Walter Scott's novel *Old Mortality* and Byron's "The battle of Waterloo" from *Childe Harold.*[40] His choice of texts carried a political message. The hegemonic enterprise that Samuel Kirkham understood as the primary objective of the teaching elocutionary skills to American youths is perhaps the reason he took the liberty to rewrite and alter two stanzas from Byron's *Childe Harold* (II, 55–72), adding such lines as "Yet doubting pagans dreamed of bliss to come" and "Of Christian martyrs, prophets gone before."[41] The tolerance and scepticism that permeate the original lines have, in his hands, been transformed into a plea for Christian monism.

In the handbooks that primarily taught elocution, articulation, and public reading (their heyday lasted from ca. 1820 to 1860) *Childe Harold* fared well. In one of the most influential early anthologies of this category, Ebenezer Porter's *Analysis of the Principles of Rhetorical Delivery As Applied in Reading and Speaking* (1827), "Battle of Waterloo" was singled out for the practicing of "emphasis," and three other specimens from the poem were adduced as reading exercises (from Canto III, 397–405, III, 590–607, and IV, 1252–69).[42] A few other examples of how *Childe Harold* was used in these handbooks should be mentioned. Dwyer used a passage from it (Canto II, 837–45) to illustrate the art of *alliteration,*[43] Jonathan Barber resorted to the "Ocean" section (IV, 1585–1656) to demonstrate the technique of *pausing,* which he also graphically illustrated[44] and John Swett, principal of the San Francisco Girls' High and Normal School, told his students that the "Ocean" section should be read "with slow movement, media stress, expulsive oratund quality, and strong force."[45] George Vandenhoff, on the other hand, made use of "The dying gladiator" (IV, 1252–69) differently, explaining that this "extract from *Childe Harold,* affords an opportunity . . . for great variety and quick transition of tone, in accordance with the change of Expression from *Pity* to *Indignation,* mounting to *Revenge*"[46] and, finally, William Russell, the most famous and influential of all these elocutionists, adopted a very censorious view of Byron. In *Ortophony* (which by 1890 had reached its seventy-second edition!), he made use of only "The night before the battle of Waterloo," which he believed could be used to practise selections projecting emotions and gestures of terror and horror.[47]

By the midcentury the elocutionary handbooks were gradually superseded by literary handbooks where emphasis was more strenuously laid on literature per se, and less on moral meditation and abstract thinking, although reading in its declamatory form and the teaching of it still played important roles. If we persist in examining the mediating function of Byron's *Childe Harold* we will notice no major shifts. Thomas Budd Shaw's widely published manuals of English literature, which were adapted for use in American schools and were the first "real" literary textbooks in American education, are typical of the emergent school book tradition. However, it remained solidly within accepted norms of the Byron reception. It included the traditional stock material of the poem we are investigating, "The night before the battle of Waterloo," "The ocean," and "The dying gladiator."[48] Other midcentury educationalists followed suit. Ephraim Hunt advised his students to memorize the selections he presented. From *Childe Harold* he chose "The dying gladiator" and "The ocean," as the student then, he said, "will . . . *form habits* of expressing his own thoughts with greater form and elegance."[49] What he is suggesting, and what this class of books were very particular with, is that Byron must not be read without qualified and competent guidance. I will quote at some length the preamble to the selection of Byron in George S. Hillard's *The Franklin Sixth Reader* as an example of this type of moral censorship. The writer begins by lauding Byron for his unrivalled description and expression of passion. "His poetry," he claims, "abounds with passages of melting tenderness and exquisite sweetness," "his leading characteristic is energy," and his "words flash and burn like lightning from the cloud." Yet, he concludes,

> much of Lord Byron's poetry is objectionable in a moral point of view. Some of it ministers undisguisedly to the evil passions, and confounds the distinctions between right and wrong; and still more of it is false and morbid in its tone, and teaches, directly or indirectly, the mischievous and irreligious doctrine, that the unhappiness of men is just in proportion to their intellectual superiority.[50]

The Franklin Sixth Reader then includes bits and pieces from *Childe Harold* under the rubric "Greece, in 1809" (II, 693–728, 792–835, 855–64) and "Alpine scenery" (III, 590–98, 796–832, 860–77, 896–904, 914–22). Francis H. Underwood is equally affirmative that Byron's "creative genius, linked with the sullen hate of a fallen angel and the lawless passions of a sensualist, must give an instant, dazzling warning to the youth. . . ." *Childe Harold,* he contends, is "comparatively free from the grave faults that belong to Byron's poems in general" and he includes six extracts from it, which is—notwithstanding his reservation and apology—quite a tribute to Byron.[51] That this caution lasted for a long time is evident from many later textbooks for schools. Horace Hills Morgan, to give one example, excluded all of Byron, except a meaningless quote about the horse in *Mazeppa* in his *Literary Studies,* which was intended for "young" students, but included nine long passages from *Childe Harold* in his other literary manual, *English and American Literature.*[52] The users of the latter textbook were college and university students. McGuffey's famous *Eclectic Readers,* of which more than 122 million copies were published before their decline in the 1920s, did not represent Byron despite the book's middle-class and nationalistic bias, which, we have seen, could work in favor of Byron.[53] The reason for their exclusion is another even stronger bias: Byron's reputation as an "impure" writer.[54]

OTHER WORKS

Childe Harold's Pilgrimage was the Byron favorite by all standards among the textbook producers through the whole century, as much admired as another of Byron's long poems, *Don Juan,* was despised and rejected. It is not difficult to see why. Its reputation as Byron's most infamous and venomous poem with particular potential to harm young minds was solid on both sides of the Atlantic. In general, nineteenth-century educators refused to discuss it, much less include it in their works. Samuel Kirkham's quotation about "Fame" (I, 1737–52), Henry Mandeville's about "The shipwreck" (II, 401–24), and Horace H. Morgan's on the connections of Don Juan's England and his fiancée (II, 87–96, III, 86–88) are exceptions.[55] J. Willis Westlake's attitude is far more telling. He conceded in his *Common-School Literature: English and American with Several Hundred Extracts to be Memorized* (1876) that Byron's most brilliant poem is *Don Juan* but that its "general tone" is "misanthropic, irreligious, immoral, and therefore unhealthful" (33). The only extract from Byron that passed his censorship was a passage from *Marino Faliero* (4.1.68 ff).[56]

Don Juan, with its multifaceted theme and voice and its wealth of social ironies and criticisms, could not serve as a point of reference and a sourcebook for America's pursuit of its own self-image. The poem was perceived to be simplistic, aggressive, and mundane. The preference for mythical and alien hinterlands, the agonized inwardness of a suffering subject, and the thematics of freedom and individual and political self-rule directed the educators elsewhere. In main they looked for two basic concepts to which they could relate their lessons on elocution: romanticism and nationalism. Paradoxically, if you like, extreme rugged individualism promoted concessions to collective solutions. Byron's fight for an independant Greece indirectly supported the American republican spirit.

Thus we find the American textbook producers choosing a number of prototypical Romantic passages from *The Corsair, The Siege of Corinth, The Prisoner of Chillon, Manfred, Marino Faliero,* and *Mazeppa* that may be said to illustrate the predicaments of Romantic hero. Such a typical passage is the section in *Manfred* (I, ii, 7–56) where the lonesome hero, while languishing on the brink of the Jungfrau, contemplates suicide, but is solaced in the end by the shepherd's pipe. The search for the tense constellation of landscape as well as man and the exlusiveness of the Wilderness theme was also Byron's. The pining prisoner in his cell, contrasting the futility of his life with the permanence of the timeless lakes and mountains that he can see through his barred cell window, inspired Albert F. Blaisdell to select *The Prisoner of Chillon* (324–37) for his school edition of English and American literature. The poem should be "of deep abiding interest to young people," he believes.[57] *The Siege of Corinth,* interestingly, provided McGuffey with his only Byron quote (197–238)—the romantic tableau of moonlight and blue waters mixed with an ominous feeling of threat that so often accompany Byron's landscape illuminations. But McGuffey added a cautionary explanation:

> In real poetic genius Byron should be placed next to Shakespeare and Milton; but, unfortunately, he did not give the world the best fruits of it. This was largely owing to the fact that his moral nature lacked the purity essential to perfection of expression.[58]

For his *Essay on Elocution* (1828 and 1856), another very popular school primer, Dwyer sought out the homecoming passage from *The Corsair* (III, 555–66) with welcoming "sportive dolphins" and friends that "trim the beans." "Ocean's troubled foam" is set in healthy contrast to the pacific moonlit community on the small island.[59] The McGuffey educational ideal of "purity of expression" has been attained.

The scenery and the debate that contain the initial 100 lines of *Marino Faliero* 4.1 were satisfactory for this reason, too. The Patrician Lioni rests by the moonlit lattice of his house, meditating on the contrast between the beauty and serenity of the Levant night and the debauchery and "sad labour of the toilet" of the masquerade from which he has just returned. It was another ideal Byronic showpiece— the individual man gaining fresh insights into human character through exposure to a strip of immaculate scenery.[60]

The Turkish tale *The Giaour* was as well known, it seems, to American students of eloquence and literature as some of Shakespeare's plays. As we have seen on a number of occasions, the concentration on a few central passages with little or no bearing on the overall storyline of the tale may in itself paradoxically be an indication of a text's broad acceptance. The implication of such an "absence" of narrative center is that it—and in this case *The Giaour*—was part of a larger Byronic "narrative" mythology and thus unworthy of being reconstructed by the textbook producer as an individual story. *The Giaour* canon then included two major segments, each focusing on antagonistic aspects of Greece—the old and the modern, freedom and political suppression, spirituality and degeneracy. To this must be added the topic of Byron's private crusades in Greece. The significance of *The Giaour* must then be understood in terms of the thematics of the American democratic project that was launched along with the invocation of the Old World's collapsing.

The Giaour—and the other poems that will be dealt with in this section (*The Bride of Abydos,* "Darkness," and "The Destruction of Semnacherib")—reflects less the meditations of an agonized psychologizing Romantic hero and significantly more the projection of ideological patterns of thought. The dividing line between these two registers is the choice of medium: the vacillation of the elocutionary manuals between the oratory of drama and the oratory of reflection. The first section of *The Giaour* (7–67) ponders on the "Fair clime! where every season smiles / Benignant o'er those blessed isles;" the second (68–141) on its loss of innocence and degeneration into sloth and "villain-bonds and despot-sway." It is along this axis of Greek regression that the selections for the textbooks are being made, with a small preponderance for the latter, more disillusioned set of images. These lines (68–141) also differ from the previous ones as being more adaptable for "pure" elocutionary purposes through their cadences of anger and sorrow. The verse is crisp and direct. Both Sanders, Russell, and Campbell credited this passage as the best ever produced by Byron: Sanders marked it as a fine "instruction in taste and morals" (noting also that he had excluded everything "unsound and unseemly in sentiment or diction"),[61] Russell picked the passage on death to illustrate "profound repose,"[62] and Loomis J. Campbell thought the rhetoric concerning the crouching slave were capable of stirring "the soul as only the truest poetry can."[63]

A multifaceted image of Byron is developing from this material, contradictory and ambiguous. In the American reception of the tale, Byron's *The Giaour* reflected two such antithetical sides: one celebrating and giving "gestalt" to the innovating power of nature, natural man, history, and tradition, and the other delineating the destructive powers of the same entities. Sanders chose, we remember, the second aspect and considered its morality instructive for young people.

The splendor and incontinence associated with the Orient, whose aftermath we saw plague Lioni of *Marino Faliero,* were conceptualized as distorted and collapsed versions of the image of propriety and soberness the educationalists wished to project. The favorite passage from *The Bride of Abydos, A Turkish Tale* was the introductory passage (I, 1–19), which Thomas B. Shaw, mistakenly or knowingly, called "The Crime of the East" (the "correct" title was "The Clime of the East"). This much-anthologized piece of poetry is dressed in extravagant colors and metaphors that no one today would misjudge as belittling or insidious. But for the eduationalists the Orient of Byron's poetry was not a landscape; it was a moral, a foil to pursue other dreams.

It is in this light that one has to understand the astonishing success of two of Byron's minor poems: "The Destruction of Semnacherib" and "Darkness." The first describes the destruction and ruin of the heathen Assyrian prince with all his "cohorts . . . gleaming in purple and gold." Apart from the juxtaposition of the Orient and the West, the old and the new, the corrupt and the sane—all popular themes— associations to Napoleon or to "tyrants" were inevitable.[64] "Darkness" is apocalyptic in theme and language, too. It is hard to understand its extremely favored position among the American educationalists. Its horror theme depicting a terrestrial catastrophe of desertion and abandonment, although a popular theme with the Romantics would not, one thinks, appeal to such an enthusiastic and optimistic people as the Americans "in formation." Perhaps the reason for its appeal simply derives from the subtlety of its narration. Through a winding linkage of staggering and horrifying images culminating in the total collapse of light and life, darkness is set to rule. The thrill of the poem rests in this narrative, gyrating structure that cannot slow down, nor terminate—only collapse and break. As with a dream, only the awakening can cure. The philosophical rationale for the frequent inclusion of the poem in the literary handbooks may, then, have been cautionary and religious: look what chaos can produce and consider the everlasting powers of redemption and salvation![65]

In conclusion, then, nineteenth-century American textbooks in rhetoric and literature mediated to their readers values that were dominant in society, such as republicanism, nationalism, mercantilism, utilitarianism, and romance. To be accepted, Byron's poetry needed to be filtered through this sieve. In one sense the appropriation of his work narrowed the inlet. The centripetal force, one could say, was successful: Byron was both rejected and restricted. But, simultaneously, one would also have to accept the increasing impact of the conflicting centrifugal force. *The Pilgrimage of Childe Harold,* the only singular, larger poem by Byron that was accepted at full, was, as we have seen, extensively utilized at all levels in liberal arts education, ranging from teaching rhetorical skills to discussing literary modes. In selecting particular extracts for inclusion and commentary, the educationalists acculturized and refamiliarized readers to the content of the poem. This occurred dialectically, not only siding it with the negative movement of wholesale rejection and restriction, but also with the larger concurrent appropriations of Byron and his works that occurred during the century.

Scott: Honor and Patriotism

Although it is evident that the composers of the American elocutionary and literary handbooks picked their items from a repository of gems sanctioned by both convention and tradition, it is also manifest that they gave a lot of thought to principles of selection and discrimination. The writers of the manuals eschewed one major issue that for a modern composer of a history of literature is a gigantic problem: how to produce a textbook that is simultaneously innovative and conservative. In other words, how to slip away from canon and tradition without being seen or caught.

We have repeatedly stressed that Americans adhered to the English canon with a loyalty that seemed to border on lethargy. They did not seem to bother about finding new material to which to apply their theories about vocal and dramatic presentation. In most cases they simply rehearsed and repeated whatever tradition provided. But this was only one aspect of their works. The individuality of their works was formulated by applying the material in a most imaginative and varied way.

This is not to say that the "conservative" or repetitive aspect of the formation of these textbooks is an unrewarding point for study and that by contrast their innovative, utilitarian content a rewarding one. It is not so simple. Any examination of how American elocutionary manuals reflected the cultural dimensions of appropriation must proceed along the dual track of "tradition" and of "change."

Most of these comments have a bearing on Sir Walter Scott as well. Scott, we need only briefly repeat here, occupied the position in American cultural and literary production that up to the mid-century only Byron could challenge and after this period, Dickens. Thus it is to be expected that, from an early start (the 1820s) till the last decade of the century, passages from his works were resorted to, quoted, paraphrased, abridged, and commented upon by the elocutionists.

MARMION

From a purely quantative perspective, *Marmion* scored best among Scott's poems. There was general agreement about which sections of the poem were best suited for reading lessons or the like. Three passages stand out in their popularity with the educators: the song "Lochinvar" (also variably named "Lady Heron's Song" or "Lochinvar's Ride") in Canto 5, the sections in Canto 6 that describe Marmion's expulsion by Douglas (13–15), and Marmion's death at Flodden (28–30). In fact, to my knowledge, no other single passage from this poem was selected by the educationalists, which may underscore what I said earlier about these manuals' ebullient conservatism. However, their resistance to using the first five Cantos (with the exception of the song "Lochinvar") and their acceptance of Canto 6 is logical. The favorite passages, and Canto 6 as a whole, depict the full range of Marmion's treachery and alienation. In the first, Douglas denies hospitality to the English intruder. At this humiliating affront to the royal emissary, Marmion, proud and "swarthy," shakes "his gauntlet at the towers." The second passage, describing Marmion's death at Flodden, is significant: the treacherous intruder is punished and dies in agony in the arms of an administering monk and in the presence of the pitying but truth-saying woman, Clare. The fact that Marmion's deathbed scene also includes sentiments of magnanimity and compassion added to its validity. Together these passages reiterate symbolically, one may claim, American resistance, the American struggle against a domesticating, malevolent force which, like Marmion's circuitous Scottish journey, stealthily tries to wrest power from a foreign land.

Two of the most famous schoolbooks of the latter part of the century, George S. Hillard and Homer B. Sprague's *The Franklin Sixth Reader and Speaker* and William McGuffey's *Fifth Eclectic Reader,* used the battle section of Scott's Marmion.[66] *The Franklin Sixth Reader* quoted extensively from it (stanzas 25–28; a few lines were omitted to improve comprehension), citing *The Edinburgh Review* in its praise of the realistic and animated battle scene (140). McGuffey, as was customary, amalgamated, without acknowledging it, two passages of Canto 6 (verses 27 and 32) into one, and renamed it "Description of a Battle" (35). The selections made by these two handbooks were characteristic and full of significance; it is the Englishman's (Marmion's) death at Flodden that is the poem's raison-d'être.

Outside of this ideological and cultural frame, the passages con-

taining Marmion's treachery and the death scene were variously used
to illustrate, for instance, "personation,"[67] variation of "melody and
movement,"[68] and above all energetic style and dramatic action. No
wonder that *Marmion* was appropriated for the American stage as
soon as its text was introduced (1811). Though the romantic ballad
"Lochinvar," the third and highest-ranked specimen in the elocutionists' selection from *Marmion,* seems to fall outside the framework of
heroic dying, it has a parallel theme with that of the poem as a whole.
It celebrates the promise of male fulfilment and conquest. Lochinvar
emerges as another questing Marmion, as triumphant in love as Marmion was in dying. Lochinvar is an agent of completeness and fru-
ition; Marmion, one of of destruction and instability. Thus,
"Lochinvar," seen from this perspective, is a counterpoint to "Marmion." The two stories—one of failure and the other of success—
balance each other.

The medievalism of *Marmion,* its projection of the courtly codes
of gallantry and chivalry, and its inviting ballad form, appealed enor-
mously to readers who loved Scott's world of make-believe and adventure. The problem was that a few passages of the poem were
far too outspoken and erotic to pass the scrutiny of latter-century
educators. Thus, stanzas 4 and 5 were normally omitted to qualify
"juvenile representation."[69] Such lines as

> "I long woo'd your daughter, my suit you denied;
> Love swells like the Solway, but ebbs like the tide—
> And now am I come, with this lost love of mine,"
>
> .   .   .   .
>
> The bride kissed the goblet: the knight took it up,
> He quaff'd off the wine, and he threw down the cup.
> She look'd down to blush, and she look'd up to sigh,
> With a smile on her lips, and a tear in her eye.
> He took her soft hand, ere her mother could bar,—
> "Now tread we a measure!" said young Lochinvar.

were far too audacious. Significantly, McGuffey, always concerned
about his young readership, had the poem moved from the *Fifth
Reader* (1857), where it first appeared in 1844, to the *Sixth Reader.*[70]
However, very few elocutionary handbooks, governed as they were
by the canon, could afford to omit this poem. Mark Bailey (1865)
suggested that the poem be read with "median stress," in a lively
way[71] and Edward Napoleon Kirby, in addition to a similar recom-
mendation for its reading, also suggested that the poem could be
dramatized. "Observe," he said, "the haughty attitude of the father,
the deferential-indifferent attitude of Lochinvar. High pitch, quick
rate, medium stess, frequent wide intervals."[72] In his reading, the

ballad is turned into a domestic melodrama, featuring a possessive father and an imperial lover; the third character in the drama, the daughter, is a pawn for the masculine domination of the two.

THE LADY OF THE LAKE

The Lady of the Lake was received differently. First of all, no single passage or single Canto is favored over any other passage or Canto. The coverage of the poem is even, which does not mean to say that it is impartial. Early textbook writers such as Dwyer, Porter, and Russell favored the first four, more peaceful, cantos,[73] while antebellum anthologists found the last two cantos, with their descriptions of medieval war scenes, more rewarding for their purposes.

The producers of the elocutionary handbooks and the literary histories collected their examples from the various adventures of the poem's protagonists. For example, Canto 1 with its magical world of Loch Katrine and the romantic meeting between the disguised King James V of Scotland and Ellen Douglas provided Dwyer with the material he needed; Canto 2 and the hectic dialogue of Sir Roderick and the King was extensively used in the many editions of Russell's textbooks, and in Canto 3 and Canto 4 with their bloody clan skirmishes and fights, the textbook writers found material to illustrate speech rhythms and expressive modes of gesticulation. Cantos 5 and 6, finally, were often treated as one extended passage, spanning the "death struggle" of Rhoderick Dhu and the battle scene of Beal' an Duine.

The rhetorical application of the samples naturally conformed to the nature of their perceived content and form. Russell taught his students that "the chief use of *dialogue,* as regards elocution, is, to inspire appropriate *feeling, modulation,* and *action.*"[74] He instructed them in reading or better "dramatizing" the two sections from Canto 2 (stanzas 28–32 and 34–35), with Rhderick Dhu, Douglas and Malcolm Graeme; constantly shift positions in the room to emphasize changes in the emotional content of the passages, he admonished. Teaching elocution through the oral production of literary texts, involving two or more characters, was a common technique. It underscores the affinity of elocution practices with those of drama. John Swett, principal of the San Francisco Girls' High school and Normal School, explains that the "animated and impassioned" passage from Canto 5, delineating the "death struggle" between Roderick and Fitz-James (stanzas 16–17, "Now, yield thee, or The praise that Faith and Valour give") must be delivered in concordance with its theme, i.e., with "fast movement and radical stress."[75] From here the step to actual arrangements of the poem for more straightforward stage productions was a short one. In Mary Cobb's *Poetical Dramas for Home and School,* intended for teachers of "high schools, academies, and Sunday schools," the whole poem has been curtailed to serve purposes of this kind. Stage directions had been inserted, costumes suggested, and the text cut, to project the "voices" of five male and two female characters.[76] A further development occurred when the "drama of elocution" was taken up by amateur actors and turned into public performances. An incident from such a performance of *The Lady of the Lake,* given at Concord, Massachusetts, probably in the 1870s, is related by George Bradford Bartlett in his *Parlor Amusements for the Young People.*

> "The Lady of the Lake" also had a most successful run, until the dying Highlander brought down the house by rolling over upon the back curtain, thus exposing the dressing-room, and the bare walls of the old henhouse. A pair of old cavalry swords were the favorite properties, as this served also as goads in driving home the cows from their distant pasture.[77]

The range of appropriations was, as always, wide. So, samples from the dialogues of *The Lady of the Lake* were employed to teach proficiency in the English language; Lewis Baxter Monroe, in his *The Fifth Reader* (1871) used the well-known passage in Canto 4 (stanza 30, "Thy name and purpose, Saxon!") for a word-substituting exercise to improve on the vocabulary of his young students.[78]

Marmion and *The Lady of the Lake* are abundantly represented in the handbooks, *The Lay of the Last Minstrel, The Lord of the Isles,* and other poems and ballads feature only marginally. The description of Melrose Abbey in Canto 2 (stanzas 1–9) and the "love song" at the very beginning of Canto 3 of *The Lay* were quoted by a few educators.[79] Russell, as proved by his choice of specimens from *The Lady,* was also an innovating reader of *The Lord.* From here he selected examples to stage an "exhibition" (Canto 2, stanzas 6–32) and to illustrate "anger, excitement and rage" (Canto 2, stanza 15). To demonstrate the magic of description, he, characteristically, chose the last scene of *The Lord* that depicts the battle of Bannockburn in which Robert Bruce defeated the English army under King Edward (Canto 6, stanzas 31–34).

But these were odd samples whose use had little or no precedent. However, the famous chant to patriotism at the begining of Canto 6 of *The Lay* was an exception to this. The piece, often called "Love of Country," was one of the most-quoted poems in the whole American Scott canon. The reasons for this are eminently summed up by George R. Cathcart in his *The Literary Reader* (1874). Scott, he claims, was a man of "honour" and "unyielding fortitude" who dealt with "common topics, images, expressions" and "intense national-ity."[80] These verses, which George Vandenhoff taught should be read energetically and forcefully, with "only middle pitch,"[81] touched, one must assume, very strongly the American nostalgia for communality and patriotism.

> Breathes there the man, with soul so dead,
> Who never to himself hath said,
> This is my own, my native land!
> Whose heart hath ne'er within him burn'd,
> As home his footsteps he hath turn'd,
> From wandering on a foreign strand!
> If such there breathe, go, mark him well;
> For him no Minstrel raptures swell;
>
> . . . .
>
> The wretch, concentrated all in self,
> Living, shall forfeit fair renown,
> And, doble dying, shall go down
> To the vile dust, from whence he sprung,
> Unwept, unhonour'd, and unsung.

It is a stern and threatening lesson in nationalism that the American textbook writers present their readers and auditors.

NOVELS

Scott's novels were employed far less than his poems, which does not mean that they were unknown; the very wide and extemporane-ous usage of them suggests that they had a wide acceptance, only that descriptive prose, however popular, could not compete with po-etry and drama as a source for rhetorical emulation. As "literature," it could be treated differently. Mason Wade told the story that as a young man Parkman "put into verse the whole description of the Tournament in Scott's *Ivanhoe,* and then used [it] afterwards in decla-mation, and it was so well liked that other boys used it for the same purpose."[82] No doubt, the passage was the extract from the end of Chapter VIII that both Barber and McGuffey had inserted in their "Readers."[83]

Ivanhoe, with *Rob Roy,* were also the most cited of Scott's novels. Apart from the tournament scene, it is a scene in Chapter 29, engag-ing Rebecca and Ivanhoe as witnesses to the storming of Front-de-Bœuf's castle, which attracted a great deal of attention. It is easy to understand why. It included many of the stereotypes and rhetorical ingredients that the nineteenth-century educationalists were looking for in English literature. To describe the scene briefly: Rebecca communicates to Ivanhoe, who is lying motionless and injured on his back in the little cell, what takes place outside the window. The dialogue, with the ebulliently paternalizing, self-pitying, and inquisitive Ivanhoe and his high-strung respondent, turns the little scene into a lively domestic drama that was used extensively. Both Porter and Barber used it as a source for training declamation;[84] *McGuffey's New Sixth Eclectic Reader* and *The Sixth Franklin Reader* also included it, obviously for the same purpose, but after some alterations and abbeviations that improve the dialogue.[85] Its longevity as a popular reading piece is manifested by its frequent inclusion in Thomas B. Shaw and William Smith's many manuals of English literature.[86] All the brief introductions to this fragment make note of the racial gap between Rebecca, the Jew, and Ivanhoe, the Gentile and Saxon.

Another of Scott's strong women is featured in the second extract that enjoyed some popularity with the educators: Helen MacGregor in *Rob Roy* and the spectacle with the drowning of Morris, the spy (end of chapter 31). It is one of Scott's most famous eyewitness scenes and features Frank Osbaldistone as the shaken and pitying narrator of Helen's brutal drowning of Morris, the conspirator against Rob Roy. The passage was often picked to illustrate modes of anger and hatred. Anna T. Diehl Randall, a teacher of reading at a New York normal and training school, categorized the passage under the rubric "vivid narrative" and showed how Helen MacGregor's passion develops from "sympathetic horror," successively, to "terror," "scorn," "horror," and "revenge."[87] In her presentation of the passage she is quoting verbatim Russell in his *Orthophany* (1862),[88] another demonstration of how tight and conservative was the tradition within which the educators operated. From a literary and a thematic point of view, the scene with the drowning of Morris was interesting for its contrast of two worldviews—that of Osbaldistone's humanism and Helen MacGregor's chauvinism and brutality. Naturally, such an ambiguous piece of oratory had its educational attraction, permitting conflicting kinds of readings. Extracts from *The Heart of Midlothian* that featured strong and independent women also found their way into the textbooks as well. Thus the famous meeting of Jeanie Deans and the Queen and Jeanie's eloquent appeal for her sister's life (end of chapter 37) also gave pleasure outside the stage.[89]

In most of these specimens there lurks the notion of class that American readers were extremely sensitive to. Jeanie Deans's peasant argot contrasts not unfavorably with the Queen's English; present throughout the interview is Jeanie, the Scotchwoman, and her aborted rebellion. There are similar innuendos in another set piece, Ephraim Macbriar's speech to the Scotch insurgents in *Old Mortality* (end of chapter 18). Scott's delineation of this young preacher, "worn out by vigils, by fasts, by the rigour of imprisonment," as Macbrian stood in front of his audience must have acted as a direct prompt.

> He folded his hand, raised his face to heaven, and seemed lost in mental prayer. . . . When he spoke, his faint and broken voice seemed at first inadequate to express his conceptions. But the deep silence of the assembly, the eagerness with which the ear gathered every word, . . . had a corresponding effect upon the preacher himself. His words became more distinct, his manner more earnest and energetic; . . .

"Your garments are dyed—but not with the juice of the wine-press; your swords are filled with blood," he starts his address in a language that Scott himself described as "produced by the beams of the sun streaming through the storied representation of saints and martyrs on the Gothic window of some ancient cathedral." *The American Orator's Own Book,* which professed that its main function was to teach eloquence as a means to advance democracy in the country, chose this passage as one of its samples for exercise.[90] But Macbriar's words, of which the following are an example, must have also have had another, less technical, function for the editor of such a book:

> Set up a standard in the land; blow a trumpet on the mountains; let not the shephard tarry by his sheepfold, or the seedsman continue in the ploughed field; but make the watch strong, sharpen the arrows, burnish the shields, name ye the captains of thousands, and captains of hundreds, of fifties, and of tens: . . . for the passages of the destroyers are stopped, their rods are burned, and the face of their men of battle hath been turned to flight.

Here was an eloquence that would stir any American patriot, on whichever side he or she happened to be in the civil strifes. Barber's choice of a section of *Redgauntlet* for his *The Elocutionist* where Redgauntlet entreats his nephew Darsie to join him on a raid on Carlisle to revenge alleged outrages against the Scots (chapter 19) was another showpiece. Barber has edited the "address" radically, lifting out Darsie's evasive answers, thus eliminating the force of the dialogue and Darsie's role in it and emphasizing the codes of honor and loyalty.[91]

In no little measure these textbooks contributed to or reflected the cult of chivalry (gallantry, honor, courtesy), the cult of woman, the cult of caste and military affairs that not only inspired antebellum Southern life, but had a much wider regional and temporal function, reflecting cultural parochialism on a national scale. In making these literary choices the elocutionists directly contributed to the ongoing discussion about the epistemology of American literature.

Charles Dickens and Children

In his *School Reader* of 1843 Jesse Olney explained that his main selective principle was to "catch curiosity with the narrative,—heart with the pathetic,—and buoyant fancy with the amusing, as well as to interest the reflective powers with substantial truth."[92] Characteristically, and in full agreement with this programmatic, he included in his textbook (52–53), "Death of a school boy," the famous pathetic scene in chapter 16 where Paul Dombey dies. Olney's aims might stand as a rubric for the nature of the Dickens's specimens in the nineteenth-century American literary handbooks. They included deathbed scenes in the simplest prose form, ludicrous and comical tableaux, and homiletic pieces of narration that carried "substantial truth." It is primarily as moralist that Dickens figures in the educational field, not the comedian and the teller of stories involving homely mores that the contemporary American theater projected.

One main aspect of Dickens's attraction for the educators was his preoccupation with the grim fortunes of Victorian children. Their deaths at early ages, the oppressiveness of the educational system, and the vicissitudes of innocent and immature life among urban crooks and rural sweethearts were subjects that no American handbook of rhetoric or literature would bypass. Dickens "excels," said the editor of *The Franklin Fifth Reader,* "in scenes which paint sickness and death, especially of the lovely and young."[93] Like the offerings in so many other similar manuals, its selections from Dickens included only incidents with dying children—"The Child's Story" (no. 4 among *Christmas Stories*), "Little Nell's garden" (from *The Old Curiosity Shop*), and "Death of Paul Dombey" (*Dombey and Son,* chapter 41). Few American textbooks of the kind we are discussing would forego including these two. A third passage with a dying youth was Jo in *The Bleak House* (chapter 47).

It is perplexing, however, to imagine that these sentimental melodramas could be very useful in practising rhetoric, though M. S. Mitchell offers "Death of Little Nell" as an illustration of the "semi-tonic melody."[94] But, as has been pointed out already, these textbooks, whether they professed to teach elocution or rhetoric, projected primarily what was inscribed in the popular literary conventions of the day. If Dickens's elaboration on Nell's or Paul's dying offered a poor foundation for the teaching of rhetorical strategies, it was excellent material for the promotion of the virtues of perseverance and determinism for the young mind. It is the agony of the approaching death that these textbook excerpts dwell on. Both Monroe's and George Stillman Hillard's manuals abridge the scene with the dying Paul in the same manner, by cutting out the intermediary passages and highlighting the woesome end.[95]

Nell's death in *The Old Curiosity Shop* receives even more attention from the educators. The "ars moriendi" of the Victorian novel here reaches its novelistic peak: the gruesome details of her dying that the reader of Dickens's novel learns about in retrospect and the eyewitness description of her burial are quoted at a greater extent than any other sample from Dickens. Most extracts from the novel combine the two chapters where Nell's death is narrated (end of 71 and beginning of 72) to create an atmosphere of virtuous young death. McGuffey chose two instances of child death for his *New Sixth Eclectic Reader:* Nell's death, of course, but also the section in chapter 25 with the "teacher and the sick scholar."[96] Hillard used the graveyard scene from chapter 54 with Nell and the sexton for his *Fifth Reader* and Nell's death for the Sixth, with the comment that she "is of the sweetest and purest of all [Dickens's] creations," gliding "like a sunbeam of grace and innocence through many a troubled scene: but the burden of life is too heavy for her delicate spirit, and she thus gently lays it down" (154).[97] The extracts expose the sufferings of the small and helpless child and inscribe them with the adult or male interpretation of the causes of their lot. Nell's death is messianic, it is "the burden of life" that succumbs her, not her own ill fate, social or individual. The lesson the texts present of exemplary forebearance and laconic humility is strangely at odds with aspects of nineteenth-century American cultural ethics—like intrepidity and boldness of thought and action. However, one must be aware of the dual perspective. One strategy of application did not outmaneuver the other. The harping on the deaths of young schoolchildren could also be called on to promote antagonistic ideas of endurance and struggle.

The double perspective is more prominent in the Dickensian classroom scenes where the child often is both victim and hero. Clearly, this is the way McGuffey used the famous breakfast scene at Dotheboys Hall in *Nicholas Nickleby* (chapter 8) for his *Fifth Reader*. The two themes seem to cooperate. However, McGuffey, as was his habit, has both abridged and edited the sections describing the Squeers school, the breakfast, and the beginning of the philosphy lesson. He has reduced the most gruesome aspects of the conditions at school. References to the physical circumstances of the schoolboys have been omitted or reduced: gone are phrases such as "the crooked foot," "the hare-lip," and the "bleared eye"; descriptions that "there was childhood with the light of its eye quenched"; and comments about adult cruelty and neglect. The scenes with Mrs. Squeers calls the little boy with the curly hair to wipe her fingers on it and Mr. Squeers thanking God for the breakfast have been omitted altogether. Dickens's agony and criticism have been mitigated and the adult guilt reduced. The child is still at the center, but her or his struggle and humiliation have been mitigated.[98]

A couple of passages in *David Copperfield* promoted a healthier and less sombre view of the active child—the episodes with David running away from his aunt (chapters 12 and 13) and his falling in love with Dora Spenlow (chapter 26). In each case the subject and the initiator of the action is a young person who wants to reform his life and improve his situation. To this category of youthful intrepididity and the adventure of the road can be added the passage from *Martin Chuzzlewit* (chapter 36) where Tom Pinch travels to London. Edward Napoleon Kirby found this passage suitable for his *Vocal and Action-Language: Culture and Expression*.[99]

The affection of Dickens for the burlesque and the melodrama, so extensively represented by contemporary American theater, was only marginally appropriated by the textbook producers. The bald and naturalistic sea scene in *David Copperfield* (unique for Dickens) ("Tempest," chapter 55), the homely introductory tableau of "Chirp the first" in *The Cricket on the Hearth*,[100] and especially the lighhearted ripostes of Scrooge and Marley in *A Christmas Carol* were found to be congenial passages to enourage reading and recitation. Kirby chose a brief passage characterized as "The Cheerful Locksmith" from the less-known novel *Barnaby Rudge* (chapter 156) to practise "animated narrative." He advised his students that the "cheerfulness" of the passage should be retrieved through reading "on quite a high pitch, making wide intervals when required, to lower intervals."[101]

It is between the experiences defining the low and the high, between tear-jerking sentimentality and burlesque farce, between the death of the virtuous young and the exemplary pathos of aging that the school manuals pick their Dickens specimens and in the process of organizing them for the inclusion reformulate them. The selection from the canon of Dickens favored the world—if not *of,* at least—*about* the child, but it was partly motivated and prejudiced by another American pastime, the burlesque. Death and burlesque are conspiratorial partners in the arena of life; in its American counterpart Dickens was one of the most entertaining mediators.

Again, as in the case of the elocutionists' Shakespeare, burlesque and dialogue were linked in a symmetrical fashion. Training in the dialogue mode seemed to prescribe the choice of comedy. For an extract from *Martin Chuzzlewit* (chapter 44) in his *American Elocu-*

tionist, Russell used this as an epigraph: "An Unsuccessful Attempt
to Raise the Wind." He explained that the dialogue that he had wrung
out of the Dickens text "demands attention to the full expression of
free, playful feeling, in *voice* and *action.* . . . The object of practice
. . . is to impart *ease* and *animation* to the speaker's general manner."[102] But Russell, as did all the best teachers of elocution of the
day, went further in contextualizing and dramatizing the piece for his
students: he carved out for them the roles of Tigg, Peckniff, and
Slyme and described in a note the way he visualized them. Tigg
would represent the "shabby genteel, in its last stage" with dashing
manners, Pecksniff, "a smooth, well-dressed man," grave and cold,
and Slyme "a miserable looking wretch, worn out with low dissipa-
tion." Slyme would be dull, "indicating partial inebriety."[103] The
scene for their meeting was a bar. However, in the printed version,
Slyme is never given a line, although he is present throughout the
tableau.[104] Slyme's verbal silence could thus be used even by a rhetorician whose professed specialty was "enunciation."

But of all of Dickens's works it was was *The Pickwick Papers* that
scored highest as a seedbed for the elocutionary laughter. Some of
the most popular episodes were Pickwick's "romantic adventure with
a middle-aged lady in yellow curl-paper" that often was named "The
dilemma" (chapter 22), Wardle's story about Gabriel Grub (chapter
29), Mr. Winkle's skating (chapter 30), and Sam Weller's Valentine
(chapter 33). Apart from the hilarious and the bizarre quality that
these extracts convey, their attraction for Americans lay in their col-
loquialisms and back-talk quality. Here the teachers of elocution and
literature found a wealth of material that passed as a mild corrective
to the "vulgar" talk of the New York streets and a proliferation of
low-comedy stereotypes.

The most popular scene of them all was the the trial episode in
chapter 34 of *The Pickwick Papers.* No selection of Dickens would
miss the animated speech of the pompous Serjeant Buzfuz. It had
most of the ingredients of a dramatic and a rhetorical hit: it was
structured as a trial—and nineteenth-century readers and audiences
loved the well-devised trial—it reflected affection and pretense of a
kind that Americans often associated with a British way of life, and
it was stylized and ornamental to the point that its exaggeration became a rhetorical gimmick worthy of any student's admiration.

Other British Writers

THE ROMANTICS

Among the Romantics, Shelley and Wordsworth were only used peripherally in the manuals on rhetorics; Keats not at all. Shelley's "To

a Skylark" received some attention. Mark Bailey thought it "full of rapturous beauty, [whose reading] requires the 'purest tone' and the smoothest and happiest 'media stress,' prolonged with swelling fulness on the emphatic words"[105] and Barber offered Wordsworth's "Lucy," adorned with graphs to indicate pauses and emphasis, as a sample for reading practices.[106] But these examples are inconsequential: in their isolation they highlight the absence of these two British poets from the mainstream of nineteenth-century American reading. American readers were repelled by the stigma of intellectualism that from the beginning was attached to the Romanctics, including Keats.[107]

Coleridge fared a little better. A number of his poems were anthologized, and his poem "Hymn before Sun-rise, in the Vale of Chamouni" was a hit by any standard. It is not difficult to understand why. It had some of the characteristics that defined poems that were successful in America: the awesome mountain landscape with torrents and ravines, the solitary, agonized observer-mendicant, and pantheistic rapport betweeen an unknowing, cruel Nature and an overpowering Godhead. The poem's directness of address and individual tone made it appropriate for a variety of rhetorical usages. Russell used it to illustrate "poetic apostrophe,"[108] Hillard included it (except the last stanza—perhaps, the invocation to the morning mist surrounding the foot of Mount Blanc in the lines, "Rise, O Ever Rise, / Rise like a cloud of incense from the Earth!" was considered inappropriate) in his *The Franklin Sixth Reader,*[109] and John Swett taught that the poem must be thoroughly analyzed grammatically, before it could be read: in "media stress, with orotund quality, strong force, and slow movement."[110]

TENNYSON AND THE BROWNINGS

With the emergence of another generation of English poets, headed by Lord Tennyson and the Brownings, the mode and level of the American reception of English literature for pedagogical and rhetorical usage changed. First of all, the mode of reception diversified. This means that far more British writers were being annotated and anthologized (naturally this movement was congruent with the "Americanization" of the American textbook). A second feature is that more emphasis was laid on the interpretive literary reading and analysis and continously less on the literary text as a platform for elocution and rhetoric, although there is considerable confusion between these two areas through the very end of the century.

Of the Victorians only Lord Tennyson and the Brownings were well received by the Americans. From the 1870s on, these writers were featured in American textbooks. For the American readership, Tennyson in fact came to represent the protoypical English poet because of his, as the Americans considered it, air of lofty aristocratic craftsmanship. We can remind ourselves of Walt Whitman's complicated fascination with the poet that can be defined as a combination of self-effacement and adolescent rebellion.[111] The most popular of Tennyson's many anthologized poems was "The Charge of the Light Brigade," a poem that had its background in a newspaper clipping about the Crimean War of 1854. The poem recounts the futile, (un)heroic charge and the subesquent massacre of the "noble six hundred" by a battery of Russian cannons. The ballad can be seen as posing the question of whether there are any causes worth dying for at all. However, in I. H. Brooks' *Common School Elocution and Oratory,* the "charge," renarrated by a sergeant survivor, is presented as a patriotic demonstration of heroics and revenge—"only blood could quench our thirst for revenge."[112] But the overt pedagogical function of the prose passage, which was claimed to be an extract from the *Boston Commercial Bulletin,* was to practise "short pauses." Notably, however, Tennyson's fatalistic and melacholic dirge has been turned into an adolesecent American showpiece of bravery and quixotism; the motive of training for "pausing" is secondary.

The other poems by Tennyson that were included with some frequency by the educationalists were "Bugle Song" (one of six songs in the blank-verse poem "The Princess" which is placed between different sections, here between III and IV), stanza CVI of "In Memoriam A. H. H." ("Ring out, wild bells, to the wild sky"), "The Death of the Old Year," "Break, break, break,"and extracts from "Lady Clare" and "Lady Clara Vere de Vere." The first four of these all lament the passing of time, tensions between the past and the present, separation of loved ones, and the ensuing nostalgia and wonderment. Joshua Leavitt chose four lines (1–3, 5) from "The Death of the Old Year" to illustrate "stress of voice"; in reading these lines, he says, stress has to be placed on the middle of the syllable, "that is, the voice commences soft, swells, and then ends soft."[113] Only through such a reading would, in his view, the poem's elements of "pathos and solemnity" develop.

The two poems "Lady Clare" and "Lady Clara Vere de Vere," including a host of others on women and feminist subjects, were definitely new themes in the American literary and elocutionary manuals. Elizabeth Barrett Browning was well liked by the Americans. Educators dealing with the mother-woman-child relationship quoted extensively from such poems as "The Cry of the Human," "Mother and Poet," and "The Cry of the Children." The lush medievalism of the poem "Rhyme of the Duchess of May" had some supporters and

Hillard, in his *The Sixth Reader,* gave her a prominent place, calling her "a woman of rare and high genius, marked by imagination and originality of treatment, and hardly less so by her intense sympathy with every form of suffering." He quoted her tender and musical poem "The Sleep" in its entirety.[114]

Robert Browning had more or less the same following. Also in his case his relationship with Italy and his medievalism were attractive features. The "cavalier" couplets of the poem "How They Brought the Good News from Ghent to Aix" were quoted with some regularity. The poem describes a nightly dramatic horse ride through a moonlit landscape, the purport of which was to save lives. Tennyson's languid notes about ravenous Time and cruel Destiny were countered in the American reception by E. B. Browning's emotional sensibility and Robert Browning's forlorn picturesqueness. Optimism and pessimism were two sides of the same coin.

4

British Writers on the American Stage

The topic of Byron, Scott, and Dickens on the American stage presumes a discussion of two kinds of discourses that seemingly have very little in common: oratory and extravaganza. Yet, overdone—intentionally or not—the rhetorical stance in their works easily passes into the area of the absurd and flimsy. The British plays produced and adapted in America in the nineteenth century stepped precariously on the tightrope between these opposite poles. It is in this contraposition that the displacement of the works of the Old World is most apparent. The melodrama may be said to fall in between these two theater idioms, through its appeal to the mediating aspirations of high morality, good nature, and democratic America. The great variety of usages that the British writers were subjected to on the American stage may make an exploration of works under such headings as "oratorical," "melodramatic," and "burlesque" arbitrary; these categories intersect and mingle, sometimes even within one single performance, in which a serious first half can be followed, for instance, with a farcical afterpiece. However, an organization of the material based tentatively on modes of appropriations, rather than on single topics or individual writers, is more illuminative of the phases of acculturalization that concern us here. One will then find that Byron and Scott feature in all the sections, that Dickens is prominent in the melodrama section (and less so in the others), and that, comparatively speaking, burlesque discourse is by far the most rewarding and voluminous arena for the particular brand of my investigation. A clear majority of all British writers admired by the Americans were travestied, from Milton to Tennyson. Shakespeare could be pigeonholed in any category, but as so much has already been written about his overall impact, my section on him focuses on the tendency to extravagant discourse in the history of his American reception.

The chapter highlights then the complex issue of the integration of, what I have called, the A-and the B-text; it develops and extends the earlier statements about the vitality inhered in the *gap* between the two. The concepts I used in Chapter 2 to categorize and define the literary adaptions—integration, emulation, and comment—fail to make full sense of the richness and variety that went into the American appropriations of the British plays which we are concerned with in this chapter. Yet, as a formula of pointing to the cultural drama that these negotiations ensue—and that we also saw characterized the bilateral formulations of the educational handbooks—they are still quite valid. It is clear to me then that the partisanship of these appropriations was related to their Janus-faced character. In this chapter on American theater I will further demonstrate how American culture-formation employed "imitation"—in the the very broad sense I have been using the term—to achieve its ends.

From Oratory to Melodrama

Oratory and nationalism: Scott, Murphy, and Lamb

Patriotism and nationalism formed oratory's ideological backbone. To boast selfhood and cultural independence through an idiom and a style whose very substance had formed the foundation of oppression could be a daring enterprise. The desire to contribute to a national literature was, no doubt, as strong among playwrights as among writers of prose and poetry and educationalists. The challenge was how these ambitions were to be gained: whether through refining domestic subjects and ideas, or through imitating and emulating foreign works that had achieved international or universal acclaim. In this section I will consider four "British" works and their American adaptations that "outshone" their origins.

Early in 1812[1] James Nelson Barker of Philadelphia started to work on Walter Scott's *Marmion*[2] at the request of William Burke Wood, the Philadelphia stage manager. Wood believed that the play would do better if it was not announced as an American production. So Thomas Abthorpe Cooper, the famous actor, concocted the idea that it was dramatized by the British playwright Thomas Morton. Wood reminiscenced:

> We had it sent to our theatre from New York, where it was made to arrive in the midst of rehearsal, in the presence of actors, packed up exactly *like pieces we were in the habit of receiving from London. It was opened with great gravity, and announced without any author being alluded to.* None of the company were in the secret . . . not even the prompter.[3] [emphasis Wood's]

Due to this trick, or "finesse," as William Dunlap calls it, it "ran like wildfire through our theatre,"[4] starting in New York on 13 April 1812 with Cooper himself as Marmion.[5] Later Cooper resigned the role to [Edward Shaw] Simpson.[6] It played for six weeks at the Park. In Philadelphia it played at the Chestnut Street Theatre from 1 January 1813 for seven nights, and through mid-February, "with great success," with John R. Duff as Marmion and Mary Ann Duff as Clare de Clare.[7] Then happened what no modern history of American theater fails to mention. Wood announced the name of the author and the play, and as a consequence, he believed, "ceased to attract."[8] Barker himself, although hesitantly, seemed to have shared this view. In the Preface to the second edition of the play (1816), he explained that the "reception of it met with in these cities [New York in the spring of 1812, and at Philadelphia the following winter], was much too gracious, too widely different from that usually given to American plays, not to have been, in part at least, fairly attributable to the general belief that it was a trans-atlantic production."[9]

The assumption that the play survived due to the trick they played on the audience does not suggest the whole truth. The attempt at concealing the American authorship of the play was partly a response to the established colonial myths about the inferiority of native talent that colonial powers cherish wherever they operate, partly a measure to safeguard the integrity of the theaters that were playing *Marmion*. In fact, Wood and Cooper were taking quite deliberate risks in producing Barker's play, for it was loaded with political innuendoes that no Philadelphia or New York theatergoer would fail to understand. Dunlap also warned the producers of the play that King James's speech in 4.3 might "'unkennel' the 'occult' design."[10] This is a section from the exchange between Marmion, the English traitor and invader, and James, the Scottish defender and "outlaw":

James. . . . Do not ask us here
To throw our armour off, and cower at home,
Patient, till England find a time to treat?

Marmion. Till Henry come from France.

James. Why went he thither
But to wage unjust war?

Marmion. Your highness' pardon,
He went to quell the general enemy,
Of you, and all.

James. The general enemy!
Spare me, my lord, the stale, distasteful tale,
I know it all. The nation the most selfish,

Presuming, arrogant, of all this globe,
Professes but to fight for others' rights,
While she alone infringes every right.

———

Even in days of truce! I burn to speak it—
Murder and pillage, England's constant agents,
Roamed through our land, and harboured in our bays!
Our peaceful border sacked, our vessels plundered,
Our abused liegemen robbed, enslaved and slaughtered.
My lord, my lord, under such injuries,
How shall a free and gallant nation act?
Still lay its sovereignty at England's feet—
Still basely ask a boon from England's bounty—
Still vainly hope redress from England's justice?
No! by our martyred fathers' memories,
The land may sink—but, like a glorious wreck,
'Twill keep its colours flying to the last.[11]

But to the surprise of the proprietor of the theater the two producers insisted that there was to be no censoring of it: James's speech "must remain as a powerful 'touch at the times'."[12] They defended the historicity informing the play, as well as their own professionalism. The play was indeed an effective political statement.

On one of its representations at the Chestnut Theatre only a few weeks before the war against England started, the audience was, Durang recalled, "in a great state of excitement." After King James's words "My lord, my Lord, under such injuries," the father of the author, Jacob Barker, a pompous military officer, rose from his seat, and, swinging his cane, exclaimed: "No, sir! No! We'll nail them to the mast, and sink with the stars and stripes before we yield." The dialogue on the stage could not be resumed for a long time after Barker Senior's outburst.[13]

The play was seen to harbor "duplicity" and an "occult design"; its projection of parallels that alluded to the contemporary and the very concrete warlike situation outside Philadelphia gave it a vitality that was unexpected.[14] A reviewer of the third edition (1826) in the *American Quarterly Review* claimed that the play was truly American in sentiment. He quoted the illustrious speech by James, but in his quotation reduced wittily the play's aggressiveness by making the last line read "Still keep its colors flying at the mast," instead of the original's "'Twill keep its colours flying to the last."[15]

Barker had written a political allegory that denounced British intrusion and hegemony and lauded American struggle for independence. He had employed historical analogues to emphasize his point. He had not only emulated and dramatized Scott's *Marmion,* appropriating deftly the master discourse and underwriting the Scottish, and thus American, rebellion against it. He would go on developing and radicalizing his views. In the Preface to the first edition he had courteously explained that he had made two major alterations in his presentation of Marmion, first by bringing Wilton's supposed guilt closer to the time of the action, and second by softening the punishment of Constance. But otherwise, he was anxious to point out, he had followed Scott closely. Obviously stimulated by the warm reception of the play, in the Preface to the second edition of 1816, his tone has become ebullient and aggressive. Supported by Holinshed, whom he has consulted, he now faulted Scott for

> having selected his country's overthrow for the subject of the poem, while the splendid histories of Bruce and Wallace so obviously claimed his preference: first, as they were the histories of earlier and more chivalrous times, and therefore, it would seem, more attractive to mr. Scott's taste; and better suited to his peculiar genius for the gothic; but still rather as they were the histories of the bright hours, of the faded glories of his courts. . . . [T]o our utter surprize, the Scottish bard pauses in the lay of Scotland's former triumphs over England, to pay to the same England, here ultimate enslaver, a compliment at his country's expense, by way of apology for his boldness. Such devotness to a master or a conqueror may, perhaps, become the mercenary minstrel of feudal lord; but it requires all our admiration of mr. Scott's genius to make us forget, that, any of the strains of his "Harp of the North," those of independence are not sometimes heard. (ii–iii)

He then provides a couple of other comments about his play that demonstrate to the full his political motivations for both writing the play and seeing it through in all three editions:

> The reader is desired to recollect, that at the time this play was written, we were on the verge of war with England: the dialogue in the fourth act, between James and Marmion, might else appear overcharged. And yet James imputes nothing to England which England's history does not record as her deed. England did sack the peaceful border, even while a pending negotiation was prostrate by her evasions; she did [enter] the Scottish harbours, to burn and pillage, to enslave and murder. . . . [S]uch was England to Scotland in the sixteenth century; and such, precisely such, has she recently been to America. And it was not the least of the author's gratifications, on the representation of the play, that the coincidence was perceived and felt by an audience of his countrymen. (v)

Parenthetically, the rebellious rhetorics of *Julius Caesar* could also be made good use of. Not uncommonly, passages from it were used to kindle instincts of war and heroism, but also, which is more surpring, to celebrate peace. This latter kind of play was performed on 12 April, 1815, at Albany Theatre which, it was reported, was decorated with American standards and illuminated with one hundred "wax tapers."[16]

Another Scott play whose early American production projects a cultural differential was *Mary of Scotland; or, The Heir of Avenel,* founded on Scott's *The Abbott.*[17] It was produced at the Park on 18 May 1821 by "a gentleman of this city." The play puffed a Catherine Seyton, who "will sing Ye Banks and Bars of Bunny Doon, accompanied by herself on the harp." The enterprise fell flat, "in spite of the fact a prologue 'written by a gentleman of this City' was recited." Odell's explanation that "the Scott vein had been worked out, except for a few finds" was wishful thinking; the play was simply embracing too much.[18] The preface discusses the pros and cons of adapting foreign material. The printing of the play, it is explained, has been undertaken, tentatively to

> determine how far the progressive interest, and diffused action, of "The Abbott" could be concentrated so as to produce dramatic effect, and also to ascertain the disposition of the public to encourage indigenous efforts. However the author may have succeeded in the former of these objects, the issue of the attempt has proved that, if so few American plays are exhibited on the stage, the cause is not so much to be sought for in the dearth of patronage, as in the absence or indolence of that genius which is necessary to call it into action. The success of "Mary of Scotland," in its first representation, was unique and unequivocal, and this auspicious result will induce a series of dramatic productions from the same press. (iii)

Paradoxically, as it may seem to us, the project to ascertain and promote indigenous talent through the reworking of foreign source material was not only hazardous in inviting comparison with the original, it also suggested rebellion in its thematic and patriotic deflation of the source. The Prologue to the play, which its writer recited on the evening of its firstnight at the Park, points to these analogues:

> A tale of other lands and other times,
> Of sovereigns' wrongs and politicians' crimes
> Our drama shows, and if our feeble stage
> Revive the memory of that golden age,
> And cause again these frequent tears to flow
> Which generous eyes have wept for Mary's woe,
> We cry content, . . .

Great effort was taken to guarantee a success for this unhappy American piece.[19] Another pathetic Prologue of appeal was delivered during

the same night, written by a friend and spoken by Mrs. [John?]
Barnes, one of the actresses:

> O'er all our drama breathe thy charm awhile,
> That we, this night, may win—our Patron's smile.
> Oh! let it not be said the opening bloom
> Of native genius withers here in gloom,
> Rouse up the town—revive the drooping heart
> Of the true votaries to the scenic art;
> Support our author's, and our dramatic cause,
> Send a rich house, and your full applause. (viii)

Back in Philadelphia, another actor/manager of the Chestnut Theatre, Francis Blissett, declared that he wanted to "avoid the legitimate
line" and "trust to the exciting causes of the day for a subject." He
was also speaking up for a truly national play that was to treat the
daily concerns of his people. Once again Barker was commissioned
to write a play. This time he produced an imitation of Arthur Murphy's *The Upholsterer* (1770). "The Embargo, or, What News?" was
played at the Chestnut on 16 March 1808. In a letter to William Dunlap (1832), Barker commented on the background and reception of
the play:

> The subject of an embargo, then existing, was rather ticklish, and some
> of the patriotic sentiments were somewhat coldly received by a portion
> of the audience; but a majority were of the right feeling, and bore me
> triumphantly through. Very much to their credit, several of our merchants
> were distinguished for the applause they bestowed. I do not know what
> became of the manuscript. . . .[20]

Durang defined the play as a manifesto, infused with American ideals
of democracy and freedom of speech and prejudiced by anti-British
emotions.[21] It did not become the stock piece it was meant to be; the
subject was probably far too controversial and, in fact, dangerous,
which Barker of course realized. Reese D. James, a historian of Philadelphia theater, somewhat cynically enlisted the play as a provoca-
tion, an "invitation to the rowdies to make themselves obnoxious."[22]
In the same year, it was shown at Baltimore, Charleston, New Orleans, and Boston, which points to the fact that at least the play was
not seen as another local skit.[23] Barker took a special pleasure, one
may assume, in dismantling British plays to serve militant causes.
From the way the plays were received, the audiences sensed that the
scripts were inscribed with colonial antagonisms.

Another play that can be linked with the 1808 "embargo" play was
Charles Lamb's "Mr. H." It was originally performed at Theatre

Royal, Drury Lane, on 10 December 1806 with Lamb himself as Mr.
H. Despite his "double" presence in it, it was a complete failure, not
revived until 1855, and then under the dubious rubric, "as a curiosity."[24] The play enjoyed an altogether different reputation in America.
It was produced in New York in March 1807, but real success was
won in Philadelphia. It played there first on 19 February 1812 and
then in 1813, 1814, 1816, 1817, 1818, 1820, 1828, 1831, and 1841 (it
was additionally performed at Baltimore and Washington).[25]

The play is about Mr. Hedgehog who lives at Bath under the assumed name of Mr. H. His secrecy gives rise to all sorts of specula-
tions, especially among the eligible and marriage-prone young women
in the city who start seeking his company. As Mr. H is fairly well-
off, one of the candidates, Melesinda, agrees to marry him. But as
soon as his real name has been discovered, the whole village turns
against him—its womanfolk and his servants, friends, and business
partners. Good luck returns, though. As if by miracle, he is accred-
ited another name and again marriage-minded women queue at his
feet. He eventually accepts Melesinda, or rather she accepts him,
and on this note the play ends.

The reasons for this rather vacuous play's success in America are
obvious. First of all it satirizes, even in it original form, English
intolerance, English hypocrisy, and English obsession with surface
impressions. Second, it is concerned with language and the "naming
of things," which theme a multicultural and multilinguistic country
like America would find particularly intriguing. The play was discussing the discrepancy between the meaning and the letter, the signi-
fier and the signified. Third, Hedgehog, finding the society around
him both intolerant and repugnant, reflects whether he would rather
emigrate to a part of the world where names do not prejudice their
holders. The American audiences were quick to fill in the empty
spaces in Lamb's text; Hedgehog could as well take refuge in the
"new" country and find himself accepted.[26]

ORATORY AND ORIENTALISM: BYRON, SHAKESPEARE, AND BRITISH ACTING

In its purest form Byron's verse had little chance of sustaining the
interest of an American audience for very long time, even if such a
native spirit as Edwin Forrest animated the lines and filled the stage.
Of course the managers realized this and were quick to devise solutions, sympathetic both to the eye and the ear. First of all there had
to be action, which William Charles Macready mistakenly believed
should center around the hero (himself) of the piece. Orientalism,
for instance, in all its fantastic aspects, was appropriated to provide

an exotic frame for Byronic action, such as the depiction of the pining hero in a cave or on a mountain top. Emblems suggesting strange, fearful customs and exotic rituals suffused the bizarre outlandish world. Colorful costumes, odd pieces of architecture, manly swords, and gaudy plumes became stock properties of theatrical evenings that contained not only a single play, but also usually a farce, some music, and other features. To many spectators, such a milieu was the only true representation of Byron.

Two British actors and interpreters play important, although partly sad, roles in the history of Byron's, and other British writers', stage production in the nineteenth century. They are Junius Brutus Booth, Sr. and Macready. Booth came to Philadelphia on 17 February 1823 as an unknown actor to pick up a job with Warren & Wood at the Chestnut Theatre. He did not do well initially and was suspended from acting *Richard III* after only three performances. He acted, however, in *The Two Foscari* on 31 March 1823, where he did Francis Foscari with Henry Wallack as Jacopo Foscari. It was the play's first night in Philadelphia.[27] Booth failed here as he would fail in his other performances in America at this stage. *The Two Foscari* did not survive the next Philadelphia season, nor was it staged to my knowledge anywhere else in the country after this. A commentary in Macready's acting copy of *The Two Foscari* explains, however, that the play was "first performed at Baltimore. W: S. October 12th. 1822. At Holliday Street. Warren & Wood managers."[28]

While in Philadelphia Booth must also have considered introducing Byron's *Sardanapulus* to the American audience. Apart from indicating his attempts at adapting the play, an acting copy of the play at Harvard Theatre Collection, which bears his signature, lists a number of Warren and Wood actors for the main parts: William Augustus Conway as Sardanapulus, Henry Wallack as Salamenes, and Mary Ann Duff as Myrrha. It is doubtful whether it was performed at the beginning of April [2–7], 1823 as noted in the acting copy. It probably never came out of the rehearsal stage; it is not recorded by theater annalists. Booth's version was probably thought to be too heavy for the audience, despite his alterations which were, moreover, far too ephemeral and unsubstantial to gain any favor.[29] For a Byron play to outlive its first performance, it had to be radically transformed and transposed on many levels. Disappointed with his alterations of the play, one could also assume that he preferred *The Two Foscari,* which he was redramatizing simultaneously and also was to act in.

Booth's name is also attached to a third Byron play which at this stage fared slightly better with the American audiences, *Bride of Abydos; or, The Pirate of the Isle.* The play was performed in Philadelphia on 13 November 1819.[30] It appeared again at the Chestnut on

1 January 1824 and Booth acted Selim in it on 21 February 1824.[31] Despite its sumptuous and elaborate stage costumes and outfitting, the performance did not "pay its outlay." It only ran for three nights. Durang thought that it was because Cooper was losing his popularity at the time. Neither could Booth salvage the play at this point.[32] Another attempt at rescuing it was made at the end of the year. The whole last scene had been reconstructed and new paintings had been installed. It worked, and during Christmas the house was crowded. Durang's comments are now persuasive: "This piece is really excellent of its kind. The language is chaste and dramatic, effective in incidents, and of romantic interest. It is really a worthy desecendant of Lord Byron's muse."[33] It was repeated on 9 March 1825 the next year with Watkins Burrough, instead of Booth, as Selim. Durang characterized Burrough's performance as "picturesque," "attitude-striking," and his declamations "rocking." In other words, Selim had been thoroughly "Americanized." Add to this "fascinating romance in euphonious poetical numbers" the attractions of the scenic landscapes and success was certain.[34]

Booth also played Selim at the Park in New York in April and May 1824, and he appeared there again in March 1827. In June the play was relegated to an afterpiece and Thomas Barry acted Selim.[35] At the Lafayette Theatre the play had a fresh opening in September, with new stage furniture and lighting. Mrs. Henry Wallack was Zuleika and Burroughs, again, Selim. It lasted till 1 October. *The Mirror* (quoted by Odell) wrote enthusiastically: "The effect of this arrangement is strikingly exemplified in the splendid procession scene . . . which presents a spectacle more imposing than any we had ever witnessed."[36] The play was acted a few times in New York in the 1840s and then disappeared for some time.[37]

The American audiences obviously preferred an acting style that turned away from an intellectualism defined via language analysis, and focused on action, spectacle, and declamation. Those American actors (Cooper, Burroughs, Wallack) who could produce an effect of this kind were applauded and well received. Durang, the eminent producer and adapter of many British plays, understood what his theatergoers wanted and organized the performances accordingly. Booth's attempt to transform Byron's plays into oratorical showpieces was bound to fail. It was not sufficient to be able to recite Byron's long and tedious passages and through the recitation attempt to achieve a fluster of pathos and furor. Booth's and Macready's struggle to teach their listeners that the medium was secondary to the message was not convincing.

William Charles Macready returned to New York in the autumn of 1843, after seventeen years at home. (He had dignified eastern the-

aters during a guest appearance tour in 1826.) In England he had
been performing *Werner* (perhaps Byron's only actable play) since
the early 1830s. On arriving in America, he took it up,[38] and it became
one of his favorites. He acted in it for the first time in New York, at the
Park on 4 October 1843 and at the National Theatre on 16 November.
Charlotte Cushman was his Josephine throughout the autumn, both
in Boston,[39] in New York[40] and at New Orleans.[41] Their performance
at the Park in New York on 12 December 1843 marked the height of
their New York career as an acting couple.[42]

However, Boston remained the only place in the country where he
was more or less unequivocally appreciated; on his return here in
September 1844, he was announced as the "the greatest Shakespearean reader and delineator of Europe."[43] We notice that it is as
"reader," and not an "actor" that he is announced: for pure-minded
Bostonians "theater" was still intimately associated with low character sketches and the circus. In December 1843, he gave *Marino
Faliero* with Boston's own Cushman as Angiolina, whom he immediately labeled an "intrigante," probably as she was receiving more
attention than he.[44] He only performed *Marino Faliero* a couple of
times. With *Werner* he was to be pretty successful. Even the clergy
in Boston came to his performances of this play, being "absolved
from sin by the non-theatrical locale, put up because the National
Theatre had been destroyed by fire, and the announcement that *Hamlet* could be read."[45] James E. Murdoch, who was the stage manager
of the National Theatre in 1840–41, explained Macready's Boston
success in the following terms: "[His Werner] stood out in natural
lineaments, a human being bowed down by an insupportable affliction
and claiming the . . . sympathy of his fellow-creatures. How entirely
did the auditors become engrossed with the settled misanthropy of a
despairing mind. . . ."[46] However, Murdoch was clear about Macready's problems with his American audiences. "He did not pass
the current coin in the market of dramatic values. In fine, his performances lacked the so-termed startling originality of effect."[47] But Macready worked and tried hard. He went south. He performed Werner
at Charleston, at Savannah,[48] and at St. Charles Theatre in New Orleans, for the first time in this town.[49] From here he went Mobile,
where the play had been given already in 1835, probably with Barton
as Werner. He continued to St. Louis, Cincinnati, Buffalo, Montreal,
and then back to New York, where he gave his last performance of
the play, on 30 September 1844, before going home for good.[50]

The lack of "sensibility" on part of his audience was a direct reflection, Macready believed, of the crude nature of American society.
This conviction was also the reason for the misery he felt when traveling in the country. "The state of society here and the condition of

the fine arts are in themselves evidences of the improbability of an artist being formed by them," he reflected in his diaries.[51] After a rather cool reception of a performance in Boston on 4 October 1843, he commented self-pityingly: "From what I can learn the audiences of the United States have been accustomed to exaggeration in all its forms, and have applauded what has been most extravagant; it is not therefore surprising, that they should bestow so little applause on me. . . ."[52] A domestic perspective is provided by Noah Ludlow, the American actor, who worked together with Macready during his American tour. Ludlow castigated his "sameness of manners," "peculiar and unnatural intonations of voice," and lack of "grace, spirit, or naturalness." Macready was "holding the mirror to art, not to nature"; he had no passion; he should have been a preacher, not an artist, were Ludlow's callous remarks.[53]

Macready made relentless efforts to edify and enchant the Americans. Having acted Hamlet at Baltimore on 28 December 1843, he bitterly notified in his diary the shortcomings of his fellow actors: "[I] cut up from the beginning to the end—striving, struggling, variety against the *wretches* [his emphasis] that were sent on with me."[54] On another occasion, on 8 January 1844, in the South, he was just as heart broken, it seems, by the lethargy of his auditors who would not respond to what Walt Whitman termed his "mental" interpretation of Shakespeare: "Acted Hamlet, I scarcely know how. I strove and fought up against what I thought the immobility of the audience."[55] Although his complaints were justifed in that the audiences generally did not appreciate and understand his sophisticated style of acting, they did come to see him and hear him declaim. He also admitted that *Hamlet* had brought him more money than any other play.[56] Paradoxically, his interpretation of Shakespeare did more to further American burlesque, one could say, than it did to extend an appreciation of Shakespeare proper.

It was also around this time, we saw, that his controversies with Forrest started to develop. He saw him acting Othello at the National Theatre on 21 October 1843, only a couple of weeks after his arrival in New York, and decided that Forrest was lacking in artistry and comprehension. "He is now only an actor for the less intelligent of the Americans,"[57] he commented. Forrest's "robustious style gains applause in the coarse melodramas of 'Sparatacus' and 'Metamora',," but otherwise he is beyond the requirements of the "legitimate drama."[58] But the truth was that Forrest was in full command of his public who loved his overflowing and luxuriant style of acting. In May 1844 Thomas S. Hamblin at The Bowery Theatre produced *Werner,* in Odell's words, "foolishly courting comparison by playing the same parts in close juxtaposition in time to the distinguished En-

glishman."[59] The Bowery, true to its early burlesque tradition of
sneering at the high and laughing with the low, was simply parodying
and sensationalizing Macready's *Werner,* which catechizing Odell,
upholder of another theater tradition, failed to appreciate.

Macbeth was also part and parcel of Macready's repertoire along
his American circuits. As is well-known to any student of American
theater, it is particularly in relation to this play that he encountered
unsurmountable problems with his audience. A notably ugly comment on Anglo-American relationships is the bloody skirmish that
took place outside the Astor Place Theatre on 7 May 1849, when a
clash between Forrest adherents and the local militia caused the
deaths of more than twenty people.[60] Directly, it was occasioned by
Macready's rivalry with Forrest about the interpretation of *Macbeth,*
but, indirectly, it probably reflected the animosity that may develop
between colonizers and their onetime subjects. In any case, Forrest,
the storm and lightning actor, epitomized, in Macready's view, the
loud-mouthing, ranting style that he increasingly associated with the
lack of taste of American audiences: "The state of society here and
the condition of the fine arts are in themselves evidences of the improbability of an artist being formed by them," he thought.[61] Simply,
Forrest could not act; Macready made this abundantly clear in derogatory remarks scattered throughout his letters and diaries: "He is
now only an actor. But he is something better—an upright and well-
intentional man."[62] Charlotte Cushman, who on occasions acted with
Macready in *Macbeth,* was also a target for much ridicule. So James
Rees thought her characterization of the Queen weak, her voice "vulgar, low, unmusical."[63]

The cases of Booth/Macready in America demonstrate that oratory, to be successful, had to court the dangerous company of an
infiltrator. Forrest could live with the "burlesque" joker; Macready
and early Booth could not. No longer capable of boosting patriotism
and nationalism, "pure" oratory as a theatrical discourse was dying
out. The Amerians had opted for the melodrama.

It is most likely that several of Byron's poems, especially *Childe
Harold* and *Don Juan,* were dramatized, but information about them
is scarce. In any case a play called "Corsair" was performed in Philadelphia in 1814 and went on the summer circuit to Baltimore and
Washington, appearing only once in each city. One could speculate
to what extent this play reflected the animosities, then ablaze, between the two countries; in January and February 1814 the Philadelphia stage was an arena for various kinds of patriotic celebrations. On
14 May, on the very evening when "Corsair" was given, the *Baltimore
Patriot* reported that "the evening's entertainment will, as far as possible, be rendered approriate and commemorative" of the capture of

the brig *Épervier* by the American warship *Peacock*.[64] It is likely that the play served to underpin the patriotism of the evening as did, in a much more expressive way, Barker's "The Embargo, or What News?" (1808) and *Marmion* (1812–13).

To what extent, or whether, Edwin Holland's melodrama *Corsair* had any connection with the Philadelphia production is also impossible to say. It first appeared at Charleston on 18 February 1818, "with special music by Charles Gilfert"[65] and played three times.[66] The text emphasizes the oppression of the individual, the values of nationality, the urge for freedom, action, and romance. It draws freely on Byron, almost copying him, but had transformed his rhymed couplet into blank verse.[67] In other words, it had become a very romantic Southern melodrama. This is perhaps the reason it did not draw any attention outside the region—until it of course was turned into a burlesque.

We have already witnessed how in 1824 at the Chestnut Theatre, Durang reconstructed *Bride of Abydos* to make it more visually attractive and intelligible for the common man and woman. The next year at Joe L. Cowell's Theatre in Boston, Watkins Burrough followed Durang's initiative and added to the script a few extra oriental spices. Burroughs acted Selim and Agnes Robertson Zuleika. Walter Leman saw them as "the very beau-ideal of Oriental splendor."[68] But the oriental lure had its risks. Noah Ludlow reports how he chose to add *Bride of Abydos* to his repertoire to curb a slackening audience reception of his shows in the province, but discovered that people were "afraid to go the theatre, lest they should be talked about by those who were members of the Church where the clergy were continually consigning *actors . . .* to the *infernal* regions" (his emphases).[69] Byron's works, it was believed, had the potential to do this; on the stage they could be even more threatening.

It was Durang who would do the near-impossible: start developing Byron's stiff closet drama of *Sardanapulus* into an enjoyable, even popular, American play. Prior to him Macready had been working on the play for some time in 1834 and also had begun to play it: he traveled with it through London, Bristol, Dublin, and Bath. Most of the time he was disillusioned with his performance of it.[70] Wisely, he did not produce the play during his American tours. Even earlier in 1823, Junius B. Booth, we saw, had grappled with it, without eventually succceeding in bringing it to the boards.

Durang made a number of alterations that were far more drastic than Booth's cuttings and technical emendations. Among other things, he transposed the dream at the beginning of the fourth act to the second to "leav[e] the last act divested of dull recitations, and invested with more stage action." In all, it must have been an fantastic theater event with two hundred people on the stage and one hundred turned way at the doors—if we can believe Durang's own words.[71] It played at the Walnut Street theater (American Theatre Company) from 23 November 1836, through 29 November, with E. S. Conner as the leading star, bringing in a receipt of $929, which was big money.[72]

Before the play came to Philadelphia, it had been performed at the National Theatre in New York (on 28 October 1836), with James William Wallack as Sardanapulus.[73] He was to tour the country with it. He brought the play to New Orleans in February 1837, a city with a special taste for Byronic extravaganza;[74] *Bride of Abydos* had previously been received here with great acclaim.[75] Odell was quick to characterize *Sardanapulus* as "war-house for spectacular trappings."[76] Its reputation increased at the speed of its gradual evolution into one of the most bizarre soap operas of the time. *The Corsair Gazette* included in its April 1839 installment a hilarious satire by N. P. Willis of the stage craze that the play had created. His satire is also a parodic comment on the New York audience's love of violent melodrama. He skillfully weaves into his satire both comments about both the performance and the public's reactions to it:

> [on the play]
> SARDANAPULUS was a Nineveh's king;
> And if all be quite true that the chronicles sing,
> Loved his song and his glass,
> And was given, alas!
> Not only to bigamy,
> Nor even to trigamy,
> But (I shudder to think on't) to rankest polygamy:
> For his sweetheart and wives were so vast in amount,
> They'd take a week or two *only* to count! . . .
> *[on the play and the audience]*
> Some in gigs, some in cabs, some on horsebacks so gay,
> And some in an omnibus hired for the day. . . .
> *[on the play]*
> Such squalling, and bawling, and sprawling,
> And jobbing, and robbing, and nobbing!
> Such kicking and licking, and racing and chasing,
> Blood spilling and killing, and slaughtering and quartering;
> You'd swear that old Nick, with Belphegn his clerk,
> And Moloch his cad, were abroad on a lark: . . .
> *[on the play and the audience]*
> [L]et's all, my brave boys, die like heroes to-night
> Raise high in this Hall a grand funeral pile,
> then fire it, and meet our death—down with a smile.
> While quick at his heels rushed the rest of the rout,
> Leaving alone,

The king on his throne,
With a torch in one hand which he waved all abroad,
And a glass in the other, as drunk as a lord![77]

An example of the breadth of the Shakespeare appropriations is John Bernard's eyewitness report of a performance of *Romeo and Juliet* at the Tavern Assembly Rooms in an equally unknown city in Virginia, probably sometime during the second quarter of the century. Here it is melodrama that serves as vehicle and tenor for what should be appreciated as a valid cultural expression, although our reviewer and the audience might not have agreed. The Shakespeare performance, Bernard reported, was interspersed with dancing and singing and concluded with "the celebrated song of 'Yankee Doodle'." The two actors recited passages from the play and addressed in turn various invisible characters. When the audience showed signs of restlessness, Romeo broke into playing a hornpipe, "to which the fife set up an ear-piercing accompaniment: "Juliet who also sensed the impatience of her listeners consequently changed the form of her delivery and started to sing. In the second act they changed into dialogues. They produced a tableau, which, could be called "vivant," we are informed, as the two lovers lay on the stage for ten minutes motionless. Then followed more singing and pantomimes, and at this point, Bernard noticed, the spectators were exhausted. At the announcement that Romeo and Juliet would sing another seventy-three verses, the audience, our witness concluded, "departed from the room with the utmost expedition."[78]

MUSIC AND MELODRAMA: SCOTT

The Lady of the Lake was the Scott romance par excellence. It was also the first of its kind on the American boards. It was produced on 31 October 1811 at Richmond, and then during the same season (1811–12) at all major theaters along the eastern seaboard.[79] What is unique in the history of this play is its stability. It did not disintegrate into hybrids of various kinds; the two versions of it, Thomas Morton's and J. E. Eyre's (Thomas Dibdin), were far too similar to stimulate a leveling of the "text." Of the two, Morton's version was more flexible and it also became the main respitory for the operatic versions of the play (*Donna del Lago* was first performed at the Bowery in 1833) as well as for the melodramas.[80]

Another feature of the American theater history of *The Lady of the Lake* is its longevity. Except *Rob Roy*, no other Scott melodrama was able to sustain its melodramatic vitality as long as *The Lady of the Lake* without disintegrating and collapsing into the burlesque convention. After its initial success during the first decade of the century, it went through a second period of revivals and changes in the early 1830s (Scott's death in 1832 gave vigor to the appropriation of it), and a third in the fifties. The last *Lady of the Lake* on an American stage was seen at Niblo's Garden in New York on 25 May 1874. None of these revivals substantially changed the play. Another reason for its stability was the very thinness of its story line: it did not offer the dramatist enough material or stimulus to motivate alterations. The staging of it also became a model for the other popular Scott melodramas based on *Bride of Lammermoor, Guy Mannering,* and *Rob Roy*.

The Lady of the Lake was particularly well received at its preliminary stage in the Philadelphia-Baltimore-Washington area and at Charleston. Its popularity derived mainly from the romance tradition of richly ornated stage paintings and other spectacular accessories of voice and sound that became this play's hallmarks. In the course of a performance at Baltimore on 2 May 1812, for instance, a "living elephant . . . richly caperisoned, attended by guards, drivers, etc" accompanied the retinue on the stage.[81] All the early playbills usually provided detailed annotations of its scenography and its producers. The *Virginia Patriot* at Richmond (1811) noticed in its review that the "melo-dramatic romance" is admirably supported by a "scenery [that has been] painted by Mr. West, The Banners and Trophies by Mr. Graime."[82] The scenery, the properties, and the dresses used by the Olympic at Philadelphia were noticed to be both new and costly. "Without any exaggeration, it was unparalleled at that day," said Charles Durang.[83] It was performed throughout January 1812 and the beginning of February with the Duff couple in the title roles and then picked up, always bringing in good money, two or three times each year up to 1820, when it disappeared for some time from the Philadelphia and Baltimore boards to appear again in the thirties. Philadelphia records demonstrate that the play was shown thirty-seven times between 1835 and 1855 and that the two versions of it were produced: the melodrama, which was far more popular, and a musical that only scored minimal success.[84] It was the most popular Scott play in St. Louis with thirteen performances in all during 1830 and 1839 (1830, 1, 1832, 2, 1835, 1, 1839, 9).[85]

The play, now from Eyre's pen, had, however, an imposing comeback at the Chatham Garden, New York, on 19 September, 1825, when its leading man Henry Wallack produced it. It was simultaneously shown at the Lafayette. Charles Durang insisted that this play was "one of the most precious melo-dramatic gems ever contemplated or beheld on any stage." Obviously he knew what he was saying as it ran throughout the season, for a total of one hundred fifty nights.[86] It succeeded, it seems to me, because it continued to be "localized": the unknown New York dramatizer received a benefit on 31 December, local artists were employed to paint and construct the scenery, and Ferdinand Durang reconstructed the "Tramp March."[87] The announcement of the play in *The American* on 22 September 1825 (quoted by Odell) gives the following details:

> Act I, scene 3, an authentic view of Loch Katrine, several Islands in perspective, scattered on the Lake, with a distant view of Ben Venne and Ben An, by Mr. Coyle,—scene 2, interior of Douglas' Retreat, by P. Grain; around the walls are hung several trophies of the fight and chase—scene 3, another view of the Lake. Act 2, scene 1, the Mountain and Cataract, with a Rude Bridge thrown across a deep Glen, by P. Grain—scene 2, a Romantic Pass and Cataract, by Coyle—scene 3, Landscape View by P. Grain; a Scots Pas de Deux by Mr. and Mrs. Conway, and a characteristic Dance by the Corps de Ballet, under the direction of Mr. Conway—scene 4, Bower—scene 5, the Pass of Benlede, by Coyle—scene 9, a distant view of Stirling Castle. Act 3, scene 1, the Guard-Room of the Castle by Grain, Junior—scene 2, the Court Yard of the Castle, by F. Grain—scene 3, the exterior of Stirling Castle, by F. Grain—scene last, an authentic and beautiful view of Stirling Castle, by Coyle.[88]

In all, ten original paintings had been produced for this particular performance by the four scenic artists. The paintings may be said to respond to the contemporary Romantic landscape stereotyping that was part of the iconography of the day.[89] Yet the pictures illustrating *The Lady of the Lake* (whether inspired by the poem or its stage version) must have had their own significations, as they could even inspire a traveler's view of the Mississippi:

> Seldom have I gazed upon a scene more eminently imposing than that of the these hoary old cliffs, when the midsummer-sun, rushing upwards from the eastern horizon, bathed their splinterd pinnacles and spires and the rifted treetops in a flood of golden effulgence. The scene was not unworthy of Scott's graphic description of the view from the Trosachs of Loch Katrine, in the "Lady of the Lake."[90]

The melodrama was repeatedly played in New York in the 1850s and the 1860s.[91] It was last seen in a very costly performance at Niblo's Garden on 25 May 1874. The New York reviewer repudiated it strongly, explaining that its framework of "pretty scenery, marches, countermarches, and dancing" was old-fashioned and irrelevant to a modern audience. This was the same kind of criticism other belated melodramas were subjected to at this time.[92]

Rob Roy Macgregor; or, "Auld Lang Syne," originally written by Isaac Pocock,[93] was a drama of loyalties and of rebellion that appealed to the Americans even more than did *The Lady of the Lake*. *Rob Roy* became the most popular of all of the Scott based melodramas and musicals, favored by both Boston and New Orleans; in the West only Shakespeare would surpass it in popularity.[94] In fact, the Park performed Isaac Pocock's *Rob Roy* on 8 June 1818, eight weeks before it reached an audience in Edenburgh.[95] The Chestnut of Philadelphia was even faster and gave it in April 1818. It was revised here on 1 January 1819 with Henry Wallack as Rob Roy. "He looked the bold outlaw to the very law. . . . In the majestic positions, he exhibited vigor without uncouthness. His ruggedness was modified by the gentle impulses of mountain hero, while in the pathetic parts . . . the heart of the brave man poured out its wrongs like nature moaning in soft sounds."[96] Durang's words reflect the assumptions about the wilderness hero that were current throughout the century. Rob Roy, the Scottish mountain hero became an American western outlaw. Like *The Lady of the Lake*, it provided ample space for the projection of picturesque landscape, rugged wilderness, steep rocks, gorgeous costumes, and torn rags, an idiom that lent itself superbly to high-flown American rhetoric, and to the music and singing that later in the century grew in importance, turning the romance into an operatic musical. Unlike *The Lady*, it had a plot to sustain it, but like it, it was not travestied by any of the New York avant-garde theaters in the midcentury.

To illustrate the romantic concepts of *Rob Roy* let me cite a playbill from Boston Theatre where it was to be performed "for the third time" on 24 December 1819. The music was selected by Mr. Bray, the scenery by Mr. Worrall. Rob Roy was acted by John Duff and Helen McGregor by [Elizabeth H.] Powell. As often was the case with a Boston playhouse, a local (unknown) writer had dramatized it. The scene descriptions listed such locations as the interior of a public house; Osbaldistone Hall; Osbaldinstone library; the house of Bailie Nicol Jarvie; a Glasgow jail; the interior of Jeanie MacAlpine's hut; a romantic pass, bordering the Loch with wild scenery; and the cave of Rob Roy.[97] Another playbill of a performance at the Boston Theatre, on 19 May 1826, announced that new scenes have been worked out, but painted from the original sketches. They included: a Romantic pass on the borders of Loch Catherine, a view of the Rocky Glen of Abersford, and Loch Catherine, with the boats of Rob Roy seen in the distance, rowing to the martial sounds of the Highland War Pipers. In addition ten songs were sung and Scotch dances, accompanied by bagpipes, were executed.[98] The foreign (Scottish) elements seem to be overwhelming. However, the play could only have been convincing if its American filiation (Scotland-America, object-subject, victim-oppressor) was active. This "interaction" created a tension that gave this play—and of course other plays based on Scott, Byron and Dickens—its independence and credibility.

Henry Wallack and Ann Duff became this play's particular devotees. They toured widely with it for a couple of decades and were appreciated as the prototype Rob Roy and Helen McGregor. Ann Duff, it was said, exhibited the same "naturalistic" power as her partner. A review of the play performed on 12 March 1826 at the Bowery with Wallack described her performance as "nature itself"; a "burst of feelings . . . comes wailing through the rocks of the Highlands" and "her agonized parental emotions" rock the mountains.[99] Charlotte Cushman—who also did this role for some years (1836–39)—adopted more or less the same postures as made her famous as Meg in *Guy Mannering*.

With a monotonous regularity, *Rob Roy* was revised in New York each year throughout the 1820s, 1830s, and 1840s, alternating between the Park, the Chatham Garden, Lafayette Theatre, the Bowery, and Blachard's Amphitheatre, where in 1830 it was turned into a mixture of equestrian performance and dramatic exhibition.[100] Statistics prove that the play remained a hit; it was performed thirty times between the years 1823–32 in Philadelphia and forty-six times in New York[101]; it was acted each year between 1835 and 1855 in Philadelphia, or in all seventy-nine times making it the overall number one of the Scott-based plays in this city.[102] In the South its reputation remained as high: at Charleston, where it had its firstnight on 3 May 1819, it was repeated regularly throughout the next three decades.[103] Noah M. Ludlow's theatre toured with it in Cincinnati, Louisville, Mobile, St. Charles, New Orleans, and St. Louis in the 1830s and 1840s.[104] No wonder that cities and steamboats in the South were named after the Scottish hero.[105]

In the midcentury the melodrama evolved into a musical, an opera, and a "comic opera." The play would either be performed as a *mélange* of these or in the more or less "pure" form. From this time onward, the play was also seldom acted solo; customarily one or two acts from it were performed together with other similar popular showpieces. Such a typical "arty" operatic "magnum-show" took place at the Castle Garden, New York, on 12 August 1851, as a complimentary benefit to Ethelbert A. Marshall. First the third act of *Rob Roy* with John Henry Anderson, the famous magician known as "The Wizard of the North," was performed, then in a succession—extending the whole entertainment into a twelve-hour show—the dance "Pas de Deux," the sketch "How to Pay the Rent," the dance "Pas Seul Dance," the "Polka Mazourka," an act from Charles J. Kean by Alexandre Dumas, Grand Italian Opera Company with the third act of "Romeo and Julietta," and the second act of "Lucia di Lammer-

moor" with Caesar Badiali. Just the operatic part of the entertainment
took four hours. After an intermission at 6:30 p. m. followed scenes
from *School of Scandal,* at 9:30 a grand divertissement by the Rous-
set family, a tightrope walking by Blonini, and at 11 p. m., to end it
all, a display of fireworks.[106] In such surroundings *Rob Roy* was performed toward the end of the century, but it retained its renown as a
site for moving music, strong feelings, and romantic stage paintings.
It was Boston's favorite opera, playing continuously at the Boston
Museum from 1848 throughout the seventies. "This play made use
of the paraphernalia which pleased the belated Gothic taste of the
times: mountain views, the interior of the old chapel in the Osbaldistone castle, and a rich valley, mountaineous pass."[107] New Orleans
and San Francisco also loved the music of this play and its adaptability for spectacular drama. On 4 February 1850 John Rowe opened
the Olympic Circus at San Francisco, with a bill consisting of an
omnibus package that included *Othello,* the first play by Shakespeare
to be performed in San Francisco, and *Rob Roy* "with horses."[108] On
20 August 1863 John Murray also did *Rob Roy,* "grand spectacular
operatic drama of Caledonia," two days before *Guy Mannering.*[109]

Interestingly, Helen Western appeared in *Rob Roy* at The Broadway Theatre in New York on 18 June 1866, after that Adah Isaacs
Menken played *Mazeppa* for three weeks to full houses. Apart from
Rob Roy, Western's bill included Irish songs and dances, gymnastic
performances by Professor Donnelson and La Petite Angelo, and
Black-Eyed American, with Menken as William, in another of her
male roles. To crown the American interest in *Rob Roy,* a revamping
of it was made at the very end of the century by Harry B. Smith
(text) and Reginald de Kovern (music), called "Rob Roy; or, The
Thistle and the Rose. An Opera in Three Acts," 1894.[110] It ran for
twenty-two weeks at the Herald Square Theatre beginning October
1895.

Rob Roy had a long and tenacious life, even though it was not so
lively as many other Scott melodramas; John William Calcraft's *Bride
of Lammermoor,* for instance, had several lives.[111] Like a few other
melodramas based on Scott's novels, and several on Dickens's novels, it would bifurcate into many generic avenues. It began in the
1820s as a romantic melodrama, with its regional base in the South.
It was first played in New Orleans in 1820, seven years before being
taken up by theaters in Philadelphia and New York, and it retained
its Southern attraction through the 1860s when it went off the bills.
In the South it was a particular favorite at Charleston. Its operatic
version, James Wright Simmons's "Master of Ravenswood," was first
produced here in 1824 and played side by side with the more conven-

tional domestic melodrama that Anna Cora Ritchie re-adapted in 1845 and toured the country with for a couple of years.[112]

The continually revised operatic versions of *Guy Mannering,* based on Daniel Terry's *Guy Mannering; or, The Gipsey's Prophecy* and/or Bishop's version of it, remained a constant playbill favorite with the theaters from 1816 up to the midcentury, when it gave way to Gaetano Donizetti's *Lucia di Lammermoor* (1836), which was first produced in New York on 15 September 1843 in Italian (in English two years later).[113] Boston and the South were the centers for the popularity of its musical versions. It was the second Scott play/musical in popularity in St. Louis (after *Rob Roy*) and the third in Philadelphia (after *Rob Roy* and *The Lady of the Lake*). The melodramatic version and the operatic version of *Guy Mannering* complemented and enriched each other: songs, for instance, often passed over from the one genre to the other. The operatic version by Donizetti, *Lucia di Lammermoor,* coexisted for some time with the other generic forms. But by the beginning of the sixties it had ousted all the other dramatizations of the play and became an enormous success in practically all parts of the country, from San Francisco to New Orleans. Boston especially took it to its heart; here it was produced almost every single year through the late 1880s, and it is still produced there and elsewhere.

But *Guy Mannering* is permanently associated with Charlotte Cushman through her impersonation of Meg Merrilies. Cushman was a frightening stage personality in whose presence, we are led to believe, it was hard to remain unengaged. Many male commentators on her performances were provoked by the directness and realism of her interpretations, all the more so as she seemed to refute or challenge notions of womanhood and femininity. But most of all, they were involuntarily attracted to her art which at its best fused intellectualism and emotionalism. The illustrations of her impersonifications, even for a modern viewer studying contemporary photos of her Lady Macbeth, Nancy Sykes, or Meg Merrilies, exude a lurid will power and self-control that are perplexing. It is easy to understand the almost reverent fascination she was to exercise over her American audiences for almost half a century. The way she dominated her audiences sprang from her ability to integrate the stage character with her own personality, up to an agonizing point of self-effacement. Her interpretation of Scott's Meg early became legendary. She acted it for nearly forty years, for the first time in New York at the Old Bowery on 15 May 1837 and the last at the Boston Globe on 5–8 May 1875 (she died a year later).

Guy Mannering remained a highly theatrical showpiece throughout the century, most often laid in a stylized romantic setting containing various American cultural ingredients; the bill for 27 October 1828, when the play was performed at the Bowery, explained that "Sixteen Indian Warriors will appear on the stage in their national Camulet or pipe dance."[114] But Cushman introduced new features into the play. Before her the melodrama had focused on the male hero, Henry Bertram and his relations with Meg. Cushman changed the focus, appropriating Scott's text and Terry's dramatization of it to suit her vision and her understanding of the character. She developed Meg, the distraught gypsy woman, into a poor working-class mother suffering from guilt and remorse, shattered by loyalties to her gender and the demands made on her by the aggressive outside world. Nineteenth-century theatergoers saw the gap between Scott's characterization of Meg, as the superstitious crazy gypsy woman, and Cushman's subtle rendering of her—and wondered at it. An editorial note in one of the American editions of the play, based on her performance at Booth's Theatre, New York (she appeared there in 1871, 1872, and 1874), qualified her interpretation of Scott in this way: "It has been said— we think hypocritically—that the Meg Merrilles [sic] of Miss Cushman, great as it is admitted to be, is not that of Scott;—if it is her own creation, the greater the genius of the Artist."[115] Cushman, it was repeated, had supernatural powers, just like Meg, "as one that exercises a supernatural power over a superstitious people."[116]

Interestingly enough, Cushman's last New York performance at Booth's on 31 October 1874 was still thought to be moving, her demonstration of motherly love, passion, and tenderness, pathetic but significant. However, the play itself was rejected as totally outmoded and "utterly without dramatic value."[117] With the new generation of Megs entering the stage, the strength of Cushman's hold of her audience became more apparent. Fanny Janauschek who thrilled the American audiences with her "dual" representation of Lady Dedlock and Hortense, based on Dickens's *Bleak House,* played Meg on 1 April 1877 at the Union Square Theatre. In an obvious attempt to distance herself from the tradition that Cushman had developed, she returned to the original (Pocock's) version of Scott's novel. But it did not work: the audience was still under the spell of Cushman. Janauschek was criticized as being too vigorous and mechanical, lacking the femininity and subtlety of Cushman's portrayal.

Ada Rehan fared no better. Twenty years later on 12 March 1897, when she appeared at Daly's Theatre in "Meg of Merrilies; or, The Witch of Ellangowan." This composition made by Robert Chambers mainly out of Daniel Terry's and Bishop's musical plays was intended as a modern thriller story. The meeting with Bertram is placed in an early scene, the cave episode concluded with the arrest of the smugglers, and Meg's death caused by a bullet intended by Hatteraich for

Glossin. But the spirit of Cushman's psychological portrayal seemingly haunted both the producers and the recipients of the play. The *New York Times* reviewer saw the new performance against the tradition developed by Cushman: he noted that the first two acts were similar to hers and regretted that Rehan's Meg had been transformed into a "sibyl in a red dress."[118] Gone was the deeply distressed woman of Cushman's creation that had intrigued theatergoers ever since the 1830s. But by this time Meg was also definitely gone from the American theatres. She could only endure in the way Cushman had envisioned her.

EARLY POPULAR MELODRAMA: DICKENS

Dickens on the American stages was a wild affair. The theater companies competed furiously for audience support. They knew that if they could find the right angle or the right touch money would flow in. Thus there was an ongoing tentative, speculative, and experimental traffic going on among the different theaters—especially in New York—in the search of the most appropriate line to adopt for dramatization. Besides the urge to hit upon the most winning episode from the Dickens canon, they also had to accept constant revisions and accomodations before beginning to pursue and elaborate the chosen version. As a consequence, there could exist simultaneously several plays from the same novel. Adherence to audience participation was a double-edged instrument: it could guide the managers and the dramatists in the most profitable direction when choosing the convenient literary idiom, but it could also generate resistance when conveyed in the acting style of particular actors and actresses—and prevent success. The arena in which the *first* Dickens "texts" operated was highly volatile and unpredictable. All of Dickens's most popular texts, starting from *The Pickwick Papers* (1836–37) and culminating in *David Copperfield* (1849–50), generated on their first appearence an outburst of vital theatrical activity that was to mold their future reputation and the forms of their appropriation. Thus as a preamble to more specific considerations of this process, in this section I will examine the initiating and formative stage of the most popular of Dickens's texts on the American stage.

The first Dickens play on the American stage was "The Pickwick Club, or the Age We Live" produced in 1837, in Philadelphia, where it was seen five times during the year, and in New York at the Bowery on 24 July the same year; here "very happy hits were made." It ran through July.[119] But as we will see further on, the first productions that attempted to embrace the "total" text, either in terms of its plot or characters, failed. The next year Philadelphia produced William

Thomas Moncrieff's "Sam Weller, or The Pickwick Papers"[120] and New York's Park did the same with Charlotte Cushman as Emily Wardle, W. R. Blake as Sam Weller, and Henry Placide as Joe, "the fat boy" servant to Wardle.[121] But their tableaux failed, even if they now sought to narrow their focus and tell a tale that centered on Weller. As was usual with the Park productions, it was overdone; there were thirty-two in the cast. *The Knickerbocker* wrote: "After all the characters have been seen, and each given a taste of his peculiar quality, the fun of the things is over." It only ran for a week. Five days after the Park presented its Sam Weller on 20 February 1838, the Bowery gave a new version, smaller in size (for some time the two shows ran simultaneously); it also failed.[122] At the end of 1839 the Park tried again with the revival sketch "Sam Weller! or, The Pickwick Club!"[123]

From now onward scenes from *The Pickwick Papers* would be presented as sideshows or afterpieces. The first years of its production had shown that the material was good only after a radical dramatization and that Weller was the only character in it that could engage an American audience. These early Dickens productions were forerunners of what was to come.

It was *Oliver Twist* and *Nicholas Nickleby* that really started the stage craze for Dickens in America. On 9 November 1838 *Oliver Twist* was published in England in one volume. Only two months later theatregoers in Philadelphia and New York could see an American version of part of the novel, which demonstrates at what speed the dramatizers worked. In Philadelphia, Francis Wemyss was the first to dramatize the play, using an English version of it. He called the play "Oliver Twist, or the Athens House Boy." It appeared at the Walnut on 1 January 1839.[124] In New York *Oliver Twist* was first shown on 7 January 1839 at The Franklin. Meanwhile the Park was rehearsing its own version called "Oliver Twist, or, The Parish Boy's Popularity," which had been written by James Rees.[125] It was produced on 7 February 1839.[126] Again as in its production of *The Pickwick Papers,* it was far too cumbersome, with as many as twenty-seven persons in the cast. But it was a formidable show. Agnes Richardson here did her first Oliver and Charlotte Cushman her first Nancy Sykes, thus laying the ground for the femininization of Dickens's children and adolescents on the American stage. In these early productions the focus was leveled at the lower class world of Oliver and Nancy, which would remain another priority in the American productions of Dickens.

This was an extremely hectic time for the interpreters of Dickens's novels at American theaters. Only about three weeks after *Oliver Twist* had appeared in New York, Nicholas Nickleby made his entrance at The National Theatre on 25 January 1839 which meant that the dramatization was based on the serialization of the novel (that had started in March 1838 with twenty monthly numbers). The novel appeared in book form in Great Britain in October 1839. Thus most Americans had their first contact with the world of Smike through the theater. The National Theatre production was a broad kaleidoscopic presentation of the novel with seventeen in the cast. Ann Duff Waring [Mrs. James William Wallack] was the first American Smike. As usual the Park followed suit. On 30 January it produced its *Nickleby* with a smaller cast and with Agnes Richardson as Smike and Cushman as Fanny Squeers. It ran for nearly the rest of the season, quite often in the company of *Oliver Twist*. From 11 February they actually ran together for week when Agnes Richardson was a great hit as both Smike and Oliver and Cushman as Fanny and Nancy.

The "craze for Dickens adaptations was soon to infect the stage," commented Odell sardonically in his New York theater annals.[127] *Nicholas Nickleby* appeared at the Walcot, in Philadelphia, on 25 February 1839, where it was shown seven times during 1839 and eleven during 1840.[128] In Boston, Joseph S. Jones, the manager of the Tremont theater, brought out the play in June 1839, and again on 8 and 9 September 1840.[129] The cast included: Squeers, Mrs. Squeers, Nicholas, Smike (a Miss Rock), and Alfred Mantalini. "It was the delight of the juveniles," it was reported.[130] On 1 April 1839 the play was at the Franklin in New York, with Mitchell as Squeers.[131] The dimension of the Dickens farce and caricature was being initiated by the portrayals of Weller and Squeers. The two traditions of the Dickens drama in America; the comic melodrama and the burlesque, were thus established at an early stage. *Nicholas Nickleby* was also performed in New Orleans during the season of 1839–40, which is another indication of Dickens's rapid and expansive popularity.[132]

It was also around this time that Dickens paid his first visit to America—with much clamor. The visit generated a fervid activity especially at the theaters and lecture halls: no major city failed to offer its patrons some new or rehashed dish from the Dickens canon. So on the first evening of February 1842, the Bostonians honored him with a magnificent dinner with "entertainments" and "stage performances."[133] Typically for Boston, some eighty years later, in 1925, this honorary dinner was rehearsed in its minutest detail: the same food, the same dresses, the same speeches and songs (Oliver Wendell Holmes's verses were produced *verbatim* and J. M. Field's comic Irish song was sung).[134] Dickens nostalgia has always been an active element in Boston's cultural life. Boston *Evening Transcript* of 20 May 1925 writes about a Dickens pageant that took place in 1860 with "Poke Bonnets and Beavers, Crinolines, and Swallow-Tails" and Dickens characters mingling with the throng.[135]

The lionizing of Dickens in New York was less reverent, in fact it always bordered on the mock-heroic.[136] On 11 December 1841—before his arrival here on 16 February 1842[137]—as an aperitif the Olympic offered Mitchell's witty sketch "Boz, or a Man Overbored," an Americanized takeoff from W. T. Monrieff's original play. The Bowery naturally offered the same show in February. But the main talk of the town during this month of Dickens celebration was the three balls in Dickens's honor that were said to have eclipsed any such festivities previously held. They took place at the Park: the first on 14 February, the second (with dumped prices) on 16 February, and the third on 18 February. Between the dances, a Dickens pageant was organized. The *Evening Post* of 15 February contained the following description of these *tableaux vivants,* which is quite illuminative of what the Americans preferred:

> A curtain, painted like the frontispiece of the *Pickwick Papers,* was drawn up at the sound of a gong, when the artists procured for the occasion were discovered in attitudes and positions. . . . These were:
> 1. Mrs. Leo Hunter's dress, *dejeuner.*
> 2. The middle-aged lady in the double-bedded room.
> 3. Mrs. Bardell faints in Mr. Pickwick's arms.
> 4. Mrs. Bardell encounters Mr. Pickwick in prison.
> 5. The red-nosed man discourseth.
> 6. Mr. and Mrs. Mantilini in Ralph Nickleby's office.
> 7. Oliver Twist at Mr. Maylie's door.
> 8. Little Nell, her grandfather, the military gentleman, and Mr. Slum's unexpected appearance.
> 9. Little Nell leading her father.
> 10. The stranger scrutinizing Barnaby's features in the widow's cottage.
> 11. The Pickwick Club.
> 12. Washington Irving in England and Charles Dickens in America.[138]

The next play that caused both exitement and rivalries between the theaters when it arrived in America was *The Cricket on the Hearth* (published in England in book form in December 1845 and in America at the beginning of 1846). One reason for the initial confusion that hampered the play's run of luck was that from the start there were three English dramatizations of the book to choose from.[139] The American adapters had to glean from these and come up with their own independent adaptation. At this early stage the result was often a compromise. Albert Smith's version of the play had the highest acceptance rate, but was adjusted to suit the abilities of the stock company and meet the audience expectations. Such a play was acted at the Park on 21 February 1846, but Mrs. G. Jones's version of the play had already been given at the Chatham on 11 February 1846. The Chatham variant could not compete, however, and it went off the boards, whereas the Park version played fairly well.[140]

Simultaneously, another version of Smith's play was playing in Philadelphia; Peale's Philadelphia Museum and the Arch theater performed it from 19 February 1846 onward. It was acted fifty-one times during this year and remained one of the most popular of Dickens's plays in Philadelphia throughout the forties and the early fifties.[141] But in Boston, where Smith's play was given at the Boston Museum on 2 and 3 March 1846, the *Cricket* did not meet with the approbation New York and Philadelphia had lavished on it. A reviewer in the *Transcript* gave the following explanation:

> Though all the resources of the Boston Museum were liberally applied in its production and despite the exertions of the performers, the tameness and paucity of incident and the transfer of whole dialogues from the book to the stage were so extremely uninteresting that it requires a great deal of effort to sit out the performance. We cannot estimate very highly the taste of the London critics who have applauded this miserable adaptation, calling it the best of the many with which the Metropolitan stage is now inundated, but we have a strong feeling of pity for the audiences, upon whom the others are inflicted.

Obviously the critic had in mind a reorganization of Smith's text, rather than a new adaptation from the book. The play, the critic felt, had to be revitalized. He continued:

> We have many Dramatists among us, whom we are certain could raise a substantial superstructure even on such flimsy foundation, among others we would name Mr. S. S. Steele. . . .[142]

We are reminded here also that Dickens would not succeed on the American stage without an input of local ingredients. Evidently, the success of a play was far more dependent on the creativity and integrity of the local dramatist/adapter than on the persuasions of the English text, whether the base was the Dickens manuscript or a London dramatization of it.

Except for Philadelphia the success of *The Cricket on the Hearth* was momentous and contained within the year of 1846. During this year it was generally played at the main American theaters. Then it gradually petered out and during the next decade was played only sporadically. It would need the magical local coloring of Dion Boucicault to survive.

The next great Dickens play on the American stage was based on *Dombey and Son,* which was published in volume form in April 1848 in England. However, the novel was issued in parts in America, even before the accompanying plates had arrived; the first seventeen with the imprint Wiley and Putnam and the last two with that of John Wiley. The first publishing was done between 1846 and 1848 and the novel came out in all the main publishing centers, Boston, New York, and Philadelphia.

The problem with this play was where to place the focus, which character to highlight, what idiosyncracies to emphasize, whose language and idiom to imitate or ridicule. This uncertainty explained why the play was so widely fragmentized and its storyline so unstable even during its very first season at the New York theaters. John Brougham's first version, called "Bunsby's Wedding,"[143] appeared at the Burton's on 24 July 1848 and made the theater the most respected company in America at the time. Brougham himself played both Major Joseph Bagstock and Captain John Bunsby, Burton, Captain Alfred Cuttle. The play was withdrawn after only four days. The first night, it was reported, was under the expenses, the second reached eighty dollars, the third seventy-seven, and the fourth seventy-two dollars. Burton did nothing, it seems, of Cuttle, and Oliver B. Raymond did everything of dim-witted Toots. Dismayed at his own failure, and of course of Raymond's success, Burton took the play off the boards. But he did not give it up; he went on adapting it, especially his own role, amplifying "the part by the introduction of stage-business and by-play."[144] It reappeared on 16 August 1848. He had enlarged the cast by four: Brogley, the Native (Joseph Bagstock's Indian servant who has become "dark"), Rob the Grinder, and Flowers, Mrs. Skewton's maid. The characters he introduced are all minor, servants and workers. He had also shuffled a few roles. The play was an immediate and enormous success. By 2 September it had run twenty times; "it took the audience by storm."[145] Burton began his fantastic career as a comedian with this play and his rendering of Captain Cuttle, the soft sailor with the tarpaulin hat, his pipe and his laconic multilingual speech, combining sentimentality and suspense with a wry kind of talk.[146]

On 7 September 1848 an extract from Brougham's play was set up at the Burton's. The one-act was called "The Capture of Captain Cuttle and Bunsby's Wedding." It was a concoction with only six characters in it. The playbill read: "Toots' adventures with the Chicken and Susan Nipper; Cuttle's artifices with Mrs. MacStinger, ending in Bunsby's marriage, with the attempt to escape and final desperation of the happy Bridegroom."[147] This is one example of the many variants of the play.[148]

The comic tradition that Burton and Brougham represented was early challenged by the melodramatic and sentimental. On 13 November 1848, Thomas S. Hamblin and the Park staged their version of Dickens's *Dombey and Son,* called "Edith; or, Dealings with the Firm of Dombey and Son." It was set up by Charles Melton Walcot in overt opposition to Brougham's,[149] elegant, with new costumes, new accessories, and an enlarged cast—"unprecedented for a comedy." Also according to Ireland, it embodied much more of the original story.[150] But it did not work. Henry Placide and Walcot as Cuttle and Toots could not compete with the simple, everyday representations of Burton and Raymond (as Florence Dombey) at Burton's.[151] It only played through 25 November. The audience would not, it seems, accept two versions of Cuttle. Burton would go on playing Cuttle till his death twelve years later, thus not only monopolizing the role, but also determining the formulas of the play.[152] It was the farce of *Dombey and Son* and not its generic variant, the sentimental comedy, that would get the upper hand.

Burton was also first out with his personification of Micawber in *David Copperfield.* The play had been adapted by W. K. Northall and was shown at the Burton's with moderate success from 30 (November?) December 1850 onward, with Burton and George Jordan as David (and another thirteen in the cast). The playbills demonstrate that it was continuously being changed and revised through 1856. Meanwhile the play was also being adapted by Brougham and on the evening of 6 January 1851 there were three Micawbers in New York, as the play had also been taken up by the Bowery.[153] Many of the "curious," said Odell, were prompted to see all the three on successive nights.[154] This was the zenith of the Dickens fever in New York. The New Yorkers really had a go at Dickens. The version at the Bowery omitted Rosa Dartle, Dora, Martha Endell, Clara Peggotty, and Barkis, some of whom were absent in the Burton adaptation.[155] It ran for a week, and then left the play to Brougham and Burton. At the Bowery, a woman impersonator, Susan Denin, acted David in the first act, and Charles Pope did David in the second; John R. Scott played Peggotty and William Augustus Fenno Micawber.

John Brougham's adapation was first shown at his own Brougham's Lyceum on 6 January 1851 with as many as seventeen characters in the cast. He had reduced David Copperfield, James Steerforth, Emma Micawber, and Rosa Dartle to subordinate positions. The focus was on Micawber, Uriah Heep (John E. S. Owen), and Daniel Peggott (Harry Lynne). "Mr. Brougham shows less of the brandy-and-water side of Micawber's character than Burton."[156] It lasted till 25 January and then went "down in defeat before Burton's," Odell commented.

Again it was Burton's interpretation that was liked best by the New Yorkers.

The other Dickens premières that occurred during the century did not arouse the same intense interest at their first appearance as the plays we have been discussing, and will not be dealt with in this context. A few stopped at their first showing ("One Hour; or, The Carnival Bell" from *Master Humphrey's Clock,* 1838; "A Christmas Carol," 1844; "The Battle of Life," 1847; "The Chimes," 1849; "No Thoroughfare," 1866; "The Seven Poor Travellers," 1866; "A Message from the Sea," 1868; "The Holly Tree Inn," 1892; "A Tale of Two Cities," 1899), others had a few repetitions ("The Haunted Man," 1848; "Hard Times," 1854; "Edwin Drood," 1870), and a third category of Dickens plays failed at first showing but were appropriated later (from *Barnaby Rudge,* 1841; *Martin Chuzzlewit,* 1845; *The Old Curiosity Shop,* 1852, *Bleak House,* 1852; *Our Mutual Friend,* 1860[157]; and *Great Expectations,* 1862).

LATER SENTIMENTAL COMEDY: DICKENS

Sentimental comedy in the nineteenth-century sense sought to moralize and educate its audience into acceptance and determinism by dramatizing the poles spanning abnegation and fulfillment, death and rejuvenation. Theater could foster, it was generally believed, stability and harmony—Dickens's plays especially—by demonstrating the attenuating and harmonizing force of laughter in overlapping boundaries, not only between people, but also between the array of inconclusive sentiments that inhabit a human being. Laughter, it was understood, could arise out of any context and even make the sadness and tragedy of death tolerable.

I will pursue two other axes of thinking: one is concerned with issues of gender and age; the other with locality and region. The first looks into the dramatic function of the actress and her relations with the gender and the age of the character, most often the child she is impersonating; the other studies the regional differences between Boston and New York and the ways in which local theatrical traditions were influential in formulating a specific Dickensian drama discourse.

The main reason for the many strands of appropriations of Dickens novels on the American stage is of course their fantastic popularity with the American readers, although such a statement suggests the ancient question about the chicken and the egg. Indeed, it happened that a dramatization of a Dickens story reached a theater audience before a reading public. His texts were like popular ballads that were dispersed and diverged across time and space. The fate of *Oliver*

Twist offers such an example. It was first produced, we saw, in 1839 and would be acted till the very end of the century. It was early sentimentalized and femininized. Agnes Richardson and Charlotte Cushman had performed the first David and Nancy. Cushman's Nancy was, like most of her personifications of women/children, monstruously realistic, bordering on the grotesque. Yet she was convincing and considered naturalistic and truthful. Cushman made Nancy an emblem of suffering and good faith. Her rendering of Nancy's death was hideous, yet redeeming and apocalyptic. Oliver in turn represented innocence and naïveté, values that were contrapuntal to the masculinity underlying the street and gang violence that any New York theater audience was familiar with.[158] However, the play did not take effectively as a sentimental comedy until the early 1860s. Throughout the fifties, as we will see, it was subjected to another theater discourse.

Thus at the Winter Garden on 2 February 1860, Joseph Jefferson III "arranged" it anew. "This was another most admirably represented play. J. W. Wallack's Fagin was a masterpiece of art, and Miss [Matilda] Heron's Nancy, though inferior to Miss Cushman's, was full of intensity and abandon so essential to the character."[159] Cushman gave up playing Nancy after 1861. Her mantle was eagerly adopted. Other Nancys in the sixties, seventies, and eighties were Lucille Western, Alexina Fisher Baker, Rose Eytinge, Fanny Davenport, and Kitty Blanchard. Elita Proctor Otis took over the role in the nineties. The play was acted almost each year at a New York theater throughout the century. Seventy years of acting Fancy had not much altered the interpretation and understanding of her; she remained the good-hearted, self-destructive prostitute, lover, and friend of Bill the criminal, an epitome of values cherished by the American audiences across two generations. She was seen as part of a value system that only woman could reproduce and represent. This explains her great popularity with the most accomplished American actresses. Noteworthy also is that on the nineteenth-century stage, her fiendish and brutal counterparts and instigators Fagin and Bill were secondary and complementary characters. They were borrowed from the burlesque genre and were seldom performed in these plays in a realistic fashion. That the two traditions cooperated even within the same performance can be seen in the following famous instance of "sentimental" cum "grotesque" acting. On 11 June 1866, Lucille Western acted in *Oliver Twist* at the Boston Theatre, supported by E. L. Davenport and J. W. Wallack.

Their rendering of [Oliver Twist] stands in theatrical history as one of the most dramatically horrifying performances ever seen on the stage. Miss

Western was Nancy Sykes, Wallack the Fagin, and Davenport Bill Sykes. The murder scene sent ladies in the audience into fainting fits and drove strong men from the theatre, unable to endure any longer the effect of their terribly natural acting.[160]

Lucille Western had glued a thin slice of raw beef to one side of her face and was pulled across the stage!

Oliver Twist was the great favorite of New York. One reason was that the play was early associated with Burton's urban comedy; second the plot of *Oliver Twist* spun around an underworld of petty criminality, depravity, and violence that an audience in New York would find easier to recognize and assess than, say, a Boston audience. A third reason was that the play, through its projection of Nancy and rejection of Oliver, provided an opportunity for the woman actor to excel in a stellar role. It was well known also that New York theaters remained far more generous toward and tolerant of women both on the stage and in front of it than the provincial theaters.

As sentimental comedy, *David Copperfield* also involved feminization of the main characters. As in *Oliver Twist,* the chief character is either made secondary or redundant, and replaced by a woman character; women actors performed the main roles whether male or female. Little Emily, Clara Peggotty, another devoted, nursing woman, is the exemplary heroine of the play who taught values such as devotion and loyalty. Also, the male comic figures of Micawber and Heep served as her narrative foils.

Andrew Halliday's *Little Emily,* first shown at the Olympic Theatre, in London on 9 October 1869, was produced at Niblo's Garden on 20 December 1869; it ran for three weeks with seventeen in the cast.[161] But it was not particularly popular in New York which seemed to have preferred to laugh at Micawber and Heep. It was in Boston that *Little Emily* became a great hit toward the end of the century. The most famous producer of this play was George Fawcett Rowe, who usually acted Micawber in it. The play was often called "Little Emily, or, The Emigrant's Farewell."[162] In the last act Emily and her "happy family departs for the great West,"[163] instead of for the Australia of the original.

Bleak House, first dramatized by John Brougham in 1853, waited till 1877 to be rendered into a sentimental drama. The dramatization took place at the Boston Theatre and the script, called "Poor Jo!," was written by B. E. Woolf and centered on another juvenile, the illiterate crossing-sweeper Jo. The playbill from the performance at the Boston Theatre on 23 July 1877, listed Mary Cary as Jo, thus another woman actor in the role as a persecuted and dying Dickensian youth. The play outline indicated that it was organized as a thriller embedded in a morality: Act I is entitled "Setting Snares"; Act II "Discoveries"; Act III "Murder"; Act IV "Retribution"; and Act V "Moving On."[164]

As sentimental and pathetic drama *Oliver Twist, David Copperfield,* and *Bleak House* all centered on plots preempting children with women performers to project such (female) virtues as stoicism and endurance and highlight such (male) vices as recklessness and inconsistence. The next two plays I will consider, *The Cricket on the Hearth* and *Nicholas Nickleby,* are less oblique in their treatment of a thwarted adult world that had lost its innocence and sensitivity. The history of these two plays' nineteenth-century reputation is heavily inscribed by Dion Boucicault who made dramatizations of each that were immediately successful. *Dot,* his adaptation of *The Cricket on the Hearth,* remained popular till the end of the century.

Boucicault has been called a trickster, a sentimentalist, and a charlatan, who "fostered in his most influential works a brainless, crowd-pleasing, spectacular, and simplisitic kind of entertainment."[165] This would be a fair characterization of Boucicault, if the connotations of the epithets used here were made positive instead of negative. He had a delicate ear for what the audiences wanted. He knew he could trick them, but also that the "trick" had to be accepted."What is success! It is the fitness of [a work] to [meet] the requirements of the moment. . . . Failure then is a mistake of public wants. What should we say of a rifleman who having missed his mark laid his fault on the target for not being hit—such is the blame often laid on the public for want of appreciation."[166] Boucicault was also a literary critic and an influential advocate for the theater as an art form and a working place.[167] He was clear about his profession: he wanted to educate and entertain and knew that what people in the streets talked about, what the office workers read, and the newspapers columnists gossiped about was well worth turning into plays. Nothing was more natural to him than to use his stage craft to make Dickens available for his theater audience.

In adapting *The Cricket on the Hearth,* third of the Christmas Books, which we remember had been extensively performed in Albert Smith's version along the eastern coast in 1846, Boucicault worked from a French version entitled *Le Marchand de Jouets d'Enfants* (1848) which it is believed he saw at rehearsals in Paris, retranslated, and adapted for the company, and especially for Joseph Jefferson, then at the newly reconstructed Winter Garden, where Boucicault's plays were produced. The story also goes that he did not know it was by Dickens, and on learning this he changed the title to *Dot.*[168] His main revisions were that he revealed the secret of Edward's identity at the beginning of the play and inserted a fortune-telling episode as well as a fairy prologue. Smith had kept Edward a secret to the end of the play.[169] Boucicault's adaptation makes a little drama out of Dickens's (and Smith's) sentimental little story.

It opened on 14 September 1859 with Agnes Richardson, Boucicault's wife, as Dot, the subtle, but domesticated wife of John Peerybingle. Joseph Jefferson insisted on having the play followed by a farce to counter the last pathetic scene of the play.[170] Their disagreement resulted in Albert Smith's text being used for some time as there was more room in it for stellar roles.[171] But this did not work and *Dot,* re-adopted, "chirped alone." *Dot* was a smashing success: it ran without interruption till the end of October when it was joined by Boucicault's second successful adaptation of Dickens, that of *Nicholas Nickleby,* called "Smike."[172] Together they made the Winter Garden and Boucicault famous.[173]

But it was Jefferson as Caleb Plummer, rather than Agnes Richardson or Dot, that drew people to the Winter Garden. His Plummer, said Odell, "was simply the most exquisite, most natural piece of acting conceivable. It passed from tears to smiles as easily as life passes from sorrow to joy; it was nature itself—one of the great performances of the theatre."[174] To compare a performance with nature herself was the highest praise that a nineteenth-century critic could give. Yet the play never had a long New York run. It was customarily played two to three times a decade up to the end of the century, sometimes to very negative publicity. Jefferson also abandoned the play for a long time, playing it only sporadically along his circuits after his early success in the sixties. Instead, another actor, John E. Owens, was to monopolize the role and make it his own. A playbill from Broadway Theatre boasts that on this evening—30 March 1865—Owens gave his 183rd appearance of Caleb in *Dot* and his fifteenth at this theatre.[175] But this experience did him little good. After a performance at Booth's on 6 November 1871 a New York critic admonished him for drenching his performance in a "senile pathos" and "tedious balderdash. . . . Most of the characters alternate, with much unanimity, between idiotic laughter and maudlin pathos."[176]

Jefferson started to play it again after an interval of almost a quarter of a century, but then went back to Albert Smith's version of the play, which the *New York Times* reviewer of his performance at the Garden Theatre on 14 October 1895 did not appreciate: "There was no possible illusion in Dot's love, or John Peerybingle's jealousy."[177] In another performance of it in 1900 at the Miner's Fifth Avenue Theatre, on 23 April, Jefferson had significantly altered and "raised" the role of Tilly Slowboy, Mrs. Peerybingle's teenage housemaid. She was acted by a small girl.[178]

Dot had a different history at other theaters in the country. Quite remarkably, it ran for two whole months, from 26 December 1859 till the end of January, 1860, at the Varieties Theatre in New Orleans with John E. Owens. This theatre also revived the play both in March and in April the same year and for several years on it was offered at Christmastime.[179] *Dot,* or revised forms of it, was also one of Boston's great favorites. It was first given at the Boston Museum on 15, 16, 18, and 24 February 1860, and as an afterpiece in April and May the same year. The playbill listed W. Warren as Caleb and Miss J. M. Davenport as Dot.[180] Again as in New Orleans, Boston would play it at least once a year to 1900, while subjecting the play to constant revisions. In Boston theaters there was always a great deal of experimentation going on (we remember the criticism of the absence of local adaptation in the staging of *The Cricket* in 1846). In 1877 *Dot* was rearranged by Fred Williams, an Irish-born actor and stage manager at the Museum, who translated and adapted a number of plays for the theater. The "beautiful Christmas Fairy Story, Dot" was announced in playbills to take place on 26 November 1877, "in preparation for the Christmas Holidays."[181] At this stage, it seems, Boucicault's text was being applied. By 24 December, the date of the firstnight, the title had been changed into the one used by Smith. As the synopsis printed in the Boston Museum playbill also indicated, Fred Williams had reorganized the play using Smith's *Cricket* as his staple text, infusing into it segments from Boucicault's *Dot.*[182] The prompt copy of the play used by George W. Wilson, who played Plummer, demonstrates other consequences of the demands for local treatment. References to the English version are unequivocally omitted; the use of English dialect words has been reduced; a number of cuts have been made, many of which relate to the English setting; a few words have been "Americanized" (master>employer, desire>wish), etc.[183] The play ran to 5 January 1878, with a revival on 22 February 1878.

In *The Cricket on the Hearth* and *Dot* the issue is family stability and human solidarity, quite approriate Christmas themes. The play celebrates the function of the father as the nob of the family unit. It presents conventional "masculine" characteristics as opposed to the "feminine" ones of homecoming, caring, and jealousy. The only stellar role (Caleb Plummer) is male and its occupants are also all male, Jefferson, Owen, and S. Wilson. The play was more favored outside New York, quite in line with the tradition.[184] The same can be said about the other very popular Boucicault production, "Smike" that, we saw replaced *Dot* at the Winter Garden at the end of October 1860. On Thanksgiving Day (24 November) the two plays were given in succession.[185] The title role was Agnes Richardson's "whose gifts of pathos were well suited to elicit tears for the unfortunate waife."

Thereby she started another series of female impersonators of young
Dickens males on the American stage. Jefferson acted the decent
Newman Noggs.[186] But as with *Dot,* Boucicault's "Smike" did not do
well in the metropolis, which always was more inclined to favor the
farce and the burlesque; it provided more pleasure in the comedy
tradition of the play wrung out of subplots involving Newman Noggs,
the Mantilinis, and Kate Nickleby. Coincidentally, Byron and Dickens came together on the New York stage of the Winter Garden during
the first week of 1861—and in the same actor—as Jefferson did Newman Noggs in "Smike" and, for the first time, *Mazeppa,* in the burlesque billed "Mazeppa, or the Fiery, Untamed, Rocking Horse."[187]

In New York Boucicault's "Smike" virtually stopped playing in
the sixties and *Nicholas Nickleby* was replaced as melodrama by
adaptations coming from the hands of George Fawcett Rowe and
Andrew Halliday. Rowe contrived a happy ending to his drama by
introducing a living Ralph who asks his long-lost son Smike for forgiveness. Smike is eventually restored and reinstated in the Nickleby
family. At the performance at Booth's Theatre on 6 October 1875,
Smike was acted by a woman. Halliday's play was produced at the
Union Square Theatre, on 8 May 1877. *The New York Times* review
of the play was ambiguous, faulting the play's lack of plot and inter-
locking incidents, but endorsing its pathos and extravaganza (a horse
and couch was brought onto the stage). "People like it for the reality
of contrivance."[188]

In Boston the play as melodrama was acted regularly till the end
of the century, often around a male stellar role, but with a female
Smike. Also in Boston, Boucicault's "Smike" did not survive the
sixties. But another version did: a performance at the Boston Theatre, starting 20 October 1866 with John S. Clarke as Newman Noggs
went on for two weeks. It was billed "Nicolas Nickleby; The Beautiful Domestic and Comic Drama" and consisted of four tableaux:
"The Departure," "Smike and His Mother," "Nicholas Flogging the
Schoolmaster," and "The Drunkard's Last Drink [Newman
Noggs]."[189]

Two additional plays should be noted in this context: *Martin Chuzzlewit* and *Barnaby Rudge.* "Martin Chuzzlewit," although played in
1845,[190] would not for obvious reasons appeal to the Americans without being heavily altered. Horace Wigam dramatized it in 1868, with
John Sleeper Clarke playing "Sairey" Gamp, the drunken mid-wife
and nurse. Thus Edward Smith Willard secured the piece for his repertoire, having retouched the manuscript, assisted by Elwyn A. Bar-
ron, once a Chicago dramatic critic.[191] Another melodramatic version
of *Martin Chuzzlewit* was performed in Boston at Col. Sinn's Mon-
tank Theatre in mid-November 1897, called "Tom Pinch. A Play in
Three Acts, Being a Dramatization of Certain Incidents in Charles

Dickens's Martin Chuzzlewit." The playbill read: Act I. Tom Pinch's idol. A Room at Mr. Pecksniff's. Act II. The Idol Shattered. Mr. Pecksniff's Garden. Act III. Tom Pinch's Love. Fountain Court.[192]

Barnaby Rudge had been performed in 1841 in Philadelphia[193] and dramatized in Boston on the occasion of Dickens's visit there in 1842,[194] but was rearranged and shown on 3 October 1870 at Lina Edwin's Theatre in Boston with Stuart Robson as Simon Tappertit and his sister as Miss Miggs.[195] It had been dramatized for the Robsons by H. A. Weaver,[196] an actor at the Boston Theatre, and J. B Bradford.[197] The playbill from 7 October listed nineteen persons in the cast, which is more than half of the original number of characters in the book.[198]

Before we leave Dickens we have to account for his second visit to America and the activities that it engendered. This visit received even more publicity than his first, but was less succcessful. By now his views on copyright and slavery were well-known to the Americans. He read from his works at Steinway Hall in New York on 9, 10, 12, 13, 16, 17, 19, 20, 26, 27, 30, and 31 December 1867; on 3, 9, and 10 January 1868; and on 13, 14, 16, 17, and 20 April 1868 when he took his last farewell of his American public. Prior to this visit in 1867, the organizers had received 200 letters containing requests for his autograph. In Boston, where he again (in December) chose to start his tour, streets were swept, the State House and the Old South Church were repainted, and "Little Nell" cigars were made. Holmes, Lowell, Charles Eliot Norton, and Edwin Whipple (but not Emerson) came to listen to him. Also present were a number of shorthand writers, although Ticknor and Fields sold copies of his readings in paper cover to prevent piracy and competition.[199] Dickens had brought "No Thoroughfare," based on *The Christmas Books* and written with Wilkie Collins, to Boston. As had been the case with the the play derived from *Barnaby Rudge,* it was refashioned and burlesqued by two Boston actors, L. R. Shewell and Fred Williams, at the Boston Museum. It was also played there on 30 December 1867 and on 1 February 1868. Dickens was furious. R. M. Fields, the manager, actually prevented him from receiving any shares. Dickens offered the New York producers of the play his assistance, if they retained his version and did not "localize" it. They refused. Their version played at the Park on 6 January 1868. The American readers had long been out of Dickens's control.

Burlesque

SHAKESPEARE

"Legitimate" Shakespeare drama could not compete at all on its own merits; it functioned mainly, it seems, as a springboard for new acting

versions that parodied either the actor who had the singular trepidity
to take Shakespeare "seriously," or the very conventions that had
been formed around a particular scene or passage. Many an actor
who tried to play scenes from Shakespeare's dramas relying on mannerisms of declamation and eighteenth-century character acting had
to face an unfriendly and disbelieving American audience that was
especially furious when the Shakespearean interpreter colored his
(very seldom her) interpretation with ethnicity. The American actors
and adapters used all their resources to jargonize, say, Hamlet's language of and rave at his procrastinations. For an English traveler,
used to listening to William Charles Macready's Hamlets, an American travesty of the play must have been nearly unbearable. The Englishman Henry Fearon, traveling in the the country in the 1810s,
saw such a the play in Pittsburgh. He was stupefied at what he understood to be the lack of breeding in the audience, and embarrassed at
their uncivilized behavior: "solemn, serious, and dull." In addition,
he thought, the acting was monstrous:

> The affecting entrance of the deranged Ophelia, who, instead of rosemary,
> rue, &c. had an ample supply of turnips and carrots, did not move a
> muscle of their *intelligent faces* [his italics]. The ladies, indeed . . .
> evinced by the frequent use of their pocket handkerchiefs, that their sym-
> pathies were engaged on the side of the love-sick maiden.[200]

Fearon's aesthetics of reception would not agree with a local Ophelia
using turnips and carrots as props to establish comic transgressions.
For him it is as if the actress and her audience had formed a conspiracy against his metropolitan viewpoint.

There was thus a definite tendency in America to sneer and poke
fun at the famous Shakespearean stage figures and their equally famous interpreters. But in their inverted or burlesqued form, Shakespeare's plays were above all employed to castigate the melodramatic
or rhetorical structure that they were part of, to laugh at the moral
failures of their heroines and the Yankee simple-mindedness of their
husband-heroes. Various ethnic stereotypes, such as the ebullient
Yankee, the drinking Irishman, the ne'er-do-well Rip Van Winkle, and
the pathetic Negro were all conceptualized through the medium of a
Shakespeare travesty. To make Falstaff look and speak like a stage
Irishman or low-comedy "happy" Negro must have been a powerful
challenge to any producer of these plays. The travesties and parodies
of Shakespeare, then, relatively speaking, signify more about the
ways in which Shakespeare was transgressed and transformed than
about the political and melodramatic mode of his adaptations. Naturally, many of the travesties and parodies that were produced in the

country throughout the century were imported and as such were part of an international Shakespeare theater tradition; in turn, these travesties were often transformed or rewritten.

Hamlet and *Richard III* were, as we have already noted, both the most popular of Shakespeare's plays throughout the century[201] and the most emphatically burlesqued. The travesties of *Hamlet* had an early start in the country and were constantly played wherever there was a stage. The earliest were adapted from English, yet at an early stage in their cisatlantic history they were "Americanized." Such a travesty of *Hamlet* was shown at the New Park Theatre in New York on 28 February 1798, remarkably only a month after the opening of the theater; in Philadelphia on 7 March 1812; and at Baltimore on 13 and 22 May in the same year.[202] John Poole's travesty of *Hamlet* (1811), we know, was introduced in America in 1828 by George Holland. His production of *Hamlet* signaled the beginning of the "legitimate burlesque" in America and its reputation spread: a *Hamlet* travesty, "written by the author of the rejected addresses," was shown on 10 February 1831 in New Orleans;[203] in San Francisco theatergoers were titillated by a parody showing Hamlet and his mother dancing a cancan;[204] and both Mitchell and Burton humored the New Yorkers with similar take offs on *Hamlet* and other "serious" plays in the forties and fifties.[205] Mitchell's *Hamlet* travesty was on the boards for a week starting 13 February 1840 and was back on 20 March 1843.[206] However, the most successful American *Hamlet* burlesque during the century may have been a new American version of it by Thomas C. De Leon, of Mobile, who had arranged it for George L. Fox at the Olympic in New York, on 14 February 1870. Here it played for ten consecutive weeks. Typically, it was more, says Laurence Hutton, a burlesque of Edwin Booth than of *Hamlet*. Booth had played Hamlet in New York for one hundred consecutive nights, "probably the longest run that any tragedy whatever had at that time enjoyed."[207] So Hamlet intrigued and amused the New Yorkers for almost seven months in a row.

Richard III was along with Hamlet one of the the most popular of all Shakespeare's protaganists in America during this century,[208] and as such was travestied early on; William B. Wood observed in 1855 that "the so called original *Richard III*" failed, "notwithstanding its gorgeous armors, appropriate scenery, banners, &c."[209] The imitations and travesties of well-known actors' configurations of *Richard III* were extremely popular. Among these are James H. Hacket who produced travesties of Kean's Richard III and Thomas McCutcheon of J. B. Booth's (in "The Man about Town").[210] "These peculiar representations," says Alice I. Perry Wood, "furnish significant evidence of the popularity of the tragedy, the extreme familiarity of the audiences with it, and illustrate the opportunity in the play for striking and extraordinary situations, which so easily pass over into the grotesque."[211] Edwin Booth's recasting of *Richard III*[212] demonstrates that—in comparison with Washington Irving's acting edition of the same play—he had made a number of changes in the text to minimize the risk of being ridiculed. He had cut thirteen of the twenty-seven characters, shifted lines, omitted whole passages, reconstructed scenes, and added to Gloucester "a fine strain of innate royalty."[213] But to little avail. Forrest, more in alliance with his audience, had far more ruthlessly "altered and amended" his *Richard III* and would thus normally eschew the irony of the pit.[214] Generally speaking, the effort to make audiences bend to a "literary" concept of Shakespeare was futile, functioning mainly as a prompt for the burlesque theater. The temptation to wrest a laugh out of the rhetorical flourishes of a Hamlet or a Richard III was irresistible.

Richard III, then, lent itself to all sorts of theatrical ventures. The parodying of it got on its way in the 1840s. It went through all kinds of genre transformations and appeared in processions, histrionics, and "prodigies." At the Bowery Theatre in 1840, Charles Kemble Mason used the battle scene in Act V primarily to exhibit his horses. O. E. Durivage's burlesque at the Olympic on 10 February 1842, then given twenty-nine times in a succession (in all it was played forty-three times during 1841–42), included, Odell recalled, such local "heroes" as Richard, cad to Omnibus No. 3, and afterwards its driver; Henry King, an old omnibus driver; Bucky Gammon, a third omnibus driver; Richmond, a cab driver; and Dutch Bess of New York.[215] Charlotte Crampton, the famous striptease actor, played "Richard Ye Third" at the Chatham Theatre; in San Francisco in the fifties and sixties she was also reported to have done fantastic tricks with her horses.[216] The king was once more on horseback in a battle scene composed by Harry Seymour at the New Bowery Theatre in 1862. The infant phenomenon of the American stage also affected this play: on 10 December 1849 the two sisters Kate and Ellen Bateman, whose combined age was not more than ten years, did their version of the play at the Broadway Theatre. They also did Shylock, Macbeth, and other Shakespearian personages.[217] Perhaps to counter its reputation as a boisterous and noisy place often in need of police supervision, the African Grove in New York, which exhibited a "black" jungle as a pleasure "garden," offered its patrons a variety of "cultural dishes." Richard III was part of such a program that looked like this:

In addition to ice-cream, punch, and other refreshments *al fresco,* certain entertainments were offered. Among these was a performance in the "upper apartment," of Richard III, in which "a little dapper wooly-haired waiter [*sic*] at the city Hotel personated the second Plantagenet," in "robes made up from discarded merino curtains of the ball room."[218]

All the other roles were carried by women.

Antony and Cleopatra attracted the burlesque dramatists too; at the Olympic it was performed as "a dramatic eccentricity" with Charles Wolcot as Antony, billed as "a gentleman of the town," and [Mrs.] H. C. Timm as the grisette Cleopatra. It had its tenth performance here on 18 March 1843. The producer was the well-known local actor-playwright, Joseph M. Field. This travesty (or "burletta," as it was called) was followed by burlesques of *Hamlet* and *Romeo and Juliet*.[219] The "legitimate" play of *Antony and Cleopatra* followed the burlesque version, which was not altogether a normal procedure. It was produced by the Park on 27 April 1846.[220] Twelve years later, in 1858–59, it popped up at the Broadway theater; this time in an elaborate and weird partnership with Dryden's *All for Love*.[221] Boston Theatre, finally, gave a multishow on 28 June 1876 that, apart from the "burletta" *Antony and Cleopatra* with H. S. Murdoch and Mrs. Fred Williams, included singing, acrobatic feats, riding of "velocipedes," harp-playing, pantomimes, and feats of magic.[222]

In his notes, Macready explained that he had "revised the play of 'King Lear' for American performance," which must have been an insurmountable task and a sign of poor theatrical judgment, as this play had no precedent as a "legitimate" play, either in America or in Europe during this century. But Macready did scenes from it along his American circuit.[223] It was of course more delectable to the audiences as a parody. Such a skit was performed, for example, in January 1851 in San Francisco, along with a burlesque about the Swedish opera singer Jenny Lind, one of darlings of the period.[224] *Macbeth*, it stands to reason, was burlesqued throughout the century and even published which speaks for its popularity; such an example is W. K. Northall's travesty in Samuel French's Minor Drama series [6], [1843].[225]

Romeo and Juliet was shown relatively early on the American stage: during the first season of the New Park Theatre of New York in 1798.[226] It took much longer for it to be transformed into a travesty. It was produced at the Olympic, San Francisco, in September 1866, called "Roman Nose and Suet."[227] "The irreverent vulgar," says MacMinn,

suffered no lack of opportunity to laugh at what the cultured element took so seriously. For example, one night in the spring of 1857, when *Macbeth* was being given, with all the weight of the "legitimate," at the American Theatre, a burlesque of that same masterpiece was being presented with full complement of the ludicrous by the blackface troupe at

Maguire's Opera House. But the height of the ridiculous must have been
reached by the San Francisco Minstrels in their "Inauguration Ball; or,
The Shakespearian Festival." Not only were Hamlet and Richard
bracketed, but Lady Macbeth was merged with Meg Merrilies [from
Scott's *Guy Mannering*]. . . .[228]

"The Shakespeare Festival," the most renowned art occasion of them
all, has here been thoroughly dismantled through disrespectful and
mocking acts of deviation: "low" and "high" are juxtaposed, ethnici-
ties mingle, genres and incongruous characters are confronted. The
laughter moves "downward," departing from the "happy" state of a
Hamlet and Meg and ending in their downfall. The strong, the familiar, the public, the "civilized," "English" are all being desacralized to
create a sense of diversity and heterogeneity.[229]

The two comedians, Burton and Brougham, had a natural affinity
for the ludicrous and the grotesque and found in Shakespeare's plays
themes and situations that they were soon to elaborate. In most cases
they were in tune with public expectations and negotiated skillfully
between the lore and code associated with Shakespeare and the recognition that in order to succeed as an entertainer in New York one
also had to speak the language and idiom of the street. However,
nothing was so precarious as the taste of New York audiences. So
quite often, Brougham, and to a lesser degree Burton, went wrong
in seeking an outlet for their ambitions. They simply miscalculated
the audience support.

This happened with their efforts to turn *The Tempest* into a local
sketch called "The Enchanted Isle."[230] It was performed at Burton's
in January 1849.[231] It did not help much that it was the first time it
was played in the country and that "the size and weight of Mrs.
Brougham as *Ariel,* materially heightened the absurdity of the representation."[232] It failed. John Brougham also tried his hand at *King
John* (at the Bowery on 7 July 1850), but was unsuccessful again.[233]
Much Ado about Nothing was another of the plays of Brougham's
production that failed; it was shown at his Bowery Theatre on 12
December 1856 with Brougham as Dogberry.[234]

He was more successful with his version of *Henry IV.* John Daly
had adapted the play earlier in the century, but it was hardly known
and probably never acted in its entirety. What was appreciated, however, was the Falstaff figure.[235] Falstaff could incarnate, and often did,
both the stage proptype of the drunken Irishman, or the witty lower-
class New Yorker. Such burlesques and medleys were legion on the
American midcentury burlesque stage. We find Falstaff performed at
Brougham's in 1856. It was announced as the "Great Shakespearian
Play, with Mr. C. K. Mason as Hotspur" and to be followed by the

comic burletta, "The First Part of King Henry Fourth or, The Humours of Sir John Falstaff (with Lynne as Falstaff)."[236] Brougham and Burton went on acting Falstaff in different combinations throughout their careers; on 1 February 1858, they performed a play called "The Merry Wives of Windsor" with Burton as Falstaff and Brougham as The Host of the Garter.[237] *The Merry Wives of Windsor* had a first night at the Richmond Theatre, Virginia, where it was advertised as "Shakespeare's corrected Comedy," which was a clever way of admitting that the play had been tampered with.[238]

The Merchant of Venice[239] had a vivid following, for which there are at least two reasons: it contained the ever so popular (in American mass entertainment) trial scene and it provoked backtalk along racial and ethnic lines. George M. Baker produced a burlesque of the scene called "The Peddlar of Very Nice," which was to be used in amateur "theatricals" in the midcentury, and—to give an example from another cultural sphere—H. M. Smith's Circus Company, which commissioned both pantomimists and ballet dancers, produced the scene at Davenport in 1856 and 1859.[240] Tom B. Johnstone was Shylock in New York, at Burton's, in 1853, and Myron W. Leffingwell produced Francis Talfourd's "Shylock; or, The Merchant of Venice Preserved, a Jerusalem Hearty Joke" in September, 1867, at 24th Street Theatre. It was a cabaret with witty comments on avarice and hypocrisy with racist allusions interspersed. Jessica was depicted as a young New York yuppie dreaming about going to "Paree" and Antony an adventurous street thug.[241]

But the best known "Merchant of Venice" was John Brougham's. His *Much Ado about a Merchant of Venice* had its first night on 8 March 1869 at Brougham's, at Fifth Avenue and 24th Street. Brougham himself played Shylock, Miss Effie Germon Lorenzo, and Louise Young Prior Portia.[242] The text of the prologue catches something of the flavor and idiom associated with this burlesque:

SCENERY from Sketches taken on the spot, or nearer. COSTUMES copied from the Fashion Plates of the period. MUSIC by the most celebrated composers, unblushingly appropriated, disconnected and placed in unaccustomed positions. Tableaux and incidental choreographies.[243]

The play opens with a four-page introduction in clamorous style, heavy with pseudo-Elizabethan jargon, and pulpit rhetorics.

Lotta Crabtree, who also acted in Brougham's play (in San Francisco, in 1869[244]), played Desdemona in a burlesque of the third act of *Othello* in New York at the Academy of Music in 1877 for a benefit romp.[245] It had previously been shown in San Francisco, in 1849 and

1850, with "black" minstrels.[246] Lotta Crabtree also played it in San Francisco, on 11 September 1879.[247]

BYRON: *CORSAIR* AND *SARDANAPULUS*

We have discussed how Edwin Holland and Durang turned Byron's *Corsair* and *Sardanapulus,* respectively, into melodramas that from the start verged on the burlesque mode. In the midcentury, the transformation was complete.[248] William Brough at Maquire's Opera House in San Francisco travestied *Corsair* on 17 September 1859 under the title "Corsair, or The Little Fairy at the Bottom of the Sea."[249] An extra element in it was the vocalized ballet. The story involved Medona who has been abducted from a slave market in Alabama by the black-moustached corsair Conrad and the intimacies of their settling down into middle-class American life. Conrad listens to the seaspirits and decides to opt for a new British [!] lifestyle:

> Agreed;
> I've long been weary of the life I lead,
> So I'll reform
>
> .   .   .   .
>
> Turn steady; and go in for domesticity;
> Stand for church warden, and the vestry ritual,
> Aye, and pay rates and taxes like a Briton.

A midcentury revival of *Sardanapulus* was undertaken by The Bowery Theatre. It was adapted (and performed on 4 September 1854) by Hamblin and Mary Shaw who had made fun of *Mazeppa* as early as in June 1839.[250] The main novelty was that *Sardanapulus* in 1854 was impersonated by a woman; "a bad practice," summarized Odell.[251] The sensationalizing of Byron's *Sardanapulus* reached its zenith, however, with Charles Calvert's adaptation of it at Booth's Theatre, New York, on 14 August, 1876.[252] In his preface to the play Calvert outlined his purpose, which was to project a play that enshrined the achievements of time in all spheres of life, reflected upon parallels and contradictions, discussed the nature of bondage and servility, and pondered the downfall of empires. The dramatization tried to combine the Yankee preference for the oriental Byronic tale and violent stage action with an intellectual aspiration to discuss the causes and impacts of historical events. He had changed the position of a few scenes and deleted a few passages; otherwise he followed Byron's text rigorously. However, on the New York stage, Calvert's intellectual ambitions were totally squelched; Henry C. Jarrett and Palmer's dramatization effects, processions, tableaux, songs, dances made the play, and especially the fire scene, the most talked-about event in New York for a long time. The "pyrotechnicist to the Queen of England" had been invited, said Odell, to organize the conflagration at the end of the play. A huge ballet consisting of twenty-four "Negro boys" and forty-eight "extra ladies" were strutting around, and the two main characters, Signor Ernesto Mascagno and Mlle. Bartoletti, "won all the honors of the day," said a scathing review in New York *Herald*."There was a fine tragic burst when standing on his toes he [Mascagno] pirouetted across the stage and jumped at least four feet in the air, which drew forth thunder of applause from the admirers of Byron's immortal genius. . . ."[253] For several days this review was attacked by indignant playgoers who were fascinated by the extravanza and thought the report about the play utterly unfair. That it was the reviewers who were out of touch with the popular taste of the days is obvious: the play ran for one hundred thirteen consecutive nights.[254]

BYRON: *MAZEPPA* AND ADAH ISAACS MENKEN

In *Mazeppa* melodrama and circus came together to form one of the most popular—if not the most popular—stage performances witnessed in America in the nineteenth century. The history of this carnivalesque performance begins with Adah Isaacs Menken, the first American vaudeville artist. Here was everything that an audience looking for exitement and fun could ask for: romance, adventure, pathos, exitement, circus, burlesque, and from the sixties, when Menken started to act in it, vaudeville and erotic comedy. But what must be kept in mind is that it was Byronism that formed the inspirational frame for the the play's ongoing success. Without its grounding in a concept that contained elements such as libertinism, liberalism, and anarchism, all associated with Byron, the play would not have survived the thirties and the forties. Along its itinerary throughout time and space it was also sustained by direct and indirect references to Byron, to his works and life.

But even more important, the story of *Mazeppa* in America is a hothouse of transactions of the most varied kind. The metonymic world of the other ("Europe") is here, kept at bay, as it were, by being so throughly invaded. Byron's readerly romance has been transposed into the theater of the local carnival, his hero has been transsexualized and erotized, and the sublime has been degraded into the grotesque. Before we have seen these approriations operate separately, but not within the same "text." This is why *Mazeppa* is such an interesting case. "Burlesque depends," says Robert C. Allen, for its effect upon a preexistent hierarchical ordering of culture into high and low, worthy and unworthy, appropriate and inappropriate, solemnity and frivolity, importance and puerility. Burlesque works, in large measure, by upsetting this order. . . . [Its] two main vehicles of deposition are travesty, by which the high is made low, and the mock-heroic, by which the low is made high. [255]

The American reception history of *Mazeppa* falls roughly into two periods, the dividing line being the year (1861) of Menken's first performances in it. The texts that were used by the American producers from its start were H. M. Milner's, which was first performed on 4 April 1831 at the Royal Adelphi in London. Milner's text was used both at the Broadway Theatre in New York and Walnut Street Theatre in Philadelphia in 1833.[256] The second was an anonymous version, often called *Mazeppa; or, The Wild Horse of the Ukraine,* and first played at the Royal Coburg as early as 1823. The title also crops up in America.[257] A third version, *Mazeppa; or, The Wild Horse of Tartary,* written by the American John Howard Payne in 1825 and often listed as an American play,[258] paradoxically was, to my knowledge, not performed at all. But these national signfiers make little sense; the American adaptations were so thoroughgoing that most of the characteristics of the originals were obliterated and furthermore, one could ask, polemically, what is "American" about a script that never was performed or, alternatively, what remains of "British" in a play that was so totally transfigured.

One could characterize the almost three decades of *Mazeppa* performances, prior to Menken's emergence, as the period of "the fiery steed," or that of the "wild Ukrainian horse." So much attention was lavished on the equestrian art that the horse and the rider exhibited that comments about the play's other qualities are rare and when they occur even seem peripheral. But it is this play's popularity we are concerned with here.

Milner's drama was first played on 13 February 1833, typically in New Orleans, a city which took a particular pleasure in the opéra bouffe and the art of histrionics and where also, coincidentally, Menken was born.[259] Joseph M. Fields was reported to have ridden—as so many others would do after him—across the stage lashed to a local circus horse.[260] Next in order to launch *Mazeppa* was New York's Richmond Hill Theatre, with the "admirably trained horse, Napoleon"[261] and the Bowery Theatre, where it ran for forty-eight successive nights with George Gale and his wife as Mazeppa and Olinska.[262] From here it moved to Philadelphia where Gale was as successful as he had been in New York. In the meantime Albany was conquered. The Duffy and Forest Company performed here on 10

September and Maywood & Co on 10 November 1833. William Duffy, an accomplished artist was "riding up clattering stairs to the top of the stage."[263] "He took the usual chances, lashed to the back of the 'fiery steed' and carried the house by storm with the vigor and dash of the performance."[264] On the other hand, the show at Albany on 7 December 1833 was reportedly tame, as the horse was too "docile and gentle."[265] So within half a year most of the eastern seaboard big cities (except Boston)[266] had witnessed the acrobatics of Mazeppa and his horse, and the show penetrated further, slowly, into the mainland.

In the process it was also adopting new techniques and new ideas of how to shock an audience that never seemed to get tired of sensational surprises. From the beginning of 1837 the play entered a new and even more quixotic phase. It was given at the Bowery, Odell writes, on 20 February 1837, with "Mr [George A.] Cooke's unrivalled stud of Horses, amounting to 50 in number." There was a nuptial procession with six ponies, a "Grand Car" drawn by six spotted horses, tournaments, broadsword combats, all set against Romantic backgrounds of terraces of castles, mountains, precipes, alpine bridges, cataracts; there were songs and tales. The show lasted four entire weeks. It must have been great fun. The Bowery was so thronged and thrilled that the management publicly made it known that "a full and efficient police force has been engaged, and will be actively engaged in preserving good order."[267] The police, "actively engaged," were no doubt part of the show! The next season it was played twenty-one successive nights, from 2 April to 5 May, 1838, at the American Theatre Company, at Walnut Street in Philadelphia, with the same George A. Cooke as producer and Charles Foster, the son of the manager, in the main role.[268] Jefferson remembered how "his graceful figure and youthful appearance fitted him perfectly for the romanctic love of the *Princess*."[269] Durang's delineation of the event is memorable in itself:

> The wild and odd appearance of the animal, springing and bounding on her *entrée,* struck the audience with something like awe. The rider entered, and quickly bowed to general reception, which was followed by a feeling of silent perturbation, which seemed to pervade the house; but, when he mounted on the bare back of the Mazeppa-like steed, and, at a furious gallop, struck attitudes, executing the the various feats with care and grace, the hitherto silent but intense curiosity burst forth in crashes of tumultous applause. . . . The ladies waved with their handkrechiefs, standing on the seats in excited enthusiasm. . . .[270]

It was given seventy-two times between 1838 and 1854,[271] which makes the play one of the most popular plays given in Philadelphia during the whole century, even when compared with the Shakespearean hits. We also have to account for its reappearance in New Orleans, where it ran for a week starting on 26 November 1838. It was then replaced by another horse play. Horses and their riders were part of almost every performance in this city for many years in the midcentury. The horseman, a certain Lewellen, we are told was cast as a Byronic chieftain.[272] It was also repeated a number of times in the next decade. *Mazeppa* was number four in the internal ranking of plays produced in New Orleans during 1831–51; it had in all eighty-two performances to be compared with sixty-nine in Philadelphia.[273]

But from the mid-forties onward there was a slackening of interest in *Mazeppa;* it is as if the play's potential to entertain and shock had been exhausted. So from Cincinnati on 6 December 1847 Maud and Otis Skinner reported unenthusiastically that "the ladies were cheerfully frightened" and "the horse sustained no injury."[274] Had it not been for Adah Isaacs Menken, the play would have no doubt disappeared from the boards.

There had always been women impersonating Mazeppa. Clara Woodhall and Mary Shaw had tried the role in the 1830s.[275] The first woman to make an attempt at it, at a later stage in its production history, was Charlotte Crampton who in 1859 at the Chatham Theatre went up the "run" on the horse's back without being lashed to it, a "feat never before acccomplished."[276] But these women actors were only rehearsing a formula already established.

Menken brought new dimensions to the *Mazeppa* show: nudity, eroticism, and a perfect command of her medium as a sexist entertainer. A vaudeville artist and "proto-feminist,"[277] she may be labeled an innovator for these reasons. But for my argument she is important because in her art she was appropriating more extensively than any one before (or after) her the most tantalizing aspects of Byronism, namely its associations with androgynous transgressions, subordination, and wanton exorbitance. She herself idolized Byron, wrote poetry in his vein, dressed like him, had a haircut modeled on his (Mark Twain called her a "manly young female"), and did nothing to refute the rumors that she was his illegitimate daughter (of course other women Mazeppas were to claim the same thing). There was a contrived nimbus of Byron extravaganza around her that she exploited to the maximum, to her artistic and commercial advantage. Having seen her climb the ramp lashed to the horseback in flesh-colored tights, pretending to be naked, there were critics who deemed her performance a "matchless and inspired realization of Byron's sublime ideals."[278] Others were less convinced. After a performance at the Broadway Theatre on 30 April 1866, "the virtuous *Tribune,*" as Odell labeled the New York paper, "fulminated . . . in Olympic wrath that doubtless sent many to the theatre." The *Tribune* wrote—and I quote it at some length as it is revealing of the complex attitudes of the day concerning not only Menken and Byron, but also the élite's displacement of popular art forms:

> The audience . . . was the coarsest and most brutal assembly that we have ever chanced to see at a theater on Broadway. . . . The purple nose, the scorbatic countenance, the glaring eye, the bull head, the heavy bower glasses, the aspect of mingled lewdness and ferocity—all was there. . . . That any purpose connected with dramatic art is served by their [physical proportions of the body] public exhibition, . . . we fail to perceive. . . . The appearance of Miss Menken's Mazeppa at a theater on Broadway is nothing less than a grievous discredit to the acted drama in this metropolis. (from Odell 8: 34–35)

"Burlesque was regarded as so troubling," claims Walter C. Allen, "because it represented a refiguring of feminity, a refiguring that in every way inverted the already challenged but still powerful sentimental idea of bourgeois feminity—an ideal . . . . [that] valued sincerity, simplicity, naturalness, purity, domesticity, self-effacement and self-restraint."[279]

Menken tested the play first at The Gayety Theatre at Green Street in Albany on 3 or 7 June 1861 before venturing to take it to New York. From Albany it was reported that the "tournament scene was a great sucess," "the combat scene even greater," and "the riding she did successfully." She made her début in it in New York at the Broadway Theatre on 13 June 1861, taking fourteen curtain calls from an ecstatic audience that included both Walt Whitman and Edwin Booth. It seems that the hand of Dion Boucicault was involved in producing the play.[280] But it was James Murdoch, the actor-producer, who rewrote and arranged the play for her, shortening and simplifying Milner's speeches.[281] "Theatrical history was being made the First of the American Glamour Girls was setting a precedent that would be followed for more than one hundred years."[282] Menken now started touring the country, a trip that at this stage included Hartford, Philadelphia, Pittsburg, Baltimore, New York on several occasions, and, of course, New Orleans and San Francisco.

The reports from San Francisco were exceptionally vivid. *Mazeppa* had been played here late in 1851, prior to Menken's coming to the American Theatre. Washoe playing troupes played it, as an appetizer heralding the coming of Menken to the Maquire's.[283] "Adah la Menken" was then presented at Maquire's' Opera House on 24 August 1863.[284] The play was a hybrid combination of novelty and tradition, embryonic stripteasing, pantomimes and leg show, glamor and sin, and a woman revealing her sexuality through a male role. On one such occasion a piece of Byron's coffin was demonstrated.[285] The streets leading up to the Opera House were crammed. She played for a couple of weeks and thrilled her audiences by her way of dressing: always in free-flowing yellow silk gowns. It is estimated that about 30,000 people—half of the population of San Francisco—saw her in *Mazeppa*. From here she went back to New York and then to Virginia City, where she played for the miners. She was back in San Francisco for a second and last time at the Maquire's on 12 and 17 April 1864.[286] A journalist wrote that Menken's performance was "a scandalous, obscene exhibition, a deformation of a historical character whose ghost might well exclaim: 'To what base uses may our name be turned?'"[287] "Her exhuberant vitality, her undisciplined imagination found an echo in the incessant roaring energy of the miners, in the interminable rumble of ore wagons."[288] And another report claimed that "let a pure youth witness Mazeppa once, and he is pure no longer. . . . Strip the play of the obscene and as a theatrical display it is worse than a Chinese tragedy, wooden shoes, gongs, and all the rest."[289] She polarized San Francisco theater life for more than a year. Six of its theaters opened the autumn season of 1864 with some version of *Mazeppa,* each "advertised as employing the wildest horse, the most beautiful woman, the longest ramp, the most convincing rocks." At the Bella Union music hall, the leading woman actor would be replaced after each scene[290] and on 17 February 1864, the performance at Sutliff's, we learn, featured "long-tailed Chinamen," "thieving Paiutes," "Niggers," and of course "lovely females."[291]

If the play were stripped of Menken, would it then survive? It did—with a vengeance. Even during her lifetime (she died in Paris in 1868) a number of female Mazeppas had begun to challenge her supremacy. The most successful of them were Kate Fisher, Kate Vance, and Leo Hudson. The latter died in action when her horse tumbled over during a performance at Wakefield's Opera House, in St. Louis, on 12 May, 1873.[292] On the New York stages only in the sixties alone at least *nine women Mazeppas* performed.[293] Late-century impersonators were Fannie Louise Buckingham, Maude Forrester, and Vernona Jarbeau. By the end of the 1880s *Mazeppa* had completed its course and slipped out of the theaters, silently and gently, in extreme contrast to its tumultous entrance almost fifty years earlier.

Before we leave *Mazeppa,* a few words have to said about the burlesques that were produced in the midcentury. The best-known was the one that Joseph Jefferson III did in 1861. It appeared under different names "Mazeppa; or, The Fiery Untamed Rocking Horse," "The Fiery Steed; or, the Wild Untamed Rocking Horse," and "Mazeppa; or The Fifty Untamed Rocking Horses," and was enjoyed by audiences in all the large metropoles.[294] That *Mazeppa* would enter the domain of "Ethiopian Drama" is not surprising. Charles White "transposed and arranged" "Mazeppa. An Equestrian Burlesque" for the stage. It was printed by Frederic Brady as No. III in Brady's Ethiopian Drama [in 1865].[295] It featured Mazeppa," a Jersey darkey," disguised as Satinette courting the favors of Olinska, daughter of proud Castiron, "a darkey full of airs, living above his means." Satinette is caught "serenading" and lashed to the dummy man, the "fiery untamed steed" Castiron castigates:

> Let scorching suns, and piercing blasts; devouring hunger and parching thirsts; constant bruises and endless scratches, rend the vile nigger by piece-meal. Now launch the traitor forth, and let the story of his fate strike terror to all Jersey. (13)

In the end Mazeppa's father Abder Khan, "Cream of Tartar, and boss white-washer of Jamaica, L. L. ," recruits "all our colored sogers" in his neighborhood to walk on the tyrant's house and claim his son's love. Castiron refuses: "No never. I'll stick to dis crab till I die, and wid my last drop defend her. We defy you." To which Abder Khan retorts laconically: "Then, go in lemons," which are the last words of the play. The stage directions then explain:

> Blows fish-horn [Abder Khan]—The soldiers discharge three or four shots outside.—Rush in—push down wall—subdue their men. Enter MAZEPPA with pony—gives him in charge of DROLINSKO—he kneels with OLINSKA.—Old man blesses them.—A general picture.—Hurrah, and drum.—Red fire and Curtain. (24)

The transformation of Byron's verse story *Mazeppa* into a burlesque with social overtones and rendered in the stereotypical "black" working class jargon of mid-nineteenth-century New York is the furthest we get in the displacement of the Byron Other. Perhaps this is also metaphorically speaking the ultimate end. A further distancing would break the link between the "two" poles and attenuate and eventually mute the dialogue. This would also happen; but that is another story.

When Truman J. Bachus explained in his *The Outlines of Literature: English and American* that Byron's dramas have never been acted in America, his mistake cannot have been due to ignorance, he was too close (the book first appeared in 1897) to the events themselves.[296] Rather, I believe, he was not prepared to acknowledge as "legitimate" the current literary transactions of Byron's texts. Byron on the American stage is eighty per cent burlesque and vaudeville, the rest involves melodrama, romance, and oratory. Thus Backus's silence is a reductive assessment of a very vital aspect of the culture that in the appropriations of Byron and Byronism found an outlet for its creative daredevil. Byron was immersed in the practices of American culture, on all levels. William W. Wood, the Baltimore theater manager, understood the popular demand for him. He realized that as soon as there was a new text by Byron in circulation—or even rumors of one—there was only thing to do. He said this in 1821:

> As to Lord Byron's Tragedy [*The Two Foscari* or *Marino Faliero*], we are impatient to see it, altho it was announced as a non actable drama. However, if it is possible to make it a night's entertainment it shall [be] hard work but we shall do it.[297]

His declaration is informed with defiance and resistance. He is turning not only against the common notion that Byron's dramas refuse to be acted, but also the assumption that theater is an imitative art medium. Byron's text will produce "entertainment," he implies, if it is confronted with challenging questions—questions that only the audience in Philadelphia and Baltimore could ask. It is his job as the mediator between the text and the audience to create the framework for such a dialogue. It is this procedure that Byron was subjected to by his nineteenth-century American interpreters, readers, and consumers. They kept Byron alive.

Scott: travesties

We have seen that a few of Scott's poems and novels were not travestied, mainly for reasons of their thin plot structure. But those that attained a high level of popularity were unceremoniously uncrowned. This was no mechanical and provisional activity, far afield from Lewis C. Strang's disparaging description of it.

> There was no selecting nor weighing of merits, no casting up of dramatic possibilities. . . . Every bit of fiction, no matter how ephemeral, that sold enough copies to attract a trifle more than passing attention, was seized upon by the manager. . . . [They dramatized anything] from a census report to the latest edition of Noah Webster's dictionary.[298]

Mortimer Thomson's travesty "Doesticks,"[299] based on *Lady of the Lake,* which had its first night at Niblo's Garden on 19 June 1860, coming straight after a "Japanese Performance," then, was no coincidental occurrence. Its raison-d'être is complex. It is motivated and prejudiced by the general position of Scott in the country and by topical and local persuasions. The playbill detailing the activities on the stage speaks about a number of appropriating mechanisms: genreswitchings, sexual transgressions, and irreverent language (for example, death as a laughing matter):

> In the course of the piece, ROMANCTIC VIEW OF LOCH KATRINE. The Raging Canaul. Arrival of the Great Estern."Root Hog, or Die." The Lady of the Lake."My Love is but a lassie yet." "See, the Conquering Hero Comes." "Rhoderick Dhu's mountain retreat. The murderous-minded Brian."I think I ought to stew him." "A glove is a glove."I never knew but one could wields." The Prophecy. Wonderful death of Blanche. Whistle and country whistle. MARCH OF AMAQINIAN Zouaves . . . led by . . . BEAUTIFUL GALE SISTERS. The Fight of Roderick and Fitz James. A Rocky Defile. . . .[300]

William Mitchell travestied the second act of *Guy Mannering* at the Olympic in 1843 with Dunn as Bertram, and W. K. Northall did *Bride of Lammermoor* in 1848 at the Burton's ("Lucy Did Sham Amour"). Because of its local colorization it could hardly—without fundamental trippings—have been shown elsewhere. All the melodramatic versions of *Bride of Lammermoor* were continually travestied. On many occasions, it is impossible to tell, having access only to the title or the playbill, what kind of play or which version was being performed. Then the most reliable guess must derive from a consideration of the overall program of the specific theatre and its current bills.

The interest in *Ivanhoe* could never find a firm narrative foothold: its focus alternated between the two main characters, Rebecca and Ivanoe. The early melodrama, "Ivanhoe; or, The Jew's Daughter" (1820) split into a number of romance and operatic versions in the 1830. H. A. White has counted that there were more than eighty different versions of it in circulation (even one for children). The main operatic text was "Maid of Judah"; it was performed only between 1832 and 1840.[301] By midcentury the only "Ivanoes" on American stages were parodies that survived till the end of the century. The last called "Ivanhoe Up To Date" was produced on 18 December 1893 at Niblo's, New York, by the Columbia College amateurs, The Strollers.

The burlesque tradition of *Kenilworth* was even more lasting. Like the earlier Scott plays it started as a melodrama. The theaters of New York (Park and Lafayette) and Philadelphia made their own dramatizations of it in the 1820s, using the two existant versions of it—one that endeavored to recapture the whole of *Kenilworth*'s plot and gallery—and another that focused on Amy Robsart. It was the version based on Amy Robsart that, in one form or another, extended and expanded beyond the 1840s. By the beginning of this decade this melodrama had virtually disappeared from the boards.[302] Thirty years later, however, the romance tradition of the play was renewed. After a performance at Walnut Street Theatre, Philadelphia, on 28 August 1871, of Hamphill's Amy Robsart, James Rees noted that it "affords a fine field for splendid dresses, gorgeous scenery."[303] Accordingly, on 13 May 1873, it was produced for one of the star actresses of the period, Adelaide Neilson[304] at Booth's Theatre. But time had passed this kind of "serious" costumed melodrama. It was "wearisomely conventional," says the *New York Times* reviewer, despite the production's lively dances, imposing marches, some historical information, and a beautiful heroine. But it did keep the burlesque of *Kenilworth* alive for the rest of the century.[305] In San Francisco the play seemed to have struck familiar chords and was often parodied. At Tom Maquire's Opera House it was produced on 6 August 1866, with Lady Emilia Eliza Don, assuming aristocratic hauteur, dressed as Elizabeth, Queen of England. The *Daily Dramatic Chronicle* of 7 August 1866 reported:

> It is a little too much to expect that an American audience can enjoy a burlesque like *Kenilworth,* which occupies about an hour and a half in representing when they are entirely unable to discover the point of what were—when the piece was produced some fifteen years ago at Strand Theatre [London]—its best jokes. The piece would require a little freshening up, even for the London stage at the present day. . . . People commenced leaving the theatre and the atmosphere was delightfully cool and comfortable in consequence of the audience having become so thinned out by the time of the performance came to an end.[306]

But the theatergoers kept coming to see this burlesque. It played through 22 September, despite the negative criticism it received in local reviews.[307] The popularity of the play persisted; two other women troupes, The Zavistowskis and The Beauclerc Sisters, executed the same burlesque in San Francisco, on 6 April 1871 and in January 1877, respectively.[308] In the 1880s it was revamped and called "Little Amy Robsart."[309] Lady Don also visited New York and Boston with "Kenilworth, or Ye Queene, Ye Earle, and Ye Maydenne."[310] It played for three consecutive weeks in New York at Wood's Museum and Menagerie, beginning on 29 November 1869 for a total run of one month. In 1870 and 1871 it was parodied by the Rand sisters and in 1872 and 1873 by the famous Lydia Thompson Burlesque Company. Boston also laughed at *Kenilworth.* Handsome Don's Burlesque Circus entertained an audience at the Boston Museum on 4 March 1876 with it. Their program included balancing acts, gymnastic performances, clog dances, jigs, pantomimes, and Indian chiefs.[311] Toward the end of the century the burlesque and the romance traditions of *Kenilworth* coalesced to form "comic operas" that were performed at the New York Casino in 1886 and at Palmer's Theatre and Harlem Opera House in 1891. The *New York Times* reviewer said it featured no farcical situations, no wit, no good caricature, and no picturesque action—the only acceptable feature noted was the burlesque of W. S. Gilbert's Pygmalion and Galatea."The scenery looked like the production of a Munich impressionist in a fit of emotional insanity," it continued.[312]

DICKENS: TABLEAUX

The burlesque and the farce (I use here the two terms indiscriminately) did not aspire to teach, as did the melodrama. In connection with Dickens's plays the burlesque was a manifestation of life as an optimal and unique force, neither good, nor bad. It laughed and cried seemingly without a purpose. It questioned without offering answers. It was open-ended, much like New York streetlife where it had its home; the close-knit sentimental comedy, we saw, was functional and circumscribed by the ethics of Boston homes, their conventions and mores.

The only major Dickens text that was not burlesqued or transformed into a farce was *The Cricket on the Hearth*. Its association with Christmas celebrations probably made such a tranformation improper. All the others were in one way or another played as farce or burlesque for the fun and entertainment they could provide. Seldom did the farce turn into downright social satire. If the laughter had its origin in local misdemeanors and ethnicity, it was laughter with, not against.

The Pickwick Papers offered theater managers an abundance of material for comic back-up scenes and hilarious tableaux. Burton revived "The Pickwick Club" for his theater and showed it on 26 and 30 December 1851 (also in January) together with scenes from *David Copperfield*. In his cast were Pickwick, Snodgrass, Jingle, Sam Weller, Isabelle and Emily Wardle, and Mary, a servant girl at Mr. Nupkins's, afterwards married to Sam Weller.[313] Probably to celebrate Dickens's second visit to America, Augustin Daly's cumbersome dramatization was set up at the Worrell Sisters' Theatre on 22 January 1868. The cast included Jingle, Sam Weller, Nathaniel Winkle, Tracy Tupman, Pickwick, Bob Sawyer, Sleepy Judge, Great the Nupkins, Ben Allen, Elder Weller, Mary, Arabella Allen, Martha Bardell, Betsey Cluppins, Aunt Rachael, and Lady in Curl Papers. It is an attempt to link a few episodes to compensate for the finale terminating in the Bardell-Pickwick trial. The first act deals with "the shooting party and elopement at Wardle's in Dingley Dell," the second with "the double-bedded room and the adventure of the lady in yellow curl-papers," the third with "the election and riot at Ipswich," and the fourth with "the great trial of the breach of promise." It ran for three weeks, which must be defined as a success; it was last seen here in 1879.[314]

On 26 December 1873 the Olympic produced Fred Lysters's (dialogue) and David Braham's (music) "Gabriel Grub; or, The History of the Goblins Who Stole a Sexton! A Fantastical, Farcical, Demonical, Comical, Musical, Legendary, and Terpsichorean Imagination." It was arranged and adapted by the Californian Majilton and Reynold Families.[315] Wardle's tale told to his Christmas guests about the misanthropic Grub who drinks too much, but then repairs and repents—a Victorian morale advocating teetotalism and temperance—had been transformed into a burlesque that was heightened by the fact that it was performed right at the appropriate calendar time!

Other reduced versions of were produced mostly as afterpieces in Boston.[316] "Jingle" was the name of one-act farce based on *The Pickwick Papers,* played both in New York and Boston. In the eighties Sir Henry Irving toured American theaters with it as the impersonator of an old rogue actor. A performance at the Star Theatre, Broadway and 13th Street, New York, on 12 November 1887, listed the following characters: Pickwick, Nathaniel Winkle, Snodgrass, Mr. Wardle, Tracy Tupman, George Nupkins, Mr. Perker, Sam Weller, Job Trotter, and Fat Boy. All the characters were male; the Dickensian farce found it easy to attend to the ludicrous and incongruous with the male characters of the Pickwick circle.

Nicholas Nickleby, which had started to play almost as early as *The Pickwick Papers,* contributed at least two superior male comic characters in Squeers and Vincent Crummles, the manager of an itinerant theater company. Mitchell developed these characters as part of his repertoire and played them incessantly through 1840 at the New Olympic Theatre, the Bowery, and the Park.[317] He acted the roles side by side with scenes from *Oliver Twist* and *The Pickwick Papers.* Most remarkable, however, was his sketch "The Savage and the Maiden; or, Crummles and His Daughter," written by James Henry Horncastle, a local actor at the Olympic where Michell developed the sketch. He had started to feature Crummles in it in January 1840 and continued through September—and the farce drew audiences right through the forties and the fifties. Hutton called it a "side-splitting" operation, as it often followed the first act of *Nicholas Nickleby.*[318] It was performed at least sixty times before the end of its first season.[319] Odell claims that "the ever-famous farce founded on an episode in Nicholas Nickleby" was the most "popular piece ever brought out at this theatre." Most of the fifteen cast members were from Crummles's theater company, only Smike and Nicholas were outsiders.[320] The Crummles emigrated to America, as had in fact every second actor or actress on the American stage. Thus the play had a self-centeredness that was easily identified and recognized. The American-English connection was made comic capital of in matters of language and custom.[321] The scene was one of most acted single sketches in New York in the forties and fifties. [322] To the comedy tradition of the play belongs Burton's appearance in *Nicholas Nickleby* as Squeers at his own theater in 1853, with Mrs. Bernard as Fanny, "the best Fanny ever seen in New York."[323] The play was faintly burlesqued in October 1869 at Wood's Museum and Menagerie, and on 15 July 1871 at Wallack's with a Mr. Lewis as an Indian brave and Mrs. John Gilbert as a ballet dancer of tender years.[324]

Cuttle of *Dombey and Son* and Micawber of *David Copperfield* were two other major comic roles that Burton and Brougham kept acting it throughout their careers at theaters in New York, and also throughout the country.[325] Burton's and Brougham's adaptations had their initial performances in New York, where they were also always well received. However, when on circuit they were bound to perform these characters. Brougham was to a large extent identified with Micawber. Loyally, he kept on playing these parts till his death in 1878. From the sixties through the eighties, William J. Florence made Cuttle part of his repertoire. He procured Burton's stage clothes at the sale of his effects at his death[326] and at a performance at Wallack's Lyceum on 25 June 1860, he wore Burton's toggery, thus symbolically extending an American tradition of presenting this former adventurer, devoted friend, and great talker, a person that an American audience was bound to love. But very few other American actors would try to do the Squeers, Crummles, Cuttle, and Micawber roles; these personifications had become, it was felt, so closely associated with the New York comic traditions represented by Burton and Brougham that it seemed futile even to try to imitate them, not to mention create a new interpretation. There was even a fear of burlesquing them.

John Brougham also wrote a version of *Bleak House* while enaged at Wallack's, where it was shown on 13 October 1853 with Brougham as Turveydrop, Laura Keene as Lady Dedlock, and Mrs. Brougham as Hortense.[327] Brougham's name was not attached to it for the first few days. It was quite successful, running for a month.[328] Although played now and then, it did not have a real revival until the mid-seventies when the German "tragedienne" Fanny Janauschek made herself and the play famous in her subtle rendering of its two major female roles. The playbill for 21 February 1874 at Booth's Theatre describes it in the following way: "Her Grand & Dual Personations of 'Lady Dedlock and 'Hortense' her French Maid, in the Graphic Exciting Dramatization in 4 Acts, from Charles Dickens's interesting

Novel Bleak House, entitled Chesney Wold."[329] The American adapter had taken great liberties with the source. Many of the main personalities of the novel were absent. It included: Tulkinghorn, Sir Leicester Dedlock, Bucket, William Guppy, The Honourable Bob Staples [?], Mr. Rouncewell, Jo, Mrs. Rouncewell, Esther Summerson, Volumnia Dedlock. The *New York Times* reviewer did not understand, nor appreciate, Janauschek's way of sensationalizing the play. He considered it gloomy, with no humor and no tears. But the audience liked the play immensely. They were thrilled by Janauschek's alternating between the steady dignity and proud melancholy of the lady and the passionate malice of her French maid delivered in a broken French that came "naturally" from the German actress. The play was part of her repertoire to the end of her career.[330] Her double role included sociopolitical, ethnic, and gender implications that especially intrigued the audiences of New York and Boston (if not the theater critics). In the eighties Janauschek's *Bleak House* was one of the most performed plays in New York, obviously because it was so different, odd, and provoking.

Lotta Crabtree and Dickens's *The Old Curiosity Shop*

The Dickens farce (but not the melodrama) in America was, as we have noticed, a conservatively male matter. At least this was true up to the sixties. At this point most of the plays based on Dickens's novels as farces were already conventionalized or stereotyped with one telling exception: *The Old Curiosity Shop*. Boston, it seems, was first to have a dramatization of it. Obviously it was a shorter version of Stirling's 1840 play. It was announced as "The Old Curiosity Shop! or, Little Nell & and Her Grandfather" and shown on 16 January 1852 at the Boston Museum. The cast included fourteen people. The play seems to have been a faithful representation of Dickens's text.[331] This early, unsuccessful version of the play, "Little Nelly, or the Old Curiosity Shop," was performed the next day, on 4 August 1859, at the Chatham Theatre and at the National Theatre, New York. Little Nelly was played by the "infant wonder, Little Lola."[332] At this stage the play would definitely define as a melodrama featuring a child-heroine leading a weak, stumbling grandfather, another of Dickens many explorations of the father-daughter or adult-child relationship. But in America the play would move in another direction.

It was not until 1867 when John Brougham wrote "Little Nell and the Marchioness" for Lotta Crabtree that the play really took off. It was first produced at Crosby's Opera House in Chicago, sandwiched between other plays, but it failed to attract. Brougham was obviously still working on it. It was then brought out at Wallack's Theatre on

14 May 1867 and played for twenty-eight consecutive nights to 14 August 1867. Lotta was back here in September and she was at Niblo's Garden on 1 November 1869. Like her burlesque colleague Menken, she went to New Orleans to test her "Little Nell" and was wildly acclaimed. Brougham then realized that *he* had to accommodate his dramatization to Lotta's idiosyncracies, and *not she* to his text. Her banjo-playing, operatic and popular songs, Irish jigs, and mock bravura, which she executed with naturalness and ingenuity, provided the play a framework that subalterned Dickens's story. Lotta Crabtree had a wondrous deftness and clever skill at improvisation. If we add to this her personal magnetism, we have one of most popular entertainers of all categories in the history of American popular arts. Brougham, it would seem, had freely adapted Dickens, but Lotta Crabtree as freely adapted Brougham. In fact, she was continually inserting new elements into the play. A local blackface troupe, the Sable Minstrels, was used as the chorus for her jigs, acrobats tumbled around, Daniel Quilp, the wicked dwarf, walked a tightrope, gypsies and clowns were parading, and brisk men fought with broadswords. In the final scene Nell is hoisted to heavens as Grandfather Trent kneels at her grave.[333] Quilp's evil doings originated in his passion for Nell, and Sally and Sampson Brass become instruments of vengeance, in fact "good" characters. Brougham was bound to place exceptional importance on Lotta and close each of the four acts with a melodramatic tableau, for which the novel furnished no material; Irish girls who play the banjo were not among the institutions of the old country. Also Dick Swiveller was turned into a thorough Yankee. "The gallantry with which he offers to 'fix off' certain articles for the convenience of the Marchioness would not a little surprise the members of a London free and easy," a Boston playbill stated. The playbill for the performance at Niblo's Garden, on 1 November 1869 (the preceding week Lucille Western had appeared in *Oliver Twist*), detailed her "celebrated Specialities," "the clog dance, the Jigs and the Songs, the Banjo Solos, with Other Ingredients such as Sable Minstrels, Highland Flings, Acrobatic Performances."[334] "Lotta could not act," says Odell, "but she could hold as by sheer power of her magnetic personality. That was always a wonder as to what she would break next."[335] She made the play move fast, made it also appeal to the eye through her deft costumes and skillful dances. She was the real polyglottist of the American stage.

Within these three weeks there were three Brougham adaptations of Dickens playing at the Olympic (including *Nicholas Nickleby* and *Dombey and Son*). Brougham's nose for comedy could develop in a progressively multicultural city like New York; he would not have made it in England, said rightly a reviewer of one of his perform-

ances.[336] Lotta also played at Boston Theatre for three weeks, beginning on 14 September 1868. Playbills from here, typically, do not
mention Brougham but make capital of Lotta and her idiosyncratic
art.[337]

The popularity of the play was, indeed, overwhelming. This is evidenced not only by the actual number of showings of the play with
Lotta, but also by the fact that it was in its turn burlesqued and
fragmentized. The San Francisco Minstrels burlesqued the play during the summer of 1868 at the Hall on Fourteenth Street.[338] An independent sketch, called "Dick Swiveller," by James Cassius
Williamson was played at the Broadway Theatre on 24 April 1869.

Lotta continued to act in *Nell*. She played it on 14 August 1871 at
Booth's Theater. The *New York Times* reviewer noted that Booth's
was the fourth theater in the city where the same piece was being
given. Niblo's must have been the fifth, as she performed here together with Lydia Thompson on 19 August 1871. It is quite likely
that Lydia Thompson had further burlesqued *Nell.* From here Lotta
went to Boston where she played it on 26 August. She played *Nell*
at the Park on 18 December 1876 and went on through December at
the Museum, but now for the first time against reviews that were
increasingly cool. The *New York Times* reviewer was now calling her
art inoffensive. In 1881, after seeing her again at the Park on 11 April,
the same newspaper expressed contempt at the comedy. It is empty
and Lotta, he found, was not absurd enough.

Approximately around this time Dickens's name was to be seen on
the several New York playbills, together with Brougham's.[339] In 1884
Lotta was in London at Opera Comique and the *New York Times*
reported malevolently that there was "no organized opposition"
against her. The negative reception of Lotta continued. She performed at The Standard Theatre on 5 December 1885. The newspaper
told its readers "The play was always a vulgar perversion of one of
the most wonderful romances in English literature." At this stage she
was acting along a text that had been adapted by Dickens's son and
closer to Brougham's original (from which it had continuously been
slipping) but this did not help; according to the New York reviewer
it was bad, crowded with disconnected scenes, incoherent and dull;
"the day of scrappy, incoherent dramatizations of novels has passed,"
he declared. Lotta's dancing and singing could no longer save the
play.

Despite this criticism she went on playing *Little Nell* for a few
additional years, but dropped it definitely in 1888, having played it
by then for twenty years. Another Nell emerged in Katie Putnam
who played it in the nineties. And toward the end of the century, in
Boston where Lotta Crabtee was a frequent visitor and was very

popular, Harry P. Mawson dramatized the play for the Tremont Theatre. It was shown on 22 January 1900. According to Mawson himself it was very successful.[340] It was called "Little Nell and the Marchioness" and was a return to Dickens's original text. But without Lotta Crabtree and her vaudeville style, the play could not survive.

OTHER BRITISH WRITERS

The rather "uncivilized" American "domestications" of British writers and their novels and poems are further apparent in the adaptations of Charlotte Brontë's *Jane Eyre* and Tennyson's "Enoch Arden." However, such operations reflect meaningfully on the very nature of American nineteenth-century protean concept of the Other and its relationship with the self. To dramatize a poem by Tennyson, turn it into a piece of burlesque or low comedy, and for the same stage, simultaneously, project *Jane Eyre* as a popular farce seemed natural things to do.

John Brougham also tried his hand at Brontë's *Jane Eyre*. The play was first acted at Laura Keene's Varieties Theatre on 26 March 1848, but according to Ireland, it was only moderately successful.[341] As audiences ruled the theater by their patronage, Brougham had no other choice than to go on working on the play.[342] It was performed a couple of times at The Bowery Theatre in the 1850s and in 1856 at the Tripler Hall with with Laura Keene as Jane and George Jordan as Rochester, with fifteen others in the cast. Then it dropped out of sight: the Broughamian comic idiom would not sustain the mock-heroic, the "angel woman" could not salvage the play, nor her man. The play needed another woman, the rounded contours of the burlesque performer, to survive. As we have seen so many times before, the play returned after an interval of nearly fifteen years. It was first announced to be shown on 5 October 1870 and another announcement explained that it was to be performed at "The New Stadt Theatre," on 18 February 1871, as a German opera. What happened was that the play (or the novel) had been completely inverted for the burlesque genre, which operation also legitimated "operas" of the "illegitimate" kind. It was then performed by Charlotte Thompson on 17 June 1874 at the Union Square Theatre. She would appear, along with Maggie Mitchell, as a powerful fleshy Jane Eyre throughout the 1880s. *Jane Eyre* was found attractive for a long time and was often offered as part of larger bills of attractions. On 1 November 1877, for instance, the first act of *Jane Eyre* was given at the Academy of Music, in the context of the annual Roman Catholic Orphan Asylum benefit. The anachronistic program included: "Irish eccentricities, pantomimes, first act of Fanchon, trial scene of *Merchant,* third act of Monte

Christo, balcony scene from *Romeo and Juliet,* romanza from Martha, first act of Micawber, a dagger scene from The Wife."

The arenas for the dramatizations of novels and poetry were as multiform as the representations of the actual work. We are familiar with the dramaturgical eccentricities of Charles Dickens's readings from his own works, his elocutionary mannerisms, his very specific choice of "stage" properties, or of Fanny Kemble, "the High Priestess of the inspired Bard," who toured the country (except the South!) for twenty years (1849–69) reading from Shakespeare's plays for audiences who were opposed to theater.[343] Byron's poems were also often read by both professional actors and of course professional "readers" or lecturers.[344] The lecture hall and the stage attracted audiences from different social classes and different perspectives; naturally the fora and their audiences contributed to diversification of literary expressions.

Tennyson's poems were also often dramatized or read in public lectures.[345] An evening entertainment, for instance, at the Claire Hall in the small town of Davenport in eastern Iowa in 1855 listed among other things a reading of Tennyson's "The Progress of Spring," "New Year's Eve" and "The May Queen" with "the gradual decay of a young and beautiful girl, from the bloom of health to a premature grave." The reading, it is also reported, was accompanied by music.[346]

But what is more interesting for us is the strange theatrical fate of his poem "Enoch Arden," which right from its reception in America (1869) was subject to two dramatizations, one by Arthur Matthison and another by Jule de Marguerites, which demonstrates the poem's potential for varied readings. On 21 June 1869 Marguerites's version was performed at Booth's Theatre with Edwin Adams as Enoch Arden and Blanche De Bar as Annie Lee. Joseph Jefferson mentioned in his notes that Adams "created" Enoch Arden and "touched the sympathy of his audience."[347] It held the stage for six weeks. On 26 September through 17 October 1869 Matthison's version was shown at the same theatre, now with Theodore Hamilton as Enoch, Fanny Morant as Miriam, and De Bar as Annie Lee. The sad story of the shipwrecked sailor Enoch Arden who returns home after ten years on a desert island to find his wife remarried and of his perversely heroic decision not to reveal his secrets to his former family, but simply die, penitent and recluse, was a fascinating tale for the melodramatic stage. As natural was the step from melodrama to the mock-heroic or the burlesque. So instead of having two dramatic versions of the poem, two variants of it within the same narrative category, the New York audiences were endowed with versions that were each other's symbiotic opposites. Until the beginning of the eighties the melodrama and the burlesque kept each other company.

So on 17 October 1870 a burlesque called "Enoch Arden, the Sailor Boy" was performed at Woods's Museum and Menagerie by The Lydia Thompson burlesque company. We may assume that, as in all the other burlesques that the troup performed from their arrival in the country from England in 1868, a female hero impersonated Enoch Arden, and also that the troupe interpolated dances, jigs, topical songs, and puns with their script. We know that their "Enoch Arden" attracted large audiences; they benefited naturally from the opposition of the press. It must have been a special treat for many theatergoers to find a British theater company parodying a British poet of such a lofty reputation as Lord Tennyson on an American stage.

The first work by Milton to be appropriated on the American stage was *Comus,* which contained "natural" qualifications for such an operation. In 1801 the masque was performed at Mount Vernon Garden in New York[348] and in 1805, for example, it was shown at a Charleston theatre.[349] There are to my knowledge no signs of it before it was subsumed in another theatrical tradition. On 11 September 1848 Burton produced the younger Colman's version of Comus at his Chambers' Street Theatre. He had used an arrangement made by George Loder. The cast also included "the Elder Brother," "the Younger Brother," "a Lady," "a Drunken Baccanal," "Satyres of the Woods," and "the Dancing Nymph." The burlesque ran at Burton's for nine nights in the bewildering company of Burton's "Dombey and Son." With them also ran the skit "Seeing the Elephant."[350]

Milton's *Paradise Lost* was naturally subjected to various dramatizations throughout the century, ranging from the didactic use of it in elocutionary handbooks, simple dramatic lectures, and the torchlight Mardi Gras processions on the streets of New Orleans in 1857. At Davenport in eastern Iowa on 3 August 1855 the poem is reported to have been exhibited as an unrolling panorama, what could be perceived as the equivalent of the modern news reel or motion picture.[351]

Burton and Brougham were also involved in the production of Thackeray's *Vanity Fair* (the script was Brougham's), at Burton's on 25 January 1849, and Goldsmith's *Vicar of Wakefield* by Tom Taylor on 6 May 1849. Each play was revived: *Vicar of Wakefield* at Burton's on 25 January 1858[352] and *Vanity Fair* at the Tripler Hall on 30 November 1857.[353] And what is more significant: each play failed at each showing, even when Dion Boucicault both produced and played in it, supported by Laura Keene and Agnes Robertson, at Laura Keene's Varieties in March 1860. Boucicault also tampered with Richardson's *Clarissa,* of which he produced a three-act version for Wallack's Theatre with fourteen in the cast on 12 September 1878. It also failed.[354] "Clarissa Harlowe, or, The History of a Young Lady" had previously been produced by "a lady of New York" [Laura

Keene] at Niblo's Theatre on 16 June 1856.[355] Two of Robert Southey's poems were parodied, "Thalaba, the Destroyer" (called "Thalaba, the Destroyer; or, The Burning Sword of Hodeisa") and "Wat Tyler."[356] S. T. Coleridge's "Remorse; or, The Paternal Malediction" was performed throughout the century, but it was poorly conceived and consequently failed each time (at the Park on 13 December 1813 with Cooper as Don Oidonio, and at the Chestnut in Philadelphia on 11 January 1823,[357] again at the Park on 1 January 1846, and on 26 March 1878 at The New Theatre Comique). A stage version of Mrs. Shelley's melodrama *Frankenstein* was produced at the Park in 1823[358] and Smollett's *Humphrey Clinker* was done in Philadelphia on 17 June 1833.

Conclusion

Obviously any search for cultural independence is antithetical; so also postcolonial America's. It hammered out its proud message distinctly and loudly: we can offer our new citizens the freedom of thought and expression that you miss, or which is missing, in the Old World! A number of poems and plays analyzed in this book are consciously or unconsciously inscribed by such a cultural strategy; a spirit of antagonistic self-aggrandizement and self-containment characterizes the entire nineteenth-century cultural field. We have witnessed Daughter and Son America, as it were, on the run and Mother England losing control! This "evolutionary" parameter contains resistance, rebellion, and rejection. It is around such belief systems that this book has been organized. The British voice of a Byron and a Scott was prejudiced to inhabit an antiquated world of corruption and stagnation; transmitted—and displaced—it was motivated to speak up and defend the voice of another world, that of the emergent republic.

At the same time new ambiguities emerged. The logocentrism of English literature was destabilized, we have seen, but never totally rejected, nor endorsed. Milton's *Paradise Lost* performed in the new republic the double role of upholding a conservative world view and rebelling against it. So did also Byron and Scott through the many roles they were allocated as propagandists for the national cause, anticolonial rebels, freedom fighters, universalists, and degenerates, losers, and aristocrats. The case of Dickens was equally ambivalent. This ambiguity is particularly clear in the instances where the freedom credo obtained from the British writer is employed to suppress the voice of the Other American. The code could then strike both upward (against the British) and downward (against the Native Americans), as many of the Scott-Byron-inspired racist songs did. Noteworthy, moreover, is the almost total absence and exclusion in the American appropriations of the black presence, which is a prejudice of the material, not of this author; thus it adumbrates a well-known story. The British presence, on the other hand, was active in nineteenth-century America in more than the bare figurative sense; Macready, Dickens, and the British playwrights and actors Brougham and Boucicault, for instance, were compelled to accommodate their artistry to the popular desires and fantasies of the Americans. Without this cooperation, they would have failed to communicate.

My material demonstrates, one could claim, the naissance of the totalizing viewpoint that we today call "western." So when Bayard Taylor, the New England poet and *man of letters,* travelled in the north of Scandinavia in 1857 it was as a member of a displaced race seeking new alliances. The formerly "colonized" had become a "colonizer." The Finns and the Lappish people he encounters inhabited the "frontier" and were therefore, he suggested in his book *Northern Travel; Summer and Winter Pictures of Sweden, Denmark, and Lapland,* suitable for the American labor market. (Cynically speaking, he proved to be right: at the end of the century thousands of poor Scandinavians started to pour into the States.)

The nineteenth-century American incorporation of the English voice was far from complete and inclusive. The "new texts" which emerged out of the "integration" of the two were conditional; the B-text (the American text) was symptomized by the referential system of the A-text (the British text). However, one major theme in this book has dealt with the configurations coming out of the interlinking gap. In this arena takes place the *play of difference* that signifies the American appropriations. In the hybridization of Dickens's novels, for instance, due to the specific needs of Manhattan playhouses, we are metonymically speaking witnessing a cultural drama in the way Victor Turner has described it; so also when the elocutionists inflected the voice and body to forward the "politics" of Shakespeare's *Julius Caesar,* and the writers created satires, parodies, and melodramas out of Byron's *Childe Harold* and *Don Juan.* More specifically, this drama involved transgressions of the most varied kind, of literary genres, of social classes, of gender, and of age. The mobility was endless: sometimes, as in the case of Halleck's *Fancy* and Macready's *Macbeth,* one "imitation" prompted another imitation, or subsumed another literary species (a parody or a burlesque). Byron's romance *Mazeppa* underwent a whole series of tranformations and hybridizations, where each intervention reformulated and reinscribed the Byron code without, however, losing sight of its mythic source. Fascinating are also the instances where there was a multiplicity of cooperating strata, as in Ritchie's novelistic Byron tableaux and Flagg's usage in his travelogue of a stage convention borrowed from the contemporary Scott theater.

We move on grounds which are both mainstream and popular. The displacement of the European models and the shifts of hegemony it produced were inspired by local aspirations and anxieties; the local could involve the conventions of a theater or the traditions and sentiments associated with a region or a city. We saw how the female figures in Byron's *Don Juan* inspired three local variants, how the New Yorkers loved the urban comedy and thus favored *Oliver Twist*, and how the Bostonians took to the domestic narrative and the serious comedy. But the popular field also included nonregional affinities. Each of the British writers highlighted in this book—and not only Shakespeare—performed across the whole cultural field (of which I have of course only covered a section). Scott was an American hero not only, as it is often believed, in the South, but a model for the whole country and the entire century. The same could be said about Byron and Dickens who were eagerly engaged, diachronically and synchronically, for both "pure" and "impure" purposes. In sum, we are dealing with an unruly culture attracted to impure forms, promoting negotiations of dominant and subordinate positions, and enjoying the cultural practices of recoding and transcoding.

As in most popular cultures gender dominance and gender transactions were multiple and complex. The elocutionary and literary handbooks were oriented toward a male audience and the form and content they projected were strongly affirmative of the values of their target groups: politicians, teachers, business people. However, when the same material was presented on the stage with its mixed discourse of defiance and domesticity, its gender bases became entwined and complicated. The stage (both melodrama and burlesque) projected women actresses and women's concerns, and through its transgressive play with sexuality and gender (of which the child was also a part), it questioned male assumptions. Ritchie, among others, made use of this technique in her novels. Resistance against Old World cultural dominance was then implicated in contemporary class and gender questions.

One of the alternative readings of this book treats the reputations of the British writers. There is no easy way of summarizing the receptions of these writers: they are far too complex. Shakespeare constituted a class of his own, his works being transmitted and projected from the beginning of the century as a comprehensive American oral narrative of messianic pretensions. The pulpit and the board recognized no limits—nor did the general public—to the vulgarization and appropriation of this tale. Scott seemed to have enjoyed something of the same reputation as both the poet of universal aspirations and "American" motives. His epic heroes became local "wilderness" heroes and the history of the Scotland-England interface was appropriated to discuss domestic American politics. But above all, it was Scott's ballads that were imitated, their form and their antiquariansm were adopted to project American sagas. With Byron it was the hysteric push of his poetry of manners and landscape, his vigilant republicanism, his restless activism, and disruptive personality that attracted and repelled in somewhat equal measures. To write "against" the Byron code produced more American imitations than did the more sympathetic and understanding approach to him. Dickens was an attractive source for very different reasons: within the referential system of his works the Americans could discuss problems of class and gender, moral issues, and the position of the child. But there they also discovered a looking glass to laugh at themselves.

The American production of counternarratives demonstrates the search for an epistemology of American literature and culture. In prefaces and other critical comments the debate over what was genuinely American in art and literature targeted both form and content. Was there a subject matter and an art form that could be isolated and defined as authentic, it was asked? Or, it was boldly postulated: let us find the native subject matter and then dress it in alien clothes. This masquerade took place in the open, amid both great fun and deep seriousness. Similar postulations develop in any postcolonial society and that of nineteenth-century America was no exception. Thus the high ideals of exclusivity and parochialism were constantly thwarted; the burlesque mode and, what we might call, adaptability governed. Through reassimilating defiantly—that is, resisting—the English canon, a rich vernacular practice of "talking-writing" arose, a practice of addressing the listless and moving the lethargic. It is through this mode of inflecting popular desires and beliefs that "American literature" expanded into excellence and recognition.

Appendix 1
British Writers in American
Elocutionary/Literary Handbooks

William Shakespeare

JULIUS CAESAR

ACT I

Sherwood 1855. Marullus addressing the mob 1.1.35–59.
Zackos 1861. Ibid.
Raymond 1880. Ibid.
Southwick 1894. Ibid.

Welles 1822. Cassius inciting Brutus against Caesar 1.2.89–129.
Barber 1830. Ibid.
Rush 1833. Ibid.
Vandenhoff 1846. Ibid.
Sanders 1860. Ibid.
Zackos 1861. Ibid.
Wiley 1869. Ibid.
Shoemaker 1876. Ibid.
Shoemaker 1895. Ibid.

Rush 1833. Cassius to Brutus 1.2.156–59.

Kirby 1888. Cassius and Casca 1.3.103–32.

II

Brooks 1883. Soliloquys of Brutus 2.1.10–34, 61–69, 76–85.
Graham 1877. Brutus's speech to the conspirators 2.1.114–40.

III

a

Bronson. 1846. Caesar's speech 3.1.58–78.
Leavitt 1849. Ibid.

b

Barber 1830. Antonio's oration over Caesar's body 3.1.254–75.
Rush 1833. Ibid.

Kirkham 1836. Ibid.
Barber 1836. Ibid.
Comstock 1843. Ibid.
Bronson 1846. Ibid.
Vandenhoff 1846. Ibid.
Dwyer 1856. Ibid.
Russell 1862. Ibid.
Brooks 1883. Ibid.

c

Barber 1831. Address. Brutus's speech on the death of Ceasar 3.2.12–48.
Kirkham 1836. Ibid.
Comstock 1843. Ibid.
Claggett 1845. Ibid.
Vandenhoff 1846. Ibid.
Mandeville 1851. Ibid.
Dwyer 1856. Ibid.
Zackos 1861. Ibid.
Lawrence 1871. Ibid.
Brooks 1883. Ibid.
Southwick 1894. Ibid.

d

Swinton 1886. The funeral scene of Julius Caesar 3.2.40–202. Passim.

Vandenhoff 1846. Antony's speech in the Forum 3.2.75–109.
Frobisher 1867. Ibid.
Lawrence 1871. Ibid.

IV

Russell 1862. Brutus's speech to the boy Lucius 4.2.18–24.

Barber 1830. Quarrel scene. Cassius and Brutus 4.3.1–156. Passim.
Rush 1833. Ibid.
Barber 1836. Ibid.
Vandenhoff 1846. Ibid.
McGuffey 1857. Ibid.
Sanders 1860. Ibid.
Frobisher 1867. Ibid.
Sanders 1872. Ibid.
Shoemaker 1876. Ibid.
Kirby 1888. Ibid.

HAMLET

I

Barber 1836. Dialogue. Hamlet and Horatio 1.2.159–212.
Porter 1841. Ibid.
McGuffey 1879. Ibid. [With a picture and a glossary]

Russell 1862. Advice of Polonius to Laertes 1.3.56–81.
Brooks 1883. Ibid.

Wiley 1869. The ghost scene 1.4.38–86.
Shoemaker 1876. Ibid.

III

a

Kirkham 1836. Hamlet's soliloquy 3.1.55–89.
Porter 1841. Ibid.
Comstock 1843. Ibid.
Vandenhoff 1846. Ibid.
Mandeville 1851. Ibid.
Apthorp. 1858. Ibid.
Sanders 1860. Ibid.
Wiley 1869. Ibid.
Sanders 1872. Ibid.
Shoemaker 1876. Ibid.
Brooks 1883. Ibid.
Brown 1886. Ibid.

b

Kirkham 1836. Hamlet's advice to the players 3.2.1–39.
Barker 1836. Ibid.
Porter 1841. Ibid.
Mandeville 1851. Ibid.
Sherwood 1855. Ibid.
Sanders 1860. Ibid.
Zackos 1861. Ibid.
Atwell 1867. Ibid.
Lawrence 1871. Ibid.
Sanders 1872 VI. Ibid.
Shoemaker 1876. Ibid.
Raymond 1880. Ibid.
Brooks 1883. Ibid.
Ross 1887. Ibid.
Kirby 1888. Ibid.
Soutwick 1894. Ibid.

c

Porter 1841. Soliloquy of Hamlet's uncle 3.3.38–72.
Kidd 1870. Ibid.

V

Kirkham 1836. Hamlet's reflections on Yorick's skull 5.1.202–16.
McGuffey 1879. Fifth. Ibid.

Rush 1833. Hamlet and Laertes 5.1.289–290.

Brown 1886. Hamlet's death 5.1.322–37.

OTHELLO

Welles 1822. Othello's address to the Senate 1.3.76–93.
Barber 1830. Ibid.
Barber 1836. Ibid.
Aprthorp 1858. Ibid.
Sanders 1860. Ibid.
Shoemaker 1876. Ibid.
Brooks 1883. Ibid.
Kirby 1888. Ibid.
Shoemaker 1895. Ibid.
Ross 1887. Othello's speech to Desdemona 2.1.184–93.

McGuffey 1857. The folly of intoxication 2.3.259–335.
Wiley 1869. Ibid.

Rush 1833. "Yield up, O love, thy crown, and hearted throne" 3.3.447–48.

MACBETH

Russell 1862. The dagger scene 2.1.49–64.
Atwell 1867. Ibid.
Wiley 1869. Ibid.
Mitchell 1870. Ibid.
Randall 1870. Ibid.
Sanders 1872. Ibid.
Brown 1886. Ibid.

ROMEO AND JULIET

Bronson 1845. Mercutio's speech. Queen Mab 1.4.53–94.

Apthorp 1858. The balcony scene 2.2.1–138.
Randall 1870. Ibid.
Shoemaker 1876. Ibid.
Graham 1877. Ibid.

Vandenhoff 1846. "If I may trust the flattering truth of sleep" 5.1.1–11.

ANTONY AND CLEOPATRA

Graham 1877. Cleopatra's death 5.2.280–92.

TIMON OF ATHENS

Rush 1833. "Nothing I'll bear from thee / But nakedness, thou detestable town!"
    4.1.32–33.

COROLIANUS

Barber 1836. Corolianus and Aufidius 4.5.50–153. Passim.

I HENRY IV

I

Barber 1836. Hotspur's description of a fop 1.3.29–68.
Wiley 1869. Ibid.

Vandenhoff 1846. "The lofty enthusiasm of the aspiring Hotspur" 1.3.199–206.

II

Barber 1836. Prince Henry and Falstaff 2.4.310–404. Passim.
McGuffey 1857. Ibid. [Bowdlerized.]

IV

Vandenhoff 1846. The description of Prince Henry 4.1.98–110; Hotspur's eagerness for battle 4.1.112–23.

Barber 1836. Falstaff's ragged regiment. 4.2.11–48; 65–66. [he added a couple of lines of his own to end the monologue.]

Russell 1844. Hotspur's reply to Walter Blunt 4.3.32–88.

V

Russell 1844. Henry's challenge to Hotspur 5.5.11–44. Passim.

II HENRY IV

Porter 1827. The apostrophe to sleep 3.1.5–31.
Kirkham 1836. Ibid.
Apthorp 1858. [?]

Kirby 1888. King Henry's rebuke to the Prince 4.5.92–137.

HENRY V

Barber 1830. The address of Henry V to his troops before the gate of Harfleur 3.1.1–34.
Claggett 1845. Ibid.
Vandenhoff 1846. Ibid. [to 58]
Apthorp 1858. Ibid.
Zackos 1861. Ibid.
Wiley 1869. Ibid.
Ross 1887. Ibid.
Kirby 1888. Ibid.

Kirkham 1836. The speech before the battle of Agincourt 4.3.19–67.

Hillard 1876. Ibid.

HENRY VIII

Barber 1836. Cardinal Wolsey's farewell to Cromwell 3.2.350–72.
Kirkham 1836. Ibid.
Truman 1844. Ibid.
Bronson 1845. Ibid.
Comstock 1845. Ibid.
Vandenhoff 1846. Ibid.
Sherwood 1855. Ibid.
Zackos 1861. Ibid.
Wiley 1869. Ibid.
Mitchell 1870. Ibid.
Lawrence 1871. Ibid.
Brown 1886. Ibid.
Shoemaker 1876. Ibid.
Hillard 1876. Ibid.

KING JOHN

Barber 1836. Prince Arthur and Hubert 4.1.1–134.
Leavitt 1840. Ibid.
Russell 1841. Ibid.
Hillard 1876. Ibid.

RICHARD III

Porter 1827. Clarence's dream 1.4.1–34.
Barber 1836. Ibid.
Porter 1841. Ibid.
Comstock 1845. Ibid.
Apthorp 1858. Ibid.

Wiley 1869. The soliloquy of Richard III 3.1.1–41.
Kidd 1870. Ibid.
Sanders 1872. Ibid.

Russell 1841. The downfall of Richard III 5.3.177–206.
Mandeville 1851. Ibid.

RICHARD II

Porter 1827. King Richard on the vanity of power 3.2.143–85.
Wiley 1869. 3.2.37–62; 143–185.
Kidd 1870. The king and Scroop 3.2.121–28.

THE MERCHANT OF VENICE

I

Randall 1870. Portia and Nerissa 1.2.1–131. Passim.

Zackos 1861. On Shylock. "How like a fawning publican he looks!" 1.3.41–54.

Russell 1862. Ibid.

Leavitt 1849. Shylock and Antonio 1.3.106–82.
Vandenhoff 1846. Ibid.
Lawrence 1871. Ibid.

IV

a

Leavitt 1840. The trial scene 4.1. Passim.
Leavitt 1848. Ibid.
Vandenhoff 1846. Ibid.
Lawrence 1871. Ibid.
McGuffey 1866. Ibid. [The scene first appeared in the Fourth Reader (1844); it was
    transferred to the Fifth in 1857]
Shoemaker 1876. Ibid.
Graham 1877. Ibid.
Swinton 1886. Ibid.

c

Vandenhoff 1846. Portia's speech of mercy 4.1.180–218.
Randall 1870. Ibid.
Sanders 1872. Ibid.
Graham 1877. Ibid.
Brooks 1883. Ibid.
Brown 1886. Ibid. [With Shylock's reply]
Ross 1887. Ibid.
Southwick 1894. Ibid.

V

Kirkham 1836. On music 5.1.81–88.
Kirkham 1836. Ibid.
Wiley 1869. Ibid.
Brooks 1883. Ibid.

As You Like It

Ross 1887. Duke Senior 2.1.1–17.

Vandenhoff 1846. The seven ages of men 2.7.139–66.
Sanders 1860. Ibid.
Wiley 1869. Ibid.
Lawrence 1871. Ibid.
Shoemaker 1876. Ibid.

Russell 1844. Point of honor 5.4.39 to the end of the scene. Passim.
Atwell 1867. Ibid. The whole scene.

MIDSUMMER NIGHT'S DREAM

Mandeville 1851. The power of love. Theseus's speech 5.1.4–8.
Wiley 1869. Ibid.

Russell 1862. 5.1.219–26.

MUCH ADO ABOUT NOTHING

Apthorp 1858. Leonato's grief at the loss of his daugther 4.1.119–43.

Graham 1877. 4.1.312–23.

LOVE'S LABOUR'S LOST

Wiley 1869. The power of love 4.3.324–65. Passim.

MEASURE FOR MEASURE

Graham 1877. Claudio's speech about dying 3.1.117–31.

ALL'S WELL THAT ENDS WELL

McGuffey 1857. The knave unmasked. 3.6.1 to the end of scene 4.4 [five scenes are
    compressed into three]

THE TEMPEST

Vandenhoff 1846. Prospero's invocation 5.1.32–57.
Russell 1862. Pity and tenderness. Miranda to Ferdinand 3.1.16–91.

OTHER WORKS

Apthorp 1858. "Tis now the dread of the night." *The Rape of Lucrece*. Passim.
Sanders 1872. Beauty. "Oh, how much more doth beauty." *Sonnets* 54.1.

John Milton
(The figure denotes lines.)

PARADISE LOST

I

Rush 1830. Description of Moloch 392–96.
Barber 1836. Satan rallying the fallen angels 315–30.
Comstock 1843. Ibid.
Truman 1844. Satan's address to Belzebub 80–124. Passim.
Russell 1862. Satan rallying the fallen angels 284–330.
Parker 1870. Ibid.
Russell 1890. Ibid.

II

Porter 1827. Moloch's speech 51–105; Satan's encounter with death 670–725.
Rush 1833. Satan's imperial presence in Pandemonium 1–5; Satan's encounter with death 674–76, 689–91, 706–10.
Barber 1836. Satan's encounter with death 670–725.
Porter 1841. Moloch's speech 51–105.
Russell. 1844. Ibid.
Truman 1844. Ibid.
Bronson. 1845. Belial's speech 119–225.
Bronson 1845. Molach's speech 51–105.
Sanders 1860. Satan's encounter with death 670–725.
Sanders 1860. Belial's speech 119–225.
Sanders 1860. Moloch's speech 51–105.
Russell 1862. Ibid.
Russell 1862. Satan's encounter with death 670–725.
Wiley 1869. Ibid.
Parker 1870. Ibid.
Kidd 1870. Belial's speech 119–225.
Brown 1886. Satan's encounter with death 670–725.

III

Mitchell 1870. [Unlocated]

IV

Rush 1833. Satan brought before the fallen angels 925–45; Satan's apology for his flight from Hell 950–53.
Truman 1844. The garden of Eden. [Unlocated]
Bronson 1845. Eve's love for Adam 440–91. Passim.
Parker 1870. Eve's address to the morning 641–58.
Sanders 1872. Satan's address to the sun 33–113. Passim.

V

Barber 1830. Adam and Eve's morning hymn 153–208.
Barber 1836. Ibid.
Russell 1844. Ibid.
Apthorp1858. Ibid.
Russell 1862. Ibid.
Swett 1884. Ibid.

VI

Rush 1833. Abdiel's encounter with Satan 189–93.

VII

Barber 1830. The apostrophe to light 243–60.
Kirkham 1836. Ibid.
Barber 1836. Ibid.

Russell 1841. Ibid.
Comstock 1843. Ibid.

VIII

Dwyer 1856. Adam's description of first finding himself on Earth 250–337. Passim.

X

Porter 1827. Eve lamenting the loss of Paradise 914–36.
Rush 1833. Ibid.
Porter 1841. Ibid.
Comstock 1843. Sin and death 230–63. Passim.

SAMSON AGONISTES

Vandenhoff 1846. The death of Samson 1605–59.
Wiley 1869. [Unlocated.]

COMUS

Russel 1841. 331–[?].
McGuffey 1889. [Unlocated.]

L'ALLEGRO

Russell 1862. Rustic superstitions 100–52. Passim.
Swinton 1886. [Unlocated.]

OTHERS

Barber 1830. To Mr Cyriack Skinner upon his Blindness; Sonnet on his blindness
    ("When I consider how my light is spent").
Mandeville 1851. [Unlocated.]
Sanders 1872. Sonnet on his blindness.
Campbell 1884. Ibid.
Swinton 1886. From *Il Penseroso* and *Areopagitica*. [Unlocated]

Lord Byron

CHILDE HAROLD'S PILGRIMAGE

Porter 1827. Ambition (Napoleon) III 397–405; Alpine scenery III 590–607; The
    battle of Waterloo III 181–89; The dying gladiator IV 1252–69.
Dwyer 1828. II 837–45; The ocean IV 1648–1656; Night II 181–89; Venice IV 1–9;
    Rome IV 1369–7.
Barber 1830. The ocean IV 1585–1656.
Severance 1832. Night II 181–89; The ocean IV 1585–1656. [Reprinted 1847]
The American Orator's 1836. The battle of Waterloo III 181–89.
Barber 1836. The ocean IV 1585–1656; Greece II 693–864. Passim.
Kirkham 1836. Bliss of the future state II 55–72; The ocean IV 1585–93.
Porter 1841. The battle of Waterloo III 181–89.

Comstock 1843. The battle of Waterloo III 181–89; The ocean IV 1585–1611.

Truman 1844. The battle of Waterloo III 181–89; The Coliseum by moonlight IV 1144–52.

Bronson 1845. The battle of Waterloo III 181–89. [Unspecified from IV]

Rice 1846. Alpine scenery III 653–715.

Vandenhoff 1846. The dying gladiator IV 1252–69; Rome IV 1369–77.

Sargent 1853. Alpine scenery III 860–68.

Boyd 1856. The battle of Waterloo III 181–89; The dying gladiator IV 1252–69.

Dwyer 1856. Night II 181–89; Example of alliteration III 397–405.

Sanders 1860. The battle of Waterloo III 181–89.

Zackos 1861. The ocean IV 1603–11.

Russell 1862. Night II 181–252; The ocean IV 1603–11.

Shaw 1869. The battle of Waterloo III 181–89; The dying gladiator IV 1252–60; The ocean IV 1648–56.

Hunt 1870. The dying gladiator IV 1252–60; The ocean IV 1648–56; Lake Geneva [?].

Parker 1870. The dying gladiator IV 1252–69; The dream III 75–81; Ambition (Napoleon) III 396–97; Alpine scenery III 590–98; The ocean IV 1648–56.

Lawrence 1871. The battle of Waterloo III 181–89.

Hillard 1874. Greece II 693–728, 792–835, 855–64; Alpine scenery III 590–98, 796–832, 860–77, 896–904, 914–22.

Cathcart 1874. Greece II 693–701; Rome IV 1369–77; The Ocean IV 1585–93. [The same samples in the edition of 1878]

Underwood 1875. Night II 181–252; Greece II 801–63; Ambition (Napoleon) III 397–405; Alpine scenery III 860–68; Venice IV 1–36; Ocean IV 1594–1656.

Hudson 1882. Greece II 693–701; Alpine scenery III 590–98; The ocean IV 1585–93.

Shaw 1883. Night II 181–89.

Southwick 1883. Greece 693–701; II 10–18.

Murdoch 1883. The ocean IV 1585–93.

Brooks 1883. The battle of Waterloo III 181–89.

Swett 1884. The ocean IV 1585–93; The battle of Waterloo III 181–89.

Campbell 1884. The battle of Waterloo III 181–89; Drachenfels III 496–505.

Lippincott 1884. [Unlocated]

Brown 1886. The ocean IV 1594–1611.

Kellogg 1886. An August evening in Italy IV 235–261; Greece II 693–701.

Ross 1887. 6 unspecified extracts.

Murray 1888. III 217–20.

Morgan 1889. I 109–117, 387–468; The battle of Waterloo III 181–252; Alpine scenery 635–43, 653–715; IV 1–234; 694–882; The dying gladiator IV 1252–69; The Ocean IV 1567–1656.

Russell 1890. The battle of Waterloo III 181–89.

Pancost 1894. The Ocean IV 1585–1656.

Raub 1899. The Ocean IV 1585–1674.

Blaisdell 1899. Good Night [unlocated]; Lake Leman III 797–805; The battle of Waterloo III 181–89; Gibbon and Voltaire III 977–1003; Venice IV 1–9; A woman's grave IV 883–91; Time IV 1162–70; The dying gladiator IV 1251–69; The Ocean IV 1648–56.

Summary of the main usage of *Childe Harold's Pilgrimage*
(The figures after "in" indicate end years of publication; see the list above.)

1. The Ocean. In 28, 30, 32, 36, 36, 43, 61, 62, 69, 70, 70, 74, 82, 83, 84, 89, 89, 94, 99, 99.

2. The battle of Waterloo. In 27, 36, 41, 43, 44, 45, 56, 60, 69, 71, 83, 84, 84, 89, 90, 99.
3. The dying gladiator. In 27, 46, 56, 69, 70, 70, 89, 99.
4. Alpine scenery. In 27, 46, 53, 70, 74, 75, 82, 89.
5. Night. In 28, 32, 56, 62, 75, 83, 89.
6. Greece. In 36, 74, 74, 75, 82, 83, 86.
7. Ambition. In 27, 70, 75.
8. Venice. In 28, 75, 99.
9. Rome. In 28, 46, 74.

THE CORSAIR

Shaw 1883. I 91–96.

Sargent 1853. Remorse II 331–40.
Shaw 1869. Ibid.
Shaw 1883. Ibid.
Ross 1887. Ibid.
Morgan 1889. Ibid.

Dwyer 1828. III 555–66.
Dwyer 1856. Ibid.

THE SIEGE OF CORINTH. A POEM

Parker 1870. Night at Corinth 197–238.
McGuffey 1889. Ibid.

THE PRISONER OF CHILLON. A FABLE

Shaw 1869. 107–25.
Sanders 1872. [Unlocated]
Shaw 1883. 107–25.
Swinton 1886. Whole.
Blaisdell 1899. 324–37.

MANFRED. A DRAMATIC POEM

Morgan 1889. 1.1. passim.

The American Orator's Own Book 1836. 1.2.1–56.
Shaw 1869. Ibid.
Parker 1870. Pastoral music 1.2.47–56.
Shaw 1883. 1.2.7–56.
Raub 1889. Ibid.

Parker 1870. 3.4.1–44.
Morgan 1889. Ibid.

MARINO FALIERO. DODGE OF VENICE. AN HISTORICAL TRAGEDY IN FIVE ACTS

Dwyer 1828. 4.1. passim.
Russell 1844. 4.1.1–111.

Vandenhoff 1846. Ibid.
Russell 1862. 4.1.68–85.
Westlake 1876. Ibid.

MAZEPPA. A POEM

Brown 1886. 373–463 passim.
Morgan 1889. 358–463.

THE GIAOUR. A FRAGMENT OF A TURKISH TALE

Dwyer 1828. 7–67.
Barber 1836. Ibid.
Dwyer 1856. Ibid.
Shaw 1869. Ibid.
Wiley 1869. Ibid.
Morgan 1880. Ibid.

Porter 1827. 68–141.
Kirkham 1836. Ibid.
Barber 1836. Ibid.
Vandenhoff 1846. 103–41.
Sanders 1859. 68–102.
Sanders 1860. Ibid.
Russell 1862. Ibid.
Shaw 1869. 103–41.
Parker 1870. 68–102.
Campell 1884. Ibid.
Morgan 1889. Ibid.

Shaw 1869. 200–72.

THE BRIDE OF ABYDOS

Vandenhoff 1846. 1–19.
Shaw 1860. Ibid.
Shaw 1869. Ibid.
Shaw 1883. Ibid.
Morgan 1889. Ibid.

DON JUAN

Kirkham 1836. Fame. I 1737–52.
Mandeville 1851. The shipwreck I 401–24.
Cathcart 1874. Ibid.

Morgan 1889. II 87–96; III 86–88.

Sargent 1853. [Unlocated]
Westlake 1876. [Unlocated]
Kellogg 1886. [Unlocated]

CAIN

Welles 1822. 3.1.1–69.

ODE TO NAPOLEON BUONAPARTE

Southwick 1883. 116–25.

Emerson 1835. "The Destruction of Semnacherib."
Kirkham 1836. Ibid.
Comstock 1843. Ibid.
Bronson 1845. Ibid.
Sherwood 1855. Ibid.
Sanders 1860. Ibid.
Hunt 1870. Ibid.
Southwick 1883. Ibid.
Kellogg 1886. Ibid.
Morgan 1889. Ibid.
Blaisdell 1899. Ibid.

Porter 1827. "Darkness."
Emerson 1835. Ibid.
Kirkham 1836. Ibid.
Comstock 1843. Ibid.
Massey 1856. Ibid.
Wiley 1869. Ibid.
Mitchell 1870. Ibid.
Parker 1870. Ibid.
Hunt 1870. Ibid.
Brown 1886. Ibid.
Morgan 1889. Ibid.

Morgan 1889. "Vision of Belshazzar."
Blaisdell 1899. Ibid.

Kellogg 1886. "Napoleon's Farewell."

Sir Walter Scott

THE LADY OF THE LAKE
(The figure denotes the number of the stanza.)

I

Dwyer 1828. Fitz-James and the Lady of the Lake 14–15, 16–27.
Dwyer 1856. Ibid. 14–27.
Shaw 1869. Ibid. 17–19.
Brooks 1883. 31 ff.

II

Russell 1844. 27–32, 34–35.
Russell 1862. Ibid.

III

Sargent 1853. Coronach 16.
Parker 1870. Ibid.

Campbell 1884. The Highland gathering 13–25, 18–24.
Kirby 1888. 13–24.

IV

Porter 1827. Fitz James and Roderick Dhu 30–31.
Porter 1841. Ibid.
Dwyer 1856. Quarrel between Roderick Dhu and Fitz-James 29. From "The shades
    of eve come slowly down" to "The praise that Faith and Valour give" (in V 17).
Wiley 1869. 4–5, 30–31.
Lawrence 1871. FitzJames and Rhoderick Dhu 30–31.
Monroe 1871. Ibid.

V

Swett 1884. The death struggle 16–17.
Brown 1886. Ibid.

VI

Hunt 1870. The guard-room 1–4; Soldier's song 5; Battle of Beal' an Duine 15–21.
Shoemaker 1876. Battle of Beal' an Duine.
Pancost 1894. Ibid.
Blaisdell 1899. 23 ff.

UNSPECIFIED

Sanders 1872.
Cobb 1873. [Includes plays that are slightly revised extracts from the poem]
Southwick 1883.

MARMION

I

Shaw 1869. Pitt and Fox; from the Introduction to the Canto.
Murray 1888. How to read poetry. Four lines from the Introduction to the Canto.
McGuffey 1889. Introduction to the Canto.

V

Comstock 1843. Lochinvar.
Bronson 1845. Ibid.
Vandenhoff 1846. Lady Heron's Song.
Sargent 1853. Lochinvar.
Massey 1856. Ibid.

Bailey 1865. Ibid.
Parker 1870. Ibid.
Cathcart 1874. Ibid.
Underwood. 1874. Ibid.
Shoemaker 1876. Ibid.
Raymond 1880. Ibid.
Campbell 1884. Ibid.
Kirby 1888. Ibid.
Raub 1889. Ibid.
McGuffey 1889. Ibid.
Shoemaker 1895. Ibid.
Blaisdell 1899. Ibid.

VI

a

Dwyer 1828. Marmion taking leave of Douglas 13–15.
Sherwood 1855. Ibid.
Wiley 1869. Ibid.
Shaw 1869. Ibid.
Monroe 1871. Ibid.
Raymond 1880. Ibid.
Brooks 1883. Ibid.
Southwick 1894. Ibid.
Shoemaker 1895. Ibid.

b

Porter 1841. The battle of Flodden Field and the death of Marmion; punishment of
    the wife of MacGregor 30 ff.
Sherwood 1855. Ibid.
Sanders 1860. Ibid.
Wiley 1869. Ibid.
Shaw 1869. Ibid.
Hillard 1876. 25–28; The battle of Flodden Field (till the end of the poem).
McGuffey 1879. The battle of Flodden Field. [Two pieces have been moulded into
    one: from 27, "Yet still-mid the foes," to 32; last lines beginning "The war"]
Southwick 1883. The battle of Flodden Field and the death of Marmion.

THE LAY OF THE LAST MINSTREL

II

Underwood 1874. Melrose Abbey 1–11.
Shaw 1869. Ibid.

III

Dwyer 1856. Love song. Beginning of the Canto.

VI

Vandenhoff 1846. Love of country. "Breathes there a man." 16 lines.
Sherwood 1855. Ibid.
Sanders 1859. Ibid.
Sanders 1860. Ibid.
Wiley 1869. Ibid.
Shaw 1869. Ibid.
Parker 1870. Ibid.
Hillard 1871. Ibid.
Cathcart 1874. Ibid.
Campbell 1884. Ibid.
Raub 1889. Ibid.

UNSPECIFIED

Lippincott 1884.
Blaisdell 1899.

THE LORD OF THE ISLES

Russell 1844. Death of De Argentine. "Already scatter'd o'er the plain . . . Torch never gleamed, nor mass was said" VI 31–34; another scene from II 6, starting "Brother of Lorn" and ending 32 "Unmoor, unmoor!" [The passage has been partly dramatized (cut and curtailed) for exhibition occasions]
Russell 1862. From II 15 "Talk not to me."
Swett 1894. [Unlocated]

MISCELLANEOUS PIECES

Sanders 1860. "Nora's vow."
Zackos 1861. "Pibroch of Donuil Dhu."
Underwood 1875. Ibid.

IVANHOE
(The figure denotes chapters.)

Barber. 1836. The description of a siege. Ivanhoe and Rebecca 29. "Following with wonderful promptitude of Ivanhoe."
Sargent 1853. The song of Rebecca.
McGuffey 1857. The description of a siege.
Parker 1870. Ibid.
Randall 1870. Ibid.
Underwood 1875. The song of Rebecca; the description of a siege.
Hillard 1876. The description of a siege.
Shaw 1883. Ibid.

Barber. 1836. A tournament 8. "The music also of the challenge."
McGuffey 1857. Ibid.

Blaisdell 1888. [Unlocated]

ROB ROY

Barber 1836. The reply of Rob Roy MacGregor to Osballistone; the death of Morris, the spy 31. "It was under the burning influence of revenge that the wife of Macgregor."
Russell 1862. Helen McGregor to the spy Morris; the death of Morris.
Randall 1870. Ibid.
Brown, 1886. Ibid.
Russell 1890. Ibid.

THE HEART OF MIDLOTHIAN

Underwood 1875. The visit of Jeanie Deans to the Queen 37.
Blaisdell 1899. Ibid.

Shaw 1883. The description of Richmond.

Blaisdell 1888. The character of Effie Deans.

OLD MORTALITY

The American Orator's 1836. The speech of Macbriar to the Scotch insurgents. "Your garments are dyed" 18.
Sanders 1860. Ibid.
Kidd 1870. Ibid.

Blaisdell 1888. [Unlocated]

McGuffey 1889. The battle of Bothwell Bridge 16.

ANTIQUARY

Barber. 1836. The funeral of Steenie Mucklebackit 31.
Hudson 1882. Ibid.

Shaw 1869. A sunset and the approach of a storm 7.
Blaisdell 1899. Ibid.

GUY MANNERING

Kellogg 1886. Abel Sampson 2.

THE ABBOT

Massey 1856. Mary Queen of Scots; a play by H. G. Bell. [Doubtful whether the play is derived from Scott]

Blaisdell 1888. [Unlocated]

THE MONASTERY

Lippincott 1884. [Unlocated]
Pancost 1894. A border ballad. [Unlocated]

REDGAUNTLET

Barber 1836. Redgauntlet's address to his nephew 19.

KENILWORTH

Blaisdell 1888. The description of the apartments of Amy, Countess of Leicester.

WAVERLEY

Barber 1836. The post-office in Fairport; the interview between Waverly and Fergus Mac-Ivor at Carslile, previous to the execution of Fergus and Evan Dhu 69.

Charles Dickens
(The figure denotes the chapter.)

THE PICKWICK PAPERS

Parker 1870. Pickwick's apartment and his hiring of Wellek 12.

Atwell 1867. Pickwick's romantic adventure with a middle-aged lady in yellow curl-papers 22. [Often called "Mr. Pickwick's Dilemma"]
Wiley 1869. Ibid.
Parker 1870. Ibid.
Hunt 1870. Ibid.
Sanders 1872. From 6 and 12.

Randall 1870. Wardle's story. Gabriel Grub 29.

Campbell 1884. Mr. Winkle puts on the skates 30.

Wiley 1869. Sam Weller's Valentine 33.
Brooks. 1883. Ibid.

Sanders 1860. Speeches of Buzfuz in the case of Bardels vs Pickwick 34.
Wiley 1869. Weller as witness.
Sanders 1872. Ibid.
Kellogg 1886. Ibid.

Cathcart 1874. [Unlocated]

THE OLD CURIOSITY SHOP

McGuffey 1857. The teacher and the sick scholar 25.
McGuffey 1857. The death of Little Nell 71 and 72. [The two chapters have been combined]
Randall 1870. The death of Little Nell.
Mitchell 1870. Ibid.
Hunt 1870. Ibid.
Randall 1870. Ibid.

Hunt 1870. Ibid.
Lawrence 1871. Ibid.
Hillard 1871. Little Nell's Garden 54.
Shoemaker 1876. The death of Little Nell.
Hillard 1876. Ibid.
Brooks, 1883. Ibid.
Lippincott 1884. Ibid.

DOMBEY AND SON

Olney 1843. The death of Paul Dombey 16.
Kidd 1870. Ibid.
Monroe 1871. Ibid.
Hillard 1871. Ibid.
Lawrence 1871. Ibid.
Cathcart 1874. Ibid.
Brooks 1883. Ibid.
Lippincott 1884. Ibid.
Raub 1889. Ibid.

BLEAK HOUSE

Mitchell 1870. Jo's death 47.
Shoemaker 1876. Ibid.
Brooks 1883. Ibid.

A CHRISTMAS CAROL

Randall 1870. Scrooge and Marley.
Underwood 1875. Ibid.
Shoemaker 1876. Ibid.
Brooks 1883. Ibid.
Swett 1884. Ibid.
Swinton 1886. Ibid.
Southwick 1894. Ibid.

NICHOLAS NICKLEBY

Wiley 1869. Squeers's methods 8.
McGuffey 1879. Ibid.
Kidd 1870. The duel. Captain Adams and Sir Mulberry Hawk and Lord Frederick
    Verisopht 50.
Lippincott 1884. Tim Linkinwater 35.

THE CRICKET ON THE HEARTH

Monroe 1871. From the beginning of Chirp the First. Abridged. Lines 243 ff.
Brooks 1883. Lines 346 ff.
Campbell 1884. Lines 193–97.

DAVID COPPERFIELD

Shoemaker 1876. The Child-Wife. Dora Spenlow falls in love with David Copperfield 26.

Campbell 1884. The storm and the wreck 55.

McGuffey 1889. David makes himself known to his aunt and runs away 12; Miss
    Betsy 12–13.

MARTIN CHUZZLEWIT

Russell 1844. Unsuccessful attempt to raise the wind 4.
Kirby 1888. Tom Pinch's journey to London 36.

BARNABY RUDGE

Kirby 1888. The cheerful locksmith [Gabriel Varden] 41.

AMERICAN NOTES

Cathcart 1874. [Unlocated]

UNLOCATED

Monroe 1871. An object lesson.
Cathcart 1871. The captain's song.
Brooks. 1883. Ibid.
Hillard 1871. A child's dream of a star.
Brooks 1883. Ibid.

S. T. Coleridge

Emerson 1838. "Ode To Tranquillity."
Russell 1844. "Sonnet to an Aged Beggar"; "Sonnet to Lafayette in the Dungeon
    of Olnetz."
Sargent 1853. "Love, Hope, and Patience in Education."
Parker 1870. "Love" ("All thoughts, all passions, all delights"); from "Sonnet to
    Lafayette in the Dungeon of Olnetz" 20–30.
Cathcart 1871. "The Quarrel."
Sanders 1872. "An Ode to the Rain"; "Coleridge on Himself."
Swinton 1886. "Love"; a passage from "Christabel."

Porter 1827."Hymn before Sun-rise, in the Vale of Chamouni."
Truman 1844. Ibid.
Sherwood 1855. Ibid.
Russell 1862. Ibid.
Lawrence 1871. Ibid.
Sanders 1872. Ibid.
Hillard 1876. Ibid.
Raymond 1880. Ibid.
Southwick 1884. Ibid.
Swett 1884. Ibid.
Swinton 1886. Ibid.
Russell 1890. Ibid.

Raub 1889. Ibid.
Southwick 1894. Ibid.

William Wordsworth

· Barber 1830. "Lucy"; "Three years she grew in sun and shower."
Severance 1832. From "Education."
Truman 1844. "Trust in God" from Book First, *The Excursion.*
Bronson 1845. A petit maitre would. Beauty and Air.
Sargent 1853. "Friendship"; "Character of the Happy Warrior."
Apthrop 1858. "The old Man's Song."
Mitchell 1870. From "Intimations of Immortality."
Sanders 1872 From "Intimations of Immortality"; "Milton."
Kirby 1888. "To the Cuckoo."
McGuffey 1889. From *The Excursion.*

Percy Bysshe Shelley

Bronson 1845. [Unlocated]
Claggett 1845. [Unlocated]
Bailey 1865. *To a Skylark.*
Mitchell 1870. Ibid.
Swinton 1886. Ibid.

Alfred Tennyson

Atwell 1867. "The Charge of the Light Brigade."
Wiley 1869. Ibid.
Randall 1870. Ibid.
Cathcart 1871. Ibid.
Lawrence 1871. Ibid.
Brooks 1883. Ibid.
Campbell 1884. Ibid.
Brooks 1886. Ibid.
Raymond 1880. Ibid.
Ross 1887. Ibid.
Southwick 1894. Ibid.

Mitchell 1870. "Bugle Song."
Randall 1870. Ibid.
Cathcart 1871. Ibid.
Lawrence 1871. Ibid.
Raymond 1880. Ibid.
Campbell 1884. Ibid.
Brown 1886. Ibid.

Mitchell 1870. "Ring out, wild bells, o the wild sky." From *In Memoriam. A. H. H.*
Lawrence 1871. Ibid.
Sanders 1872. Ibid.

Brooks 1883. Ibid.
Swett 1884. Ibid.
Brown. 1886. Ibid.

Parker 1870. "Lady Clare."
Brooks 1883. Ibid.
Shoemaker 1895. Ibid.

Cathcart 1871. "Lady Clara Vere de Vere."
Brooks 1883. Ibid.

Leavitt 1849. "The Death of the Old Year."
Randall 1870. Ibid.
Mitchell 1870. Ibid.

Mitchell 1870. "Sweet and Low." From *The Princess.*
Cathcart 1871. Ibid.
Soutwick 1894. Ibid.

Randall 1870. "Break, Break, Break."
Hillard 1871. Ibid.
Brown 1886. Ibid.

Others

Kidd 1870. "The Captain."
Mitchell 1870. "Godiva."
Parker 1870. "Morte d'Arthur."
Randall 1870. "Dora," "The Grandmother."
Cathcart 1871. "Enoch Arden," "The Brook."
Lawrence 1871. "The May Queen."
Sanders 1872. "The Lord of Burleigh."
Brooks 1883. "Edward Gray," ["Milkmaid's Song"], ["Woman's Cause"].

E. B. Browning

Parker 1870. "The Cry of the Human."
Randall 1870. "Mother and Poet"; "The Dead Pan"; "The Romance of the Swan's Nest."
Mitchell 1870. From "The Drama of Exile"; "The Cry of the Children" [whole]; an extract from "Rhapsody of Life's Program"; "Rhyme of the Duchess May."
Hillard 1876. "The Sleep."
Brooks 1883. "Rhyme of the Duchess May"; "The Sleep."
Russell 1890. "Rhyme of the Duchess May."

Robert Browning

Parker 1870. "How They Brought the Good News from Ghent to Aix."
Raymond 1880. Ibid.
Shoemaker 1895. Ibid.

Kirby 1888. "Hervé Riel."
Southwick 1894. Ibid.
Randall 1870. "The Pied Piper of Hamelin. No. III."
Brooks 1883. "Evelyn Hope."
McGuffey 1889. "The Italian in England."

Appendix 2

"Jeanie Deans; or, The Heart of Midlothian"[1]
Dion Boucicault's adaptation of Walter Scott's
The Heart of Midlothian

COMMENTARY

Dion Boucicault obviously had different motives for producing this play. He wanted to tell a sentimental story about the Calvinistic family virtues of loyalty and love and the accompanying corrrupting forces of betrayal and guilt; he sought to produce a play that would entertain within the framework of contemporary light melodrama, as well as perhaps disturb the very assumptions that inscribed this genre; he wanted to employ the Scottish dialect and history for their distancing and displacing effects (the events that form the backbone of Scott's novel, the Porteous Riots, took place in 1736 and Scott wrote the novel eight decades later). Thus Boucicault's "Jeanie Deans" oscillates between the unrelenting paternal rhetoric of drama centering on Davie Deans and the melodramatic sections of abduction, hiding, and escape that followed on Effie Deans's waywardness (having given birth to an illegitmate child). The play ends with family sanctity polluted and Effie sent to prison accused of infanticide. Boucicault's sympathies remain, however, with the female worlds of the two sisters—Effie, bonny and spoilt, and Jeanie, serious and compassionate. (He antipated of course that every theatergoer would know that Effie was innocent of having killed her child.) This is also corraborated by the sequel "The Trial of Effie Deans" (of which we have no text) that normally was produced as an afterpiece projecting in a series of costume tableaux the strident antitheses of the low and the high, the powerless and the powerful, family and court—themes that impregnate the main play. His Midlothian play projects, then, women's domestic distress and meditates on it as an outcome of the paternalism connected with the church and the law. One may say that it was an early American feminist play, a comment on its own time.

The playbill for its first night introduced it as "New Scottish Drama" and announced that "The Trial Scene of Effie Deans" will be "depicted" in "all possible fidelity, the forms and formalities, costumes and incidents of the Court of Justiciars, under George the Second."[2] It moved early up from the Winter Garden to Laura Keene's, where it successfully ran to 12 March 1860; in fact for fifty-six consecutive nights. It was then produced by Barnum's American Museum in April and May, and starting in July in Boston where it was on and off the boards for an entire year; it was also a hit in New Orleans.[3] About Laura Keene as Effie it was said that she was "a *genre* picture, so small, *gentil,* pretty, acceptable" and Agnes Robertson as Jeanie was also praised.[4]

The play was indeed so successful that, if you like, it itself became the object of adaptation, or rather plagiarism. According to Boucicault, Jean Davenport Lander visited Laura Keene's Theatre during its run there in the company of a secretary who took down his piece, word by word, and produced it under her name at theaters in New York and Philadelphia. In a letter to a Philadelphia newspaper, Boucicault explains that he has changed the plot by beginning in the end, by the introduction of the arrest of Effie in her father's house, by the special texture of the trial scene, and so on. He defended *his* art as a dramatist, while accusing Davenport of having committed an infringement of his copyright. "She has taken characters, incidents, scenes and dialogue which are not in Sir Walter Scott's novel and which are in my play. She has taken my language *verbatim*. I *have* improved on Scott by introducing dialogue of my own and Miss Davenport has recognized the improvement by taking my dialogue. . . . In my play 'Jeanie Deans' there is not 150 lines of Sir Walter Scott's; I have altered the plot" (his emphases).[5] He was right; it is a very Boucicault play.

Jeanie Deans; or, The Heart of Midlothian a Drama in Three Acts

by Dion Boucicault

[The play was first performed at Laura Keene's Theatre on 9 January 1860 with the following cast (those additional characters indicated by an asterisk performed—with

Jeanie and Effie—the tableau "The Trial of Effie Deans" that normally was produced as an afterpiece)]:

David Dean [a dairy farmer at St Leonard's Craigs]	Mr. C. Fisher
Geordie Robertson [son of Edmund Staunton, Rector]	Mr. F. Daly
*Mr. Duke of Argyle	Mr. M. Smith
Fairbrother [counsel for Effie]	Mr. D. Boucicault
Ratcliffe [a subordinate of Sharpitlaw]	Mr. I. G. Burnett
The *Laird of Dumbiedikes* [Jeanie's admirer]	Mr. D. Leeson
[Reuben Butler] [a schoolmaster, Jeanie's lover]	
Sharpitlaw [a constable]	Mr. C. Wheatleigh
Judge	
Crier	
Two Officers	

The Queen Caroline (wife of George 2nd)	
Jeanie Deans [daughter of Davie Deans]	Mrs. Agnes Robertson
Effie Deans [dauhter of Davie Deans]	Mrs. Laura Keene
Madge Wildfire [daughter of Mag]	Mrs. M. Macarthy
[Meg Murdockson] [Geordie's nurse]	

Act I

McLeonard's Crags. The [outside] of Davie Deans's cottage. Edinburgh in the distance. [Music.] Enter Geordie Robertson. He glances hastily round and then hides himself in the shed. Enter Ratcliffe and the two officers. They search round [and] look in at window [. . .]. Ratcliffe knocks [and] then waves the officers away. They retire behind house. Enter Davie Deans from the cottage.

Davie: Well Sirs, what's yer [wull]?

Ratcliffe: A criminal has escaped from his escort. We are in pursuit of him.

Davie: Why d'ye seek him in my house? Is the roof of Davie Deans a den for thieves? Gang yer gate, man!

Ratcliffe: It would na be the first time that Geordie Robertson sought shelter here in McLeonard's Crags.

Effie utters a cry within house.

Davie: Is Effie's voice. *[Over to door.]* Effie! lass! Effie!

Ratcliffe: [aside] Those fellows of mine have been trying the back door.

Enter Effie.

Effie: Father, two rough looking men are searching the house.

Reenter the two officers by the cottage door.

Davie: By what authority do ye come here? A Scot's house is a Scot's castle and nae man but the King himsel shall pass my lintel, unless he show me Royal Seal and Warrant.

Ratcliffe: Dinna fash yersel, Davie, for maybe I shall soon cross your door with a warrant ye little dream of now. That's yer daughter Effie, [. . .] the Lily of McLeonard's as she's called by the bullies of the Canongate.

Davie: How came my daughter's name in sic light mouths?

Ratcliffe: [going] Ask Geordie Robertson!

Davie: Geordie Robertson. The smuggler, the doomed fellow. What have I to do wi sic as he?

Ratcliffe: Ask your lassie there!

[Music.] Exeunt Ratcliffe and officers.

Davie: Effie, ye tremble. What know ye of this rakehell Robertson?

Effie: Eh, father. It's na fault o'mine. If as I trip along the grassmarket on down the Canougaht the folk say there gangs Effie Deans, the Lily of McLeonard's, the blithest lassie between the Firth and the [blyve, Clyde].

Davie: Hand yer tongue ye limmer! *[lights are being gradually lowered for change of scene.]* The devil invented looking glasses to make idolatry perpetual. For while there's a woman in the world, she'll say her prayers night and morning to a brazen image she sees in her mirror. To work. The day is closing. See yonder comes Jeanie driving the cows home to the byre. Help her to herd them.

    Reenter cottage. [Music.]

Effie: He is gone! How my heart beats!

    Reenter Geordie.

Geordie: Hist, Shot! Effie!

Effie: Geordie! *[Runs to him.]*

Geordie: Escaped, but the lawdogs are at my heels. I must remain concealed here till dark. Then I can gain the Salisbury Crags. Our schooner lies over at Kirkaldie. She can drop over across to Leith in the morning, and tomorrow night I'll creep on board; then hey for the coast of France.

Effie: What can I do to aid you?

Geordie: Damme, you're a brave girl, Effie.

Effie: No, Geordie, I am only desparate. I am yours and I will follow you to the world's end.

Geordie: There's no need to go so far, meet me tonight at Muschat's Cairn in the Salisbury Crags. There I'll give you a letter which must be conveyed tonight across the Firth. Can you find a messenger?

Effie: If not, I'll take it myself.

Geordie: Alone!

Effie: Alas! I have nothing to fear now. Nothing except my father and discovery of our love [. . .]. Nothing to dread, but that hour when my sister will look on me with shame and I shall be cast forth from yonder door.

Geordie: That shall never be! Let us fly together!

Effie: And our child, Geordie, our wee bairn, you turn from her! Oh Geordie, when I sleep I hear it cry. I feel it here upon my breast, a weight, a dead weight.

Geordie: Hush! girl! That woman Meg Murdockson and her mad daughter Madge have stolen the child.

Effie: But it lives, Geordie, it lives! They would not harm it!

Geordie: If I could get the old hag's wizzen in my five fingers I'd tell ye that . . .

    Jeanie sings without.

Effie: Hark! Tis my sister Jeanie's voice. Conceal yourself quick.

Geordie: We collect tonight at Muschat's Cairn.

    [Music.] He reenters the shed. Enter Jeanie Deans, with pails of milk.

Jeanie: Hey! Spot! hoo! Fannie, the kine are peering over the byre after me, as if I'd stole their milk. Effie, lassie, wha was that parted wi ye now?

Effie: [aside] She saw him. *[aloud]* Naebody.

Jeanie: Naebody!

Effie: If ye ask me no questions I'll tell yer no lies. I never ask what keeps the Laird of Dumbiedikes glowering round here like a waw cat.

Jeanie: He's our Laird and landlord and comes to see our father.

Effie: And Dominie Butler, the young Curate. Does he come to see our father too? Through the kirkyard I met with the Laird. The silly poor boy he served me na harm, but just ere twas dark I met with the clerk. Ha! ha! Eh Jeanie! What's the matter, lass! I was only joking.

Jeanie: Oh, Effie, if ye will learn fule sangs ye might make a kinder use of them.

Effie: [embracing her] So I ought. Oh have I hurt ye? I wish my tongue blistered ere I had vexed ye, Jeanie.

Jeanie: Never mind that, Effie. I canna be muckle vexed wi anything ye say to me but, oh, my sister, dinna sorrow our poor father.

Effie: I will not, I will not.

Jeanie: He loves ye mair than he likes to show. His auld heart is laid up in ye. For all the beauty our mother had she gave ye. Oh Effie! I canna please him as you can. But I fear me I can love him mair.

Effie: [aside] And tonight I leave my home. Tomorrow the auld man will greet for his bairn, his bit lassie. *[aloud]* Oh. Jeanie! You are strong of heart and can overcome temptation. When we were children, you could pray and ye meant it, while on my knees I was thinkin of the fields of flowers, the games and toys. And now when I am weak I sink. I have nothing to cling to to hold me upright.

Jeanie: Cling to yer home, Effie! If temptation is before yer look back and stand fast by the days of auld lang syne. Let every briar and every twig round here twine itself round your heart. *[Jeanie sings to the air "John Anderson, my Joe": "Around the cottais fire/In winter where twas cauld . . ."]*

Effie: Oh, Jeanie, Jeanie, you break my heart.

Jeanie: If there's anything heavy in it, let it break out. Wash it clean with tears, Effie. Ye'll be brighter like the flower after the rain. Tell me, sister!

Effie: No! I canna. I canna! I have made my bed and I must lie on it. These tears are not for myself, Jeanie dear, but for my father and for you. Oh, if I could bear all the sorrow, all the shame. But I canna, and that's what makes it bitter. Nae, do not ask me more. The truth will out soon enough. *[The lights very gradually out.]*

[Music.]Exit into cottage.

Jeanie: The lass has gotten married heels owre gowdie to some fletherin neer-do-well and dare not say it out. Yet she wears her blue snood round her hair as if she war a lassie still. *[Enter Reuben Butler.]* Hey Reuben, is that you?

Reuben: Am I not welcome, Jeanie?

Jeanie: And do you doubt it?

Reuben: I passed the Laird of Dumbiedikes on the Dalkeith road. His pony's head was turned this way.

Jeanie: Devil take the Laird and spare the pony! *[taking up milkpails]*

Reuben: Jeanie!

Jeanie: I canna help it. Reuben, that gowky Lair will come the morn and set watching me all day, without a word! The laddie's fou! Then he'll draw a sigh that'll come up like a bucket and make the doors slap and the windows shake.

Reuben: But your father sees his love and favors his suit. I am only a poor curate. He is a rich laird.

Jeanie: Dye think it's for his siller that I bear wi' him! Na, na, I'd gie him his ways lang ago if he brought nout but his lands and his goud to shew me.

Reuben: I can see nothing else to recommend him.

Jeanie: I can see an honest heart. Reuben fulish maybe, but soft, but I would na mair turn away a heart from my love than I would turn a beggar from my door. But I'd thank them baith for taken comfort from my hands. Coom in, it's ower dark for us to be abroad.

Reuben: Jeanie, say a word. Will you marry me?

Jeanie: You are a curate Reuben and your calling is the care of souls. I'm afraid if I marry you I shall be robbin the parish.

Exeunt. [Music. Footlights are kept to blue.]

Act 2

Salisbury Crags. Night. Enter Ratcliffe.

Ratcliffe: Where is Sharpitlaw! *[a whistle is heard without]* That's the signal. *[he whistles]*

Enter Sharpitlaw.

Sharpitlaw: Ratcliffe, is that you?

Ratcliffe: It's so dark I can scarce tell.

Sharpitlaw: What news of young Robertson?

Ratcliffe: Never fear, he won't leave the neighborhood of McLeonard's while the Lily is there. I never knew a trap baited with a woman fail in catching one of his kind.

Sharpitlaw: Here is the warrant for the arrest of Effie Deans.

Ratcliffe: We must hold that off until we can nab them both in the same net. We can always make sure of her.

Sharpitlaw: Hark!

Madge: [Outside. She sings.] "Hey for Cavalier, ho for Cavaliers, Rub a dub, rub a dub."

Sharpitlaw: What's that?

Ratcliffe: Madge Wildfire, a mad creature who followed us from the city. We could not shake her off.

Enter Madge.

Madge: Good Sir, gentles. Ye are up in the mornin airly. *[She sings.]*

"Up in the mornin early, / I'd rather gang [. . .] / Than be up in the mornin early."

Sharpitlaw: Hold yer skirling! Devil take the wench! She'll yap all round us like a cocker spaniel and warn off the game. Come!

Ratcliffe: Stay! Madge my beauty, what d'ye call the rocks?

Madge: It's Muschat's Cairn by daylight.

Ratcliffe: We'll find our game higher up in this cover. Look to your pistols.

Exeunt. Enter Meg Murdockson.

Meg: Have they gone?

Madge: Ay. And now the moon will come out. She was over modest before folks.

Meg: Shut your fool's mouth and clear your brains, ye limmer, for there's work to do tonight.

Madge: Work mother! I'm a lady. I do no work. I'm George Staunton's wife, that is I would ha' been if he'd married me.

Meg: Are ye so mad that even revenge can't rouse ye? Listen, tonight Geordie will take ship and return to his home.

Madge: She best be stout though. For the lawyers are after him and she shew them where he lies and they'll catch him and keep him till I want him.

Meg: Ye fool, they would twist his neck. Harkye, d'ye mind the mother o' Geordie's bairn?

Madge: Ay Madge, Madge Murdockson.

Meg: No child, you were his first victim. I mean his last. The girl that he brought to us, the golden haired thing, Effie Deans.

Madge: Ae, poor lassie, she that greeted and sobbed for her little one that we took awa'.

Meg: She's guilty of concealment and that by Scottish law is death. The hangman's rope is after her like a serpent, I tell ye, and I've done it—Madge—I've moved her from your road. It's brewing an' doing. Wait a wil and then ye'll see. Geordie shall escape, but ere I let him pass he shall marry you Madge as he swore to do. He has to choose between you and the gibbet.

Madge: Oh that's brave and shall we be married in a jail or in a church mother.

Meg: Go, follow those men and when they come near their cairn, skirl a snatch o'song to warn the laddie they are near.

Madge: Oh this is rare! Huntin' a lawyer in the gloamin'.

Exit. [Music.]

Meg: Now I'll rouse Geordie from his den and—Ho!—what's comin' yonder like a wraith in the mist? It is a woman.

She retires behind a rock. Enter Effie.

Effie: Here is the Cairn. Hist Geordie! I thought I saw a figure moving on this spot.

Meg: [looking out] Effie!

Effie: Eh? *[Meg disappears.]* I heard my name.

Geordie: Effie. *[Enters.]*

Effie: Quick dear. I have run all the way here. How my heart beats.

Geordie: Here is the letter. *[Gives her a paper.]*

Effie: When all are asleep tonight, I'll slip from my window, an hour will take me to Leith. There Sandie McPherson will cary me in his boat across to Kirkaldie . I can be back an hour before daylight and neer be missed.

Geordie: No Effie, remain on board the schooner until I join you there.

Effie: Oh, Geordie, must I leave my home to night—for ever?

Geordie: Nonsense, ye little fool! You can write from France to your father, say you are my wife—repentance, tears, forgiveness—and all that sort of thing. Other scenes will obliterate these rude crags and other loves replace the memories of your heart.

Effie: Never, never! I should be unworthy of your love if I could forget my dear father and my gentle sister Jeanie.

Geordie: Well, remember them as much as you like, only fetch the schooner round and be in her when I reach her. Farewell Effie!

Effie: Farewell. *[They embrace. Exit Effie.]*

Geordie: She's a brave girl.

Meg advances.

Meg: The devil speed her.

Geordie: Meg!

Meg: Aye, George Staunton. Meg Murdockson, your nurse, and little did I think when you lay on my breast four and twenty years ago what a fiend I was nourishing.

Geordie: It never occurred to me where I got the bad qualities of my nature. Now I recognize the source.

Meg: I hold ye now as I held ye then, helpless and in my power.

Geordie: I defy you to harm me.

Meg: Do ye then, do ye, when one cry from my lips would do it. The crags are full of law dogs.

Geordie: Shout for 'em, Meg. Why don't ye shout, you would sooner throttle yourself than do it.

Meg: I don't know whether it's love or hate that keeps me still.

Geordie: And I don't care.

Meg: You ruined my child.

Geordie: You tempted me with her.

Meg: Was my ambition any excuse for your crime? But now, a condemned felon. She is your equal! Will you marry her?

Geordie: No. Dye think I'll be led by you to the altar with a rope round my neck.

Meg: Then take your doom for you shall never escape with your [. . .] yonder.

Madge outside. She sings. [Music.]

Meg: They're coming! That's the warning. Dye hear it?

Geordie: I do. [. . .] I don't tremble, no, but you shake with fear for the life of your foster child.

Meg: Devil, devil. Go and go hide yourself, you'll be seen caught, taken to jail. They come , they come.

Geordie: Ha! ha! I knew it.

    Exit.

Meg: I could not do it. My heart shook when I tried, but he shall marry Madge yet.

Dumbiedikes: [outside] Deel take the powny! Ho!

Meg: There's a struggle in the dark yonder. Two figures—ha—one falls, the other flees down the mountain.

    She retires behind rock. Enter Dumbiedikes.

Dumbie: The devil's in my pony I had his head turned for Dumbiedikes, when round he twirled and set for McLeonards. "Home," says I! "Nay," says he! "Supper," said I in a wheedlin tony. "Jeanie," says he in a whinny. My heels went up and I went down and he left me sprawling like a fish on dry land. He's half way to Deans's cottage by this time.

    Enter Ratcliffe , Sharpitlaw, and officers to each.

Ratcliffe: Hush. There he is.

Sharpitlaw: Have you the manacles?

Ratcliffe: He's a devil. See to your arms.

Sharpitlaw: And think you of the hundred £ reward that's on his head.

Dumbie: What'll Jeanie say when the pony knocks at the door. She'll say . . .

Sharpitlaw: In the King's name, you're my prisoner.

Ratcliffe: [siezing Dumbiedikes] Drop your weapons or you're a dead man.

Dumbie: Don't, don't shoot. Take all I've got! There's a silver watch in my breeches fob and I've pennies and a bawbee in my auld leather pouch. Take it all, but don't shoot.

Ratcliffe: This is not our man.

Sharpitlaw: I tell you I saw a struggle.

Dumbie: You did, and you saw I got the worst of it?

Ratcliffe: Oh! Yer tried to hold him fast.

Dumbie: I did. I stuck to him.

Ratcliffe: And he fled. Can ye guess the road he took?

Dumbie: I'd tak my oath on't he's trotted off to Davie Deans's cottage.

Sharpitlaw: You were right, Ratcliffe. That's the trap to catch him.

Ratcliffe: I suppose you are in the same job as we are, I mean
you are after the fugitive.

Dumbie: Well, I'd like to put a good halter around his neck.

Ratcliffe: And you know there is a hundred pounds offered for him?

Dumbie: A hundred pounds! I'll sell him for ten and I'll tell you just how to catch him. Just go to Deans's cottage and you'll find him munching hay in the stable.

Sharpitlaw: What! Geordie Robertson!

Dumbie: No! My pony, Rory Beau.

Ratcliffe: Why now, I look again. It is the Laird of Dumbiedikes.

Dumbie: Every inch of him.

Sharpitlaw: Fool! Have we been loosing precious time with you?

Dumbie: That's what surprises me.

Ratcliffe: You take that side of the rocks. We'll descend by this path.

    Exeunt Ratcliffe, Sharpitlaw, and the officers.

Dumbie: That's four maniac folk just escaped from the hospital. *[Madge advances.]* A hundred pounds for Rory Beau!

Madge: [taking his arm] It's a braw night, Laird o'Dumbiedikes.

Dumbie: Is it a woman or a grenadier—

Madge: Hush [. . .].—There's wild folk in the craigs tonight. I've watched yer, but they won't harm ye while I'm nigh.

Dumbie: Then I'll stick to you. I'm thinking those fellows were all mad men.

Madge: Mad as hares.

Dumbie: Thank heaven I've found somebody in their senses about.

Madge: [*taking his arm*] Come! Stop! What have you done with the child?

Dumbie: The child!

Madge: Hush! step soft or you wake it up. softly.

Dumbie: Don't you see I'm treadin on pigeons eggs.

Madge: Hush!

   Exeunt. Music.

Act 3

   Davie Deans's cottage. Davie is discovered seated at a table with Butler. Jeanie is laying the supper.

Davie: Reuben Butler, you ask me for my daughter. Jeanie, lass, d'ye hear him?

Jeanie: Ay father, I've heard him these twa years.

Davie: And what dye say?

Jeanie: I'm willing, when you can spare me?

Davie: Eh, Sir. It's a hard thing for an auld man to part wi all he has in life, my two bairns, my Leah and my Rachel. For twenty years they have grown eside me, Jeanie so good and Effie so winsome. The fireside will be aye lonely for the auld father when they're gone.

Jeanie: But why need it so? Reuben can live here father.

Davie: Na. Na. Jeanie. It's ower much for a girl to be a daughter, wife and mother too. I would na ask it.

Jeanie: Then I'll be a daughter ainly. I wad na gie up that name for the proudest in the land and I wad na change my home for the palace of Dalkeith.

   Enter Effie.

Davie: Come here, my bit lassie! Why the dew is on your gowdan hair and you aire cauld. Effie!

Jeanie: Ye look as if ye'd seen a bagle.

Effie: Let me help you to dress the table, Jeanie.

Davie: No, sit there, and let me look into your face Look there, Reuben! There is all my wealth, all my pride, the King of Scotland could gie a mon letters and estate but he never could mak him father of twa such children.

Jeanie: What! That's [. . .] scruffin at the window? Have the kine broke loise? [*she opens window*] Why it's Rory, the Laird's powny. There he trots straight for the stable. But where's the Laird?

   Enter Dumbiedikes.

Dumbie: Here, Jeanie, and I'm droukit to the skin wi fear. I've—there's a regiment of thieves and madmen in the crags wi pistols and [whingers]—wha wanted to gie a hundred £ for Rory and shoot me because I wasn't somebody else. Then a mad woman took me in charge and led me in search of dead babbies that seemed buried under every stone in Salibury Crags. I've had an awful night.

Jeanie: Sit down, Laird, and compose your legs.

Dumbie: If ye had the smallest drop of strong water, it might stay the wobbles in me for I'm shook indeed.

Davie: Set to the board and put food in you. There's more courage in that than in drink. Water is truth and every ither drink is a lie. Water cleaneth a man and makes of him a Christian. Water brings up his food from the South and it is the only earthly thing that God has permitted to rise up and inhabit the heavens and sky. There is a blessing in it and in everything that lives by it.

Jeanie: Effie winne ye coom.

Effie: No, no, let me bide here on the hearth. I've na appetite for food.

Jeanie: [aside] Why Effie, ye are greetin!

Effie: Hush, let me greet. I must, I must, or my heart will break. Keep them from seeing it.

Dumbie: Food is better than drink! So it is Davie. Well, here's your health in a slice of mutton. [*eats*]

Davie: Eat Laird, eat Reuben, and then we'll gather round the fire and Reuben shall read to us from the auld Bible and instead of the draught of death ye shall drink from the waters of life.

> *Effie kneels on the hearth as if in prayer and then creeping behind her father kisses his plaid.*

Dumbie: Where's Effie?

Effie: [rising] Here, but, oh, I am sick and I would go, go to rest, but do not, let me ponder you. No, don't rise father, but kiss me and—bless me—if you will.

Davie: Bless you? My bit lassie. May heaven keep you!

> *Effie rises. Pause for music.*

Jeanie: Effie, you can scarce walk, what's the matter?

Effie: Naething! Good night Jeanie. Good night! [*She is going, but returns and embraces Jeanie.*]

> *Enter Ratcliffe.*

Ratcliffe: I'm sorry to intrude on ye at meal time.

Dumbie: That's the fellow that wanted to give me a hundred £ for my pony.

Davie: What's yur bisness here, al sic are hom o night.

Effie: We may hinder the gentleman Jeanie. Let us go.

Ratcliffe: No! My pretty lassie, you must stop. *[Enter Sharpitlaw.]* Your name I think is Euphemia Deans.

Davie: Well Sir, she'll no deny it.

Sharpitlaw: Then Euphemia Dean, on order of this warrant made by the High Court of Judication, duly instructed on the premises for the crime of murder done on the body of your infant child, within the jurisdiction of this court and against the heart of the Realm and the dignity of our sovereign Lord the King, you are my prisoner.

> *Enter the two officers.*

Jeanie: Effie my sister, it canna be!

Davie: Murder—my—my lassie—My Effie—speak. Speak, why don't ye—if ye can't—if yer wrath chokes ye as mine does—look—Look at me and . . .

Effie: Oh! Take me away! Take me away! [*They place handcuffs on her.*]

Jeanie: Oh fi! No, no! Don't harm her.

Ratcliffe: It is a sorry formality, lassie, but in capital cases it is my duty to do this.

Davie: Murderess. She! My child! Let me look at her. Stand back Laird, hand off, there Reuben Butler. Let me look on this thing that I have made to blast my old age! Murderess and ye have dared to haunt my house, to sleep under my roof, to pollute my hearthstone. Begone, and following your steps let your father's curse . . .

> *Effie utters a cry.*

Jeanie: No! no! [*Throws herself on Davie's neck.*] Do not curse your child!

Davie: My child!! My . . . [*after a struggle he bursts into tears and sets at table in convulsive grief. Jeanie kneels at his feet.*] Tableau.

Appendix 3

"Mazeppa *in New York 1861–1888*"

1861

Idah Isaacs Menken. Broadway Theatre. 13 June, 1861.

Idah Isaacs Menken. New Bowery Theatre. 16–28 June, 1862.

Idah Isaacs Menken. The Broadway Theatre. 30 April, 1866 for three weeks to crowded houses. She returned in mid-August to The Broadway; she had performed in New York in December 1863.

Idah Isaacs Menken. Wood's Broadway and Broome Street house. [Date unknown] 1866.

Kate Fisher. New Bowery Theatre. 18 January, 1864.

Kate Fisher. New Bowery Theatre. 30 October, 1865.

[Kate Fisher]. [New Bowery Theatre] 12 November, 1866.

Kate Fisher. New Bowery. 30 October, 1866.

Kate Fisher. New Bowery. 4 November, 1867; 9 March, 1868; 24 May 1869; 19 July, 1869.

Kate Fisher. The Olympic. [Date unknown] 1869.

Leo Hudson. New Bowery Theatre. She made her first appearence in the city on 9 November, 1863, also on 17–20.

Leo Hudson. Barnum New Museum. October 1865.

Leo Hudson. New Bowery Theatre. 9 April, 1866; also 19 August, 1866.

Leo Hudson. Barnum's. 27 May, 1867.

Leo Hudson. New Bowery. 4 October, 1869.

Leo Hudson. The Olympic. 18 October, 1869.

Kate Vance. New Bowery Theatre. 2 May, 1864.

Addie Anderson. New Bowery Theatre. 30 January, 1865.

Lizzie Wood. New Bowery Theatre. 26 June, 1865.

Oceana Judah. Barnum's. 16 October, 1865.

[Artist unknown]. New Bowery Theatre. 23 November, 1866.

Florence Temple. Brooklyn Opera House. [Date unknown] 1867.

Kate Raymond. The Olympic. 8 February, 1869.

1870

Kate Raymond. The Bowery. 4 July, 1870.

Kate Fisher. The Bowery. 2 October, 1871; and Christmas 1871.

Kate Raymond. The Globe Theater. 7 July, 1872.

Helene Smith. The Bowery. 15 August, 1873.

Kate Fisher. The Bowery. 29 June, 1874.

Kate Fisher. Wood's Museum and Menagerie. 10 May, 1875.

Kate Fisher. The Broadway Theater. 11 October, 1876.

Fanny Louise Buckingham. The Broadway Theater. American début. 2 July, 1877.
[Star unknown]. Niblo's Garden. 5 September, 1878.

1880
Maude Forrester. Windsor Theatre. For two weeks. 10 May, 1880.
Maud Forrester. Aberle's Theatre. 3 January and 23 May, 1881; 17 October, 1881.
Fanny Louise Buckingham. The Bowery. 12 November, 1888 (Jacob's Thalia
    Theater).
Vernona Jarbeau. The last woman to perform Mazeppa. Place and date unknown.

See Odell 8:41, 174, 308, 311, 538, 607; 44, 45, 175, 180, 606, 672; 47, 405, 468;
    537, 609, 673; Brown, index, 3:642; Glenn Hughes, *A History of American
    Theatre*, 192.

Notes

Chapter 1. Imitation as Resistance

1. Albert J. von Frank, *The Sacred Game: Provincialism and Frontier Consciousness in American Literature, 1630–1860* (Cambridge: Cambridge University Press, 1985), 155.

2. Bernard Smith, *Forces in American Criticism: A Study in the History of American Literary Thought* (New York: Harcourt, Brace and Company, 1939), 11, 14.

3. Patrick A. Halpin, *Precepts of Literature: A Text-Book* (New York: Baker & Godwin, 1881), 57.

4. This view is very common, see e.g. Stephen Spender, *Love-Hate Relations: English and American Sensibilities* (New York: Random House, 1974), xxvi.

5. Russel Blaine Nye, *The Cultural Life of the New Nation, 1776–1830* (New York: Harper & Brothers, 1960), 261–62.

6. *An Essay on American Poetry, with Several Miscellaneous Pieces on a Variety of Subjects, Sentimental, Descriptive, Moral, and Patriotic* (New Haven: Hezekiah Howe, 1818), 5.

7. From a letter written to Philip C. Pendleton in 1841, in *The Letters of William Gilmore Simms,* ed. Mary C. Simms Oliphant, Alfred Taylor Odell, T. C. Duncan Eaves (Columbia: University of South Carolina Press, 1953–56), 1:216.

8. William Crafts, *A Selection in Prose and Poetry from the Miscellaneous Writings of the Late William Crafts* (Charleston: C. C. Sebring and J. S. Burges, 1828), 275–76.

9. John Bristed, *America and Her Resources; or, A View of the Agricultural, Commercial, Manufacturing, Financial, Political, Literary, Moral and Religious Capacity and Character of the American People* (London: Henry Colburn, 1818), 310.

10. Ibid., 313.

11. S. G. Goodrich, *Recollections of a Literature, or Men and Things I Have Seen: In a Series of Familiar Letters to a Friend* (New York and Aubuvin: Miller, Orton & Co., 1857), 2:106.

12. William Ellery Channing, "On National Literature," *Old South Leaflets* 6.141 (Boston: Directors of the Old South Work [1904]), 13.

13. John G. C. Brainard, *Poems. A New and Original Edition, with an Original Memoir of His Life* (Hartford: S. Andrus and Son, 1847), xlvi–xlvii.

14. William Gilmore Simms, *Donna Florida. A Tale* (Charleston: Burges and James, 1843), 2.

15. [I. S. Clason], *Horace in New-York* (New York: James M. Campbell, 1826), pt 1: vii.

16. Harriet Martineau, *Society in America* (New York: AMS Press, 1966), 3:219.

17. Gian Biago Contë, *The Rhetoric of Imitation: Genre and Poetic Memory in Virgil and Other Latin Poets,* trans. from the Italian, ed. Charles Segal (Ithaca and

London: Cornell University Press, 1986), 24; see also Alexander Lindey, *Plagiarism and Originality* (New York: Harper & Brothers Publication, 1952).

18. Conté, *Rhetoric of Imitation,* 40.

19. See Victor V. Turner, "Dewey, Dilthey, and Drama: An Essay on the Anthropology of Experience," in *The Anthropology of Experience,* ed. Victor Turner and Edward M. Bruner (Urbana: University of Illinois Press, 1986).

20. Constance Rourke, *American Humor: A Study of the National Character* (New York: Harcourt, Brace and Company, 1931), 48.

21. Percy H. Boynton, *The Rediscovery of the Frontier* (Chicago: University of Chicago Press, 1931), 41.

22. Russel B. Nye, *The Unembarrassed Muse: The Popular Arts in America* (New York: Dial Press, 1970), 156.

23. William E. Dodd, *The Cotton Kingdom: A Chronicle of the Old South* (New Haven: Yale University Press, 1919), 62–63.

24. See e.g., Jay B. Hubbell, *The South in American Literature, 1607–1900* (Durham, N.C.: Duke University Press, 1954), 182–87.

25. Graham Pollard, Introduction, in Isidore R. Brussell, *Anglo-American First Editions 1826–1900. East to West. Describing First Editions of English Authors Whose Books Were Published in America before Their Publication in England* (New York: R. R. Bowker Co., 1935), 11–12.

26. James C. Derby, *Fifty Years among Authors, Books and Publishers* (New York: G. W. Carleton & Co., 1884), 141.

27. James D. Hart, *The Popular Book: A History of America's Literary Taste* (New York: Oxford University Press, 1950), 70.

28. Ibid., 70.

29. Frank Luther Mott, *Golden Multitudes: The Story of the Best Sellers in the United States* (New York: Macmillan, 1947), 68.

30. Ibid., 69.

31. Rollin G. Osterweis, *Romanticism and Nationalism in the Old South* (New Haven: Yale University Press, 1949), 41.

32. Mott, *Golden Multitudes,* 67.

33. Ibid., 79–84.

34. Quoted from Earl Bradsher, *Mathew Carey: Editor, Author and Publisher. A Study in American Literary Development* (New York: Columbia University Press, 1912), 95. Carey & Lee published six editions of the book between November 1836 and 1838; 7,850 copies in all. See *The Cost Book of Carey & Lee: 1825–1838,* ed. David Kaser (Philadelphia: University of Pennsylvania Press, 1963).

35. Hellmut Lehmann-Haupt, *The Book in America: A History of the Making, the Selling, and the Collecting of Books in the United States* (New York: R. R. Bowker Company, 1939), 93. See also Frank L. Schick, *The Paperbound Book in America: The History of Paperbacks and Their European Background* (New York: R. R. Bowker Company, 1958).

36. Ray Charles Billington, "The Frontier and American Culture," *America's Frontier Culture: Three Essays* (College Station: Texas A&M University Press, 1977), 66–67.

37. Bradsher, *Mathew Carey,* 54.

38. See e.g., George Harrison Orians, "The Rise of Romanticism, 1805–1855," in *Transitions in American Literary History,* ed. Harry Hayden Clark (Durham, N. C.: Duke University Press, 1953), 161–244; Ralph Leslie Rusk, *The Literature of the Middle Western Frontier* (New York: Columbia University Press, 1925); William E. Dodd, *The Cotton Kingdom: A Chronicle of the Old South;* Francis Pendleton Gaines, *The Southern Plantation: A Study in the Development and the Accuracy of*

a Tradition (New York: Columbia University Press, 1925); M. F. Heiser, "The Decline of Neoclassicism," in *Transitions in American Literary History,* 93–159.

39. See Ray Charles Billington, "The Frontier and American Culture," 52–72; Louis B. Wright, *Culture on the Moving Frontier* (Bloomington: Indiana University Press, 1955); Russell Blaine Nye, *The Cultural Life of the New Nation, 1776–1830* (New York: Harper & Brothers, 1960); *New Dimensions in Popular Culture,* ed. Russel B. Nye (Bowling Green, Ohio: Bowling Green University Popular Press, 1972); Linden Peach, *British Influence on the Birth of American Literature* (New York: St. Martin's Press, 1982); Nicolaus Mills, *American and English Fiction in the Nineteenth Century: An Antigenre Critique and Comparison* (Bloomington, London: Indiana University Press, 1973); Constance Rourke, *American Humor: A Study of the National Character;* Frank Luther Mott, *Golden Multitudes.* The influence of British writers on individual American writers is well documented; see e.g., Ernest E. Leisy, *The American Historical Novel* (Norman: University of Oklahoma Press, 1950) and George Dekker, *The Historical Romance* (Cambridge, New York, Melbourne: Cambridge University Press, 1990).

40. Shakespeare's American reputation is extremely well documented. But see in particular *Shakespeare in the South: Essays on Performance,* ed. Philip C. Kolin (Jackson: University Press of Mississippi, 1983); Lawrence W. Levine, *Highbrow/Lowbrow: The. Emergence of Cultural Hierarchy in America* (Cambridge, Mass.: Harvard University Press, 1990), 13–81; Raoul Granqvist, "Some Traits of Cultural Nationalism in the Reception of Shakespeare in Nineteenth Century U.S.A," *Orbis Litterarum* 43 (1987):1–26.

41. See George F. Sensabaugh, *Milton in Early America* (Princeton: Princeton University Press, 1964); Lester Fred Zimmerman, "Some Aspects of Milton's American Reputation to 1900," diss., University of Wisconsin, 1949; John A. Weigel, "The Milton Tradition, in the First Half of the Nineteenth Centuy," diss., Department of English, Western Reserve University, 1939.

42. Agnes Marie Sibley, *Alexander Pope's Prestige in America, 1725–1835* (New York: King's Crown Press, 1949); see also Guy A. Caldwell Jr., "The Influence of Addison on Charleston Periodicals, 1795–1860," *Studies in Philology* 35 (1938): 456–70.

43. William Ellery Leonard, *Byron and Byronism in America* (1907; New York: Gordion Press, 1965).

44. Samuel C. Chew, "Byron in America," *The American Mercury,* 1.3 (1924): 335–44.

45. G. Werner Krug, *Lord Byron als Dichterische Gestalt in England, Frankreich, Deutchland, und Amerika* (Potsdam: Richard Schneider, 1932), and Frank Lentricchia, "Byron in America. The Later Nineteenth Century," diss., Duke University, 1963.

46. Jay B. Hubbell, *Southern Life in Fiction* (Athens: University of Georgia Press, 1960); Hubbell, "Literary Nationalism in the Old South," in *American Studies in Honor of William Kenneth Boyd by Members of The Americana Club of Duke University,* ed. David Kelly Jackson (Durham, N. C.: Duke University, 1944), 175–220; Hubbell, *The South in American Literature, 1607–1900* (Durham, N. C.: Duke University Press, 1954); see also Dodd, *The Cotton Kingdom: A Chronicle of the Old South; M. F. Heiser,* "The Decline Neoclassicism," in *Transitions in American Literary History,* 93–159.

47. Annabel Newton, *Wordsworth in Early American Criticism* (Chigago, Ill.: University of Chicago Press, 1928); Hyder Edward Rollins, *Keats' Reputation in America to 1848* (Cambridge, Mass.: Harvard University Press, 1946); also Hyder Edward Rollins and Stephen Maxfield Parrish, *Keats and the Bostonians: Amy Low-*

ell, Louise Imogen Guiney, Louis Arthur Holman, Fred Holland Day (Cambridge, Mass.: Harvard University Press, 1951); Julia Power, *Shelley in America in the Nineteenth Century; His Relations to American Critical Thought and His Influence* (Lincoln, N.: University of Nebraska) vol. 40, no. 2, 1940.

48. George Harrison Orians, *The Influence of Walter Scott upon America and American Literature before 1860. An abstract of a thesis* (Urbana, Ill.: University of Illinois, 1929); "Walter Scott, Mark Twain, and the Civil War," *South Atlantic Quarterly* 40 (1941): 342–59; "The Romantic Ferment after Waverley," *American Literature* 3.4 (1932): 408–31; "The Rise of Romanticism, 1805–1855," in *Transitions in American Literary History*, 161–244.

49. Hamilton James Eckenrode, "Sir Walter Scott and the South," *North American Review* 206.2 (1917): 595–603; Grace Warren Landrum, "Sir Walter Scott and His Literary Rivals in the South," *American Literature* 2.3 (1930–31):256–76; William E. Dodd, *The Cotton Kingdom: A Chronicle of the Old South;* Francis Pendleton Gaines, *The Southern Plantation: A Study in the Development and the Accuracy of a Tradition;* M. F. Heiser, "The Decline of Neoclassicism," in *Transitions in American Literary History*, 93–159; Rollin G. Osterweis, *Romanticism and Nationalism in the Old South* (New Haven: Yale University Press, 1949); Edd Winfield Parks, *Ante-Bellum Southern Literary Critics* (Athens: University of Georgia Press, 1962).

50. David A. Randall, "Waverley in America," *The Colophon. A Quarterly for Bookman* 1.1 (1935):39–55; Harold F. Bogner, "Sir Walter Scott in New Orleans, 1818–1832," M.A. thesis., Tulane University, 1932, *Louisiana Historical Quarterly* 21.2 (1938): 420–517; Ralph Leslie Rusk, *The Literature of the Middle Western Frontier.* See also Bernard Smith, *Forces in American Criticism: A Study in the History of American Literary Thought* (New York: Harcourt, Brace and Company, 1939); John Tebbell, *The American Magazine: A Compact History* (New York: Hawthorn Books, 1969); Reginald Horsman, *Race and Manifest Destiny: The Origins of American Racial Anglo-Saxonism* (Cambridge, Mass.: Harvard University Press, 1981); Mory McLaren, "The Waverley Novels Abroad—Particularly in America," in *Sir Walter Scott. The Man and Patriot* (London: Heinemann, 1970), 137–47.

51. Henry Adelbert White, *Sir Walter Scott's Novels on the Stage*, Diss. 76 (New Haven: Yale University Press, 1927).

52. Edward F. Payne, *Dickens Days in Boston* (Boston and New York: Houghton Mifflin Company, 1927).

53. *Charles Dickens in America*, ed. Clyde William Wilkins (New York: Charles Scribner's Sons, 1912); *Dickens in Cartoon and Caricature*, comp. William Clyde Wilkins, ed. B. N. Matz (Boston: Plimpton Press, 1924).

54. Herman Leroy Edgar and R. W. G. Vail, "Early American Editions of the Works of Charles Dickens," in *Charles Dickens: His Life as Traced by His Works*, ed. Charles W. Cavanaugh (New York: The New York Public Library, 1929), 14–31; *Dickensiana of the Literature Relating to Charles Dickens and His Writings*, comp. Fred G. Kitton (1886; New York: Haskell House Publishers Ltd., 1971).

55. George Edgar Montgomery, "Dickens on the American Stage," *American Magazine* 8 (1888):190–207; Paul Wilstach, "Dramatisations of Dickens," *The Bookman* 14.1 (1901–2):52–62. See also Frank Dubrez Fawcett, Appendix A, *Dickens the Dramatist, on Screen, and Radio* (London: Allen, 1952).

56. See James Grant Wilson, *Thackeray in the United States, 1852–3, 1855–6. Including a Record of a Variety of Thackeraryna . . . with Six Score Illustrations and a Bibliography*, vol. 1 (London: Smith, Elder, & Co., 1904); Eyre Crowe, *With Thackerary in America, Illustrated* (New York: Charles Scribner's Sons, 1893); Harold S. Gulliver, "Thackeray in Georgia," *The Georgia Review* 1 (1947):35–43.

57. John Olin Eidson, *Tennyson in America: His Reputation and Influence, from*

1827 to 1858 (Athens: University of Georgia Press, 1943); Cornelius Weygandt, *The Time of Tennyson: English Victorian Poetry As It Affected America* (New York: D. Appleton-Century Company, 1936).

Chapter 2. Appropriations in Literature

1. Samuel B. Beach, *Escalala. An American Tale* (Utica: William Williams, 1824), vi.

2. The following poems on "Indian" themes, American history, war, and legend are not examined in this discussion, but listed here to indicate the scope of this genre (the letter B[yron] and S[cott] included after the author's name identifies the code): James Wallis Eastburn and his friend [Robert Charles Sands] [S], *Yamoyden, a Tale of the Wars of King Philip in Six Cantos* (New York: James Eastburn, 1820); Henry Whiting [S], *Sannilac, a Poem with Notes by Lewis Cass and Henry R. Schoolcraft* (Boston: Carter, Hendel and Babcock, 1831); William H. C. Hosmer [S], *Later Lays and Lyrics* (Rochester, N. Y.: D. M. Dewey, 1873); *Redburn; or, The Schoolmaster of a Morning* [S] (New York: Wm. M. Christy, 1845); Alfred B. Street [S], *Frontenac; or, The Atotarho of the Iroquois. A Metrical Romance* (New York: Baker and Scribner, 1849); see also his "Onnawah" [B, S] in *The Poems* (New York: Clark & Austin, 1850); Frances Jane Crosby [S], *Monterey, and Other Poems* (New York: R. Craighead, 1851); William Grayson [S], "Chicora," in *The Hireling and the Slave, Chicoro, and Other Poems* (Charleston: McCarter, 1856); William Allen [B], *Wunnissoo; or, The Vale of Hoosatunnuk, a Poem, with Notes* (1826; Boston: John D. Jewett and Co., 1856); John Greenleaf Whittier [S], "Pentucket" [written in 1838], in *Narrative and Legendary Poems. Vol. I* (Boston and New York: Houghton, Mifflin Co., 1900), 33–36; and his "Mogg Megone" [written in 1834] in *Personal Poems: Occasional Poems; The Tent on the Beach; With the Poems of Elizabeth H. Whittier* (Houghton, Mifflin and Co., 1900). Of this poem Whittier said: "It suggests the idea of a big Indian in his war-paint strutting about in Sir Walter Scott's plaid" (ibid., 357).

3. [Charles Fenno Hoffman], *Greyslaer: A Romance of the Mohawk. By the Author of "A Winter in the West," and "Wild Scenes in the Forest and Prairie"* (New York: Harper & Brothers, 1840).

4. Homer F. Barnes, *Charles Fenno Hoffman* (New York: Columbia University Press, 1930), 199.

5. Charles Fenno Hoffman, *Wild Scenes in the Forest and Prairie. With Sketches of American Life* (New York: William C. Colyer, 1843), 1:145–53.

6. Seba Smith, *Powhatan, a Metrical Romance, in Seven Cantos* (New York: Harper & Bros., 1841), 48.

7. Andrew Coffinberry, *The Forest Rangers: A Poetic Tale of the Western Wilderness in 1794. Connected with and Comprising the March and Battle of General Wayne's Army, and Abounding with Interesting Incidents of Fact and Fiction. In Seven Cantos* (Columbus: Wright & Lagg, 1842), 216.

8. *The Writings of Robert C. Sands, in Prose and Verse with a Memoir of the Author* (New York: Harper & Brothers, 1835), 1:111–12.

9. See James Reed, *Sir Walter Scott: Landscape and Locality* (London: Athlone Press, 1980).

10. [Frederick W. Thomas], *Emigrant, or Reflections while Descending the Ohio. A Poem* (Cincinnati: Alexander Flash, 1833), 41–43.

11. Edmund Flagg, *The Far West; or, A Tour beyond the Mountains* (New York: Harper & Brothers, 1838), 1:236.

12. Flagg, *The Far West*, 1:73–74.

13. Charles Fenno Hoffman, *The Vigil of Faith and Other Poems* (New York: Harper & Brothers, 1845), 10–11.

14. Charles Fenno Hoffman, *The Vigil of Faith and Other Poems*, 23.

15. Quoted by Homer F. Barnes, *Charles Fenno Hoffman*, 96–97.

16. See Homer F. Barnes, *Charles Fenno Hoffman*, 144–45.

17. William Ellery Leonard, *Byron and Byronism in America*, 85.

18. Lucretia Maria Davidson, "Chicomico," in *Poems. With Illustrations by F. O. C. Darley,* ed. M. Oliver Davidson (New York: Hurd and Houghton, 1871), 18.

19. Davidson, "Chicomico" in *Poems*, 22.

20. I. e. [Robert C. Sands], *The Bridal of Vaumond; a Metrical Romance* (New York: James Eastburn and Co., 1817) and *The Lay of the Wilderness, a Poem, in Five Cantos; by a Native of New-Brunswick* (Saint John: Printed by Henry Chubb, 1833). Sands, whose views on the American imitations we have already referred to (above, p. 40), omitted this early poem of his (he says it was written in 1813) from his 1835 *Writings,* because it was so severely criticized, obviously because of its links with Scott's "Lay of the Last Minstrel" (whose meter he had copied) and with Byron's "The Deformed Transformed" (on which he had founded his story). See *The Writings of Robert C. Sands,* 1:7 and 8.

21. P. Hamilton Myers, *Ensenore, and Other Poems* (1840; New York: Dodd & Mead, 1875).

22. George Hooker Colton, *Tekumseh; or, the West Thirty Years Since. A Poem* (New York: Wiley and Putnam, 1842), 68. See also poems such as "War Song of the Comanches" and "Song of the Nabajo" by Albert Pike, in his *Prose Sketches and Poems Written in the Western Country (with Additional Stories)* ed. David J. Weber, foreword by Tom Popejoy (Albuquerque, N. M.: Calvin Horn Publishers, 1967), 130–40.

23. Carlos D. Stuart, in *Ianthe, and Other Poems* (New York: C. L. Stickney, 1843), 111, 114.

24. James Nack, "The Minstrel Boy," in *The Legend of the Rocks and Other Poems* (New York: E. Conrad, 1827), 59.

25. P. M. Wetmore, "Introductory Memoir," in James Nack, *Earl Rupert, and Other Tales and Poems. With a Memoir of the Author by P. M. Wetmore* (New York: George Adlard, 1839), xvi.

26. [Emma C. Embury,] *Guido, a Tale; Sketches from History and Other Poems. By Ianthe* (New York: G. & C. Carvill, 1828). *Childe Harold* III: 371–73 prefaced her poem "The Lament of Columbus"; the lines 375–78 were added to the 1869 printing of the poem (in *The Poems of Emma C. Embury* [New York: Hurd and Houghton, 1869]). She used lines from Shakespeare's *The Tempest* (2.1.155–58) as a motto for her poem "The Shipwreck of Camoens."

27. Among the poems she included for her debut as a reader (in Boston in 1841) she chose Byron's "The Dream" and Scott's "The Lay of the Last Minstrel." See David W. Thompson, "Early Actress-Readers: Mowatt, Kemble, and Cushman," in *Performance of Literature in Historical Perspectives,* ed. David W. Thompson (Lanham: University Press of America, 1983), 631.

28. [Anna Cora Ritchie], Preface, *Pelayo; or, The Cavern of Covadonga. A Romance, by Isabel* (New York: Harper & Brothers, 1836), v–xii.

29. George H. Boker, *Plays and Poems* (Boston: Ticknor & Fields, 1857).

30. Bayard Taylor, *Eldorado or Adventures in the Path of Empire* (New York: G. P. Putnam & Son, 1868); *A Journey to Central Africa; or, Life and Landscape from Egypt to the Negro Kingdoms of the White Nile* (New York: G. P. Putnam, 1854); *Northern Travel; Summer and Winter Pictures of Sweden, Denmark and Lapland* (New York: G. P. Putnam, 1858). The latter book was translated into Swedish.

31. Bayard Taylor, from "Bedouin Song," in *Poems of the Orient* (Boston: Ticknor and Fields, 1855). See also his *A Book of Romances, Lyrics, and Songs* (Boston: Ticknor, Reeds, and Fields, 1852).

32. James E. Brooks and Mary E. Brooks, *The Rivals of Este, and Other Poems* (New York: J. & J. Harper, 1829), 82–84; James E. Brooks's "I met thee in my dreams last night" (176–77) is epigraphed by lines from *Manfred* (I: 223); his "An Elegy" on Byron's death, by two lines from *The Giaour* (1249–50).

33. C. F. Hoffman, "Song—Rosalie Clare," in *Wild Scenes in the Forest and Prairie. With Sketches of American Life*, 1: 193–95; it is also printed in *The Poems of Charles Fenno Hoffman. Collected and Edited by His Nephew, Edward Fenno Hoffman* (Philadelphia: Porter & Coates, 1873), 188–89. The lines from *Mazeppa*, "Away!—Away! My breath was gone. . . ." (375–82), preface Hoffman's story "The Ghost-Riders. A Legend of the Great American Desert" (in *Wild Scenes,* 127) and the famous lines on "young Lochinvar" (from Scott's *Marmion*) another story in the same book: "Petelesharoo, or the Last Offering from the Great Star" (211). Also noteworthy is that *Wild Scenes* first appeared in London in 1839 (printed by Richard Bentley).

34. "I think I could repeat one-half of the 'Lady of the Lake', and quite as much of 'Marmion'," Halleck said. See Nelson Frederick Adkins, *Fitz-Greene Halleck: An Early Knickerbocker Wit and Poet* (New Haven: Yale University Press, 1930), 191 and James Grant Wilson, *The Life and Letters of Fitz-Greene Halleck* (New York: D. Appleton and Co., 1869), 162.

35. *The Poetical Works of Fitz-Greene Halleck* (New York: D. Appleton and Co., 1858), 9–14; "Alnwick Castle" (ibid., 15–21).

36. St. Leger L. Carter, *Nugae, By Nugator: or Pieces in Prose and Verse* (Baltimore: Woods and Crane, 1844), 176–80 and 42–43. The volume also contains an imitation of Milton, called "Darkness" and further line-by-line quotations from Byron's *Mazeppa*, Scott's *Marmion*, Dickens's *The Pickwick Papers,* and Milton's *Paradise Lost* (II:66, 996, III:481–83).

37. *The Poetical Works of James Gates Percival with a Biographical Sketch* (Boston: Ticknor and Fields, 1854); Julius H. Ward, *The Life and Letters of James Gates Percival* (Boston: Ticknor and Fields, 1866), 116.

38. Micah P. Flint, *The Hunter and Other Poems* (Boston: Cummings, Hilliard, and Co., 1826), 113.

39. Richard M. D. Emmons, *The Freedoniad; or, Independence Preserved. An Epic Poem on the Late War of 1812* (Philadelphia: William Emmons, 1832), 3:17; Milton is also behind the structure and contents of Theodore Sedwick Fay's *Ulric; or, The Voices* (New York: D. Appleton & Co., 1851), another massive, martial exercise in verse.

40. Quoted from Homer F. Barnes, *Charles Fenno Hoffman,* 97–98.

41. *Childe Harold's Pilgrimage to the Dead Sea; Death of the Pale Horse; and Other Poems* (New York: James Eastburn and Co., 1818), 10–11.

42. *The Pilgrimage of Ormond, or Childe Harold in the New World* (Charleston: W. Riley, 1831). The poem is prefaced by six lines from *Childe Harold* (IV: 1228–33). Cf. James Gilmore Simms, *Atlantis. A Story of the Sea in Three Parts* (New York: J. & J. Harper, 1832).

43. William D. Gallagher, *Erato, Number I* (Cincinnati: Josiah Drake, 1835); *Erato, Number II* (Cincinnati: Alexander Flagg, 1835).

44. Gallagher, *Erato, Number II,* 46.

45. William R. Wallace, "Childe Harold," in *The Battle of Tippecanoe, Triumphs of Science, and Other Poems, Delivered on the Battle Ground, November 7, 1835* (Cincinnati: P. McFarlin, 1837), 83–87.

46. George H. Calvert, *Cabiro: A Poem. Cantos I and II* (Baltimore: N. Hickman, 1840); *Cabiro: A Poem. Cantos III and IV* (Boston: Little, Brown and Company, 1864).

47. Phæbe Carey, "Poems and Parodies," in Walter Hamilton, *Parodies of the Works of English and American Authors* (London: Reeves & Turner, 1886), 3:213; Hamilton lists two additional parodies of Byron by Phæbe Carey: "To Mary," which seems to be a parody of Byron's "Well, thou art happy" and "To Inez" (source unknown).

48. [Nathan Ames], *The Baby and the Bards. Childe Harvard, a Romance of Cambridge. By Senor Alguno* (Boston: Redding & Company, 1848); another edition appeared in 1851.

49. See Nelson Frederick Adkins, *Fitz-Greene Halleck: An Early Knickerbocker Wit and Poet*, 87–88.

50. Fitz-Greene Halleck, *Fanny with Other Poems* (New York: Harper & Brothers, 1839), 49.

51. James Grant Wilson, *The Life and Letters of Fitz-Greene Halleck,* 231–32.

52. Adkins, 111.

53. James Grant Wilson, *The Life and Letters of Fitz-Greene Halleck*, 239.

54. [G. C. Verplanck,] "Appendix. Extract from the Fourth Canto of Don Juan," in *Dick Shift; or, The State Triumvirate, a Political Tale and The Epistles of Brevet Major Pindar Puff* (New York: J. Seymour, 1819), 207–12.

55. See Leonard, 40.

56. See James Grant Wilson, *The Life and Letters of Fitz-Greene Halleck*, 234. I have not seen this work. Isaac Starr Clason also wrote a "continuation" of *Don Juan,* called *Don Juan. Canto XVII–XVIII* (see p. 63) and *Horace in New York* (see p. 80). See also Rufus W. Griswold's comments in his *The Poets and Poetry of America. With an Historical Introduction* (Philadelphia: Carey and Hart, 1842), 188: "The two cantos . . . have much of the spirit and feeling, in thought and diction, which characterize the work of BYRON."

57. William Barker Walter, Preface, *Sukey* (Baltimore: N. G. Maxwell, 1821), iii–vi.

58. William Crafts, *A Selection in Prose and Poetry from the Miscellaneous Writings of the Late William Crafts* (Charleston: C. C. Sebring and P. S. Burges, 1828), 346.

59. *A Selection in Prose and Poetry from The Miscellaneous Writings of the Late William Crafts*, 349.

60. See his "Lord Byron. Don Juan, Cantos 3, 4, 5," in *A Selection in Prose and Poetry from The Miscellaneous Writings of the Late William Crafts*, 254–55.

61. *Writings of Hugh Swinton Legaré* [ed. Mary Swinton Legaré] (Charleston, S.C.: Burges & James, 1845), 2: 155.

62. *The Letters of William Gilmore Simms* (1830–1844), 1:361.

63. See letter to Griswold, dated 6 December 1846, in *The Letters of William Gilmore Simms*, 2:222.

64. In Rufus Dawes, *Geraldine, Athenia of Damascus, and Miscellaneous Poems* (New York, Samuel Colman, 1839), 19–112; N. Parker Willis, *The Complete Works of N. P. Willis* (New York: J. S. Redfield, 1849), 849–61; and George Lunt, *Julia. A Poem, by Wesley Brooke, pseud.* (Boston: Ticknor and Fields, 1855).

65. Willis's poems "The Gypsy of Sardis" and "Melanie" recall *The Bride of Abydos* and *Manfred.* See Cortland P. Auser, *Nathaniel P. Willis* (New York: Twayne Publishers, 1969), 111–13; see also Leonard, 58–59.

66. Carlos D. Stuart, *Ianthe; and Other Poems* (New York: C. L. Stickney, 1843), 14–15.

67. Isaac Starr Clason, Don Juan. Cantos XVII–XVIII (New York: Charles Wiley, 1825).

68. Henry Morford, The Rest of Don Juan; Inscribed to the Shade of Byron (New York: Burgess, Stringer & Co., 1846).

69. Robert C. Sands, The Writings, 1:7.

70. Robert C. Sands, Preface, The Bridal of Vaumond.

71. The Writings of Robert C. Sands, 1:113.

72. From scene III, "The Tournament," in The Bridal of Vaumond.

73. Jonathan M. Scott, Blue Lights, or The Convention. A Poem in Four Cantos (New York: Charles N. Baldwin, 1817), viii.

74. [Joseph McCay], The Frontier Maid; or, A Tale of Wyoming. A Poem in Five Cantos (Wilkesbarre, Pa.: Steuben Butler & Samuel Maffet, 1819), 207.

75. The Frontier Maid, 206.

76. For an imitation of Charlotte Brontë's Jane Eyre, see "Agnes Reef: A Tale," in Strange Visitors; a Series of Original Papers, Embracing Philosophy, Science, Government, Religion, Poetry, Art, Fiction, Humor, Narrative, and Prophecy. By the Spirit of Irving. . . . (New York: Carleton, Publishers, 1869), 65–131.

77. [John Bailey], The Sultana; or, A Trip to Turkey. A Melodrama, in Three Acts, Founded on Lord Byron's Don Juan (New York: C. N. Baldwin, 1822). I have no information of where, when, or if, the play was performed. A play called "Don Juan" was, however, performed in the Washington (1810, 1818) and Baltimore (1810, 1811, 1813) theaters. But it is doubtful if they were based on Lord Byron's poem. See Reese D. James, Index, Old Drury of Philadelphia. A History of the Philadelphia Stage, 1800–1835. A Thesis in English (Philadelphia: University of Pennsylvania, 1932). The poem must have been transformed for the stage, probably as a burlesque, as most of Byron's works were dramatized in one way or another.

78. [Maturin Murrey Ballou], Fanny Campbell, The Female Captain. A Tale of the Revolution. By Lieutenant Murrey (New York: E. D. Long & Co., 1844); another edition appeared the next year in Boston published by F. Gleason. They differ only slightly.

79. John Neal, Randolp, a Novel by the Author of "Logan"—and "Seventy-six" [Baltimore] (Published for whom it may concern, 1823).

80. John Neal, Otho: A Tragedy, in Five Acts (Boston: West, Richardson, and Lord, 1819).

81. Frederick W. Thomas, Howard Pinckney (London: J. Clements, 1841).

82. Thomas's quotations in Howard Pinckney are worth annotating, as they reflect the direction of the literary taste of the day. They are: Byron, Childe Harold III, 9–11, another on page 13 I have been unable to trace, Parisina 558–61, Dream 44–63, Corsair I, 365–66, Manfred III, 296–97, 293–95, Dead 23–25; Burns, "The Merry Miller," 8 stanzas; Milton, Comus 74–77; Suckling, two lines, untraced; Lovelace, "The Health," two stanzas; Shakespeare, Anthony and Cleopatra, 1 line, untraced, Othello (on page 74) untraced.

83. [Frederick William Thomas, Clinton Bradshaw; or, The Adventures of a Lawyer (Philadelphia: Carey, Lee & Blanchard, 1835), 2:147. Like Howard Pinckney, this novel is sprinkled with quotations from English literature, with Byron as the given favorite. The Byron quotes are from Faliero II, 483, Childe Harold III, 262–79, and from Don Juan, Sardanapulus, and Mazeppa. He quotes from Scott's The Bride of Lammermoor, The Lady of the Lake and Marmion. Thomas's Sketches of Character and Tales Founded on Facts (Louisville: The Office of the Chronicle of Western Literature and Art, 1849) adduces numerous comments, accompanied by quotations, on Shakespeare, Milton, Byron and Scott. The quotations from Byron include: Manfred I, 271–72 and Don Juan II, 1–4.

84. She read from Scott's *The Lay of the Last Minstrel* in Boston in 1841 and from this time onwards she was one of the most popular American women readers of poetry. See Eric Wollencott Barnes, *The Lady of Fashion. The Life and the Theatre of Anna Cora Mowatt* (New York: Charles Scribner's Sons, 1954), 71–77, and *Autobiography of an Actress; or Eight Years on the Stage* (Boston: Ticknor, Reed, and Fields, 1853), 149.

85. Apart from the quotations we will discuss below, *Evelyn* contains the following quotations from Byron: *Corsair* II, 446, *Childe Harold* III, 91, *Lara* I, 371–72, *Sardanapulus* I, 320–25 (rep. 320–21), 470–74. In addition to these from Byron, there are quotations (as chapter headings or integrated textual references) from Shakespeare (*Henry IV* 2.03.44–46, *The Taming of the Shrew* 5.01.127–28), Crabbe, Scott, Shelley, and Coleridge. Ritchie's *The Fortune Hunter: A Novel of New York Society* (Philadelphia: T. B. Peterson, 1854) contains chapter headings with quotations from Coleridge, Keats, Hannah Moore, and Byron (*Childe Harold* II, 771, IV, 88, *Corsair* I, 273). *Her Twin Roses: A Narrative* (Boston: Ticknor and Fields, 1857) has a single quotation from Byron's "Ode to Napoleon Buonaparte. Additional stanza," 19–26. She gradually dropped this technique. Her novel from 1866 *The Mute Singer* contains no direct quotations.

86. A. C. Ritchie, *Evelyn; or, A Heart Unmasked. A Tale of Domestic Life* (Philadelphia: G. B. Zieber and Company, 1845). *Evelyn* was inspired by the novels of the Swedish writer Fredrika Bremer.

87. These are the scenes: 1. Conrad's Parting with Medora (I, 466–81); 2. The Dervise (II, 29–30, 45–56); 3. Conrad Undisguised (II, 141–51); 4. Conrad's Rescue of Gulnare (II, 196–203, 221–24); 5. Gulnare's Visit to the Dungeon (II, 392–404); 6. Medora in Conrad's Absence (III, 66–69, 74–75); 7. Gulnare's Second Visit to the Dungeon (III, 304–7); 8. Gulnare's Entreaty (III, 466–71); and 9. The Death of Medora (III, 597–608).

88. That the Gulnare of Byron's poem could stimulate male writing is evident from many quarters. See e. g. Rufus Dawes's poem "Gulnare" in *Geraldine, Athenia of Damascus, and Miscellaneous Poems*, 306–7.

89. James W. Simmons, *Manfredi; A Tragedy, in Five Acts* (Philadelphia: Moses Thomas, 1821).

90. James W. Simmons, *Valdemar; or, The Castle of the Cliff, a Tragedy* (Philadelphia: H. C. Carey and I. Lee, 1822).

91. See Edd Winfield Parks, *William Gilmore Simms as Literary Critic* (Athens: University of Georgia Press, 1961), 68–87. His letters and his works are full of quotations from British writers, especially Shakespeare (in his *Letters* he quotes from *Childe Harold* III, stanza 2, III, 817–18, *The Bride of Abydos* I, 11, 342–43, *Don Juan* I, stanza 216 and from Scott's *Rob Roy, Fair Maid of Perth*, and *A Legend of Montrose*.

92. *The Letters of William Gilmore Simms*, 3:202–3.

93. Simms was insistent. He went on working on the play and he approached Forrest as late as 1860. See *Letters*, 3:218.

94. In *Norman Maurice; or, The Man of the People. An American Drama* (Charleston: Walker and Richards, 1852), 166–69.

95. George Melville Baker, *Amateur Dramas for Parlor Theatricals, Evening Entertainments, and School Exhibitions* (Boston: Lee and Shepard, 1867), 227–48. This adaptation is also printed in his *The Exhibition Drama: Comprising Drama, Comedy, and Farce, Together with Dramatic and Musical Entertainments, and School Exhibitions* (Boston: Lee and Shepard, 1875); here is also a burlesque of the trial scene in *Merchant of Venice*, called "The Peddlar of Very Nice."

96. George B. Bartlett, *The Grand Dickens Cosmorama. Comprising Several*

Unique Entertainments Capable of Being Used Separately or in Combination, for School, Home, and Hall (Boston: Lee & Shepard, 1885), 6–7.

97. In *Mrs. Jarley's Far-Famed Collection of Wax-Works. In Two Parts. Arranged by G. B. Bartlett, of Concord, Mass., and Performed by the Amateurs under His Direction for Charitable Purposes in Most of the Cities of the United States* (New York: Samuel French & Son, 18?.) "Buoyant" consists of scenes from *Nicholas Nickleby, David Copperfield,* and *Our Mutual Friend* (this scene is a pantomime centred on poor Jenny Wren and her drunken father); "Dotage" includes scenes from *Cricket on the Hearth, David Copperfield,* and *Bleak House.*

98. A similar work is *Dialogues Dramatized from the Works of Charles Dickens with Full Directions for Performance, Preparation of Costumes, Etc.* (Chicago: T. S. Denisson, Publisher, 18?-). It presents in all twelve dramatizations: "Copperfield's Proposal," "The Prentice Knights" (*Barnaby Rudge*), "Spearlow and Jorkins" (*David Copperfield*), "The Refreshment Room," "Mugby Junction" (*Christmas Stories*), "Return of Sol Gills" (*Dombey and Son*), "Mr Pecksniff" (*Martin Chuzzlewit*), "The Friendly Knave" (*Our Mutual Friend*), "Squeer's School" (*Nicholas Nickleby*), "Mrs Gamp's Tea-party" (*Martin Chuzzlewit*), "Bamble's Courtship" (*Pickwick Papers*), "The Circumlocution Office" (*Little Dorritt*), "Bardell vs. Pickwick" (*Pickwick Papers*).

99. "Sam Weller's Visit to His Mother-in-Law," in *The New York Drama* 3 (1877): 29, 159–60; Frank E. Emson, "Bumble's Courtship: A Comic Interlude, in One Act," ibid., 4 (1878):45, 286–87.

100. Robert Henry Newell [Orpheus C. Kerr], *The Cloven Foot: Being an Adaptation of the English Novel "The Mystery of Edwin Drood," (By Charles Dickens) to American Scenes, Characters, and Nomenclature* (New York: Carleton, 1870). In *Strange Visitors* (52 ff.) there is an ironic account of William Thackeray's trip to America and his greed for money, a vice that was also ascribed to Dickens. The piece is called "W. M. Thackeray: His Post Mortem Experience."

101. John McVickar, *Tribute to the Memory of Sir Walter Scott, Baronet* (New York: George P. Scott and Co., 1833), Preface and 3.

102. [Thomas] Barry, *A Masque and Pageant in Honour of the Genius of the Minstrel of the North, Entitled A Vision of the Bard* (New York: James Kennaday, 1832). The scenes were the attack of Dirk Hatteraick on Henry Bertam and Dandie Darmont and Meg Merrilies among the mountains *(Guy Mannering);* the return of Rob Roy after his capture *(Rob Roy);* Jeannie Deans's travel to London and the attempt of Mrs. Bachristie to drive her away *(The Heart of Midlothian);* the attempts to burn Rebecca and her saviour *(Ivanhoe);* the meeting of Fitz James and Ellen from *The Lady of the Lake;* the death of Marmion *(Marmion);* and to end the performance a recital of the last stanzas (starting "Harp of the North, farewell! the hills grow dark,") of *The Lady of the Lake.* "The solemn Thing," says Odell, "was repeated many times, and doubtless was well meant." In George C. D. Odell, *Annals of the New York Stage* (New York: Columbia University Press, 1927–49), 3 (1832–33):614.

103. P. Hamilton Myers, "Sir Walter Scott," in *Ensenore, and Other Poems,* 168.

104. William B. Walter, "Ogilvie," in *Poems* (Boston: John Cotton; Jr. & Co., 1821), 55–60.

105. Rufus Dawes's "Ode, on the Death of Sir Walter Scott" is quite similar in style and content; in *Geraldine, Athenia of Damascus, and Miscellaneous Poems,* 323–28.

106. Grenville Mellen, "Ode on Byron," in *The Martyr's Triumph; Buried Valley; and Other Poems* (Boston: Lilly; Wait, Colman, and Holden, 1833), 199–203. The volume also includes two other odes to English writers, "Ode on Shakspeare" (187–93) and "The Inspiration of Milton" (194–98).

107. Richard Henry Wilde, "To Lord Byron," in Rufus W. Griswold, *The Poets and Poetry of America*, 79.

108. Charles Fenno Hoffman, "Byron," in *The Poets and Poetry of America*, 271; the poem was also printed in Hoffman's *The Echo; or, Borrowed Notes for Home Circulation* (Philadelphia: Lindsay & Blakiston, 1844), 46 and in his *The Poems of Charles Fenno Hoffman*, 208, which indicates the importance Hoffman ascribed to the poem.

109. Walter Colton, "Byron," in *The Poets and Poetry of America*, 257.

110. Lucretia Maria Davidson, "Byron," in *Poems*. The poem was written in 1823; she was a teenager then.

111. James W. Simmons, *An Inquiry into the Moral Character of Lord Byron* (London: Ivertson and Palmer, 1826), see 50–51; the quotations are from *Childe Harold* III, 806–23, 914–17.

112. James G. Brooks, *Anniversary Poem. Delivered at New Haven, Conn.* (New York: G. & C. Carvill, 1826).

113. James G. Brooks, "An Elegy," in Brooks, James G. and Mary E. Brooks, *The Rivals of Este, and Other Poems*, 200–202.

114. James Nack, *The Immortal; A Dramatic Romance; and Other Poems. With a Memoir of the Author by George P. Morris* (New York: Stringer and Townsend, 1850), iii–iv; *Strange Visitors*, 27–28.

115. [James Kirke Paulding], *The Lay of the Scottish Fiddle: A Tale of Havre de Grace. Supposed to be Written by Walter Scott, Esq. First American, from the Fourth Edinburgh Edition* (New York: Inskeep & Bradford, 1813).

116. See Walter Hamilton, *Parodies of the Works of English and American Authors*, 3:84.

117. Solyman Brown, *An Essay on American Poetry*, 5.

118. McDonald Clarke, "The Gossip," in *The Gossip; or, A Laugh with the Ladies, a Grin at the Gentlemen, and Burlesques at Byron, a Sentimental Satire; with Other Poems in a Series of Numbers. No One* (New York: Gray & Bunce, 1823), 192 and 193.

119. McDonald Clarke, "Byron to the Devil," in *The Gossip*, 103–4.

120. Leonard, 76–77.

121. George Lunt, *The Grave of Byron, with Other Poems* (Boston: Hillard, Gray, Little, and Wilkins, 1826); *The Lay of the Last Pilgrim. By the Author of "The Pigimage of Ormond"* (Charleston, S. C.: Printed by W. Riley, 1832). Five lines from *Childe Harold* (IV, 1216–20) serve as an epigraph to the latter book.

122. [Isaac Starr Clason], *Horace in New-York* (New York: James M. Campbell, 1826), 28–29.

123. Grenville Mellen, *Our Chronicle of '26. A Satirical Poem* (Boston: Wells and Lilly, 1826); see also [A. M. Ritchie], *Reviewers Reviewed. A Satire by the Author of Pelayo* (New York: [publisher unknown] 1837).

124. [J. L. Martin], *Native Bards; A Satirical Effusion; with Other Occasional Pieces* (Philadelphia: E. L. Carey & A. Hart, 1831).

125. Lambert A. Wilmer, *The Quacks of Helicon: A Satire* (Philadelphia: J. W. Macclefield, 1841), 25.

126. [A. J. H. Duganne], *Parnassus in Pillory. A Satire. By Motley Manners, Esq.* (New York: Adriance, Sherman & Co., 1851), 13, 22, 45.

127. *The Mongrelites; or, The Radicals—So Called, a Satiric Poem, By—* (New York: Van Evrie, Horton, & Co., 1866), iv.

128. *Dolby and Father. By "Buz"* (New York: P. S. Wynkoop & Son, 1868).

129. The New York audiences were as a rule enthused by Dickens's powerful reading from his own novels at Steinway Hall. See *Charles Dickens' Readings 1867.*

Clippings from New York Newspapers. Pasted in One Volume. [Includes] Nicholas Nickleby at the Yorkshire School. As Condensed by Himself, for His Readings. With an Illustration by S. Eytinge, Jr. (Boston: Ticknor and Fields, 1868).

Chapter 3. British Writers in American Elocutionary/Literary Textbooks

1. See my "Some Traits of Cultural Nationalism in the Reception of Shakespeare in Nineteenth Century U. S. A."

2. *The American Orator's Own Book; or, The Art of Extemporaneous Public Speaking, Including a Course of Discipline for Obtaining the Faculties of Discrimination, Arrangemeent and Oral Discussion; with a Debate, as an Exercise in Argumentative Declamation; and Numerous Selections for Practice* (Philadelphia: James Kay, 1836), 1–2.

3. *An Essay on Elocution: with Elucidatory Passages from Various Authors. To Which Are Added Remarks on Reading Prose and Verse, with Suggestions to Instructors of the Art* (Albany: Weare & Little, 1856), iii–iv.

4. See Ruth Miller Elson, *Guardians of Traditions: American Schoolbooks of the Nineteenth Century* (Lincoln: University of Nebraska Press, 1966); John A. Nietz, *Old Textbooks* (Pittsburgh: University of Pittsburgh Press, 1961); John A. Nietz, *The Evolution of American Secondary School Texbook* (Rutland, Vt.: Charles E. Tuttle Company, 1966).

5. Samuel Kirkham, *An Essay on Elocution, Designed for the Use of Schools and Private Learners* (New York: Robinson, Pratt, & Co., 1836).

6. See Raoul Granqvist, "The Self and the Other in Walt Whitman's Mirror: English Literature and Culture from an American Perspective," *American Studies in Scandinavia* 21.1 (1989): 11.

7. The bibliographies in Appendix 1 include all the instances of writer-related references that I have been able to find; however, only a sample of these are commented on in the text.

8. See Lawrence W. Levine, *Highbrow/Lowbrow: The Emergence of Cultural Hierarchy in America* (Cambridge, Mass.: Harvard University Press, 1988).

9. Levine, *Higbrow/Lowbrow,* 37–38.

10. Ibid., 37.

11. James Rush, *The Philosophy of the Human Voice; Embracing Its Physiological History; Together with a System of Principles* . . . (Philadelphia: Grigg & Elliott, 1833), 129.

12. William Russell, *Orthophony; or, the Cultivation of the Voice in Elocution. A Manual of Elementary Exercises, Adpated to Dr. Rush's "Philosophy of the Human Voice," and the System of Vocal Culture Introduced by Mr. James E. Murdoch* (Boston: Ticknor and Fields, 1862), 236 ff.; 263, 265.

13. James Rush, *The Philosophy of the Human Voice,* 289.

14. George Vandenhoff, *The Art of Elocution; from the Simple Articulation of the Elemental Sounds of Language, to the Highest Tone of Expression of Speech, Attainable by the Human Voice* (London: Wiley and Putnam, 1846), 148–49.

15. James Rush, *The Philosophy of the Human Voice* 288–89; see also Wilhelm T. Ross, *Voice Culture and Elocution* (New York: The Baker & Taylor Co., 1887), 219.

16. William H. McGuffey, *McGuffey's Fifth Eclectic Reader* (New York, Cincinnati, Chigago: American Book Company, 1920), 35; and Samuel Kirkham, *An Essay on Elocution, Designed for the Use of Schools and Private Learners* (New York: Robinson, Pratt, & Co., 1836), 168.

17. George Vandenhoff, *The Art of Elocution*, 185–86.

18. F. Taverner Graham, *Reasonable Elocution. A Textbook for Schools, Colleges, Clergymen, Lawyers, Actors, etc.* (New York & Chicago: A. S. Barnes, 1877), 181–89. For her other applications of the "speech" category, see Shakespeare in Appendix 1.

19. George Vandenhoff, *The Art of Elocution*, 186.

20. Jonathan Barber, *A Practical Treatise on Gesture, Chiefly Abstracted from Austin's Chironomia; Adapted to the Use of Students, and Arranged According to the Method of Instruction of Harvard University* (Cambridge: Hilliard and Brown, 1831), 96.

21. Vandenhoff, 148.

22. J. C. Zackos, *Analytic Elocution: An Analysis of the Powers of the Voice, for the Purpose of Expression in Speaking Illustrated by Copious Examples, and Marked by a System of Notation* (New York: A.S. Barnes & Burr, 1861), 173–76.

23. George S. Hillard and Homer B. Sprague, *The Franklin Sixth Reader and Speaker; Consisting of Extracts in Prose and Verse, with Biographical and Critical Notices of the Author* (Boston: Brewer and Tileston, 1876), 148–52.

24. James Rush, *The Philosphy of the Human Voice*, 130.

25. Jonathan Barber, *The Elocutionist, Consisting of Declamations and Readings, in Prose and Poetry; for the Use of Colleges and Schools* (New Haven: A. H. Maltby, 1836), 50–51, 362–66, 366–70, and 385–90.

26. *The Franklin Sixth Reader*, 262–66.

27. Joshua Leavitt, *American Lessons in Reading and Speaking, for the Use of the Middle Class in Common Schools* (Andover, Mass.: Gould, Newman & Saxton, 1840) 159–63; William Russell, *Orthophony* (1862) 236 ff.; B. W. Atwell, *Principles of Elocution and Vocal Culture: in Which the Rules for Correct Reading and Speaking, and Directions for Improving and Strengthening the Voice are Given* (Providence: Bangs Williams News Co., 1867), 83.

28. Stanley W. Lindberg, *The Annotated McGuffey: Selections from the McGuffey Eclectic Readers 1836–1920* (New York: Van Nostrand Reinhold Company, 1976), 233–37.

29. Stanley W. Lindberg's observation (ibid. 236) that Iago ran the risk of really appearing "honest," as the *Reader* did not provide its readership with the whole context is, I believe, not correct. One of the reasons why a fragment like "The folly of intoxication" could develop into a cliché in the first place was the fact that its context was recognized.

30. Odd passages from *Samson Agonistes*, "Comus," "L'Allegro," and "Il Penseroso," and a couple of his sonnets (on "blindness") were anthologized.

31. Andrew Comstock, *A System of Elocution, with Special Reference to Gesture, to the Treatment of Stammering and Defective Articulation* (Philadelphia: J. Kay and Brother, 1843), 184.

32. See e. g. Richard Green Parker and J. Madison Watson, *The National Fifth Reader, Containing a Complete and Practical Treatise on Elocution; Select and Classified Exercises in Reading and Declamation; . . .* (New York: A. S. Barnes, 1870), 200–202. Parker and Watson's introduction is another example of a multiple approach to "elocution," with notes on pronunciation and intonation, a glossary, and comments on interpretation.

33. James Rush, *The Philosophy of the Human Voice*, 158.

34. Ibid., 158.

35. Ibid., 128–29.

36. Cf. Russell, *Orthophony* (1862), 236 ff.

37. James Rush, *The Philosophy of the Human Voice*, 308–9.

38. Commentary, *Lord Byron: The Complete Poeticals Works*, ed. Jerome J. McGann. *Childe Harold's Pilgrimage* (Oxford: At the Clarendon Press, 1980), 2: 264–65.

39. The three extracts from *Childe Harold* ("The battle of Waterloo," "The night before the battle of Waterloo," and "The dying gladiator") can be linked through their common theme with the two other very popular poems "Destruction of Sennacherib" and "Darkness" and, similarly, the piece on Greece in *Childe Harold* with the passage from *The Giaour* (68–140) that often was called "Address to Ancient and Modern Greece."

40. *The American Orator's Own Book*, 212, 289.

41. Samuel Kirkham, *An Essay on Elocution* 165; see also Jerome McGann, ed. *Childe Harold*, 284–85.

42. Ebenezer Porter, *Analysis of the Principles of Rhetorical Delivery As Applied in Reading and Speaking* (Andover: Mark Newman; Boston: Hilliard, Gray & Co., 1827). Another book by the same writer called *The Rhetorical Reader; Consisting of Instructions for Regulating the Voice, with a Rhetorical Notation . . .* (Andover: Gould and Newman, 1841) also included "The battle of Waterloo." This edition (1841) was the seventy-fifth!

43. John Hanbury Dwyer, *An Essay on Elocution: with Elucidatory Passages from Various Authors. To Which Will Be Added, Remarks on Reading Prose and Verse* (New York: Published by the author, sold by G. & C. Carvill and E. Bliss, 1828) 34, 277, and 293; the sixth edition (1856) printed the same passages except the one from Canto II.

44. Jonathan Barber, *A Grammar of Elocution; Containing the Principles of the Arts of Reading and Speaking; . . . Adapted to Colleges, Schools, and Private Instruction: . . . Taught in Yale College* (New Haven: A. H. Maltby, 1830), 273–77; his *The Elocutionist* added the "Greece" sections (II, 693–864 passim).

45. John Swett, *School Elocution; a Manual of Vocal Training in High School, Normal Schools, and Academies* (New York: D. Appleton & Company, [1884]).

46. Vandenhoff, *The Art of Elocution*, 205–6.

47. Russell, *Orthophony* (1862), 267.

48. Thomas Budd Shaw, *Outlines of English Literature. A New American Edition. With a Sketch of American Literature by Henry T. Tuckerman* (Philadelphia: Blanchard and Lea, 1856); cf. *A Complete Manual of English Literature, ed. William Smith. With a Sketch of American Literature by Henry Theodore Tuckerman* (New York: Sheldon and Company, 1867); *Choice Specimens of English Literature; Selected from the Chief English Writers, and Arranged Chronologically. Adapted to the Use of American Students by B. N. Martin* (New York & Chicago: Sheldon & Company, 1869). See also Parker and Watson, *The National Fifth Reader*.

49. Ephraim Hunt, *Literature of the English Language; Comprising Representative Selections from the Best Authors, also Lists of Contemporary Writers and Their Principal Works* (New York, Chicago: Ivison, Blakeman, Taylor, and Co., 1870).

50. George S. Hillard and Homer B. Sprague, *The Franklin Sixth Reader and Speaker*, 295. *The Franklin Fifth Reader* (1871), understandably, did not include any Byron.

51. Francis H. Underwood, *A Handbook of English Literature Intended for the Use of High Schools, As Well as a Companion and Guide for Private Students, and for General Readers. British Authors* (Boston: Lee & Shepard, Publishers, 1875), 395. The extracts were the following: II, 181–252; II, 801–63; III, 397–405; III, 860–68; IV, 1–36; IV, 1594–1656.

52. Horace Hills Morgan, *Literary Studies from the Great British Authors* (St. Louis: G. I. Jones and Co., 1880), 312; see also his *English and American Literature*

for Schools and Colleges (Boston, New York, Chicago: Leach, Shewell, and Sanborn, 1889). The extracts are: I, 109–17; I, 387–468; III, 181–252; III, 635–43; III, 653–715; IV, 1–234, IV, 694–882; IV, 1252–69; IV, 1567–1656.

53. See Stanley W. Lindberg, xv–xvii.

54. See p. 106 below.

55. Samuel Kirkham (1836) offered the two stanzas from the poem to illustrate the usage of simile and to train reading. Horace H. Morgan daringly included the two passages in his *English and American Literature for Schools and Colleges,* despite his earlier remonstrance of Byron's "coareseness," "immature views," and—the worst of all—"sensuality" (cf. also Introduction to his *Literary Studies for the Great British Authors* 1880).

56. Willis J. Westlake, *Common-School Literature: English and American with Several Hundred Extracts to Be Memorized* (Philadelphia: Christopher Sower Co., 1876), 33–34, 115.

57. Albert F. Blaisdell, *First Steps with American and British Authors* (New York, Cincinnati, Chicago: American Book Co., 1899), 146; Shaw and Smith used another chilling section from the poem for the same purpose; in *Choice Specimens* (107–25).

58. McGuffey's *High School and Literary Reader* (Cincinnati and New York: Eclectic Press, 1889), 140–41.

59. Dwyer, *An Essay on Elocution* (1828), 277 ff.

60. See Dwyer (1828); Russell, *The American Elocutionist; Comprising "Lessons of Enunciation," "Exercises in Elocution," and "Rudiments of Gesture"* (Boston: Jenks and Palmer, 1844); Vandenhoff (1846); Russell, *Ortophony* (1862); and J. Willis Westlake, *The Common-School Literature.* A passage from *Manfred,* called "Midnight at Coliseum" (III, iv 1–44) is similar in its preoccupation with the moonlit landscape; it is quoted by Richard Green Parker and J. Madison Watson (1870), and by Morgan (1889).

61. Charles W. Sanders, *The School Reader. Fifth Book. Designed as a Sequel to Sanders' Fourth Reader* (Chicago: Ivison, Blakeman, Taylor & Co., [1859]), 357.

62. Russell, *Ortophony* (1862), 269.

63. Loomis J. Campbell, *The New Franklin Fifth Reader, with a New Elocutionary Treatise, Essentials of Reading, by Mark Bailey* (1884: New York: Taintor Brothers & Co., [1886]), 329.

64. Other references to the concepts of "freedom" and "tyranny" can be found in Albert P. Southwick. See his use of the poem "Ode to Napoleon Buonaparte" in *Short Studies in Literature. For the Use of Schools* (Philadelphia: Eldredge & Brother, 1883) and also Horace H. Morgan (1889) and Blaisdell (1899) ("Vision of Belshazzar").

65. Similar in content is a brief passage from *The Corsair* (II, 331–65), often called "Remorse," which was used by a number of handbooks: Epes Sargent, *Selections in Poetry for Exercises at School and at Home* (Philadelphia: Thomas, Cowpertwaite & Co, 1853); Shaw, 1869; Morgan, 1889.

66. Hillard and Sprague, *The Franklin Sixth Reader,* 139–47 and McGuffey, *McGuffey's Fifth Eclectic Reader,* 35.

67. Dwyer (1828).

68. George L. Raymond, *The Orator's Manual; a Practical and Philosophical Treatise on Vocal Culture, Emphasis and Gesture, Together with Selections for Declamations and Recitation* (Chicago: S. C. Griggs and Company, 1880).

69. Charles Massey, Introduction, *Massey's Exhibition, Reciter, and Drawing-Room Entertainments; . . . Adapted for the Use of Schools and Families* (New York: Samuel French, [1856]).

70. Stanley W. Lindberg, 344–45.

71. Mark Bailey, *An Introductory Treatise on Elocution; with Principles and Illustrations, Arranged for Teaching and Practice. Yale College* (Boston: Brewer and Tileston, 1865), lvii.

72. Edward Napoleon Kirby, *Vocal and Action-Language: Culture and Expression* (Boston: Lee and Shepard, 1888), 148.

73. In Dwyer (1828 and 1856); Porter (1827 and 1841); Russell, *Exercises in Elocution, Exemplifying the Rules and Principles of the Art of Reading* (Boston: Jenks and Palmer, 1841); *Ortophany, or Vocal Culture. A Manual of Elementary Exercises for the Cultivation of the Voice in Elocution,* ed. Francis T. Russell (Boston: Houghton, Mifflin and Company, 1890); Russell, *The American Elocutionist.*

74. Russell, *The American Elocutionist,* 300.

75. John Swett, *School Elocution,* 349 and 387. See also Isaac H. Brown, *Common School Elocution and Oratory: A Manual of Vocal Culture Based upon Scientific Principles* . . . (St. Louis: I. H. Brown & Co., 1886), 163.

76. Mary L. Cobb, Preface, *Poetical Dramas for Home and School* (Boston: Lee and Shepard, 1873), 7–35.

77. George Bradford Bartlett, *Parlor Amusements for the Young Folks* (Boston: James R. Osgood and Company, 1875), 8–9.

78. Lewis Baxter Monroe, *The Fifth Reader* (Philadelphia: Cowperthwait & Co., 1871), 133.

79. See e. g., Underwood, Shaw (1869 etc.), and Dwyer.

80. George R. Cathcart, *The Literary Reader: Typical Selections from Some of the Best British and American Authors, from Shakespeare to the Present Time* (New York and Chicago: Ivison, Blackman, Taylor, and Company, 1874), 63–67.

81. George Vandenhoff, *The Art of Elocution,* 174.

82. Mason Wade, *Francis Parkman: Heroic Historian* (New York: Viking Press, 1942), 11; see also 17.

83. Barber, *Elocutionist,* 191–223; McGuffey, *New Sixth Eclectic Reader. Exercises in Rhetorical Reading, with Introductory Rules and Examples* (Cincinnati, New York: Van Antwerp, [1857]), 172–75. McGuffey rewrote the end of his selection, as was his custom, adding the sentence "but that to the 'Disinherited Knight' the meed of victory was fairly and honorably awarded" to the paragraph ending in ". . . permit this species of encounter." His extract started with the sentence, "The music of the challengers breathed. . . ."

84. Porter, *The Rhetorical Reader,* 373 ff.; Barber, *The Elocutionist,* 220 ff.

85. McGuffey, *New Sixth Eclectic Reader,* 161–64; also in *Franklin Sixth Reader,* 164–69, which prunes curses such as "God of Zion" and "God of Moses."

86. E.g. in Shaw and Smith, *Choice Specimens,* 336–38.

87. Anna T. Diel Randall, *Reading and Elocution: Theoretical and Practical* (New York: Ivison, Phinney, Blakeman & Co., 1870), 56–57.

88. 277, 280–82.

89. See e.g., Underwood, 277–88.

90. *The American Orator's Own Book,* 289 ff.

91. *The Elocutionist,* 128–31.

92. Jesse Olney, Preface, *The School Reader; Consisting of Instructive and Progressive Lessons in Prose and Poetry* (New Haven: Duffie and Peek, 1843).

93. Hillard, *The Franklin Fifth Reader,* 76.

94. M. S. Mitchell, *A Manual of Elocution Founded upon the Philosphy of the Human Voice* (Philadelphia: Eldredge & Brothers, 1870), 71–72.

95. Monroe, *The Fifth Reader,* 275; Hillard, *The Franklin Fifth Reader,* 150–52.

96. *McGuffey's New Sixth Reader,* 77–79, 384–88.

97. *The Franklin Fifth Reader,* 145–47, and *The Franklin Sixth Reader,* 154–59.

98. *McGuffey's Fifth Eclectic Reader,* 247–51. Another episode printed by Monroe's *Fifth Reader* (223–26) involved an insensitive and brutal teacher and an intelligent little boy (Master Square).

99. Edward Napoleon Kirby, *Vocal and Action: Language: Culture and Expression,* 180–83.

100. In describing the accident that happened to Mrs. Peerybingle at the very beginning of the First Chirp, *Monroe's Fifth Reader* takes the precaution of replacing the word "legs" with "stockings."

101. Kirby, 147.

102. Russell, *The American Elocutionist,* 307.

103. Russell, *The American Elocutionist,* 307 and note.

104. Another lively scene in the same vein, employed by Robert Kidd for his *A Rhetorical Reader, for Class Drill and Private Instruction in Elocution* (Cincinnati: Wilson, Hinkle and Co, 1870) 187–92, was the duel between Captain Adams and Sir Mulberry Hawk in *Nicholas Nickleby* (chapter 50).

105. Mark Bailey, *An Introductory Treatise on Elocution,* lxv.

106. Barber, *Grammar of Elocution,* 318–20.

107. See Annabel Newton, *Wordsworth in Early American Criticism* (Chicago, Ill.: University of Chicago Press, 1928).

108. Russell, *Ortophony* (1862), 236 ff.

109. *The Franklin Sixth Reader,* 282–85. The extract was illustrated by a stereotype of a Swiss mountain landscape.

110. Swett, *School Elocution,* 15.

111. See Raoul Granqvist, "The Self and the Other in Walt Whitman's Mirror: English Literature and Culture from an American Perspective," 1–15.

112. I. H. Brooks, *Common School Elocution and Oratory: A Manual of Vocal Culture Based upon Scientific Principles* (1885; St. Louis: I.H. Brown & Co., 1886), 200–04.

113. Joshua Leavitt, *Selections for Reading and Speaking, for the Higher Classes in Common Schools* (Boston: John P. Jewett & Co., 1849), 37.

114. Hillard, *The Sixth Reader,* 419 ff.

Chapter 4. British Writers on the American Stage

1. Charles Durang noted in his survey of the Philadelphia stage life that a certain Mrs. Ellis of England "was near forestalling" (in another context in the same work he mentions that her play was given at Pepin & Breschard's Circus) Baker's *Marmion* by a version that was shown at the Olympic, Chestnut Street, in April 1812. In Durang, "History of the Philadelphia Stage, 1749–1855. Partly Compiled from the Papers of his Father, the Late John Durang, with Notes by the Editors" [Philadelphia: University of Pennsylvania Library, 1854–59] n. pag., Harvard Theatre Collection; Joseph N. Ireland, *Records of the New York Stages, from 1750 to 1860* (New York: T. H. Morell, Publisher, 1866–67), 1:222, 258–59, and 283; Joseph N. Ireland, *A Memoir of the Professional Life of Thomas Abthorpe Cooper* (New York: Dunlap Society, 1888), 38.

2. *Marmion; or, Flodden Field, a Drama Founded on the Poem by Walter Scott. From the first London edition; of 1812* (New York: Longworth, 1812).

3. William B. Wood, *Personal Recollections of the Stage; Embracing Notices of Actors, Authors, and Auditors, During a Period of Forty Years* (Philadelphia: Henry Carey Baird, 1855), 188; see also George C. D. Odell, *Annals of the New York Stage* (New York, 1927–49) 2:383.

4. William Dunlap, *A History of the American Theatre* (London: Richard Bentley, 1833), 2:315. He admits: "I never felt very proud of the circumstance." It was repeated in 1815 and in 1817; see Odell 2:439, 475, 478, 479, and 480.

5. According to Joseph N. Ireland in *Records of the New York Stage, from 1750 to 1860* (New York: T. H. Morell Publishers, 1866), 1:283, its firstnight was on 13 February.

6. See Ireland, *A Memoir of the Professional Life of Thomas Abthorpe Cooper*, 38.

7. Ireland, "Memories of Mrs. Duff," ed. E. J. W., n.pag., [in the handwriting of Joseph N. Ireland] Harvard Theatre Collection.

8. Odell 2: 383. See also James Rees, *Scrapbooks. Old Play Bills with Remarks* (Philadelphia, 1874–78), 1:19: "By this stratagem the piece obtained an impartial trial, although with foreign color upon it, and thousands lavished applause where otherwise it would not have endured the strains of an American muse. . . . After this discovery, no one went to see the piece, and it was withdrawn." But it was played in the South; for instance at Charleston in 1820 and 1824. See William Stanley Hoole, Index, *The Ante-Bellum Charleston Theatre* (Tuscaloosa, Ala.: University of Alabama Press, 1946).

9. The same title as of 1812 (see above). Published by D. Longworth, et. al., Dramatic Repository, Shakespeare-Galley, April 1816, ii.

10. Dunlap, 2:315.

11. James N. Barker, *Marmion; or, The Battle of Flodden Field. A Drama, in Five Acts. With a Portrait of Mr. Duff, in the Character of Marmion*, 3rd ed. (Philadelphia: A.R. Poole, and Ash & Mason, etc., 1826), 40–41.

12. Dunlap, 2:315.

13. Durang, "Philadelphia Stage."

14. Cf. Moray McLaren, *Sir Walter Scott: The Man and Patriot* (London: Heinemann, 1970), who claims (72–77) that Scott's *Marmion* depicts the Scottish loss of chivalry and integrity.

15. "American Drama," *American Quarterly Review* (1827), 1:353. See also Index, in *Three Centuries of English and American Plays: A Checklist. England: 1500–1800, United States: 1714–1830*, ed. G. William Bergquist (New York: Readex Microprint Corporation, 1963).

16. H. P. Phelps, *Players of a Century: A Record of the Albany Stage. Including Notices of Prominent Actors Who Have Appeared in America* (New York: Benjamin Blom, 1972), 50–51. Edward Willard (Philadelphia 1890) is listed as the writer of an "American" play related to *Julius Caesar*. See Robert F. Roden, *Later American Plays, 1831–1900* (New York: Dunlap Society, 1900).

17. The whole title is *Mary of Scotland; or, The Heir of Avenel. A Drama, in Three Acts. Founded on the Popular Novel of "The Abbott," and Originally Performed at the Theatre, New-York, with Universal Applause* (New York: Henry I. Megarey, 1821). I have used the copy AC 8 A 100.821 at Houghton Library, Harvard University.

18. Odell, 2:595; Ireland, 1:378; Henry Adelbert White says about this local play that "though a bit long, [it] is a noble instance of dramatic condensation, without following Scott slavishly." *Sir Walter Scott's Novels on the Stage* (New Haven: Yale University Press, 1927), 156.

19. It was not played until 31 January 1857, at The Chatham Theatre.

20. Dunlap, 2:313.

21. Durang, "Philadelphia Stage."

22. Reese D. James, *Old Drury of Philadelphia: A History of the Philadelphia Stage, 1800–1835* (Philadelphia: University of Pennsylvania, 1932), 12.

23. Dunlap, 2:313; Hoole, Index.

24. In *The Works of Charles Lamb,* ed. E. V. Lucas, Poems and Plays (1903; New York: AMS Press, 1968), 5:180–211; see also Arthur Hobson Quinn, *A History of the American Drama, from the Beginning to the Civil War* (New York: Appleton-Century-Crofts, 1951), 162. The differences in the work's popularity also came out in its publishing history: it was not printed in England until 1818, and then as part of Lamb's *Complete Works,* whereas in America it came out separately in Philadelphia in 1813 as Carey's imprint, and in 1825 as Thomas H. Palmer's.

25. James, 664.

26. On the American stages the play was pruned of details that could suggest America. See *Works of Charles Lamb* 5: 368, and note 207.

27. See James, Index.

28. *The Two Foscari,* Macready's Acting Copy, Harvard Theatre Collection. James gives the dates 8 and 9 November 1822 for its American premiere at Baltimore (see Durang "Philadelphia Stage" and James 43 and 385). Macready started to work on the play in 1834, and on 16 April 1838, he gave his first English performance of it, among the spectators was Dickens. See his *The Diaries of William Charles Macready, 1833–1851,* ed. William Toynbee (New York: G. P. Putnam's Sons, 1912), 1:124, 233–34, 410, 412, 424, 450 [hereafter Diaries]. See also his *Macready's Reminiscences, and Selections from His Diaries and Letters,* ed. Sir Frederick Pollock, Bart. (London: Macmillan and Co., 1875), 1:416, and 460; 2:85, 93, 103–04, and 106 [hereafter *Reminiscences*].

29. Lord Byron, *Sardanapulus, A Tragedy. The Two Foscari, A Tragedy. Cain, A Mystery* (London: John Murrey, 1821). Copy used by Junius B. Booth. Harvard Theatre Collection. According to James (Index) it was not acted in Philadelphia until 1836.

30. James, Index. It was repeated in the Philadelphia theaters on 19 February 1828, on 20 and 25 January 1831, and on 2 July 1834. It had been given at the Park, New York, on 25 May 1818.

31. See his acting copy of *Sardanapulus* etc., Harvard Theatre Collection.

32. Durang, "Philadelphia Stage."

33. Ibid.

34. Ibid. See Herman Arthur Wilson, *A History of the Philadelphia Theatre, 1835 to 1855* (Philadelphia: University of Pennsylvania Press, 1935) for its further reputation in this area. It was staged in 1837, 1840, 1841, and 1843 and then vanished from the boards. The play had also a run at Charleston, on 17 and 26 May 1824, on 31 January, 2 March, 11 April 1825, and on 25 March 1841. See Hoole, Index.

35. Odell, 3:105, 108, and 251; "The Starks, the Bakers, the Chapmans," in San Francisco Theatre Research, ed. Lawrence Estavan, 3:17 (San Francisco, 1938). MS at Harvard Theatre Collection.

36. Odell, 3:343–44. The play was repeated at the Lafayette on 18 July 1828; it was also given at Barnes' Theatre on 8 January 1833.

37. At the Chatham on 24 May 1841, and at the Bowery on 10 September 1842. Odell, 4:489 and 624.

38. It had been given at the Park on 16 December 1828 with Thomas Barry as Werner and repeated on 14 and 18 March 1831. It was a failure. See Odell 3:387 and 499. His prompt book of the play at Harvard Theatre Collection (TS 2732.588) demonstrates the range of his work on the play, in cutting it, paraphrasing it, and even adding a number of rewritten passages to it.

39. On 30 September and 7 October at The Drama Melodeon, on 12 and 24 October, on 4 and 28 November; and at Baltimore on 26 December. See Playbills in "Macready and Forrest; and Their Contemporaries," in "Actors and Actresses of

Great Britain and the United States, from the Days of David Garrick to the Present Time," ed. Matthew Brander and Laurence Hutton, 4.1 part 2 (New York: Cassell & Company, 1886). MS at Harvard Theatre Collection.

40. At the Park on 7 through 12 December and at the same theater on 19 through 25 September 1844. See Playbills in "Macready and Forrest," 4.2 part 1 and 2; and Odell, 5:5, 10, 11, 17. Further on 26 October (Odell: "It did not seem to have a great success in the theatre"), on 30 November, and 20 December 1843.

41. At St. Charles Theatre on 14 February 1844. See playbills in "Macready and Forrest," 4.1–2, Harvard Theatre Collection.

42. Playbills in "Macready and Forrest" 4.2.

43. Playbills in "Macready and Forrest" 4.1.1–2. See also See James E. Murdoch, *The Stage, or, Recollections of Actors and Acting from an Experience of Fifty Years* (Cincinnati: Robert Clarke & Co., 1884), 121.

44. *Diaries* 2:222, 234, 243, 273, 275, 404, 486, 410, 413 (Boston). John Agg's production of it had been presented in New York in September 1821 at the Park, "with but little success" (Ireland 1:389). Donizetti's opera *Marino Faliero* was first produced in Italian (!) in New York on 15 December 1843.

45. Alan S. Downer, *The Eminent Tragedian William Charles Macready* (Cambridge, Mass.: Harvard University Press, 1966), 269.

46. Murdoch, 121.

47. Murdoch, 117.

48. From here it was reported that "some women in the dress circle shrieked in the last scene and the play ended with the house in a state of ferment." Alan S. Downer, *The Eminent Tragedian William Charles Macready,* 261.

49. Playbills in "Macready and Forrest" 4.2; *Reminiscences* 1:239 and 248.

50. Odell, 5:5, 10, 11, and 17. See also "Macready and Forrest" 4.2 and *Reminiscences* 1:239 and 248.

51. *Diaries,* 2:229.

52. *Reminiscences,* 1:218.

53. Noah M. Ludlow, *Dramatic Life as I Found It* ([1880]; Bronx, N.Y.: Benjamin Blom, 1966), 597–98; see also Joseph Jefferson, *"Rip Van Winkle." The Autobiography of Joseph Jefferson,* ed. Alan S. Downer (Cambridge, Mass.: Belknap Press, Harvard University Press, 1964), 33, 339–40.

54. *Diaries,* 2:329f.

55. *Reminiscences* 2:226. Cf. Ibid., 239.

56. *Reminiscences,* 2:248.

57. *Diaries,* 2:230.

58. *Reminiscences,* 1:320.

59. Odell, 5:25, 87.

60. *The Journal of William Charles Macready,* 1832–1851, ed. J. C. Trewin (London: Longman's, 1867), 254–55.

61. *Diaries,* 2:229.

62. *Diaries,* 2:230.

63. Rees, *Scrapbooks,* 1:51.

64. James, 151.

65. *American Theatre Companies, 1794–1887,* ed. Weldon B. Durham (New York: Greenwood Press, 1986), 153.

66. Hoole, Index.

67. See Arthur Hobson Quinn, *A History of the American Drama, from the Beginning to the Civil War,* 192.

68. Walter M. Leman, *Memories of an Old Actor* (San Francisco: A Roman Co., 1886), 14.

69. Ludlow, *Dramatic Life as I Found It*, 347. He produced the play in Cincinnati in late 1829, and on 19 October 1845 in St. Louis where it ran four nights in succession: a sure mark of success.

70. *Diaries*, 123–239, passim.

71. Durang. See also Wilson, *Philadelphia Theatre* 10, 59–60, 163.

72. Durang, "Philadelphia Stage" and "The Memoir of John Durang: American Actor, 1785–1816," ed. Alan S. Downer (Published for The Historical Society of York Country and for the American Society for Theatre Research by the University of Pittsburg Press, 1966). It was repeated on 23 April 1842 at the Arch Theatre.

73. Ireland, 2:203.

74. John S. Kendall, *The Golden Age of New Orleans Theatre* (Baton Rouge: Louisiana State University Press, 1952), 148.

75. The play opened in New Orleans in February 1828, at The Camp Street Theatre with James Caldwell as manager. It ran four successive nights . . . "[and was] witnessed by crowds" (Kendall, 47); see also Nelle Smither, *A History of the English Theatre at New Orleans, 1806–1842* (Philadelphia: University of Pennsylvania, 1944) 4 and James H. Dormon, Jr., *Theater in the Ante Bellum South, 1815–1861* (Chapel Hill: University of North Carolina Press, 1967), 260–61.

76. Odell, 3:105.

77. Willis, *The Corsair. A Gazette of Literature, Art, Dramatic Criticism, Fashion and Novelty*, [1–2]: 65 ff.

78. Bayle Bernard [John Bernard's son], *Early Days of the American Stage; Being a Selection from the Pages of One of Its Managers.* From *Tallis's Dramatic Magazine* (London, 1850–51) and *The Manhattan Magazine* (New York, 1884) 613–14, Harvard Theatre Collection.

79. In Philadelphia on 1 January 1812, at Charleston on 28 February 1812, in Boston on 30 March 1812, and in New York on 8 May 1812 (although Odell claims that it was produced in New York as early as on 12 June 1811).

80. Odell, 3:693.

81. James, 105.

82. Martin Staples Shockley, *The Richmond Stage, 1784–1812* (Charlottesville: University Press of Virginia, 1977), 342, 343, 347.

83. Durang, "Philadelphia Stage."

84. See Wilson, Index, *Philadelphia Theatre.*

85. William G. B. Carson, Appendix, *The Theatre of the Frontier. The Early Years of St. Louis Stage* (New York: Benjamin Blom, University of Chicago, 1932).

86. Durang, "Philadelphia Stage."

87. Ibid.

88. Odell, 3:202. The play was repeated in October-December 1826, in February 1827, and then each year through 1830.

89. As an itinerant actor in the South in 1842, Joseph Jefferson remembered how he worked out a contract for his father to paint two scenes from *The Lady of the Lake:* one "representing Loch Katrine, with the ladyship paddling her own canoe in the distance, and a mountain torrent in the foreground with a bridge made famous by the combat of Fitz-James and Roderick Dhu." *"Rip Van Winkle": The Autobiography of Joseph Jefferson*, 24–26.

90. Edmund Flagg, *The Far West; or, A Tour Beyond the Mountains* (New York: Harper & Brothers, 1838), 1:73.

91. At the Bowery on 21 February, 1852, on 8 May, 1854, and in September 1860; at the Chatham on 18 January, 1858; and at the New Bowery Theatre on 30 May 1864. In 1864 E. L. Davenport and J. W. Wallack added to it scenes from *Oliver Twist* (Eugene Tompkins, *The History of the Boston Theatre 1854–1901*. Compiled

with the assistance of Quincy Kilby [Boston and New York: Houghton Mifflin Company, 1908], 126).

92. See Odell, 9:408, 409.

93. See Don L. Hixon and Don A. Hennessee, *Nineteenth-century American Drama. A Finding Guide* and William R. DuBois, *English and American Stage Productions: An Annotated Checklist of Prompt Books, 1800–1900* (Boston: G. K. Hall, 1973) for a list of the American editions.

94. Ralph Leslie Rusk, *The Literature of the Middle Western Frontier* (New York: Columbia University Press, 1925), 1:417.

95. Odell, 2:505.

96. Durang, "Philadelphia Stage."

97. Playbill, Boston Theatre, Harvard Theatre Collection.

98. Playbill, Boston Theatre, Harvard Theatre Collection. Durang (in "Philadelphia Stage") complains that the "martial airs on the military bagpipes [by a 'gentleman from Scotland'], the nasal groans, and screaching dissonant notes—put us in a gallopade."

99. From Ireland, *Memories of Mrs. Duff*, 79–80.

100. See Indexes in Odell 2, 3, 4, and 5.

101. Hoole, Index.

102. See Indexes in James, and in White, *Sir Walter Scott's Novels on the Stage*.

103. Dormon, *Theater in the Ante Bellum South, 1815–1861*, 274, n. 46.

104. Ludlow, 430, 347, 352, 361, 398, 566, 682, 437, 459, 960.

105. [William Newham Blane], *An Excursion through the United States and Canada during the Years 1822–23 by an English Gentleman* (London: Baldwin, Cradock, and Joy, 1824), 121 and Charles Cist, *Cincinnati in 1841; Its Early Annals and Future Prospects* (Cincinnati: E. Morgan and Co., 1841), 437.

106. T. Allton Brown, in *A History of the New York Stage: from the First Performance in 1732 to 1901* (New York: Dodd, Mead and Company, 1903), 1:93–94. At The Academy of Music on 4 September 1856 a similar gigantic performance took place. This time the second and third acts of *Rob Roy* were performed with Mme Elizabeth Ponisi as Helen and John Dyott as Rob Roy. After this occurred the musical extravaganza "The Invisible Prince, or The Island of Tranquil Delights," the third act of *The Lady of Lyons, All the World a Stage, and The Widow's Victim* (Brown, Index, New York Stage, 1).

107. Claire McGlinchee, *The First Decade of the Boston Museum* (Boston: Bruce Humphries Publishers, 1940), 79.

108. Edmond M. Gagey, *The San Francisco Stage: A History* (New York: Columbia University Press, 1950), 22.

109. Margaret G. Watson, Appendix, *Silver Theatre: Amusements of the Mining Frontier in Early Nevada, 1850–1864* (Glendale, Calif.: Arthur H. Clark Company, 1964).

110. See Roden, List and Index, *Later American Plays 1831–1900*.

111. James W. Simmons dramatized *Bride of Lammermoor* and gave it the title *Valdemar; or, The Castle of the Cliff. A Tragedy* (Philadelphia: H. C. Carey and I. Lee, 1822); see Quinn, 192–93. It was acted in New York in 1827, and a few times in later years (Odell, 3:285, 338, 390, 391, 489).

112. See Laurence Hutton, *Curiosities of the American Stage* (New York: Harper & Brothers, 1891), 177.

113. "The Heart of Midlothian; or, The Lily of St. Leonard's" (1819), originally adapted by Thomas J. Dibdin (Charles Dibdin Pitt), was rarely played in America before being dramatized by Dion Boucicault as "Jeanie Deans" (see the whole text of Boucicault's play and the Commentary in Appendix 2) in 1860. It was first pro-

duced at the Park on 19 May 1819 (Odell, 2:533), then in [1826] and 1839–1840 at
the same theatre (Odell, 4:119, 281, 353) (in Philadelphia and Baltimore also in 1819
and 1820; in Boston in 1848 with Mrs. Judah as Meg). The Bowery of New York
also produced the version "Whistler; or, The Fate of the Lily of St Leonard's"
on 23 December 1833. Boucicault also produced "The Spae Wife," based on *Guy
Mannering,* expressly for the Boston Museum. It was never acted, except for a
single copyright performance at the Elephant and Castle Theater in 1886. He also
made a gaelized version of it, which he also abandoned. This play, "Cuisla-M-Chree"
("Throb of My Heart"), was played at Hollis Street Theatre on 20 February 1888.
Boucicault had placed the action in Ireland and centered it on an old Ulster family.
The playbill explains that "this proud race would accept no horrors from the English
Court, but . . . stood fiercely at bay." See Harold Freeze Follard, "The Plays of Dion
Boucicault: Studies in Nineteenth Century Theatrical History" (Harvard University
thesis, 1938), 1:165–67. The playbill (TS 931.2. Harvard Theatre Collection) quotes
the following lines from the play: "A crowned King I cannot be, / No title less
contenteth me; / I'll keep the crown I won by steel. / For I am Owen Roe O'Neill. /
To my own blood I will be true, / To my own lord allegiance yield."

114. Odell, 3:406; see his Index for a listing of the play's American run.

115. *Guy Mannering; or, The Gipsey's Prophesy, as Presented at Booth's Theater*
(New York: Henry L. Hinton & Co., Publishers, 1876), iv. See *Helen Potter's Impersonations* (New York: Edgar S. Werner, 1981) for her imitation of Cushman's Meg
(152–57).

116. Rees, *Scrapbooks* 1:51.

117. *New York Times,* 6 November 1874 (7).

118. *New York Times,* 13 March 1897 (9:2).

119. Ireland, 2:204.

120. Wilson, Index, *Philadelphia Theatre.*

121. See William L. Keese, *A Group of Comedians* (New York: Dunlop Society,
1901), 29.

122. Odell, 4:160; 203–4, 251, 160, 551.

123. Playbill, Dickens file, Harvard Theatre Collection.

124. Wilson, Index, *Philadelphia Theatre.*

125. Solomon Franklin Smith, *Theatrical Management in the West and South for
Thirty Years. Interspersed with Anecdotical Sketches: Autobiographically Given by
Sol. Smith* (New York: Harper & Brothers, 1868), 131.

126. Odell, 4:283, 284, 289; 305, 353, and 362.

127. Odell, 4:296; 282–83. See also Ireland, 2:244.

128. Wilson, Index, *Philadelphia Theatre.*

129. Tremont Theatre, Forfeit Books, TS 1793.92, Harvard Theatre Collection.
Field also produced "Boz," a "Masque phrenologic." When it was shown (on 21
January 1842) Dickens was present at the Boston theater. Scenes from his *Nicholas
Nickleby* were also given in January and for the performance on 24 February when
Dickens was back at the theater. The masque consisted of the usual introduction to
some of the major Dickens's characters. Field also composed several so-called Boz
waltzes and the comical song "The Wery Last Observation of Weller Senior" after an
Irish air that became a hit with the Bostonians and would remain so for a long time.

130. William W. Clapp, *A Record of the Boston Stage* (New York, London: Benjamin Blom, 1968), 359.

131. Odell, 4:311. On 19 October 1839, *The Corsair* ([1–2]:503) provided an extract
from the (to me) unknown play, "Smike's Death."

132. Kendall, 174, 193, 393.

133. See William Glyde Wilkins, *Charles Dickens in America* (New York: Charles Scribner's Sons, 1912). Field's song is reprinted (65–66).

134. Boucicault file, Harvard Theatre Collection.

135. Dickens file, cutting, Harvard Theatre Collection.

136. See e. g., *Dickens in Cartoon and Caricature,* compiled William Glyde Wilkins, ed. B. N. Matz, privately printed for the Bibliophile Society (Boston: Plimpton Press, 1927).

137. Cf. A. J. Leavitt and H. N. Eagan, "The Arrival of Dickens. An Ethiopian Sketch" (New York: Samuel French, n. d).

138. *Charles Dickens in America,* 113.

139. *The Cricket on the Hearth. A Fairy Tale of Home* (New York: Harper & Brothers, Publishers, 1846) was one of the first American issues based on Albert R. Smith's dramatization which was performed for the first time at the Lyceum Theatre, London, 1845. See also Ireland 2: 524. Edward Stirling's version bore the same name, but had two instead of three acts. It was played on 31 December 1845 at The Adelphi Theatre, London. A third was produced at the City of London Theatre on 7 January 1846. This was subtitled *A Fairy Tale of Home in Three Chirps;* by W. T. *Townsend.* There was an edition of it published in Boston [1846], another in New York (Wiley & Putnam, 1846, no LV of Wiley and Putnam's Library of Choice Reading); and in Philadelphia [1846]. *The Cricket on the Hearth. A Fairy Tale of Home in Three Chirps* (Lacy's Acting Editon. London: Thomas Hales Lacy [1869], by [W. T.] Townsend) was played at the Bowery in May 1850.

140. Odell, 5:178–79, 199.

141. See statistics in Wilson, *Philadelphia Theatre.* It was performed fourteen times in 1847; four times in 1848; twice in 1849; twelve times in 1850; nine times in 1851; five times in 1854, and twice in 1855.

142. From McGlinchee, *The First Decade of the Boston Museum,* 119.

143. See Margaret G. Mayorga, Index, *A Short History of the American Drama. Commentaries on Plays prior to 1920* (New York: Dodd, Mead & Company, 1932).

144. Jefferson, *Autobiography,* 334–35.

145. Odell, 5:429, 432, 435, 437, 438, 441, 444, and 525; Ireland 2:523.

146. See Jefferson, *Autobiography* (335) for an excellent characterization of his way of acting.

147. Odell, 5:7.

148. Mitchell's Olympic Theatre produced still another fragment or sketch called "The Nipper, or, One of the House-(hold) of Dombey." It was acted on 29 November 1848 (see Ireland, Index, 2).

149. The play is listed by Mayorga as an "American" play.

150. Ireland, 2:524–25.

151. William L. Keese, *A Group of Comedians,* 13–14, 47.

152. Odell, 5:415–16.

153. Ireland, 2:567 and 585. *David Copperfield* was repeated at Burton's on 12 September 1853; Ireland 2:621.

154. Odell, 6:50.

155. Odell, 6:29.

156. Odell, 6:49–50.

157. A playbill in the Dickens & Stage file, Harvard Theatre Collection, describes the "farewell performance of Mrs. John Wood," at the Olympic on 11 June 1866, which indicates naturally that the play had been burlesqued. The play was further fragmentized by Chandos Fulton who produced "Jeremy Wren. The Dolls'-Dressmaker, and Her Friends," at the Bowery on 14 February 1868; see TS 3339. 350, Harvard Theatre Collection.

158. In Green Street Theatre, Albany, a play was performed in June 1853 based on one of Oliver's fellow-sufferers, Little Dick. The play was called "Little Dick, The Sick Pauper Boy." It created an enormous fuss. The child impersonating Dick was so convincing that everybody, inlucing the Oliver of the play, broke down in tears. The child actor was made Eva in *Uncle Tom's Cabin* that was to run for seven years in New York. See Phelps, 286–87.

159. Ireland, 2:700; also Odell, 7:214.

160. Tompkins, 126. See also Brown, *New York Stage,* 2:217.

161. Odell, 8:591.

162. Tompkins, 125. The play "Heep vs Micawber" was shown in Boston on 9 June 1873, with John T. Raymond and F. Mackey. Tompkins, 132.

163. Playbill from the Boston Museum for 13 April 1877, Harvard Theatre Collection.

164. Playbill, Dickens & Stage, Harvard Theatre Collection [159]. See also Odell 10: 378–79. H. A. Weaver, who also worked at Boston theaters, made another adaptation of the book, called "Tom-All-Alone's." Jo was acted by N. S. Wood, a child actor.

165. Robert Hogan, *Dion Boucicault* (New York: Twayne Publishers, 1969), 106.

166. Single MS sheet in Boucicault's handwriting, Boucicault's file, Harvard Theatre Collection.

167. See Garff B. Wilson on Boucicault's role in American theatre history: Boucicault sponsored the first successful copyright law for the protection of American playwrights, introduced the road companies, introduced fireproof scenery, etc. *Three Hundred Years of American Drama and Theatre: From Ye Bear and Ye Cubb to Hair* (Englewood Cliffs, N. J.: Prentice-Hall, 1973), 91–103.

168. Quinn, 372–73. This view is refuted by Follard.

169. Follard, 1:156–58.

170. See Jefferson, *Autobiography,* 159–60; also Odell, 7:211–12.

171. John Bouvé Clapp and Edwin Francis Edgett, *Plays of the Present* (New York: Dunlap Society, 1902), 73.

172. Philadelphia produced another reduced version of the play called "Poor Smike and His Friend Nicholas," with Joseph Jefferson as Smike. It was shown ten times at Peele's Philadelphia Museum in March 1847 (Wilson, *Philadelphia Theatre,* 634).

173. Odell, 7:211–12.

174. Odell, 7:212.

175. *History of the New York Theatres: Records of the New York Stage. Charles White, Extra Illustrated,* Harvard Theatre Collection.

176. *The New York Times,* 7 November 1871 (5: 3).

177. *The New York Times,* 15 October 1895 (5: 4).

178. *The New York Times,* 24 April 1900 (8: 6).

179. Kendall, 385–86, 392, 401, 413, 427.

180. Playbill, Boucicault, Harvard Theatre Collection.

181. Playbill, Boucicault, Harvard Theatre Collection.

182. Fred Williams also made an adaptation of Andrew Halliday's sketch from *Dombey and Son,* called "Heart's Delight," which was Captain Cuttle's pet name for Florence Dombey. He played Sol Gills in the play. See Fred Williams, file, Harvard Theatre Collection.

183. Harvard Theatre Collection (TS 3169.101).

184. That Dickens's "Christmas" characters found favor with a most disparate audience is proved by the popularity George Pauncefort, the itinerant trouper, who regaled the mountain men of the Northern Rockies with selections from the book. See Lyle A. Schwarz, "A Prophetic Protagonist of the Gold Frontier: George

Pauncefort," in *Theatre West: Image and Impact,* ed. Dunbar H. Ogden, with Douglas McDermott and Robert K. Sarlós (Amsterdam, Atlanta: Rodopi, 1990), 106–7.

185. Odell, 7:211–12.

186. Follard, 1:162.

187. Brown, *New York Stage,* 1:449.

188. *The New York Times,* 9 May 1877.

189. Thompson; "John S. Clarke," in "Actors and Actresses of Great Britain and the United States," ed. Matthew Brander and Lawrence Hutton, 5.6 (New York: Cassell & Co., 1886). MS at Harvard Theatre Collection.

190. Wilson, Index, *Philadelphia Theatre.*

191. Dickens file, clippings, etc., Harvard Theatre Collection.

192. Playbill, Dickens & Stage, Harvard Theatre Collection [156].

193. Wilson, Index.

194. Joseph Stevens Jones, a Boston actor-producer, dramatized *Barnaby Rudge* and subtitled it, "Ten Thousand a Year; or The Ups and Downs of Jittlebat Jitmouse Esq." It played at the National during the week Dickens visited Boston, starting on 24 January 1842. On 31 January Dickens paid a visit to this theater to see the play. It was also given on 1–3, 17, and 22 February 1842. Edward F. Payne, *Dickens Days in Boston* (Boston and New York: Houghton Mifflin Co., 1927), 5. The English version of the play by Charles Selby and Charles Melville had been performed at the New Chatham Theatre, New York, on 27 September 1841 (Ireland 2:370) and in Philadelphia around the same time (Wilson, Index).

195. It was shown at Boston Theatre on 29 November 1870 with Mrs. J. B. Booth as Barbany Rudge and Robson as Simon Tappertit. Playbills, Dickens & Stage, Theatre Collection, Harvard University. See also Tompson, 169.

196. Clippings on Weaver, Harvard Theatre Collection.

197. Clippings on Bradford, Harvard Theatre Collection.

198. Playbill, Dickens & Stage, Harvard Theatre Collection [159].

199. From the program "Dickens: Days in Boston," from Houghton Mifflin Company, The Parker House, and The Globe Corner Bookstore present Emlyn Williams as Charles Dickens, 10 March 1984 (Boston: Globe Corner Bookstore, 1984). At Harvard Theatre Collection.

200. Henry Bradshaw Fearon, *Sketches of America. A Narrative of a Journey of Five Thousand Miles through the Eastern and Western States of America* (London: Longman, Hurst, Rees, Orner, and Brown, 1818), 211–12.

201. See David Grimsted, Appendices, *Melodrama Unveiled: American Theater and Culture 1800–1850* (Chicago: University of Chicago, 1968), 250–56.

202. Ireland, 1:176; see also James, Index.

203. Smither, *A History of the English Theatre at New Orleans.* 1806–1842, 32.

204. Gagey, *The San Francisco Stage: A History,* 94.

205. Hutton, *Curiosities of the American Stage,* 157 ff. See [Stanley Wells,] *Nineteenth-Century Shakespeare Burlesques. With an Introduction by Stanley Wells, American Shakespeare Travesties* (1852–1888) (London: Diploma Press Limited, 1978), 5. Cf. James Rush's "Hamlet" (1834) listed by Roden in *Later American Plays 1831–1900.* I have not seen this play.

206. Odell, 4:409.

207. Hutton, *Curiosities of the American Stage,* 182–85. See also his catalogue of American actors personating Hamlet, ibid. 257–77. J. M. Field acted in "Hamlet and My Aunt," another of the many travesties. See Solomon Franklin Smith, *Theatrical Management in the West and South for Thirty Years,* 168. *Julius Caesar* was also burlesqued; a cherished passage was the quarrel scene. See Hutton, *Curiosities of the American Stage,* 106; see also Russel Blaine Nye, *The Cultural Life of the New*

Nation, 1776–1830 (New York: Harper & Brothers, 1960), passim; Gerald Bordman, *America's Musical Theatre: A Chronicle* (New York: Oxford University Press, 1978), 27.

208. It was the most popular of all Shakespeare plays on the Philadelphia stage 1835–1841 with eighty-three performances, next came *Othello* with fifty-seven, and then *Hamlet* with fifty-three. The tabular arrangement for the year 1835 singles out *Richard III* as a class of its own. See Wilson, *Philadelphia Theatre,* 18–19.

209. Wood, *Personal Recollections of the Stage, Embracing Notices of Actors, Authors, and Auditors, During the Period of Forty Years,* 431.

210. He did Richard III on 6 July 1821, at Richmond, Virginia. See Martin Staples Shockley, "Shakespeare's Plays in Rickmond Theatre, 1819–1838," *The Shakespeare Association Bulletin,* 16.1 (1940): 86. This is Durang's description of Booth featuring Richard III in the trial scene: "The shaking of every fibre of the frame, the ghastly look, . . . and the turning of the eyes upwards until the orbs see the eye-brows, all produced a very peculiar and shuddering aspect." It is easy to imagine what the caricaturists picked on.

211. Alice I. Perry Wood, *The Stage History of Shakespeare's King Richard the Third* (New York: Columbia University Press, 1909), 158. For an overview of the play's American links, see ibid., 134–65.

212. See *Shakespeare's Tragedy of King Richard III, As Presented by Edwin Booth,* ed. William Winter (New York: Francis Hart & Co., 1878).

213. Booth used Colley Cibber's edition up to 1877. See Preface, *The Tragedy of King Richard III, as Produced by Edwin Booth, Wednesday Evening, May 1, 1872, at Booth's Theatre, New York* (New York: Henry L. Hinton, Publishers [1872]); another edition based on Booth's prompt book, edited by William Winter, appeared in 1878. Amateur groups found Booth's version unacceptable, see *Shakespeare's Historical Tragedy of Richard III. Adapted for Amateurs and the Drawing-Room by Mr. J. A. Arneux; and Played by Him at the Lexington Ave. Opera House, New York, 1886* (New York, 1886), 4.

214. See Kendall, 34.

215. Odell, 4:578.

216. "Ministrelsy," San Francisco Theatre Research, ed. Lawrence Estavan, 13: 82. San Francisco 1939. MS at Harvard Theatre Collection.

217. See Hutton, *Curiosities of the American Stage,* 238–41.

218. Quoted by Glenn Hughes, *A History of the American Theatre, 1700–1900* (New York: Samuel French, 1951), 106–7.

219. Odell, 4:660.

220. Ireland, 2:5.

221. Hughes, *A History of the American Theatre 1700–1900,* 188.

222. Tompkins, 230. In 1894 and 1896 Fanny Davenport played Sardow's *Cleopatra.* See ibid., 413. For commentries about the burlesque in California, see George R. MacMinn, *The Theater of the Golden Era in California* (Caldwell: Caxton Printers, 1941), 102, 187, 358.

223. For instance, in New Orleans on 18 February 1844. See *Reminiscences,* 2: 240.

224. "Ministrelsy," San Francisco Theatre Research, 13:22.

225. In San Francisco the piece was called "Sports on the Spar"; it was performed in September 1866. "Ministrelsy," San Francisco Theatre Research, 13: 89. See also Mayorga, Appendix.

226. Ireland, 1:176.

227. "Ministrelsy," San Francisco Theatre Research 13: 88. Another travesty was

produced at St. Louis on 16 June 1877; it was published. See Roden, Index, *Later American Plays.*

228. MacMinn, 444.

229. See Michael D. Bristol, chap. 3 and 4 in *Carnival and Theater: Plebeian Culture and the Structure of Authority in Renaissance England* (New York and London: Routledge, 1985).

230. "The Enchanted Island from the Tempest" in *Nineteenth-Century Shakespearian Burlesques* 5; Helen Potter, *Helen Potter's Impersonations,* 50–58.

231. Odell, 5:451, 478, 528.

232. Ireland, 2:541.

233. *Memorial of John Brougham; Illustrated with Portraits, Playbills, Obituary Notices and Autographs, collected and arranged by Charles C. Moreau* (New York: Harvard Theatre Collection, 1890), [60]. This play had been shown as early as early as in 1798 at the New Park Theatre. Ireland 1:176.

234. *Memorial of John Brougham,* 73. It was revived on 14 October 1868, but was still received unkindly.

235. At Davenport Falstaff scenes (and scenes involving Shylock and Richard III) were produced by H. M. Smith and his circus, in conjunction with "Graphic and Interesting Scenes of Nautical Life." See Joseph S. Schick, *The Early Theater in Eastern Iowa: Cultural Beginnings and the Rise of the Theater in Davenport and Eastern Iowa, 1836–1863* (Chicago: University of Chicago Press, 1939), 35; for performances in New Orleans in December 1817, see Roger P. McCutcheon, "The First English Plays in New Orleans," *American Literature* 2 (1939–1940): 183–99; see also Rees, *Scrapbooks,* 3.

236. *Memorial of John Brougham,* 29.

237. Ibid., 30.

238. Martin Shockley, "Shakespeare's Plays in the Richmond Theatre, 1819–1838," *The Shakespeare Association Bulletin,* 16.1 (1940):89. John Daly dramatized the play in 1882, see Mayorga, Appendix. John Daly had also dramatized *Love's Labour's Lost.* It was published in 1891; see Ireland, 2:541. *As You Like It* was played at the opening of the New Park Theatre on 29 January 1798 (Ireland, 1:176). The play was reorganized by John Daly and published in 1888 (Mayorga, Index, and 374); see also Solomon Smith's note about the acting/reading of a passage from the play by Mr. Lynne, "our heavy tragedian." In *Theatrical Management in the West and South,* 79–80. Daly dramatized *Midsummer Night's Dream* in 1888.

239. Mayorga lists Daly's *Merchant of Venice* (1898) as an original American play.

240. George N. Baker, "The Peddlar of Very Nice," in *Amateur Dramas as for Parlor Theatricals, Evening Entertainments, and School Exhibitions* (Boston: Lee & Shepard, 1867), 201–14; J. Schick, *The Early Theater in Eastern Iowa* 35, and Appendix. George N. Belknap, *Oregon Imprints 1845–1870* (Eugene: University of Oregon Books, 1968), 167. A playbill from a Davenport theater, 18 May 1859, announced as the main feature of the night's entertainment "Queen Katherine's Trial Scene" in *Henry VIII,*" in costume by Mrs. C. N. Sinclair" (the late wife of Edwin Forrest). See J. Schick, Appendix.

241. See Hutton, *Curiosities of the American Stage,* 165 ff.

242. Odell (8: 428–30) quotes a local review that depicts the play as stiff and heavy and actors who could not sing. It was repeated in April and in May. It was produced in Philadelphia in May 1869. See also Hutton, *Curiosities of the American Stage,* 164 ff. for other burlesques of *The Merchant of Venice.*

243. *Much Ado about a Merchant of Venice, from the Original Text—a Long Way* (New York: S. French [1850]). TS 272.50.2 at the Harvard Theatre Collection.

244. David Dempsey with Raymond P. Baldwin, *The Triumphs and Trials of Lotta Crabtree* (New York: William Morrow & Company, 1968), 173; see also Gagey, 94.

245. Dempsey, 200.

246. MacMinn, ch. 3; "Ministrelsy," San Francisco Theatre Research, 13:22; and McCutcheon about *Othello* in New Orleans.

247. See MacMinn; Dean Goodman, *San Francisco Stages: A Concise History, 1849–1986* (San Francisco: Micro Pro Litera Press, 1986) 6. Anna Cora Ritchie reminiscenses about her acting in the play, in her *Mimic Life; or, Before and Behind the Curtain. A Series of Narratives* (Boston: Ticknor and Fields, 1856).

248. A travesty of Byron's play *Manfred,* written by G. A. Beckett, was produced for the first time in the country on 25 February 1840 at Mitchell's Olympic with Mitchell as Man-fred. The other characters in the play were: Seguin, Wilson, Shirreff, City Charley, Annie Starkie, Hazard, and Celeste. According to Brown, *New York Stage,* 1:267, "it had a longer run than any piece up to that time in America." See also Constance Rourke, *The Roots of American Culture and Other Essays,* ed. Van Wyck Brooks (New York: Harcourt, Brace and Company, 1942), 121. It was also given in Philadelphia in 1842; see Wilson, Index, *Philadelphia Theatre.*

249. Ettore Rella, "A History of Burlesque." San Francisco Theatre Research Series: A Monograph History of San Francisco Stage and Its People from 1849 to the Present Day, ed. Lawrence Estavan, 14:17–18, San Francisco 1939, MS at Harvard Theatre Collection. San Francisco offered another burlesque, called "Conrad the Corsair," in the late 1878 and 1888 by Brough. It could have been the same as the one that Wallack's Theatre, New York produced on 10 August 1857 with Mrs. John Wood. See Ireland 2:660. Other late-century *Corsair* burlesques were produced at the Bijou Theatre, New York, on 18 October 1887 (with Conrad, Birbanto, Syed Pacha, Syng Smaul, Yursug, Gulnare, Ahmed, Zuliema, Hassan, Ganem, Ali, Bachsheesh, Medora). Its attractions included a trick dancing mule and a telephone that was summoned with a cowbell. It had 180 performances and was spoofed by Dockstaders Minstrels as "The Coarse Hair." See Bordman, *America's Musical Theatre,* 93. It was also produced here on 17 March 1888, and at the Grand Opera House on 25 March 1889.

250. *The Corsair,* [1–2]:174.

251. Odell, 6:366.

252. *Lord Byron's Historical Tragedy of Sardanapulus.* Arranged for Representation, in Five Acts, by Charles Calvert, for Booth's Theatre, New York, first produced 14 August, 1876.

253. From Odell, 10:174–75.

254. Quite appropriately, on 4 September 1876, at the Kelly and Leon, a skit called "Sir Dan O'Pallas, Chief of the Assyrian Jim-Jams" laughed at Calvert, and also on 13 November 1876 at the Eagle Theatre. See Odell, 10:291 and 259.

255. Robert C. Allen, "'The Leg Business': Transgression and Containment in American Burlesque," *Camera Obscura: A Journal of Feminism and Film Theory,* a special edition on Popular Culture and Reception Studies, ed. Lynn Spigel, 23 (1990):43.

256. It was printed in Samuel French's Standard Drama, The Acting Edition, No. 184 [1833].

257. For instance, at the Richmond Hill Theatre on 18 April, 1833.

258. See Quinn, 186 n. 1 and Walter J. Meserve, *An Outline History of American Drama* (Totowa, N. Y.: Littlefield, Adams & Co., 1965), 99–100. Meserve claims (119) wrongly that *Mazeppa* "introduced the fashion of equestrian drama." It did not; "horse plays" were much in vogue long before the *Mazeppa* horses had started to climb the ramps. In *The Philadelphia Stage* John Durang tells how horses were

taught to imitate death in the melodrama "Timour, the Tartar." At the end of a performance on 19 December 1816, at the Olympic Theatre, the people in the audience were so thrilled that they rose to their feet, "and, with canes, hands, and wild screams, kept the house in one uproar of shouts for at least five minutes." Payne's source was a French version which he translated and changed very little. (See DAL 2929. 43. Widener Library, Harvard University.) MacMinn claims that Payne's version was used in San Francisco in 1851 (197).

259. According to *American Theatre Companies* (65) it was played on 18 June 1830, at the Chatham Garden Theatre, which then hosted Blanchard's Amphitheatre Stock Company. I have not been able to verify this. Brown explains, however, that "equestrian and dramatic performances were given" (*New York Stage* 1: 90) here at this period.

260. Kendall, 62.

261. Ireland, 2:65.

262. Odell, 3:641. See also Ireland 2:60 and *American Theatre Companies*, 115.

263. *American Theatre Companies, 259–60.*

264. Phelps, 132.

265. Phelps, 172–73.

266. "The Forfeit Books of 1840–1842 of Tremont Theatre in Boston" (TS 1793.92, Harvard Theatre Collection) show that *Mazeppa* was given eleven times in 1841. Otherwise the information about the play in Boston is scarce, mainly because this was not the sort of play that Bostonian theatergoers favored. It was performed in Boston later in the century; by Spaulding and Rogers's Circus on 4 February, 1861, and by John H. Murray's Circus on 25 November 1872. See Clapp, 374, 394.

267. Odell, 4:163–65. The play seemed to have been picked up by the Bowery on several occasions throughout the decade. The *Corsair* reported in June 1839 that Mrs. [Mary] Shaw continues to "give satisfaction" in *Mazeppa. The Corsair* 1: 174 .

268. *American Theatre Companies, 1749–1887,* 49.

269. Jefferson, *Autobiography,* 95–96.

270. Durang, *"Philadelphia Stage."*

271. Wilson, *Philadelphia Theatre,* 189.

272. Kendall, 188–91.

273. Grimsted, *Melodrama Unveiled: American Theater and Culture 1800–1850,* 254.

274. Maud and Otis Skinner, *One Man in His Time. The Adventures of H. Watkins, Strolling Player, 1845–1863.* From His Journal (Philadelphia: University of Pennsylvania Press, 1938), n.p.

275. See Paul Lewis, *Queen of the Plaza: A Biography of Adah Isaacs Menken* (New York: Frank & Wagnalls Company, 1964), 6.

276. Brown, *New York Stage,* 1: 332.

277. Misha Berson, "The San Francisco Stage. Pt. I. From Gold Rush to Golden Spike, 1849–1869," *The San Francisco Performing Arts Library and Museum Journal* 2 (1989):76.

278. Quoted from Allen Lesser, *Enchanting Rebel: The Secret of Adah Isaacs Menken* (New York: The Beechhurst Press, 1947), 111.

279. Allen, '"The Leg Business'," 53.

280. Lewis, *Queen of the Plaza,* 152.

281. Lewis, 113–14.

282. Ibid., 66.

283. On 2 November 1863, on 14 January, and on 17, 27–29 February 1864; see Watson, Appendix, *Silver Theatre,* 215, 251 and newspaper cuttings at Bancroft Library, box Menken and Crabtree.

284. Gagey, 87–88.

285. MacMinn, 216–18.

286. "Lola Montez, Adah Isaacs Menken, Mrs. Judah," San Francisco Theatre Research, ed. Lawrence Estavan, 5:43–98, San Francisco 1938. MS at Harvard Theatre Collection.

287. From Watson, 259.

288. San Francisco Theatre Research, 5:78.

289. Franklin Walker, *San Francisco's Literary Frontier* (New York: Alfred A. Knopf, 1939), 163.

290. Ettore Rella, "A History of Burlesque," San Francisco Theatre Research, 14: 62. For several years burlesques on the Mazeppa theme were popular with the San Francisco theatre. See ibid., 76, 212–13.

291. Watson, 252.

292. Michael Bennett Leavitt, *Fifty Years in Theatrical Management, 1859–1909* (New York: Broadway Publishing House Co., [1912]) 53.

293. See Appendix 3.

294. He showed it for the first time at Tripler Hall, New York, on 7 Janury 1861 (Brown, *New York Stage*, 1:449) and probably at the same time at The Winter Garden, where, Lawrence Hutton reports (*Curiosities of the American Stage*, 199), he sang the "aria," "The Victim of Despair," "while standing on the bare back of a mock toy rocking-horse." It was also seen in San Francisco; see Dempsey, 141–43. Other burleques were "Mazeppa the Second, or the Wild Horse of Williamsburg" by C. W. Taylor, performed at The Chatham Theatre, on 12 June 1854 (Brown, *New York Stage,* 1:319); it was also given at this theatre on 28 March 1856; at Mrs. John Wood's Olympic, on 18 January 1864, with Frank Drew and Mrs. John Wood, and named "Ill Treated Il Trovatore," at Mrs. John Wood's Olympic, on 8 February 1864 (Manrico, Azucena, Count di Luna, Ferando, The Kichin, Ruiz, Leonora, Inez); at Kelly & Leon's on 19 January 1871; here the burlesque was called "His Last Legs."

295. C[harles] White, *Mazeppa. An Equestrian Burlesque. In Two Scenes. Transposed and arranged by C. White* (New-York: Frederic A. Brady, [1856]). See further Hans Nathan, *Dan Emmett and the Rise of Early Negro Ministrelsy* (Norman: University of Oklahoma Press, 1977). At White's Theatre of Varieties, in late 1852 and on 12 February 1853, Daniel Emmett performed in the parody "Old Uncle Ned or Effusions from Lord Byron."

296. Truman J. Backus, *The Outline of Literature: English and American*. Based upon Shaw's Manual of English Literature (New York: Sheldon & Co., 1897), 252.

297. Quoted by Earl L. Bradsher, in *Mathew Carey: Editor, Author and Publisher. A Study in American Literary Development* (New York: Columbia University Press, 1912), 110.

298. Lewis C. Strang, *Players and Plays of the Last Quarter* Century (Boston: L. C. Page & Co., 1903), 2:243.

299. Mortimer Thomson, "Doesticks." *The Lady of the Lake, a Travestie in One Act. As performed at Niblo's Garden, June 21, 1860* (New York: Samuel French, 1860), TS 732.12 F, Harvard Theatre Collection.

300. *Memorial of John Brougham*, 71.

301. Odell 3: 98, 554. The early melodramatic version was performed at the Walcot in January 1821 for two nights only; see Durang, "Philadelphia Stage."

302. Two other plays based on Scott's novels, Isaac Pocock's "Montrose; or, The Children of the Mist," produced at the Park on 13 May 1822, and Daniel Terry's and Pocock's "The Antiquary; a Musical," at the Park on 17 May 1822, were never revived.

303. Rees, *Scrapbooks,* 1:212.

304. Hughes, 252–53.

305. See Hutton, *Curiosities on the American Stage,* 177.

306. Rella, San Francisco Theatre Research 14:72–73.

307. "Pioneer Impresarios; Tom Maguire, Doc Robinson, M. B. Leavitt," San Francisco Theatre Research 2:18.

308. Rella, 138, 158, 159.

309. Ibid., 192–93.

310. In New York on 18 February 1867 at The New York Theatre. Lady Don was the Earl of Leicester, with Tony, Sir Walter, Michel, Queen Elisabeth, Amy Robsart, Duke of Susssex, Wayland Smith, Tressillian, Janet, Varney, and Giles. Brown, *New York Stage,* 2:381.

311. McGlinchee, 76.

312. *New York Times,* 26 October 1886 (5: 2).

313. Odell, 6:21. Cf. Charles White, "Sam's Courtship. An Ethiopian Farce in One Act. By Charles White, the popular Ethiopian Comedian, as first produced at White's Opera House. Bowery, New York, 1852," *The New York Drama, A Choice Collection of Tragedies, Comedies, Farces, etc.* 3.29 (New York: Wheat & Conett, No. 8, 1877), 31–32; "Sam Weller's Visit to His Mother-in-Law, Adapted from "The Pickwick Papers," ibid., 159–60.

314. Odell, 8:304–05.

315. Playbill, Dickens & Stage, Harvard Theatre Collection [158]. See also Odell 9:404. It failed: it was shown once.

316. Playbills, Dickens on the stage, Harvard Theatre Collection.

317. Odell, 4:340, 362, and 367.

318. Hutton, *Plays and Players* (New York: Hurd and Houghton, 1875), 24.

319. Odell, 4:405–6.

320. Odell, 4:405–6.

321. The first melodramatic version of *Martin Chuzzlewit* was produced by Thomas Higgie and Thomas Hailes Lucy, on 8 July, 1844, at the Lyceum Theatre, London. This play, very popular in England, would not, unaltered, appeal to the American audiences (see above xx). New Strand Theatre gave a burlesque version of it, written by C. Webb, in 1844 (Wilson, Index, *Philadelphia Theatre*). The first American re-adaptation of it along such lines was produced by Stephen Fiske at Mrs. John Wood's Olympic Theatre, New York, on 26 September 1864, where it played for five weeks (Odell, 7:634, 635, 636, and 680). A collation of the two texts, Webb's and Fiske's, demonstrates that the American version is much more focused on the comedy of situations, on verbal repartee, and on morality; despite its smaller cast the English version is more intent on telling Dickens's story as faithfully as possible (there were 25 persons in the American cast; 15 in the English). Fiske's dramatization is freer; he cut, abridged, and created fewer scenes. What is noteworthy is that the American side of the story is totally eliminated—in both versions, but no doubt for different reasons.

322. It was repeated a number of times during the following seasons: 25 September 1840, 15 April 1841, 5 June 1841, December 1841, 18 November 1843, and 2 February 1844, at Niblo's June-July 1844, at the Olympic again on 3–8 December 1844, 30 April 1845, December 1845, at The New York Opera House 9 March 1847, at The Chatham 6 October 1847, at the Olympic 18 October 1847, 21 April 1849, 6 February 1850 (Odell 5, Index); at The Lyceum on 23 May 1851 with Brougham as Crummles, late January 1855 at the National Theatre, 10 March 1856, and 27 April 1857 at Wallack's (Odell, 6, Index).

323. Ireland, 2:610.

324. *New York Times* review, 16 July 1871.

325. See Actors and Actresses 3, No. 15, Harvard Theatre Collection. Wheatley's Arch Street Theatre, 1857, Howard Atheneum, Boston 1859 (Captain Cuttle) and 1867 (both Dombey and Son and Captain Cuttle), Walnut Street Theatre, 1866. See also the file (at Houghton Library, Harvard University) of Brougham's itinerary 1865–66 from New York, through Philadelphia, Chicago, Cincinnati, Louisville, Milwauke, Indianapolis, St. Louis, Pittsburg, Philadelphia, Boston, and New York again (Brooklyn, Ivory, Walnut). At all these places he played *Dombey and Son and David Copperfield,* alternatively.

326. Harry P. Mawson, "Dickens on the Stage," *The Theatre* 1 (1912 February) 15.132:47.

327. Ireland, 2:623. It has been assumed that Dion Boucicault also tried to dramatize it. Such a play is listed in the Greene Collection under his autograph, but there is no evidence that the play ever existed.

328. Odell, 6:256, 297, 298.

329. Playbill, Dickens & Stage [159], Harvard Theatre Collection.

330. Odell, 9:387.

331. Playbill, Dickens & Stage, Harvard Theatre Collection.

332. Odell, 7:149.

333. David Dempey, with Raymond Baldwin, *The Triumphs and Trials of Lotta Crabtree* (New York: William Morrow & Co., 1968), 162–63.

334. Playbill in "Modern Stars" on Lotta Crabtree [18], Harvard Theatre Collection.

335. Odell, 8:135.

336. Review of Lotta Crabtree, in "History of the New York Theatres: Records of the New York Stage," TS 944.28, Harvard Theatre Collection .

337. Playbill in "Modern Stars" on Lotta Crabtree [10], Harvard Theatre Collection.

338. Dempsey, 164. Her popularity in San Francisco equalled that of Menken with whom she was always contrasted: Lotta the virtuous, Menken the anarchist. The Bancroft library (San Francisco) (77/81) holds three manuscripts by Helen Lyon Hawkins (written in 1936–37 about San Francisco theatre life in the 1850s and 1860s. They dramatize Lotta's encounters with Menken and her circle.

339. Playbills in "Modern Stars" on Lotta Crabtree [461], [49], [70], and [73].

340. Mawson, "Dickens on the Stage," 47–48. Cf. his play based on Dickens's *The Old Curiosity Shop,* MS (TS4389.452) at Harvard Theatre Collection.

341. Ireland, 2:525. The play is No. 136 in Samuel French.

342. *Life, Stories, and Poems of John Brougham,* ed. William Winter (Boston: James R. Osgood and Co., 1881), 84.

343. See Leota S. Driver, *Fanny Kemble* (Chapel Hill: University of North Carolina Press, 1933) and David W. Thompson, "Early Actress-Readers: Mowatt, Kemble, and Cushman," 634–41.

344. Byron's *Manfred,* for instance, was read at Booth's Theatre by Mrs. Booth on 26 May 1869.

345. Mayorga (374) lists a play called *The Forresters* by John Daly as based on Tennyson.

346. J. Schick, 216. Charles Whitney's "Lecture Impersonations" of 1869 listed Tennyson's "Light Brigade." See Rees, *Scrapbooks* 2:25.

347. Jefferson, *Autobiography* 248.

348. Ireland, 1:203. Odell (1:167, 245, and 327) places its first showing on 17 June 1773, with repetitions in 1786 and 1793. It was also shown on 7 September 1801 (2:126).

349. Hoole, Index.

350. Odell, 5:435–36. An extravaganza based on Milton's "Hero and Leander" was simultaneouly shown at Mitchell's Olympic Theatre (on 2 October 1848). Odell, 6:470, 473, 475, and 555.

351. J. Schick, 140; Rees, Scrapbooks 2:25, which prints the playbill of Professor Charles Whitney's "Lecture Impersonations, Including the Scene Sin and Death, a Meeting with Satan"; Michael Forsythe, "Mardi Hearty," USAIR, February 1988, 12.

352. Ireland, 2:565.

353. Odell, 5:440.

354. Follard, 2:168.

355. Ireland, 2:450.

356. "Thalaba" was first produced on the American stage at the Bowery on 13 May 1833 (Ireland 2:59); revived at the New Bowery Theatre on 4 April 1864. "Wat Tyler" had its first showing on 12 April 1841 at The Bowery; revived on 9 March 1857 at the Tripler Hall (Ireland, 2:662).

357. Booth the Elder used to read from "The Ancient Mariner." See Murdoch, 277–78, and Durang, "Philadelphia Stage."

358. Hughes, 100.

Appendix 2. "Jeanie Deans; or, The Heart of Midlothian"

1. The manuscript (TS4337.25), in Dion Boucicault's handwriting, is at Harvard Theatre Collection.

2. A playbill in "Mr. & Mrs. Dion Boucicault," in *Actors and Actresses*, ed. Broader Matthews and Lawrence Hutton (TS931.2), Harvard Theatre Collection.

3. See the Indexes in Odell and Kendall and the Boucicault file at Harvard Theatre Collection. It was produced later in the century in New York in 1865 and in 1872.

4. In "Mr. & Mrs. Dion Boucicault," in *Actors and Addresses*.

5. The original letter in the Boucicault file.

Bibliography

Primary Sources

Allen, William. *Wunnissoo; or, The Vale of Hoosatunnuk, a Poem, with Notes.* Boston: John D. Jewett, 1856.

American *[The] Orator's Own Book; or, The Art of Extemporaneous Public Speaking, Including a Course of Discipline for Obtaining the Faculties of Discrimination, Arrangement and Oral Discussion; with a Debate, as an Exercise in Argumentative Declamation; and Numerous Selections for Practice.* Philadelphia: James Kay, 1836.

"American Drama." Review of Scott's *Marmion. American Quarterly Review* 1 (1827):331–57.

American Ladies' Magazine 6 (1833):369–73, 557–59.

Ames. Nathan. *The Baby and the Bards. Childe Harvard, a Romance of Cambridge. By Senor Alguno.* New edition. And The Bards of Lind: To Wit, Longfellow . . . Boston: Redding & Company, 1848.

Apthorp, H. O. *A Grammar of Elocution: Adapted to Use of Teachers and Learners in the Art of Reading.* Philadelphia: H. Cowperthwait & Co., 1858.

Art [The] of Reading: or Rules for the Attainment of a Just and Correct Enunciation of Written Language. Mostly Selected from [John] Walker's Elements of Elocution, and Adapted to the Use of Schools. Boston: Cummings, Hilliard, and Company, 1826.

Atwell, Benjamin W. *Principles of Elocution and Vocal Culture: in Which the Rules for Correct Reading and Speaking, and Directions for Improving and Strengthening the Voice are Given.* Providence, R.I.: Bangs Williams News Co., 1867.

Backus, Truman J. *The Outline of Literature; English and American. Based upon Shaw's Manual of English Literature.* New York: Sheldon & Co., 1897.

Bailey, John. *The Sultana; or, A Trip to Turkey. A Melodrama, in Three Acts, Founded on Lord Byron's Don Juan.* New York: C. N. Baldwin, 1822.

Bailey, Mark. *An Introductory Treatise on Elocution; with Principles and Illustrations, Arranged for Teaching and Practice.* Yale College. Boston: Brewer and Tileston, 1865.

Baker, George Melville. *Amateur Dramas for Parlor Theatricals, Evening Entertainments, and School Exhibitions.* Boston: Lee and Shepard, 1867.

Baker, George Melville. *Christmas [A] Carol. In The Exhibition Drama: Comprising Drama, Comedy, and Farce, together with Dramatic and Musical Entertainments, for Private Theatricals, Home Representations, Holiday and School Exhibitions by George M. Baker.* [The Amateur Drama Series] Boston: Lee and Shepard, 1875.

Baker, George Melville. *Exbition [The] Drama: Comprising Drama, Comedies, Farce, Together with Dramatic and Musical Entertainments, and School Exhibitions.* Boston: Lee and Shepard, 1875.

Ballou, Maturin Murray. *Fanny Campbell. The Female Pirate Captain. A Tale of the Revolution. By Lieutenant Murray.* New York: E. O. Long & Co., 1844.

Barber, Jonathan. *Elocutionist [The], Consisting of Declamations and Readings, in Prose and Poetry; for the Use of Colleges and Schools.* Second ed. New Haven: A. H. Maltby, 1836.

Barber, Jonathan. *Grammar [A] of Elocution; Containing the Principles of the Arts of Reading and Speaking; . . . Adapted to Colleges, Schools, and Private Instruction.* New Haven: A. H. Maltby, 1830.

Barber, Jonathan. *Practical [A] Treatise on Gesture, Chiefly Abstracted from Austin's Chironomia; Adapted to the Use of Students, and Arranged According to the Method of Instruction in Harvard University.* Cambridge: Hilliard and Brown, 1831.

Barker, James Nelson. *Marmion; or, Flodden Field, a Drama Founded on the Poem by Walter Scott. From the First London Edition; of 1812.* New York: Longworth, 1812.

Barker, James Nelson. *Marmion; or, The Battle of Flodden Field. A Drama, in Five Acts. With a Portrait of Mr. Duff, in the Character of Marmion.* Corrected from the prompt books of the Philadelphia Theatre by M. Lopez, prompter. Philadelphia: A. R. Poole, and Ash & Mason, 1826.

Barry, [Thomas]. *A Masque and Pageant in Honour of the Genius of the Minstrel of the North, Entitled A Vision of the Bard.* New York: James Kennaday, 1832.

Bartlett, George Bradford. *A Dream of the Centuries and Other Entertainments for Parlor and Hall.* Boston: Walter H. Baker, 1877.

Bartlett, George Bradford. *Grand [The] Dickens Cosmorama. Comprising Several Unique Entertainments Capable of Being Used Separately or in Combination, for School, Home, and Hall.* Boston: Lee & Shepard, 1885.

Bartlett, George Bradford. *Mrs. Jarley's Far-Famed Collection of Wax-Works. In Two Parts. Arranged by G. B. Bartlett, of Concord, Mass., and Performed by the Amateurs under His Direction for Charitable Purposes in Most of the Cities of the United States.* New York: Samuel French, n.d. [1873–89].

Bartlett, George Bradford. *Parlor Amusements for the Young Folks.* Boston: James R. Osgood and Company, 1875.

Beach, Samuel B. *Escalala. An American Tale.* Utica: William Williams, 1824.

Bell, David Charles and Alexander Melville Bell. *Bell's Standard Elocutionist. Principles and Exercises, Followed by a Copious Selection of Extracts in Prose and Poetry, Classified and Adapted for Reading and Recitation.* New ed. Belfast: William Mullen, 1874.

Bell, Lucia Chase. "Buoyant. A Dickens Charade in Three Scenes [from *Nicholas Nickleby, David Copperfield, Our Mutual Friend*]." In George B. Bartlett, *A Dream of the Centuries and Other Entertainments for Parlor and Hall.*

Bernard, [William] Bayle [notes by his father, John Bernard]. Early Days of the American Stage, Being a Selection from the Papers of One of Its Managers [from Tallis's *Dramatic Magazine,* London 1850–1851 and *The Manhattan Magazine,* New York, 1884]. Harvard Theatre Collection.

Blaisdell, Albert F. *First Steps with American and British Authors.* Revised and enlarged edition. New York, Cincinnati, Chicago: American Book Company, 1899.

Blaisdell, Albert F. *Readings from The Waverly Novels. Edited for School and Home Use.* Boston: Lee and Shepard, 1888.

Blake, Charles. *An Historical Account of the Providence Stage; Being a Paper*

Read before the Rhode Island Historical Society, Oct. 25th, 1860. Providence, R.I.: George H. Whitney, 1868.

Blane, William Newham. *An Excursion through the United States and Canada during the Years 1822–23 by an English Gentleman.* London: Baldwin, Cradock, and Joy, 1824.

Boker, George H. *Plays and Poems.* Two vols. Second ed. Boston: Ticknor and Fields, 1857.

Booth, Edwin. *The Tragedy of King Richard III, as Produced by Edwin Booth, Wednesday Evening, May 1, 1872, at Booth's Theatre, New York.* New York: Henry L. Hinton, [1872].

Booth, Junius Brutus. "Junius Brutus Booth, the Elder. Junius Brutus Booth, the Younger. Edwin Booth." San Francisco Theatre Research. Ed. Lawrence Estavan. Vol. 4, first series. San Francisco 1938. MS at Harvard Theatre Collection.

Booth, Junius Brutus. *Lord Byron's Sardanapulus, a Tragegdy. The Two Foscari, a Tragedy. Cain, a Mystery.* London: John Murray, 1821. Copy used by Booth. Harvard Theatre Collection.

Boucicault, Dion. *Dot, in Forbidden Fruit and Other Plays by Dion Boucicault.* Edited by Allardyce Nicoll and F. Theodore Cloak. Princeton, New Jersey: Princeton University Press, 1940, 107–49.

Boucicault, Dion. "Jeanie Deans or The Heart of Midlothian. A Drama in Three Acts." Original handwritten MSS. Harvard Theatre Collection.

Boucicault, Dion. "Mutilations of Shakespere. The Poet Interviewed." *North American Literature,* 148 (1889):266–68.

Boucicault, Dion. "Shakespere's Influence on the Drama." *North American Review,* 147 (1888):680–85.

Boyd, James R. *Elements of Rhetoric and Literary Criticism with Copious Practical Exercises and Examples for the Use of Common Schools and Academies.* Fifth ed. New York: Harper & Brothers, 1846.

Brainard, John G. C. *Poems of John G. C Brainard. A New and Original Edition, with an Original Memoir of His Life.* Hartford: S. Andrus and Son, 1847.

Bristed, John. *America and Her Resources; or A View of the Agricultural, Commercial, Manufacturing, Financial, Political, Literary, Moral and Religious Capacity and Character of the American People.* London: Henry Colburn, 1818.

Bronson, C. P. *Elocution; or, Mental and Vocal Philosophy: Involving the Principles of Reading and Speaking; and Designed for the Development and Cultivation of Both Body and Mind . . .* Louisville, Ky.: Morton & Griswold, 1845.

Brooke, Stopford. *English Literature. With and Appendix on American Literature.* New York: D. Appleton and Company, 1879.

Brooks, Edward. *A Manual of Elocution and Reading. Embracing the Principle and Practice of Elocution. Designed for Academies, Seminaries, Normal Schools, Colleges, and Private Pupils in Elocution.* Philadelphia: Eldredge & Brother, 1883.

Brooks, I. H. *Common School Elocution and Oratory; A Manual of Vocal Culture Based upon Scientific Principles.* St. Louis: I. H. Brown & Co., 1886.

Brooks, James G. and Mary E. Brooks. *The Rivals of Este, and Other Poems.* New York: J. & J. Harper, 1829.

Brooks, James G. *Anniversary Poem, Delivered at New Haven, Conn. before the Connecticut Alpha of the Phi Beta Kappa, Sept. 12, 1826.* New York: G. & C. Carvill, 1826.

Brougham, John. *A Message from the Sea. A Drama, in Four Acts. Founded on*

Charles Dickens's Tale of That Name. First Performed in America. London: John Dicks, 313, Strand, [1880].

Brougham, John. *Cricket on the Hearth. A Fairy Tale of Home*. London: Thomas Hailes Lucy, [1869].

Brougham, John. *David Copperfield. A Drama in Two Acts. Adapted from Dickens' Popular Work of the Same Name. The Acting Edition*. Modern Standard Drama 16–17. New York. S. French, [1851].

Brougham, John. *Dombey and Son. Dramatized from Dickens's novel. French's American Drama. The Acting Edition, 127*. New York: Samuel French, [1856?].

Brougham, John. *Jane Eyre. A Drama in Five Acts. Adapted from Charlotte Brontë's Novel*. In Brougham, *David Copperfield*.

Brougham, John. *Life, Stories, and Poems of John Brougham*. Edited by William Winter. Boston: James R. Osgood and Company, 1881.

Brougham, John. "Memorial of John Brougham; Illustrated with Portraits, Playbills, Obituary Notices and Autographs. Collected and arranged by Charles C. Moreau." New York, 1890. Harvard Theatre Collection.

Brougham, John. *Much Ado about a Merchant of Venice, from the Original Text— a Long Way*. French Minor Drama, 308. New York: S. French [1850].

Brougham, John. *Night and Morning. A Play in Five Acts. Adapted from Bulwer's Novel*. New York: Samuel French, [1856?].

Brougham, John. *Shakespeare's Dream; an Historic Pageant with an Allegorical Introduction*. French Minor Drama, 164. New York: S. French [1850].

Brougham, John. *Songs, Choruses, and Other Incidental Harmonies in Brougham's Much Ado about a Merchant of Venice: with a Metaphysical, Critical, and Comparative Analysis of the Ancient and Modern Versions. 1869*. Harvard Theatre Collection [n. p.].

Brown, Isaac H. *Common School Elocution and Oratory; a Manual of Vocal Culture Based upon Scientific Principles* . . . St. Louis: I. H. Brown & Co., 1886.

Brown, Solyman. *An Essay on American Poetry, with Several Miscellaneous Pieces on a Variety of Subjects, Sentimental, Descriptive, Moral, and Patriotic*. New Haven, Ct.: Hezekiah Howe, 1818.

Burk, John. Cuttings etc. Harvard Theatre Collection.

Caldwell, Merritt. *A Practical Manual of Elocution; Embracing Voice and Gesture. Designed for Schools, Academies and Colleges, as Well as for Private Learners*. Philadelphia: Sorin & Bak, 1845.

Calvert, Charles. *Lord Byron's Historical Tragedy of Sardanapalus, Arranged for Representation, in Five Acts, by Charles Calvert, for Booth's Theatre, New York*. First Produced 14th August, 1876.

Calvert, George H. *Cabiro. A Poem. Cantos I and II*. Baltimore: N. Hickman, 1840.

Calvert, George H. *Cabiro: A Poem. Cantos III and IV*. Boston: Little, Brown and Company, 1864.

Calvert, George H. *Essays Aesthetical*. Boston: Lee and Shepard, 1875.

Campbell, Loomis J. *The New Franklin Fifth Reader, with a New Elocutionary Treatise, Essentials of Reading, by Mark Bailey*. New York: Taintor Brothers & Co., [1886].

Carter, St. Leger L. *Nugae, By Nugator: or Pieces in Prose and Verse*. Baltimore: Woods and Crane, 1844.

Cary, Phoebe. *Poems and Parodies*. Boston: Ticknor, Reed, and Fields, 1854.

Cathcart, George R. *Literary [The] Reader: Typical Selections from Some of the Best British and American Authors, from Shakespeare to the Present Time.* New York and Chicago: Ivison, Blackman, Taylor, and Company, 1874.

Cathcart, George R. *Selections in Prose, Poetry, and Dialogues for Declamation and Recitation: Suited to the Capacities of Youth, and Intended for the Exhibition-Day Requirments of Common Schools and Academies.* New York, Chicago: Ivison, Blackeman, Taylor, and Company, [1871].

Cavanaugh, Cortes W. *Charles Dickens. His Life as Traced by His Works. Early American Editions of the Works of Charles Dickens.* By Herman Leroy Edgar and R. W. G. Vail. New York: The New York Public Library, 1929.

Channing, William Ellery. "On National Literature," *Old South Leaflets 6.141.* Boston: Directors of the Old South Work [1904].

Childe Harold's Pilgrimage to the Dead Sea: Death of the Pale Horse; and Other Poems. New York: James Eastburn and Co., 1818.

Choate, Rufus. "The Importance of Illustrating New-England History by a Series of Romances like The Waverly Novels." Delivered at Salem, 1833. In *Addresses and Orations.* Seventh ed. Boston: Little, Brown, and Company, 1897.

Cist, Charles. *Cincinnati in 1841; Its Early Annals and Future Prospects.* Cincinnati: E. Morgan & Co., 1841.

Claggett, R. *Elocution Made Easy: Containing Rules and Selections for Declamation and Reading with Figures Illustrative of Gesture.* New York: Paine & Burger, 1845.

Clappe, Louise A. Knapp Smith. *The Letters of Dame Shirley. California in 1851.* Introduction and Notes by Carl I. Wheat. San Francisco: The Grabhorn Press, 1933.

Clarke, McDonald. *The Gossip ; or, A Laugh with the Ladies, a Grin at the Gentlemen, and Burlesques on Byron, a Sentimental Satire; with Other Poems in a Series of Numbers. Number One.* New York: Gray & Bunce, 1823.

Clason, Isaac Starr. *Don Juan. Cantos XVII–XVIII.* New York: Charles Wiley, 1825.

Clason, Isaac Starr. *Horace in New-York.* New York: James M. Campbell, 1826.

Cleveland, Charles D. *A Compendium of English Literature, Chronologically Arranged, from Sir John Mandeville to William Cowper. Consisting of Biographical Sketches of the Authors, Selections from Their Works, with Notes, Explanations, . . . for the Highest Classes in Schools and for Junior Classes in Colleges, as well as for Private Reading.* Philadelphia: E. C. & J. Biddle, 1851.

Cleveland, Charles D. *English Literature of the Nineteenth Century on the Plan of Arnold's "Compendium of English Literature;" and Supplementary to It. Designed for Colleges and Advanced Classes in Schools, as well as for Private Reading.* Philadelphia: Schermerhorn, Bancroft & Co., 1866.

Cobb, Mary L. *Poetical Dramas for Home and School.* Boston: Lee and Shepard, 1873.

Coffinberry, Andrew. *The Forest Rangers: A Poetic Tale of the Western Wilderness in 1794. Connected with and Comprising the March and Battle of General Wayne's Army, and Abounding with Interesting Incidents of Fact and Fiction. In Seven Cantos.* Columbus: Wright & Lagg, 1842.

Colton, George Hooker. *Tekumseh; or, The West Thirty Years Since. A Poem.* New-York: Wiley and Putnam, 1842.

Comstock, Andrew. *Rhythmical [The] Reader; Being a Selection of Pieces in Prose and Verse . . . Designed for the Use of Schools . . . in the Art of Reading and Speaking.* Philadelphia: William Brown, 1832.

Comstock, Andrew. *System [A] of Elocution, with Special Reference to Gesture, to the Treatment of Stammering and Defective Articulation.* Philadelphia: J. Kay and Brother, 1843 [1841].

Cooper, James Fenimore. *Notions of the Americans. Picked up by a Travelling Bachelor.* 2 vols. Philadelphia: Carey, Lea & Carey, 1833.

Coppée, Henry. *English Literature, Considered as an Interpreter of English History. Designed as a Manual of Instruction.* Seventh ed. Philadelphia: E. Claxton & Company, 1881.

Corson, Hiram. *A Primer of English Verse: Chiefly in Its Aesthetic and Organic Character.* Boston: Ginn & Company, 1893.

Crafts, William. *A Selection in Prose and Poetry from the Miscellaneous Writings of the Late William Crafts.* Charleston: C. C. Sebring and J. S. Burges, 1828.

Crosby, Frances Jane. *Monterey and Other Poems.* New York: R. Craighead, 1851.

Curry, Samuel Silas. *Lessons in Vocal Expression. Course I. Processes of Thinking in the Modulation of the Voice.* Boston: School of Expression, 1895.

Davidson, Lucretia Maria. *Poems. With Illustrations by F. O. C. Darley.* Ed. by M. Oliver Davidson. New York: Hurd and Houghton, 1871.

Dawes, Rufus. *Poems. Geraldine, Athenia of Damascus, and Miscellaneous Poems.* New York: Samuel Colman, 1839.

Day, Henry N. *Introduction to the Study of English Literature; Comprising Representative Masterpieces in Poetry and Prose . . .* New York: Charles Scribner and Company, 1869.

Dialogues Dramatized from the Works of Charles Dickens with Full Directions for Performance, Preparation of Costumes, Etc. Chicago: T. S. Denisson, Publisher [1870?].

"Dickens & Stage." Reviews, playbills etc., Harvard Theatre Collection.

Dickens, Charles. *Charles Dickens' Readings 1867. Clippings from New York Newspapers. Pasted in One Volume. [Includes] Nicholas Nickleby at The Yorkshire School. As Condensed by Himself, for His Readings. With an Illustration by S. Eytinge, Jr.* Boston: Ticknor and Fields, 1868.

"Dickens: Days in Boston," from Houghton Mifflin Company, The Parker House, and The Globe Corner Bookstore present Emlyn Williams as Charles Dickens, 10 March 1984 (Boston: Globe Corner Bookstore, 1984).

Dickensiana. A Bibliography of the Literature Relating to Charles Dickens and His Writings. Compiled by Fred. G. Kitton. First published 1886. New York: Haskell House Publishers, 1971.

Diehl [Randall], Anna T. *Reading and Elocution: Theoretical and Practical.* New York: Ivison, Phinney, Blakeman & Co., 1870.

Dodd, William E. *The Cotton Kingdom: A Chronicle of the Old South.* New Haven: Yale University Press, 1919.

Dolby and Father. By "Buz." New York: P. S. Wynkoop & Son, 1868.

Dot; or, The Cricket on the Hearth. Charles Dickens. Synopsis of the play. Programme. Park Theatre, Monday 20 January 1879. New York: Union Square Printing, 1879.

Duganne, A. J. H. *Parnassus in Pillory. A Satire. By Motley Manners, Esquire.* New York: Adriance, Sherman & Co., 1851.

Dunlap, William A. *History of the American Theatre.* In Two Vols. London: Richard Bentley, 1833.

Durang, Charles. Charles Durang's History of the Philadelphia Stage, 1749–1855. Partly Compiled from the Papers of His Father, the Late John Durang, with Notes by the Editors. Philadelphia: [University of Pennsylvania Library, 1854–59]. MS at Harvard Theatre Collection.

Durang, John. The Memoir of John Durang: American Actor 1785—1816. Ed. Alan S. Downer. [Pittsburgh]: Published for The Historical Society of York County and for the American Society for Theatre Research by the University of Pittsburgh Press, 1966. MS at Harvard Theatre Collection.

Dwyer, John Hanbury. An Essay on Elocution with Elucidatory Passages from Various Authors. To Which Will Be Added, Remarks on Reading Prose and Verse. Second ed. New York: Published by the author, sold by G. & C. Carvill and E. Bliss, 1828.

Dwyer, John Hanbury. An Essay on Elocution: with Elucidatory Passages from Various Authors. To Which are Added Remarks on Reading Prose and Verse, with Suggestions to Instructors of the Art. Sixth ed., with additions. Albany: Weare C. Little, 1856.

Dye, Charity. The Story-Teller's Art. A Guide to the Elementary Study of Fiction. Boston: Ginn & Company, Publishers, 1898.

Eastburn, James Wallis. Yamoyden, a Tale of the Wars of King Philip; in Six Cantos. By the Late Rev. James Wallis Eastburn and His Friend [Robert Charles Sands]. New-York: James Eastburn, Clayton & Kingland, 1820.

Embury, Emma [Catharine]. Guido, Tale [A]; Sketches from History and Other Poems. By Ianthe. New York: G. & C. Carvill, 1828.

Embury, Emma [Catharine]. Poems [The] of Emma C. Embury. First collected edition. New York: Hurd and Houghton, 1869.

Emerson, B. D. The First-Class Reader: A Selection for Exercises in Reading, from Standard British and American Authors, in Prose and Verse. For the Use of Schools in the United States. Boston: Russell, Odiorne, and Metcalf, 1835.

Emmons, Richard M. D. The Freedoniad; or, Independence Preserved. An Epic Poem on the Late War of 1812. 4 vols. Third ed. III. Philadelphia: William Emmons, 1832.

Emson, Frank E. "Bumble's Courtship: From Dickens' 'Oliver Twist'. A Comic Interlude, in One Act." The New York Drama. Vol. 4, No. 45., 1878:236, 286–87.

Everest, Charles V. Babylon; A Poem. Hartford: Canfield and Robins, 1838.

Favorite Authors, a Companion-Book of Prose and Poetry. Boston: Ticknor and Fields, 1861.

Fay, Theodore Sedwick. Ulric; or, The Voices. New York: D. Appleton & Co., 1851.

Fearon, Henry Bradshaw. Sketches of America. A Narrative of a Journey of Five Thousand Miles through the Eastern and Western States of America. London: Longman, Hurst, Rees, Orner, and Brown, 1818.

Felheim, Marvin. The Theater of Augustin Daly. An Account of the Late Nineteenth Century American Stage. Cambridge: Harvard University Press, 1956.

Flagg, Edmund. The Far West; or, A Tour beyond the Mountains. Two vols. New York: Harper & Brothers, 1838.

Flint, Micah P. The Hunter and Other Poems. Boston: Cummings, Hilliard, and Company, 1826.

Freeman, Nathaniel Chapman. [Peter Pindar, Jr]. Parnassus in Philadelphia. A Satire. Philadelphia, 1854.

Frobisher, Joseph Edwin. A New and Practical System of the Culture of Voice and

Action, and a Complete Analysis of the Human Passions, with an Appendix of Readings and Recitations. Designed for Public Speakers, Teachers, and Students. New York: Ivison, Phinney, Blakeman, 1867.

Gallagher, William D. *Erato, Number I.* Cincinnati: Josiah Drake, 1835; *Erato, Number II.* Cincinnati: Alexander Flagg, 1835.

Garland, Hugh A. *The Life of John Randolph of Roanoke. Complete in One Volume.* New York: D. Appleton & Company, 1853.

Gilman, Arthur. *First Steps in English Literature.* Tenth ed. New York and Chicago: A. S. Barnes and Company, [1874] [same: third ed. New York: Hurd & Houghton, 1871].

Goodrich, Samuel Griswold. *Literature, Ancient and Modern, with Specimens. By the author of Peter Parley's Tales.* Boston: Bradbury, Sodern & Co., 1845.

Goodrich, Samuel Griswold. *Recollections of a Lifetime, or Men and Things I Have Seen: In a Series of Familiar Letters to a Friend, Historical, Biographical, Anecdotical, and Descriptive.* Vol. II. New York and Auburn: Miller, Orton & Co., 1857.

Graham, F. Taverner. *Reasonable Elocution. A Textbook for Schools, Colleges, Clergymen, Lawyers, Actors, etc.* New York & Chicago: A. S. Barnes and Company, 1877.

Grayson, William. *The Hireling and the Slave, Chicora, and Other Poems.* Charleston: McCarter, 1856.

Griswold, Rufus W. *The Poets and Poetry of America. With an Historical Introduction.* Philadelphia: Carey and Hart, 1842.

Hall, James. *Legends of the West.* Cincinnati: Applegate and Company, 1857.

Hall, James. *Letters from the West; Containing Sketches of Scenery, Manners, and Customs; and Anecdotes Connected with the First Settlements of the Western Sections of the United States.* London: Henry Colburn, 1828.

Halleck, Fitz-Greene. *Fanny with Other Poems.* New York: Harper & Brothers, 1839.

Halleck, Fitz-Greene. *The Poetical Works.* New ed. New York: D. Appleton and Company, 1858.

Halpin, Patrick A. *Precepts of Literature: A Text-Book.* New York: Baker & Godwin, 1881.

Hart, John S. *A Short Course in Literature, English and American.* Philadelphia: Eldredge & Brother, 1876.

Hawkins, Helen L. Plays, etc. Unpublished material at Bancroft Library, University of California at Berkeley. No 77/81a.

Hawthorne, Julian and Leonard Lemmon. *American Literature. A Textbook for the Use of Schools and Colleges.* Boston: D. C. Heath & Co., 1897.

Hillard, George Stillman and Homer B. Sprague. *The Franklin Sixth Reader and Speaker; Consisting of Extracts in Prose and Verse. With Biographical and Critical Notices of the Authors.* Boston: Brewer and Tileston, 1876.

Hillard, George Stillman. *The Franklin Fifth Reader for the Use of Public and Private Schools with an Introductory Treatise on Elocution by Prof. Mark Bailey.* Boston: Brewer and Tileston, 1871.

History of the New York Theatres: Records of the New York Stage. Harvard Theatre Collection.

Hoffman, Charles Fenno. *Echo [The]: Or, Borrowed Notes for Home Circulation.* Philadelphia: Lindsay & Blakiston, 1844.

Hoffman, Charles Fenno. *Greyslaer: A Romance of the Mohawk. By the Author of*

"A Winter in the West," and "Wild Scenes in the Forest and Prairie." Two vols. New York: Harper & Brothers, 1840.

Hoffman, Charles Fenno. *Poems [The] of Charles Fenno Hoffman. Collected and Edited by His Nephew, Edward Fenno Hoffman.* Philadelphia: Porter & Coates, 1873.

Hoffman, Charles Fenno. *Vigil [The] of Faith, and Other Poems.* Fourth ed. New York: Harper & Brothers, 1845.

Hoffman, Charles Fenno. *Wild Scenes in the Forest and Prairie. With Sketches of American Life.* Two vols. I. New York: William Colyer, 1843.

Holland, Edwin. *The Corsair. A Melo-Drama, in Four Acts. Collected and Arranged for the Stage from Lord Byron's Poem.* Charleston: A. E. Miller, 1818 [Prologue by Mrs. Young of the Charleston Theatre. By "A Native Bard"].

Hosmer, William H. C. *Later Lays and Lyrics.* Rochester, N.Y.: D. M. Dewey, 1873.

Hudson, Henry N. *Classical English Reader. Selections from Standard Authors.* Boston: Ginn, Heath, & Co., 1882.

Hudson, Henry N. *Text-Book of Poetry, from Wordsworth, Coleridge, Burns, Beattie, Goldsmith, and Thomson. With Sketches of the Authors' Lives, Notes, and Glossaries. For Use in Schools and Classes.* Boston: Ginn & Company, 1889.

Hunt, Ephraim. *Literature of the English Language; Comprising Representative Selections from the Best Authors, also Lists of Contemporary Writers and Their Principal Works.* New York, Chicago: Ivison, Blakeman, Taylor, & Co., 1870.

Johnson, Fannie M. "Dotage. A Dickens Charade in Three Scenes [from Cricket on the Hearth, David Copperfield, Bleak House]." In George B. Bartlett, *A Dream of the Centuries and Other Entertainments for Parlor and Hall.* Boston: Walter H. Baker, 1877.

Johnston, Robert. No Thoroughfare, or the Foundlings of London. A Drama in Three Acts Dramatized from Dickens's and Collin's Christmas Story. MS in Harvard Theatre Collection.

Jones, Joseph Stevens. Clippings. Harvard Theatre Collection.

Kellogg, Brainerd. *A Text-Book on English Literature, with Copious Extracts from the Leading Authors, English and American, with Full Instructions as to the Method in Which These Are To Be Studied. Adapted for Use in Colleges, High Schools and Academies.* New York: Clark & Maynard, 1886.

Kemble, Stephen and Henry. *Flodden Field: A Dramatick Romance in Three Acts. First Performed at the Theatre Royal, Drury-Lane, on Thurday Evening, December 31, 1818.* London: R. White, 1819.

Kidd, Robert. *A Rhetorical Reader, for Class Drill and Private Instruction in Elocution.* Cincinnati: Wilson, Hinkle & C., 1870.

Kirby, Edward Napoleon. *Vocal and Action-Language: Culture and Expression.* Boston: Lee and Shepard, 1888.

Kirkham, Samuel. *An Essay on Elocution, Designed for the Use of Schools and Private Learners.* Third ed., enlarged and improved. New York: Robinson, Pratt, & Co., 1836 [1835].

Lamb, Charles. *Mr H., or Beware a Bad Name. A Farce in Two Acts. As Performed at the Philadelphia Theatre.* Philadelphia: Thomas H. Palmer, 1825.

Lamb, Charles. *Mr. H—A Farce in Two Acts. As It Was Performed at Drury Lane Theatre, December, 1806.* In *The Works of Charles and Mary Lamb.* Ed. E. V. Lucas. Vol. V. Poems and Plays. 7 vols. London: Methuen & Co., 1903. New York: AMS Press, 1968. Pp. 180–211.

Lawrence, Philip. *The Model Speaker. Consisting of Exercises in Prose and Poetry. For the Use of Schools, Academies, and Colleges.* Third ed. Philadelphia: Eldredge & Brother, 1871.

Lay [The] of the Last Pilgrim. By the Author of "The Pilgrimage of Ormond." Charleston, S. C.: Printed by W. Riley, 1832.

Lay [The] of the Wilderness, a Poem, in Five Cantos. by a Native of New-Brunswick. Saint John: Printed by Henry Chubb, 1833.

Leavitt, Joshua. *American Lessons in Reading and Speaking, for the Use of the Middle Classes in Common Schools.* Andover, Mass.: Gould, Newman & Saxton, 1840.

Leavitt, Joshua. *Selections for Reading and Speaking for the Higher Classes in Common Schools.* Boston: John P. Jewett & Co., 1849.

Leffingwell, Charles W. *Reading Book of English Classics for Young Pupils. Selections from the Standard Literature of English and America.* New York: G. P. Putnam's Sons, 1881.

Lequel, Louis. *Identity, or, No Thoroughfare. Dramatized from the Christmas Story of Charles Dickens and Wilkie Collins.* French Standard Drama. No. cccxlviii. New York: Samuel French & Son. As performed at Mrs F. B. Conway's Park Theatre, Jan. 6, 1868.

Lewis, Estelle [Sarah] Anna. *Records of the Heart, and Other Poems.* New York: D. Appleton and Company, 1857.

Lewis, Estelle [Sarah] Anna. *Records of the Heart.* New York: D. Appleton & Co., 1844.

Lunt, George. *Julia: A Poem. By Wesley Brooke, pseud.* Boston: Ticknor and Fields, 1855.

Lunt, George. *The Grave of Byron, with Other Poems.* Boston: Hillard, Gray, Little, and Wilkins, 1826.

Macready, William Charles. *Lord Byron's The Two Foscari.* Macready's acting copy. Harvard Theatre Collection.

Maertz, Louise. *A New Method for the Study of English Literature.* Chicago: S. C. Griggs and Company, 1879.

Mandeville, Henry. *The Elements of Reading and Oratory.* New edition, revised and corrected. New York: D. Appleton & Company, 1851 [1849].

Martin, J. L. *Native Bards; A Satirical Effusion; with Other Occasional Pieces.* By J. L. M. Philadelphia: E. L. Carey & A. Hart, 1831.

Massey, Charles. *Massey's Exhibition Reciter, and Drawing-Room Entertainments, . . . Adapted for the Use of Schools and Families.* New York: Samuel French, [1856].

Maturin, Charles. *Bertram: A Tragedy in Five Acts.* Modern Standard Drama. Ed. Epes Sargent. No 53. New York: Wm. Taylor & Co., [1868].

McCay, Joseph. *The Frontier Maid; or, A Tale of Wyoming: A Poem in Five Cantos.* Wilkes-Barre, Pa.: Steuben Butler & Samuel Maffet, 1819.

McGuffey, William H. *McGuffey's Fifth Eclectic Reader.* Revised edition. New York, Cincinnati, Chigago: American Book Company, 1920.

McGuffey, William H. *McGuffey's High School and Literary Reader.* Revised edition. Cincinnati and New York: Eclectic Press, 1889.

McGuffey, William H. *McGuffey's New Fifth Reader.* Modern edition. Cincinnati: W. B. Smith & Co., 1857.

McGuffey, William H. *McGuffey's New Sixth Eclectic Reader: Exercises in Rhetorical Reading, with Introductory Rules and Examples*. Cincinnati, New York: Van Antwerp, . . . and Co., [1866].

McVickar, John D. D. *Tribute to the Memory of Sir Walter Scott, Baronet*. New York: George P. Scott and Co., 1833.

Meek, Alexander Beaufort. *Romantic Passages in Southwestern History [Alabama]; Including Orations, Sketches, and Essays*. 3rd ed. Mobile: S. H. Goetzel & Co., 1857.

Mellen, Grenville. *Age [The] of Print: A Poem, Delivered before the Phi Beta Kappa Society at Cambridge, 26 August, 1830*. Boston: Carter and Hendee, 1830.

Mellen, Grenville. *Martyr's [The] Triumph; Buried Valley; and Other Poems*. Boston: Lilly, Wait, Colman, and Holden, 1833.

Mellen, Grenville. *Our Chronicle of '26. A Satirical Poem*. Boston: Wells and Lilly, 1827.

Mellen, Grenville. *Rest [The] of the Nations: A Poem*. Portland: Hill, Edwards, 1826.

Mitchell, M. S. *A Manual of Elocution Founded upon the Philosophy of the Human Voice*. Philadelphia: Eldredge & Brothers, 1870 [1867].

"Modern British Poets," *The American Monthly Magazine*, September 1836. New series. Vol 2: 235–50; cont. October 1836, ibid., 320–33.

Mongrelites [The]; or, The Radicals—So Called, a Satiric Poem. By—. New York: Van Evrie, Horton, & Co., 1866.

Monroe, Lewis Baxter. *The Fifth Reader*. Philadelphia: Cowperthwait & Co., 1871.

Morford, Henry. *John Jasper's Secret. A Sequel to Charles Dickens's Unfinished Novel "The Mystery of Edwin Drood"*. Philadelphia: T. B. Peterson, 1871.

Morford, Henry. *The Rest of Don Juan; Inscribed to the Shade of Byron*. New York: Burgess, Stringer & Co., 1846.

Morgan, Horace Hills. *English and American Literature for Schools and Colleges*. Boston, New York, Chicago: Leach, Shewell, and Sanborn, 1889.

Morgan, Horace Hills. *Literary Studies for the Great British Authors*. St. Louis: G. I. Jones and Company, 1880.

Morley, Henry. *A Manual of English Literature. Thoroughly Revised with an Entire Re-arrangement of Matter, and with Numerous Retrenchments and Additions, by Moses Coit Tyler*. New York: Sheldon and Company, 1879.

Murdoch, James E. *A Plea for Spoken Language*. Cininnati, New York: Van Antwerp, Bragg & Co., [1883].

Murphy, [Arthur], *The Upholsterer, or What News? A Farce in Two Acts. [As it is performed at the Theatres Royal in London and Dublin]*. Dublin: William Sleater, in Castle-street, 1770 [preface dated 7 April, 1758].

Murray, John O'Kane. *Lessons in English Literature. With a Short Dictionary of British, Irish, and American Authors*. Sixteenth edition. Baltimore: John Murphy, 1884.

Murray, John. *Elocution for Advanced Pupils. A Practical Treatise*. New York & London: G. P. Putnam's Sons, 1888 [1887].

Myers, P. Hamilton. *Ensenore, and Other Poems*. New York: Dodd & Mead, 1875.

Nack, James. *Earl Rupert, and Other Tales and Poems. With a Memoir of the Author by P. M. Wetmore*. New York: George Adlard, 1839.

Nack, James. *The Immortal; A Dramatic Romance; and Other Poems. With a Memoir of the Author by George P. Morris*. New York: Stringer and Townsend, 1850.

Nack, James. *The Legend of the Rocks, and Other Poems.* New York: E. Conrad, 1827.

Neal, John. *Otho: A Tragedy, in Five Acts.* Boston: West, Richardson, and Lord, 1819.

Neal, John. *Randolph, a Novel.* Two vols. By the author of "Logan"—and "Seventy-six." [Baltimore]: Published for whom it may concern, 1823.

"New [The] Engraving for the Sixth Year: Shakespeare and His Friends." *The Cosmopolitan Art Journal. A Record of Art Criticism, Art Intelligence, and Biography, and Repository of Belle-Lettres Literature.* Vol. III. 1858–1859. Pp. 136–37, 187.

Newell, Robert Henry [Kerr, Orpheus C.]. *The Cloven Foot: Being an Adaptation of the English Novel "The Mystery of Edwin Drood," (By Charles Dickens) to American Scenes, Characters, and Nomenclature.* New York: Carleton, 1870.

Newell, Robert Henry [Kerr, Orpheus C.] *The Mystery of Mr. E. Drood. An Adaptation.* London: John Camden Hotten, [1871].

No Thoroughfare. . . . By C-S D-S, Bellamy Brownjohn—and Dombey. [By L. R. Shewall and Fred Williams]. As originally published in the "Boston transcript." February 1, 1868. Performed on December 28, 1867, at the Boston Museum.

Northall, W. K. *Macbeth Travestie.* In *The Minor Drama: A Collection of the Most Popular Petite Comedies, Vaudevilles, Burlettas, Faraces, Travesties, etc.,* Vol. 5. New York: WM. Taylor & Co., [1853]. Acted at the Olympic Theatre, New York, 16 Oct., 1843. Also in Samuel French: The Minor Drama, 36. [1870?].

"Novels and Novel Reading," *The Ladies' Magazine* 1.4 (1828): 145–47.

Nye, [Edgar Wilson]. *The Best of Bill Nye's Humor: Selections from the Nineteenth-Century American Humorist.* Edited by Louis Hasley. New Haven, Conn.: College & University Press, 1972.

Olney, Jesse. *The School Reader; Consisting of Instructive and Progressive Lessons in Prose and Poetry.* New Haven: Durrie and Peek, 1843.

Pancoast, Henry S. *Representative English Literature from Chaucer to Tennyson.* New York: Henry Holt and Company, 1894.

Parker, Richard Green and J. Madison Watson. *The National Fifth Reader: Containing a Complete and Practical Treatise on Elocution; Select and Classified Exercises in Reading and Declamation; with Biographical Sketches, and Copious Notes, Adapted to the Use of Students in Literature.* New York: A. S. Barnes & Company, 1870.

Paulding, James K. [attributed to] *Jokeby, a Burlesque on Rokeby, A Poem, in Six Cantos, by an Amateur of Fashion [i. e. J. Roby]; to Which are Added, Occasional Notes, by Our Most Popular Characters.* London: Thomas Tegg, 1813. Other ed. Boston: W. Wells and T. B. Wait and New York: Co., and Eastburn, Kirk and Co., 1813.

Paulding, James Kirke. [attributed to] *Lay [The] of the Scottish Fiddle: A Tale of Havre de Grace. Supposed To Be Written By Walter Scott, Esq. First American, from the Fourth Edinburgh Edition.* New York: Inskeep & Bradford, 1813.

Paulding, James Kirke. "Othello, the Moor of Venice. By William Shakespeare." In *Salmagundi.* Second series. By Launcelot Langstaff, Esq. In two vols. New York: Harper & Brothers, 1835. I, 47–56.

Payne, John Howard. *Mazeppa; or, The Wild Horse of Tartary [1825]. In Trial without Jury & Other Plays by John Howard Payne.* Ed. Codman Hislop and W. R. Richardson. Princeton, N. J.: Princeton University Press, 1940. Pp. 163–204.

Percival, James Gates. *The Poetical Works of James Gates Percival with a Biographical Sketch.* Two vols. Boston: Ticknor and Fields, 1854.

Perry, Thomas Sergeant. *English Literature in the Eighteenth Century*. New York: Harper & Brothers, 1883.

Phillips, Maude Gillette. *A Popular Manual of English Literature, Containing Outlines of the Literature of France, Germany, Italy, Spain, and the United States of America*. Two vols. New York: Harper & Brothers, 1895.

Pike, Albert. *Prose Sketches and Poems Written in the Western Country, (with Additional Stories)*. Ed. David J. Weber. Foreword by Tom Popejoy. Albuquerque, N.M.: Calvin Horn Publishers, 1967.

Pilgrimage [The] of Ormond, or Childe Harold in The New World. Charleston: W. Riley, 1831.

Porter, Ebenezer. *Analysis of the Principles of Rhetorical Delivery As Applied in Reading and Speaking*. Andover: Mark Newman; Hilliard, Gray & Co., Boston, 1827.

Porter, Ebenezer. *The Rhetorical Reader; Consisting of Instructions for Regulating the Voice, with a Rhetorical Notation . . .* Seventy-fifth edition with an Appendix. Andover: Gould and Newman, 1841.

Potter, Helen. *Helen Potter's Impersonations*. New York: Edgar S. Werner, 1891.

Quiz, Jeremiah. *The Ass on Parnassus; and, From Scotland, Ge Ho!! Comes Roderigh Vich Neddy Dhu, Hoieroe!!! Cantos I. II written in imitation of The Lady of the Lake*. Philadelphia: Mathew Carey, 1815.

Raub, Albert N. *Studies in English and American Literature, from Chaucer to the Present Time; with Standard Selections from Representative Writers for Critical Study and Analysis. Designed for Use in High Schools, Academics, Seminaries, Normal Schools, and by Private Students*. Philadelphia: Raub & Co., 1899.

Raymond, George L. *The Orator's Manual; a Practical and High Philosophical Treatise on Vocal Culture, Emphasis and Gesture, Together with Selections for Declamation and Recitation*. Second ed. Chicago: S. C. Griggs and Company, 1880.

Records of the National Theatre. Season 1840–1841. Boston. Harvard Theatre Collection.

Redburn; or, The Schoolmaster of a Morning. New York: W. M. Christy, 1845.

Reynolds, John. *The Literature of Our Own Country Compared with That of Other Nations*. New York: J. Reynolds, 1948 [written in 1899].

Rice, E. L. *Introduction to American Literature; or, the Origin and Development of the English Language, with Gems of Poetry*. Cincinnati: Derby, Bradley & Co., 1846.

Richardson, Abby Sage. *Stories from Old English Poetry*. Boston, New York, and Chicago: Houghton, Mifflin & Company, 1897.

Ritchie, Anna Cora Ogden Mowatt. *Autobiography of an Actress; or Eight Years on the Stage*. Boston: Ticknor, Reed, and Fields, 1853.

Ritchie, Anna Cora Ogden Mowatt. *Evelyn; or, A Heart Unmasked. A Tale of Domestic Life*. Philadelphia: G. B. Zieber and Company, 1845.

Ritchie, Anna Cora Ogden Mowatt. *Fortune [The] Hunter: A Novel of New York Society*. Philadelphia: T. B. Peterson, 1854.

Ritchie, Anna Cora Ogden Mowatt. *Pelayo; or, the Cavern of Covadonga. A Romance. By Isabel*. New York: Harper & Brothers, 1836.

Ritchie, Anna Cora Ogden Mowatt. *Reviewers Reviewed. A Satire. By the Author of Pelayo*. New York: s.n. 1837.

Ritchie, Anna Cora Ogden Mowatt. *Twin Roses. A Narrative.* Boston: Ticknor and Fields, 1857.

Ritchie, Anna Cora. *Mimic Life; or, Before and Behind the Curtain. A Series of Narratives.* Boston: Ticknor and Fields, 1856.

Robson, Stuart. Modern Stars. Clippings. Harvard Theatre Collection.

Ross, Wilhelm T. *Voice Culture and Elocution.* Rev. ed. New York: The Baker & Taylor Co., 1887.

Royse, N. K. *A Manual of American Literature. Designed for the Use of Schools of Advanced Grades.* Philadelphia: Cowperthwait and Company, 1872.

Rush, James. *The Philosophy of the Human Voice; Embracing Its Physiological History; together with a System of Principles* . . . 2nd ed. Philadelphia: Grigg & Elliott, 1833.

Russell, Osborne. *Journal of a Trapper; or, Nine Years in the Rocky Mountains, 1834–1843.* Boise, Id.: Syms-York Company, 1921.

Russell, William. *American [The] Elocutionist; Comprising "Lessons in Enunciation," "Exercises in Elocution," and "Rudiments of Gesture."* Boston: Jenks and Palmer, 1844.

Russell, William. *Exercises in Elocution, Exemplifying the Rules and Principles of the Art of Reading.* Boston: Jenks and Palmer, 1841.

Russell, William. *Orthophony; or, The Cultivation of the Voice in Elocution. A Manual of Elementary Exercises, Adpated to Dr Rush's "Philosophy of the Human Voice" and the System of Vocal Culture Introduced by Mr. James E. Murdoch.* Boston: Ticknor and Fields, 1862.

Russell, William. *Ortophony, or Vocal Culture. A Manual of Elementary Exercises for the Cultivation of the Voice in Elocution. Reedited by Francis T. Russell.* Seventy-second edition. Boston: Houghton, Mifflin and Company, 1890.

Sadlier, D. & J. *A Review of English and American Literature, for the Use of Schools.* New York: D. & J. Sadlier & Co., 1887.

Sanders, Charles W. *Sanders' Rhetorical; or Union Sixth Reader: Embracing a Full Exposition of the Principles of Rhetorical Reading, with Numerous Specimens, Both in Prose and Poetry, from the Best Writers, English and American, as Exercises for Practice* . . . New York, Chicago: Ivison, Blakeman, Taylor & Co., 1872.

Sanders, Charles W. *Sanders' School Speaker: A Comprehensive Course of Instruction in the Principles of Oratory, with Numerous Exercises for Practice and Declamation.* New York: Ivison, Phinney & Co., 1860.

Sanders, Charles W. *Sanders' Union Fourth Reader: Embracing a Full Exposition of the Principles of Rhetorical Reading; with Numerous Exercises for Practice.* New York, Chicago: Ivison, Blakeman, Taylor, 1863.

Sanders, Charles W. *School [The] Reader. Fifth Book. Designed as a Sequel to Sanders' Fourth Reader. For the Use of Academies and the Higher Classes in Common and Select Schools.* Revised and enlarged. New York, Chicago: Ivison, Blakeman, Taylor & Co., [1859].

Sands, Robert C. *The Bridal of Vaumond; A Metrical Romance.* New York: James Eastbourn and Co., 1817.

Sands, Robert C. *The Writings of Robert C. Sands, in Prose and Verse with a Memoir of the Author.* Two vols. Second ed. New York: Harper & Brothers, 1835.

Sargent, Epes. *Sargent's Original Dialogues. A Collection for School and Family Reading and Representation.* New York: W. I. Pooley & Co., 1861 [1860]. Another 1875.

Sargent, Epes. *Selections in Poetry for Exercises at School and at Home*. Philadelphia: Thomas, Cowperthwait & Co., 1853.

Scott, Jonathan M. *Blue Lights, or The Convention. A Poem in Four Cantos*. New York: Charles N. Baldwin, 1817.

Scott, Walter. *Guy Mannering; or, The Gipsey's Prophecy, as Produced at Booth's Theatre. Miss Cushman as Meg Merrilies*. New York: Henry L. Hinton & Co., Publishers, 1876.

Scott, Walter. *Guy Mannering; or, The Gipsey's Prophecy. A Musical Play. Daniel Terry*. Baltimore: Joseph Robinson, 1839.

Scott, Walter. *Guy Mannering; or, The Gipsey's Prophecy. As Produced at Booth's Theatre, with Emma Aller as Meg Merrilies. December 27th, 1869*. New York: H. L. Hinton, Booth's Theatre, 1869.

Scott, Walter. *Marmion; or, Flodden Field. A Drama, Founded on the Poem of Walter Scott* [from the first London edition, of 1812]. New York: Longworths, 1812.

Scott, Walter. *Marmion; or, Flodden Field. A Drama, Founded on the Poem of Walter Scott*. London: J. Murray, 32, Fleet Street, and W. Blackwood, Edinburgh, 1812.

Scott, Walter. *Mary of Scotland; or, The Heir of Avenel. A Drama, in Three Acts. Founded on the Popular Novel of "The Abbot," and Originally Performed at the Theatre, New York, with Universal Applause*. New York: Henry I. Megarey, 1821.

Scott, Walter. *Tribute to Walter Scott on the One Hundredth Anniversary of His Birthday, by Massachusetts Historical Society, August 15, 1871*. Boston: Privately Printed from the Proceedings of the Society, 1872.

Scott, Walter. *Waverly. A Drama, in Five Acts as Performed at the Theatre Royal, Edinburgh. By John William Calcraft. 1824*. Acting copy at Harvard Theatre Collection.

Severance, Moses. *The American Manual, New English Reader; Consisting of Exercises in Reading and Speaking, both in Prose and Poetry. For the Use in Schools*. Geneva, New York: R. Robbins & Co., 1832 [1830]. Reprinted 1847.

Shakespeare's Historical Tragedy of Richard III, Adapted to Representation by Colley Cibber, as Played by Kemble, Cooke, and Kean, and Re-produced at the Park Theatre, New York, Jan. 7th, 1846.

Shakespeare's Historical Tragedy of Richard III. Adapted for Amateurs and the Drawing Room by Mr. J. A. Arneux; and as Played by Him at the Lexington Ave. Opera House, New York, 1886. And Re-produced at the Academy of Music, Philadelphia, 1887. New York, 1887.

Shakespeare's Tragedy of King Richard III. As Presented by Edwin Booth. New York: Printed, for William Winter, by Francis Hart & Company, 1878.

Shakespeare, William. *Nineteenth-Century Shakespeare Burlesques*. With an Introduction by Stanley Wells. Vol. 5. American Shakespeare Travesties (1852–1888). London: Diploma Press Limited, 1977–78.

Shakespeare, William. *The Tragedy of King Richard III, as Produced by Edwin Booth, Wednesday Evening, May 1, 1872, at Booth's Theatre, New York*. New York: Henry L. Hinton, Publisher [1872].

Shakespeare. Playbill at Boston Theatre. Shakespeare Jubilee Feb. 12, 1824. Harvard Theatre Collection.

"Shakespere is not the the Author of the Plays." *Evening Post*, Cincinnati, July 12, 1887. Accompanying this clipping is a handwritten note by the librarian who sent the material to Boston Public Library.

Shattuck, Harriette, R. *Our Mutual Friend. A Comedy, in Four Acts. Dramatized from Charles Dickens.* Boston: Walter H. Baker & Co., 1879.

Shaw, Thomas Budd and William Smith. *Choice Specimens of English Literature; Selected from the Chief English Writers, and Arranged Chronologically. Adapted to the Use of American Students by B. N. Martin.* New York & Chicago: Sheldon & Company, 1869.

Shaw, Thomas Budd. *A Complete Manual of English Literature. Edited with Notes and Illustrations, by William Smith. With a Sketch of American Literature, by Henry T. Tuckerman.* New York: Sheldon and Company, 1870.

Shaw, Thomas Budd. *Complete [A] Manual of English Literaure. Ed. William Smith. With a Sketch of American Literature by Henry Theodore Tuckerman.* New York: Sheldon and Company, 1867.

Shaw, Thomas Budd. *Outlines of English Literature. A New American Edition. With a Sketch of American Literature by Henry T. Tuckerman.* Philadelphia: Blanchard and Lea, 1856 [1852].

Sherwood, William. *Self-Culture in Reading, Speaking, and Conversation. Designed for the Use of Schools, Colleges, and Home Instruction.* New York: A. S. Barnes & Co., 1855.

Shoemaker, J. W. *Best Things from Best Authors. Humor, Pathos, and Eloquence Designed for Public and Social Entertainment and for Use in Schools and Colleges. Comprising Numbers One, Two, and Three of the Elocutionist's Manual.* Philadelphia: J. W. Shoemaker & Co., 1876.

Shoemaker, J. W. *Practical Elocution; for Use in Colleges and Schools and by Private Students. Enlarged with a Wide Variety of Selections for Practice.* Philadelphia: Penn Publishing Company, 1895.

Simmons, James W. *An Inquiry into the Moral Character of Lord Byron.* London: Ivertson and Palmer, 1826.

Simmons, James W. *Manfredi; A Tragedy, in Five Acts.* Philadelphia: Moses Thomas, 1821.

Simmons, James W. *Valdemar; or, The Castle of the Cliff. A Tragedy.* Philadelphia: H. C. Carey and I. Lee, 1822.

Simms, William Gilmore. *Atlantis. A Story of the Sea: in Three Parts.* New York: J. & J. Harper, 1832.

Simms, William Gilmore. "Death [The] of Cleopatra." In *Norman Maurice; or, The Man of the People. An American Drama.* Fourth ed., revised and corrected. Charleston: Walker and Richards, 1852. Pp. 166–69.

Simms, William Gilmore. *Donna Florida. A Tale.* Charleston: Burges and James, 1843.

Simms, William Gilmore. *Letters [The] of William Gilmore Simms.* Collected, Edited by Mary C. Simms Oliphant, Alfred Taylor Odell, T. C. Duncan Eaves. In 5 vols. Columbia: University of South Carolina Press, 1953–56.

Skinner, Maud and Otis. *One Man in His Time. The Adventures of H. Watkins, Strolling Player, 1845–1863. From His Journal.* Philadelphia: University of Pennsylvania Press, 1938.

Smaller [A] History of English and American Literature. For the Use of Schools. Ed. William Smith and Henry T. Tuckerman. New York: Sheldon and Company, 1870.

Smith, Harry Bache. *Rob Roy; or, The Thistle and the Rose. An Opera in Three Acts. Libretto by Harrt B. Smith. Music by Reginald de Koven.* Chicago: Stone and Kimball, 1894.

Smith, Richard Penn. *Shakespeare in Love*. In *The Sentinels & Other Plays by Richard Penn Smith*. Ed. Ralph H. Ware and H. W. Schoenberger. Princeton, N.J.: Princeton University Press, 1941. Pp. 103–14.

Smith, Seba. *Powhatan, a Metrical Romance in Seven Cantos*. New York: Harper & Brothers, 1841.

Smith, Solomon Franklin. *Theatrical Management in the West and South for Thirty Years. Interspersed with Anecdotical Sketches: Autobiographically Given by Sol. Smith*. New York: Harper & Brothers, Publishers, 1868.

Smyth, Albert H. *American Literature*. Revised ed. Philadelphia: Eldredge & Brother, 1896.

Southwick, Albert P. *Short Studies in Literature for the Use of Schools*. Philadelphia: Eldredge & Brother, 1883.

Southwick, Frank Townsend. *Elocution and Action*. Third ed. New York: Edgar S. Werner Publishing & Supply Co., [1904].

Spalding, William. *The History of English Literature; with an Outline of the Origin and Growth of the English Language: Illustrated by Extracts for the Use of Schools and of Private Schools*. New York: D. Appleton & Company, 1857.

Steele, Silas S. *Book of Plays; for Home Amusement. Being a Collection of Original, Altered and Selected Tragedies, Plays, Dramas, Comedies, Farces, Burlesques, Charades, Lectures, etc., . . . for Private Representation*. Philadelphia: George E. Evans, 1859.

Steele, Silas S. *Steele's Exhibition Dialogues, Consisting of Dramatic Dialogues and Easy Plays, Excellently Adapted for Amateurs in Parlor and Exhibition Performances*. New York: Dick & Fitzgerald, Publishers, 1882.

Stoddard, Charles Warren. C-R 46. MS. cards, notes, memorabilia, Bancroft Library, University of California, Berkeley.

Stoddard, Richard Henry. *The Book of the East, and Other Poems*. Boston: James R. Osgood and Company, 1871.

Strang, Lewis C. *Players and Plays of the Last Quarter Century. An Historical Summary of Causes and a Critical Review of Conditions as Existing in the American Theatres at the Close of the Nineteenth Century. Vol I. The Theatre of Yesterday. Vol II. The Theatre of To-Day*. Boston: L. C. Page & Company, 1903.

Strange Visitors; a Series of Original Papers, Embracing Philosophy, Science, Government, Religion, Poetry, Art, Fiction, Humor, Narrative, and Prophecy. By the spirits of Irving . . . New York: Carleton, Publishers, 1869.

Street, Alfred B. *Frontenac; or, The Atotarho of the Iroquois. A Metrical Romance*. New York: Baker and Scribner, 1849.

Street, Alfred B. *The Poems*. Sixth ed. New York: Clark & Austin, 1850.

Stuart, Carlos D. *Ianthe, and Other Poems*. New York: C. L. Stickney, 1843.

Swett, John. *School Elocution; a Manual of Vocal Training in High Schools, Normal Schools, and Academies*. New York: D. Appleton & Company, [1884].

Swinton, William. *Studies in English Literature; Being Typical Selections of British and American Authorship, from Shakespeare to the Present Time . . . for the Use in High and Normal Schools, Academies, Seminaries, etc*. New York: Harper & Brothers, 1886.

Taylor, Bayard. *A Book of Romances, Lyrics, and Songs*. Boston: Ticknor, Reed, and Fields, 1852.

Taylor, Bayard. *A Journey to Central Africa; or, Life and Landscape from Egypt to the Negro Kingdoms of the White Nile*. New York: G. P. Putnam, 1854.

Taylor, Bayard. *Diversions of The Echo Club*. London: John Camden Hotten, [1870].

Taylor, Bayard. *Eldorado or Adventures in the Path of Empire*. New York: G.P. Putnam & Son, 1868.

Taylor, Bayard. *Northern Travel; Summer and Winter Pictures of Sweden, Denmark and Lapland*. New York: G. P. Putnam, 1858.

Taylor, Bayard. *Poems of the Orient*. Third ed. Boston: Ticknor and Fields, 1855.

Tees, Levin C. *Botany Bay, an Original Melo-drama in Three Acts. Founded in Part on Dickens' "Great Expectations."* Philadelphia: The Penn Publishing Company, 1898.

Thomas, Frederick W. *Emigrant, or Reflections while Descending the Ohio. A Poem.* Cincinnati: Alexander Flash, 1833.

Thomas, Frederick William. *Clinton Bradshaw; or, The Adventures of a Lawyer.* Two vols. Philadelphia: Carey, Lee & Blanchard, 1835.

Thomas, Frederick William. *Howard Pinckney*. London: J. Clements, 1841.

Thomas, Frederick William. *Sketches of Character and Tales Founded on Facts.* Louisville: The Office of the Chronicle of Western Literature and Art, 1849.

Thomson, Mortimer. *"Doesticks." The Lady of the Lake, a Travestie [sic] in One Act. As performed at Niblo's Garden, June 21, 1860*. New York: Samuel French, 1860.

Tremont Theatre. The Forfeit Books of 1840–1842 of Tremont Theatre in Boston. Harvard Theatre collection.

Trimble [Lippincott], Esther J. *A Handbook of English and American Literature . . . For the Use of Schools and Academies*. Philadelphia: Eldredge & Brother, 1883.

Truman, Rickard, and Hiram Orcutt. *Class Book of Prose and Poetry; Consisting of Selections from the Best English and American Authors: Designed as Exercises in Parsing; for the Use of Common Schools and Academies*. Second ed. Boston: Robert S. Davis, 1848.

Underwood, Francis H. *A Handbook of English Literature. Intended for the Use of High Schools, as well as a Companion and Guide for Private Students, and for General Readers. British Authors*. Boston: Lee & Shepard, Publishers, 1875.

Vandenhoff, George. *The Art of Elocution; from the Simple Articulation of the Elemental Sounds of Language, to the Highest Tone of Expression of Speech, Attainable by the Human Voice*. London: Wiley and Putnam, 1846.

Vedder, Henry C. *American Writers of To-Day*. New York, Boston, Chicago: Silver, Burdett & Company, 1894.

Verplanck, Gulian C. *Dick Shift; or, The State Triumvirate, A Political Tale: and the Epistles of Brevet Major Pindar Puff.* New York: J. Seymour, 1819.

Wallace, William R. *The Battle of Tippecanoe, Triumphs of Science, and Other Poems. Delivered at the Battle Ground, November 7, 1835*. Cincinnati: P. McFarlin, 1837.

Walter, [William B.] *Sukey.* From the second Boston edition. Baltimore: N. G. Maxwell, 1821.

Walter, William B. *Poems*. Boston: John Cotton, Jr. & Co., 1821.

Welles, E. G. *The Orator's Guide; or, Rules for Speaking and Composing; from the Best Authorities*. Philadelphia: G. L. Austin, 1822.

Wells, Stanley. *Nineteenth-Century Shakespeare Burlesques*. With an Introduction by Stanley Wells. Five vols. Volume V: *American Shakespeare Travesties (1852–1888)*. London: Diploma Press Limited, 1977–78.

Wemyss, Francis Courtney. *Chronology of the American Stage, from 1752 to 1852.* New York: W. M. Taylor & Co., 1852.

Westlake, James Willis. *Common-School Literature. English and American with Several Hundred Extracts to be Memorized.* Philadelphia: Christopher Sower Company, 1876.

White, Charles. "Charles White's Bowery Speculation in 1853." *The New York Clipper,* April 6, 1872.

White, Charles. *Mazeppa. An Equestrian Burlesque. In Two Scenes. Transposed and Arranged. No. III. Brady's Ethiopian Drama.* New York: Frederic A. Brady, 1856.

White, Charles. "Sam's Courtship. An Ethiopian Farce in One Act . . . As First Produced at White's Opera House. Bowery, New York, 1852." [And] "Sam Weller's Visit to his Mother-in-Law." Adapted from *Pickwick Papers.* In *The New York Drama. A Choice Collection of Tragedies, Comedies, Farces,* etc. . . . 3.29 (1877). New York: Wheat & Conett, 1877. Pp. 31–32, 159–60.

Whiting, Henry. *Sannillac, a Poem with Notes, by Lewis Cass and Henry R. Schoolcraft.* Boston: Carter, Hendel and Babcock, 1831.

Whittier, John Greenleaf. *Narrative and Legendary Poems.* Vol. I. Boston and New York: Houghton, Mifflin and Company, 1900.

Whittier, John Greenleaf. *Personal Poems; Occasional Poems; The Tent on the Beach. With The Poems of Elizabeth H. Whittier.* Boston and New York: Houghton, Mifflin and Company, 1900.

Wiley, Charles Albert. *Wiley's Elocution and Oratory: Giving a Thorough Treatise on the Art of Reading and Speaking.* New York: Clark & Maynard, 1869.

Willis, Nathaniel Parker. *Complete [The] Works.* New York: J. S. Redfield, 1849.

Willis, Nathaniel Parker. *Rural Letters and Other Records of Thought at Leisure, Written in the Intervals of More Hurried Literary Labor.* Auburn, N.Y.: Alden, Beardsley & Company, Rochester, N.Y.: Wanzer, Beardsley & Company, 1853.

Willis, Nathaniel Parker. "Sardanapulus." In *The Corsair. A Gazette of Literature, Art, Dramatic Criticism, Fashion and Novelty.* Vol. I–II. New York, 1839–40.

Wilmer, Lambert A. *The Quacks of Helicon: A Satire.* Philadelphia: J. W. Macclefield, 1841.

Zackos, John C. *Analytic Elocution: An Analysis of the Powers of the Voice, for the Purpose of Expression in Speaking Illustrated by Copious Examples, and Marked by a System of Notation.* New York: A. S. Barnes & Burr, 1861.

Secondary Sources

Adams, William Davenport. *A Book of Burlesque. Sketches of English Stage Travestie and Parody.* London: Henry and Co., 1891. Forcloft, Pa.: Library Editions, 1978.

Adkins, Nelson Frederick. *Fitz-Greene Halleck: An Early Knickerbocker Wit and Poet.* New Haven: Yale University Press, 1930.

Allen, Robert C. "'The Leg Business': Transgression and Containment in American Burlesque." *Camera Obscura: A Journal of Feminism and Film Theory.* Special edition on Popular Culture and Reception Studies, edited by Lynn Spigel, 23 (1990):42–69.

Allston, Washington. *Lectures on Art and Poems (1850); and Monaldi (1841).* Facsimile reproductions including eight paintings with an introduction by Nathalia Wright. Gainesville, Fla.: Scholars' Facsimiles & Reprints, 1967.

American Theatre Companies, 1749–1887. Edited by Weldon B. Durham. New York: Greenwood Press, 1986.

Anderson, Edward Park. "The Intellectual Life of Pittsburg, 1786–1836." *Eastern Pennsylvania Historical Magazine* 14 (1931):9–27, 112–14, 225–36, 288–309.

Auser, Cortland P. *Nathaniel P. Willis*. New York: Twayne Publishers, 1969.

Baender, Paul. "Mark Twain and the Byron Scandal." *American Literature,* 30.4 (1953):467–85.

Barnes, Eric Wollencott. *The Lady of Fashion: The Life and the Theatre of Anna Cora Mowatt*. New York: Charles Scribner's Sons, 1954.

Barnes, Homer. *Charles Fenno Hoffman*. New York: Columbia University Press, 1930.

Barrett, Lawrence. *Charlotte Cushman. A Lecture*. Publications of Dunlap Society. No. 9. New York: Dunlap Society, 1889.

Baym, Nina. *Novels, Readers, and Reviewers; Responses to Fiction in Antebellum America*. Ithaca and London: Cornell University Press, 1984.

Beers, Henry A. *From Chaucer to Tennyson. With Twenty-Nine Portraits and Selections from Thirty Authors*. Meadville, Pa.: The Chatauqua-Century Press, 1898.

Belknap, George N. *Oregon Imprints 1845–1870*. Eugene: University of Oregon Books, 1968.

Bell, Malcolm Jr. *Major Butler's Legacy: Five Generations of a Slaveholding Family*. Athens and London: University of Georgia Press, 1987.

Berson, Misha. "The San Francisco Stage. Pt. I. From Gold Rush to Golden Spike, 1849–1869." *San Francisco Performing Arts Library and Museum Journal* 2 (1989).

Billington, Ray A. *America's Frontier Culture: Three Essays*. College Station: Texas A&M University Press, 1977.

Billington, Ray Allen. *Land of Savagery: Land of Promise. The European Image of the American Frontier in the Nineteenth Century*. New York and London: Norton, 1981.

Blair, Walter. "Burlesques in Nineteenth-Century American Humor." *American Literature,* 2 (1930–1931): 236–47.

Bode, Carl. *The Anatomy of American Popular Culture, 1840–1861*. Berkeley: University of California Press, 1959.

Bogner, Harold F. "Sir Walter Scott in New Orleans, 1818–1832." Master's Thesis in English, Tulane Unversity, 1932. In *The Louisiana Historical Quarterly* 21.2 (January-October 1938):420–517.

Bond, Beverly W. *The Civilization of the Old Northwest: A Study of Political, Social, and Economic Development, 1788–1812*. New York: Macmillan Company, 1934.

Boorstin, Daniel J. *The Americans: The National Experience*. New York: Random House, 1965.

Bordman, Gerald. *America's Musical Theatre: A Chronicle*. New York: Oxford University Press, 1978.

Bordman, Gerald. *The Oxford Companion to American Theatre*. New York: Oxford University Press, 1984.

Boyle, Andrew. *An Index to the Annuals. Vol. I. The Authors 1820–1850*. Worcester: Andrew Boyle (Booksellers), Ltd., 1967.

Boynton, Percy H. *The Rediscovery of the Frontier*. Chicago: University of Chicago Press, 1931.

Bradley, Edward Scullery. *George Henry Boker: Poet and Patriot*. Philadelphia: University of Pennsylvania Press, 1927.

Bradsher, Earl L. *Mathew Carey: Editor, Author and Publisher. A Study in American Literary Development.* New York: Columbia University Press, 1912.

Bristol, Michael D. *Carnival and Theater: Plebeian Culture and the Structure of Authority in Renaissance England.* New York and London: Routledge, 1985.

Brown, Harriet. *Grandmother Brown's Hundred Years, 1827–1927.* Boston: Little, Brown, 1929.

Brown, Herbert R. "Richardson and Sterne in the *Massachusetts Magazine.*" [Reprint from *The New English Quarterly.* 5.1 (1932)]. Southworth Press, 1932. [Pp. 65–82].

Brown, T. Allton. *A History of the New York Stage from the First Performance in 1732 to 1901.* 3 vols. New York: Dodd, Mead and Company, 1903.

Brussell, Isidore R. *Anglo-American First Editions, 1826–1900. East to West. Describing First Editions of English Authors Whose Books Were Published in America before Their Publication in England.* London: Constable & Co., Ltd., New York: R. R. Bowker Co., 1935–36.

Bush, Clive. *The Dream of Reason: American Consiousness and Cultural Achievement from Independence to the Civil War.* London: Edward Arnold, 1977.

Caldwell, Guy, A. Jr. "The Influence of Addison on Charleston Periodicals, 1795–1860." *Studies in Philology* 35 (1938):456–70.

Calverton, V. F. *The Liberation of American Literature.* New York: Charles Scribner's Sons, 1932.

Cameron, Kenneth Walter. *Research Keys to the American Renaissance; Scarce Indexes of The Christian Examiner, The North American Review, and The New Jerusalem Magazine for Students of American Literature, Culture, History, and New England Transcendentalism.* Hartford, Conn.: Transcendental Books, 1967.

Canons. Edited by Robert von Hallberg. Chicago: University of Chicago Press, 1984.

Cardwell, Guy A. Jr. "Influence [The] of Addison on Charleston Periodicals, 1795–1860." *Studies in Philology* 35 (1938): 456–70.

Carpenter, Charles. *History of American Schoolbooks.* Philadelphia: University of Pennsylvania Press, 1963.

Carson, William G. B. *The Theatre of the Frontier. The Early Years of St. Louis Stage.* New York: Benjamin Blom, University of Chicago, 1932.

Charvat, William. *The Profession of Authorship in America, 1800–1870. The Papers of William Charvat.* Edited by Matthew J. Bruccoli. [Columbus]: Ohio State University Press, 1968.

Charvat, William. *The Profession of Authorship in America, 1800–1870. The Papers of William Charvat.* Ed. Matthew J. Bruccoli. [Columbus]: Ohio State University Press, 1968.

Chavkin, Allan & Fritz Oehlschlaeger, "In Europe with Carlyle, De Quincey, and Samuel Rogers." *The American Transcendental Quarterly* 37–40 (Spring 1978): 120–34.

Chew, Samuel C. "Byron in America." *The American Mercury* 1.3 (1924):335–44.

Churchill, George B. "Shakespeare in America. An Address Delivered at the Annual Meeting of the German Shakespeare Society. April 23, 1906." *Deutche Shakespeare-Gesellschaft.* Weimar. Jahrbuch 42 (1905):xiii–xlv.

Clapp, Henry Austin. *Reminiscences of a Dramatic Critic. With an Essay on the Art of Henry Irving.* Boston and New York: Houghton, Mifflin and Company, 1902.

Clapp, John Bouvé and Edwin Francis Edgett. *Players of the Present.* Part I. New York: Dunlap Society, 1899; part II. New York: Dunlap Society, 1900.

Clapp, John Bouvé, and Edwin Francis Edgett. *Plays of the Present*. New York: Dunlap Society, 1902.

Clapp, William W. *A Record of the Boston Stage*. New York. London: Benjamin Blom, 1968 [1853].

Clark, Harry Hayden. "Nationalism in American Literature." Reprinted from the University of *Toronto Quarterly* 2.4 (July 1933):492–519.

Clarke, John S. "John S. Clarke." In "Actors and Actresses of Great Britain and the United States." Edited by Matthew Brander and Lawrence Hutton. Vol. 5.6. New York: Cassell & Company, 1886. MS at Harvard Theatre Collection.

Clinton-Baddeley, V. C. *The Burlesque Tradition in the English Theatre after 1660*. London: Methuen, 1952.

Club of Odd Volumes. Exhibition of Prints and Playbills to Illustrate the History of the Boston Stage (1825–1850). From the Collection of Mr. Robert Gould Shaw, May 3 to May 8 [Boston: s. n. 1915?].

Coad, Oral Sumner and Edwin Mims, Jr. *The American Stage* (The Pageant of America, 14). New Haven: Yale University Press, 1929.

Comparato, Frank E. *Books for the Millions: A History of the Men Whose Methods and Machines Packaged the Printed Word*. Harrisburg, Pa.: The Stackpole Company, 1971.

Conrad, Peter. *Imagining America*. London and Henley: Routledge & Kegan Paul, 1980.

Contë, Gian Biagio. *The Rhetoric of Imitation: Genre and Poetic Memory in Virgil and Other Latin Poets*. Translated from the Italian. Edited and with a Foreword by Charles Segal. Ithaca and London: Cornell University Press, 1986.

Corbett, Martyn. *Byron and Tragedy*. Basingstoke and London: Macmillan Press, 1988.

Cost [The] Book of Carey & Lee: 1825–1838. Edited by David Kaser. Philadelphia: University of Pennsylvania Press, 1963.

Crawford, Mary Caroline. *The Romance of the American Theatre*. Boston: Little, Brown, and Company, 1913.

Crowe, Eyre. *With Thackeray in America. Illustrated*. New York: Charles Scribner's Sons, 1893.

Dabney, Thomas Ewing. *One Hundred Great Years. The Story of the Times-Picayune from Its Founding to 1940*. Baton Rouge: Louisiana State University, 1944.

Davis, Curtis Carroll. *That Ambitious Mr. Legaré. The Life of James M. Legaré of South Carolina, Including a Collected Edition of His Verse*. Columbia, S.C.: University of South Carolina Press, 1971.

Dekker, George. *The American Historical Romance*. Cambridge, New York, Port Chester, Melbourne, Sydney: Cambridge University Press, 1990.

Dempsey, David with Raymond P. Baldwin. *The Triumphs and Trials of Lotta Crabtree*. New York: William Morrow & Company, 1968.

Derby, James C. *Fifty Years among Authors, Books and Publishers*. New York: G. W. Carleton & Co., 1884.

Dormon, James H. Jr. *Theater in the Ante Bellum South, 1815–1861*. Chapel Hill: University of North Carolina Press, 1967.

Downer, Alan S. *The Eminent Tragedian William Charles Macready*. Cambridge, Mass.: Harvard University Press, 1966.

Driver, Leota S. *Fanny Kemble*. Chapel Hill: University of North Carolina Press, 1933.

DuBois, William, R. *English and American Stage Productions: An Annotated Checklist of Prompt Books, 1800–1900.* Boston: G. K. Hall, 1973.

Eagleton, Terry. "Ideology and Scholarship." In *Historical Studies and Literary Criticism.* Ed. Jerome McGann. Madison: University of Wisconsin Press, 1985. Pp. 114–25.

Early American Textbooks 1775–1900. A Catalog of the Titles Held by the Educational Research Library. Washington, D. C.: Department of Education, 1985.

Eckenrode, Hamilton James. *Jefferson Davis: President of the South.* New York: Macmillan Company, 1923.

Eckenrode, Hamilton James. "Sir Walter Scott and the South." *North American Review* 206.2 (1917): 595–603.

Edgar, Herman Leroy and R. W. G. Vail. "Early American Editions of the Works of Charles Dickens," in *Charles Dickens: His Life as Traced by His Works.* Edited by Charles W. Cavanaugh. New York: The New York Public Library, 1929. Pp. 14–31.

Eidson, John Olin. *Tennyson in America: His Reputation and Influence, from 1827 to 1858.* Athens: University of Georgia Press, 1943.

Elson, Ruth Miller. *Guardians of Traditions: American Schoolbooks of the Nineteenth Century.* Lincoln: University of Nebraska Press, 1966.

Everson, Ida Gertrude. *George Henry Calvert: American Literary Pioneer.* New York: Columbia University Press, 1944.

Falk, Bernard. *The Naked Lady or Storm over Adah. A Biography of Adah Isaacs Menken.* London: Hutchinson & Co., 1934.

Fawcett, Frank Dubrez. *Dickens the Dramatist, on Screen, and Radio.* London: Allen, 1952.

Faxon, Frederick Winthrop. *Literary Annuals and Gift-Books.* Boston: Boston Book Company, 1912.

Felheim, Marvin. *The Theater of Augustin Daly. An Account of the Late Nineteenth Century American Stage.* Cambridge: Harvard University Press, 1956.

Foerster, Norman. *American Criticism: A Study in Literary Theory from Poe to the Present.* Boston and New York: Houghton Mifflin Company, 1928.

Foll, Llewellyn E. "Nineteenth Century Gift Books: A Curious Combination of Popular and Elite Art," in *New Dimensions,* 16–30.

Follard, Harold Freeze. "The Plays of Dion Boucicault. Studies in Nineteenth Century Theatrical History." Two vols. Unpublished thesis. Cambridge, Mass.: Harvard University, 1938.

Ford, George H. *Dickens and His Readers: Aspects of Novel-Criticism since 1836.* New York: Gordian Press, 1974.

Forsythe, Michael. "Mardi Hearty." *USAIR,* February 1988, 12–14.

Frick, John W. *New York's First Theatrical Center: The Rialto at Union Square.* Ann Arbor, Michigan: UMI Research Press, 1985.

Frontiers of American Culture. Edited by Ray B. Browne, Richard H. Crowden, Virgil Lokke, William T. Stafford. Lafayette, Ind.: Purdue University Studies, 1968.

Gadamer, Hans-Georg. *Truth and Method.* New York: Seabury Press, 1975.

Gagey, Edmond M. *The San Francisco Stage. A History. Based on Annals Compiled by the Research Department of the San Francisco Federal Theatre.* New York: Columbia University Press, 1950.

Gaines, Francis Pendleton. *The Southern Plantation: A Study in the Development and the Accuracy of a Tradition.* New York: Columbia University Press, 1925.

Gallagher, Kent G. *The Foreigner in Early American Drama: A Study in Attitudes.* The Hague, Paris: Mouton & Co., 1966.

Gallegly, Joseph. *Footlights on the Border: The Galveston and Houston Stage before 1900.* Gravenhage: Mouton, 1962.

Garber, Frederick. *Self, Text, and Romantic Irony: The Example of Byron.* Princeton, N.J.: Princeton University Press, 1988.

Garwood, Irving. *American Periodicals from 1850 to 1860.* Macomb, Ill.: Commercial Art Press, 1931.

Gates, W. B. "Shakespearean Elements in Irving's Sketch Book." *American Literature* 30.4 (1959): 450–458.

Gerson, Noel Bertram. *Queen of the Plaza: A Biography of Adah Isaacs Menken by Paul Lewis.* New York: Funk & Wagnalls Company, 1964.

Gohdes, Clarence L. F. *American Literature in Nineteenth-Century England.* New York: Columbia University Press, 1944.

Golding, Alan C. "A History of American Poetry Anthologies." In *Canons,* 279–307.

Goodman, Dean. *San Francisco Stages. A Concise History, 1849–1986.* San Francisco: Micro Pro Litera Press, 1986.

Gordon, George Stuart. *Anglo-American Literary Relations.* London: Oxford University Press, 1942.

Goslee, Nancy Moore. *Scott the Rhymer.* Lexington, Ky.: University Press of Kentucky, 1988.

Granqvist, Raoul. "Self [The] and the Other in Walt Whitmans Mirror: English Literature and Culture from an American Perspective." *American Studies in Scandinavia* 21.1 (1989):1–15.

Granqvist, Raoul. "Some Traits of Culural Nationalism in the Reception of Shakespeare in the Nineteenth Century U.S.A." *Orbis Litterarum* 43 (1987):1–26.

Green, Martin. "Literary Boston: The Charge of Taste at the End of the Century." In *American Literature: The New England Heritage.* Edited with an Introduction, by James Nagel and Richard Astro. New York and London: Garland, 1981. Pp. 113–29.

Grimsted, David. *Melodrama Unveiled: American Theater and Culture 1800–1850.* Chicago: University of Chicago Press, 1968.

Gulliver, Harold S. "Thackeray in Georgia." *The Georgia Review* 1 (1947):35–43.

Habermas, Jürgen. *Knowledge and Human Interests.* Translated by Jeremy J. Shapiro. Boston: Beacon Press, 1968.

Hamilton, Walter. *Parodies of the Works of English and American Authors.* (I–VI 1884–1889. Vol. I 1884; Vol. II 1885; Vol. III 1886; Vol. IV 1887, Vol. V 1888; Vol. VI 1889.) London: Reeves & Turner.

Hans, James S. *Imitation and the Image of Man.* Philadelphia, Amsterdam: John Benjamin's Publishing House, 1987.

Hart, James D. *The Popular Book: A History of America's Literary Taste.* New York: Oxford University Press, 1950.

Hassan, Ihab H. "The Problem of Influence in Literary History: Notes towards a Definition." In *Influx: Essays on Literary Influence.* Edited by Ronald Primeau. Port Washington, N.Y., and London: Kennikat Press, 1977. Pp. 34–48.

Heiser, M. F. "The Decline of Neoclassicism." In *Transitions in American Literary History.* Edited by Harry Hayden Clarke. Durham, N.C.: Duke University Press, 1953. Pp. 93–159.

Herrnstein Smith, Barbara. "Contingencies of Value." In *Canons*, 5–39.

Hewitt, Bernard. *Theatre USA, 1665 to 1957*. New York, Toronto, London: McGraw-Hill, 1959.

Hill, Frank Pierce. *American Plays Printed 1714–1830. A Bibliographical Record*. Stanford, California: Stanford University Press, 1934.

Hillebrand, Harold Newcomb. *Edmund Kean*. New York: Columbia Univerity Press, 1933.

Hixon, Don L. and Don A. Hennessee. *Nineteenth-century American Drama: A Finding Guide*. Metuchen, N.J., and London: Scarecrow Press, 1977.

Hodge, Francis. *Yankee Theatre. The Image of America on the Stage, 1825–1850*. Austin: University of Texas Press, 1964.

Hogan, Robert. *Dion Boucicault*. New York: Twayne Publishers, 1969.

Holman, C. Hugh. "'Cheap Books' and the Public Interest. Paperbound Book Publishing in Two Centuries." In *Frontiers of American Culture*. Pp. 25–40.

Hoole, William Stanley. *The Ante-Bellum Charleston Theatre*. Tuscaloosa, Ala.: University of Alabama Press, 1946.

Horsman, Reginald. *Race and Manifest Destiny: The Origins of American Racial Anglo-Saxonism*. Cambridge, Mass.: Harvard University Press, 1981.

Horton, Susan R. *The Reader in the Dickens World: Style and Response*. London: Macmillan, 1981.

Howard, Leon. "Wordsworth in America." *Modern Language Notes* 48 (1933):359–65.

Howell, Margaret J. *Byron Tonight: A Poet's Plays on the Nineteenth Century Stage*. Windlesham, Surrey: Springwood Books, 1982.

Hubbell, Jay B. "Literary Nationalism in the Old South." In *American Studies in Honor of William Kenneth Boyd by Members of The Americana Club of Duke University*. Edited by David Kelly Jackson. Durham, N.C.: Duke University, 1944. Pp. 175–220.

Hubbell, Jay B. *South [The] in American Literature, 1607–1900*. Durham, N.C.: Duke University Press, 1954.

Hubbell, Jay B. *Southern Life in Fiction*. Athens: University of Georgia Press, 1960.

Hubbell, Jay B. "Thackeray and Virginia." *The Virginia Quarterly Review* 3 (1927):76–86.

Hudson, Gladys W. *Paradise Lost: A Concordance*. Detroit: Gale Research Company, 1970.

Hughes, Glenn. *A History of the American Theatre, 1700–1900*. New York: Samuel French, 1951.

Hutton, Lawrence. *Curiosities of the American Stage*. New York: Harper & Brothers, 1891.

Hutton, Lawrence. *Opening Addresses Written for and Delivered at the First Performances in Many American Theatres, from Boston to San Francisco, A. D. 1752—A. D. 1880*. Publications of the Dunlop Society, no 3. New York, 1887.

Hutton, Lawrence. *Plays and Players*. New York: Hurd and Houghton, 1875.

Indices to American Literary Annuals and Gift Books, 1825–1865. Compiled by E. Bruce Kirkham and John W. Fink. New Haven, Conn.: Research Publications, 1975.

Ireland, Joseph N. *Memoir [A] of the Professional Life of Thomas Abthorpe Cooper*. Publications of Dunlap Society, No. 5. New York: Dunlap Society, 1888.

Ireland, Joseph N. *Memories of Mrs. Duff.* Edited by Joseph N. Ireland. Harvard Theatre Collection.

Ireland, Joseph N. *Records of the New York Stage, from 1750 to 1860.* Two vols. Vol. I New York: T. H. Morell Publishers, 1866; Vol. II 1867.

James, Reese D. *Cradle of Culture, 1800–1810: The Philadelphia Stage.* Philadelphia: University of Pennsylvania Press, 1957.

James, Reese D. *Old Drury of Philadelphia. A History of the Philadelphia Stage, 1800–1835. A Thesis in English.* Philadelphia: University of Pennsylvania, 1932.

Jauss, Hans Robert. *Aesthetic Experience and Literary Hermeneutics. Translation from the German by Michael Shaw. Introduction by Wlad Godzich.* In Theory and History of Literature, vol. 3. Minneapolis: University of Minnesota Press, 1982.

Jauss, Hans Robert. *Toward an Aesthetic of Reception. Translation from German by Timothy Bahti. Introduction by Paul de Man.* In Theory and History of Literature, vol. 2. Minneapolis: University of Minnesota Press, 1982.

Jauss, Robert. "Literary History as a Challenge to Literary Theory." *New Literary History: A Journal of Theory and Interpretation* 2 (1970):7–37.

Jefferson, Joseph. *"Rip Van Winkle." The Autobiography of Joseph Jefferson.* Edited by Alan S. Downer. Cambridge, Mass.: Belknap Press, Harvard University Press, 1964 [1949].

Johnson, Louise H. "The Source of the Chapter on Slavery in Dickens's American Notes." *American Literature* 14 (1942–43):427–31.

Kapferer, Bruce. "Performance and the Structuring of Meaning and Experience." In *The Anthropoloy of Experience.* Edited by Victor Turner and Edward M. Bruner. Urbana and Chicago: University of Illinois Press, 1986. Pp. 188–203.

Kasson, Joy S. *Artistic Voyagers: Europe and the American Imagination in the Works of Irving, Allston, Cole, Cooper, and Hawthorne.* Westport, Conn.: London, England: Greenwood Press, 1982.

Keese, William L. *A Group of Comedians.* New series. No. 15. New York: Dunlap Society, 1901.

Kellett, E. E. *Literary Quotation and Allusion.* Port Washington, N.Y.: Kennikat Press, 1969.

Kemble, Fanny. *The Journal of Frances Anne Butler, Better Known as Fanny Kemble.* Two vols in one. New York: Benjamin Blom, 1970.

Kendall, John S. *The Golden Age of New Orleans Theater.* Baton Rouge: Louisiana State University Press, 1952.

Krug, Werner G. *Lord Byron als Dichterische Gestalt in England, Frankreich, Deutchland und Amerika.* Potsdam: Richard Schneider, 1932.

Kummer, George. "The Americanization of the Burlesque, 1840–1860." In *Popular Literature in America: A Symposium in Honor of Lyon N. Richardson.* Edited by James C. Austin. Bowling Green, Ohio: Bowling Green University Popular Press, 1972. Pp. 146–54.

Landrum, Grace Warren. "Sir Walter Scott and His Literary Rivals in the Old South," *American Literature* 2.3 (1930–1931):256–76; cont. "Notes on the Reading of the Old South," ibid., 3.1 (1931):60–71.

Larcom, Lucy. *A New England Girlhood Outlined from Memory.* Boston: Houghton, Mifflin and Company, 1889.

Larson, Carl F. W. *American Regional Theatre History to 1900: A Bibliography.* New York: Metuchen, London: Scarecrow Press, 1979.

Lauber, John. *Sir Walter Scott.* Revised edition. Boston: Twayne Publishers, 1989.

Leavitt, Michael Bennett. *Fifty Years in Theatrical Management, 1859–1909*. New York: Broadway Publishing House Co., [1912].

Legaré, Hugh Swinton. *Writings of Hugh Swinton Legaré*. Two vols. Ed. [Mrs Mary Swinton Legaré Bullen]. Vol 1. Charleston. S. C.: Burges & James, Leavitt, 1846; vol 2. 1845.

Lehmann-Haupt, Hellmut. *The Book in America: A History of the Making, the Selling, and the Collecting of Books in the United States*. New York: R.R. Bowker Company, 1939.

Leisy, Ernest E. *The American Historical Novel*. Norman: University of Oklahoma Press, 1950.

Leman, Walter M. *Memories of an Old Actor*. San Francisco: A Roman Co., 1886.

Lentricchia, Frank. "Byron in America: The Later Nineteenth Century." Unpublished thesis. Department of English. Duke University, 1963.

Leonard, William Ellery. *Byron and Byronism in America*. New York: Gordion Press, 1965 (reprint from 1907).

Lesser, Allen. *Enchanting Rebel. The Secret of Adah Isaacs Menken*. New York: The Beachhurst Press, 1947.

Levine, Lawrence W. *Highbrow/Lowbrow: The Emergence of Cultural Hierarchy in America*. Cambridge, Mass.: Harvard University Press, 1988.

Lewis, Paul. *Queen of the Plaza: A Biography of Adah Isaacs Menken*. New York: Frank & Wagnalls Company, 1964.

Lindberg, Stanley W. *The Annotated McGuffey: Selections from the McGuffey Eclectic Readers, 1836–1920*. New York: Van Nostrand Reinhold Company, 1976.

Lindey, Alexander. *Plagiarism and Originality*. New York: Harper & Brothers Publishers, 1952.

"Lola Montez, Adah Isaacs Menken, Mrs. Judah." San Francisco Theatre Research. Ed. Lawrence Estavan. Vol. 5, first series. San Francisco 1938. MS at Harvard Theatre Collection.

Ludlow, Noah M. *Dramatic Life as I Found It*. Bronx, New York: Benjamin Blom, 1966 (from 1880).

Lyon, William H. *The Pioneer Editor in Missouri, 1808–1860*. Columbia: University of Missouri Press, 1965.

MacMinn, George R. *The Theater of the Golden Era in California. Illustrated*. Caldwell, Idaho: Caxton Printers, 1941.

"Macready and Forrest; and Their Contemporaries." In Actors and Actresses of Great Britain and the United States, from the Days of David Garrick to the Present Time. Edited by Matthew Brander and Laurence Hutton. 4.1.1–2. New York: Cassell & Company, 1886. MS at Harvard Theatre Collection.

Macready, William Charles. *Diaries [The] of William Charles Macready, 1833–1851*. Edited by William Toynbee. Two vols. New York: G. P. Putnam's Sons, 1912.

Macready, William Charles. *Journal [The] of William Charles Macready, 1832–1851*. Abridged and edited by J. C. Trewin. London: Longmans, 1867.

Macready, William Charles. *Macready's Reminiscences, and Selections from His Diaries and Letters*. Edited by Sir Frederick Pollock, Bart. Two vols. London: Macmillan and Co., 1875.

Madison, Charles A. *Book Publishing in America*. New York, Toronto, London: McGraw-Hill Book Company, 1966.

Maeder, Clara Fisher. *Autobiography of Clara Fisher Maeder*. Edited by Douglas

Taylor. Publications of Dunlap Society. New Series, no., 3. New York: Dunlap Society, 1879.

Mahan, Bruce E. "The Iowa Thespians." *The Palimpsest* 4 (1923):14–24.

Mailloux, Steven. *Interpretive Conventions: The Reader in the Study of American Fiction.* Ithaca: Cornell University Press, 1982.

Mankowitz, Wolf. *The Lives, Loves and Legends of Adah Isaacs Menken: A Biographical Quest.* London: Blond & Briggs, 1982.

Markels, Julian. "Melville's Markings in Shakespeare's Plays." *American Literature* 49.7 (1977):34–48.

Marryat, Frederich. *A Diary in America with Remarks on Its Institutions.* Edited by with a foreword Jules Zanger. Bloomington: Indiana University Press, 1960.

Martineau, Harriet. *Society in America.* Three vols. London: Saunders and Otley, Conduit Street, 1837. New York: AMS Press, 1966.

Matthews, Brander and Laurence Hutton. *The Life and Art of Edwin Booth and His Contemporaries.* Boston: L. C. Page & Company Publishers, 1906.

Mawson, Harry P. "Dickens on the Stage." *The Theatre* 25.1 (1912):46–49, viii.

Mayorga, Margaret G. *A Short History of the American Drama. Commentaries on Plays prior to 1920.* New York: Dodd, Mead & Company, 1932.

McCorison, Marcus A. *Vermont Imprints, 1778–1820. A Check List of Books, Pamphlets, and Broadsides.* Worcester: American Antiquarian Society, 1963.

McCutcheon, Roger P. "The First English Plays in New Orleans." *American Literature* 2 (1939–40):183–99.

McGann, Jerome J. *Beauty [The] of Inflections: Literary Investigations in Historical Method and Theory.* Oxford: Clarendon Press, 1985.

McGann, Jerome J. ed. *Lord Byron: The Complete Poetical Works.* 6 vols. Oxford: Clarendon Press, 1980–91.

McGann, Jerome J. "Introduction: A Point of Reference." In *Historical Studies and Literary Criticism.* Edited by Jerome McGann. Madison: University of Wisconsin Press, 1985. Pp. 3–21.

McGann, Jerome J. *Social Values and Poetic Acts: The Historical Judgment of Literary Works.* Cambridge, Mass.: Harvard University Press, 1988.

McGlinchee, Claire. *The First Decade of the Boston Museum.* Boston: Bruce Humphries, Inc. Publishers, 1940.

McKeon, Newton Felch, and Katharina Conover Cowles, eds. *Amherst, Massachusetts, Imprints 1825–1876.* Amherst, Mass.: Amherst College Library, 1946.

McLaren, Mory. *Sir Walter Scott: The Man and Patriot.* London: Heinemann, 1970.

McMaster, Graham. *Scott and Society.* Cambridge: Cambridge University Press, 1981.

Merod, Jim. *The Political Responsibilty of the Critic.* Ithaca, N.Y. and London: Cornell University Press, 1987.

Meserve, Walter J. *An Outline History of American Drama.* Totowa, N.J.: Littlefield, Adams & Co., 1965.

Milburn, William Henry. *The Rifle, Axe, and Saddle-Bags, and Other Lectures.* New York: Derby & Jackson, 1857.

Miller, Perry. *The Life of the Mind in America, from the Revolution to the Civil War.* 3 vols. New York: Harcourt, Bruce & World, Inc., 1965.

Miller, William. *The Dickens Student and Collector. A List of Writings Relating to Charles Dickens and His Works, 1836–1945.* London: Chapman and Hall, 1946.

Mills, Nicolaus. *American and English Fiction in the Nineteenth Century: An Anti-genre Critique and Comparison.* Bloomington, London: Indiana University Press, 1973.

"Ministrelsy." San Francisco Theatre Research. Edited by Lawrence Estavan. Vol. 13, first series. San Francisco 1939. MS at Harvard Theatre Collection.

Montgomery, George Edgar. "Dickens on the American Stage." *American Magazine,* new series, 8 (1888):190–207.

Moore, Arthur K. *The Frontier Mind: A Cultural Analysis of the Kentucky Frontiersman.* [Lexington]: University of Kentucky Press, 1957.

Mordden, Ethan. *The American Theatre.* New York: Oxford University Press, 1981.

Morris, Lloyd. *Curtain Time. The Story of the American Theatre.* New York: Random House, 1953.

Moses, Montrose J. *The American Dramatist.* Boston: Little, Brown, and Company, 1911.

Mosier, Richard D. *Making the American Mind: Social and Moral Ideas in McGuffey Readers.* New York: King's Crown Press, 1947.

Mott, Frank Luther. *A History of American Magazines 1741–1850.* Vol I. Cambridge, Mass.: Harvard University Press, 1939.

Mott, Frank Luther. *A History of American Magazines 1850–1865.* Vol II. Cambridge, Mass.: Harvard University Press, 1938.

Mott, Frank Luther. "Carlyle's American Public." *Philological Quarterly* 4 (1925):245–66.

Mott, Frank Luther. *Golden Multitudes: The Story of Best Sellers in the United States.* New York: Macmillan, 1947.

Murdoch, James E. *The Stage; or, Recollections of Actors and Acting from an Experience of Fifty Years. A Series of Dramatic Sketches.* Cincinnati: Robert Clarke & Co., 1884.

Myerson, Joel. *The New England Transcendentalists and the Dial: A History of the Magazine and Its Contributors.* London: Associated University Presses, 1980.

Nathan, Hans. *Dan Emmett and the Rise of Early Negro Ministrelsy.* Norman: University of Oklahoma Press, 1977.

New Dimensions in Popular Culture. Edited by Russel B. Nye. Bowling Green, Ohio: Bowling Green University Popular Press, 1972.

Newton, Annabel. *Wordsworth in Early American Criticism.* Chicago: University of Chicago Press, 1928.

Nietz, John A. *Old Textbooks. Spelling, Grammar, Reading, Arithmetics . . . as Taught in the Common Schools from Colonial Days to 1900.* Pittsburgh: University of Pittsburgh Press, 1961.

Nietz, John A. *The Evolution of American Secondary School Textbook.* Rutland, Vt.: Charles E. Tuttle Company, 1966.

Noel, Mary. *Villains Gallore: The Heyday of the Popular Story Weekly.* New York: Macmillan, 1954.

Nye, Russel Blaine. *The Cultural Life of the New Nation, 1776–1830.* New York: Harper & Brothers, 1960.

Nye, Russel Blaine. *The Unembarrassed Muse: The Popular Arts in America.* New York: Dial Press, 1970.

Oberhaus, Dorothy Huff. "'Engine against th' Almightie': Emily Dickinson and Prayer." *ESQ* 32.3 (1986):153–72.

Odell, George C. D. *Annals of the New York Stage.* 1–9. New York: Columbia University Press, 1928–49.

Orians, George Harrison. "Influence [The] of Walter Scott upon America and American Literature before 1860." An abstract of a thesis. Urbana, Ill.: University of Illinois, 1929.

Orians, George Harrison. "The Rise of Romanticism, 1805–1855." In *Transitions in American Literary History.* Edited by Harry Hayden Clark. Durham, N.C.: Duke University Press, 1953–54. Pp. 161–244.

Orians, George Harrison. "The Romanctic Ferment after Waverly." *American Literature* 3.4 (1932):408–31.

Orians, George Harrison. "Walter Scott, Mark Twain, and the Civil War." *South Atlantic Quarterly* 40 (1941):342–59.

Osterweis, Rollin G. *Romanticism and Nationalism in the Old South.* New Haven: Yale University Press, 1949.

Parkman, Francis. *Letters of Francis Parkman.* Edited and with an Introduction by Wilbur R. Jacobs. Vol II. Norman: University of Oklahoma Press, 1960.

Parks, Edd Winfield. *Ante-Bellum Southern Literary Critics.* Athens: University of Georgia Press, 1962.

Parks, Edd Winfield. *William Gilmore Simms as Literary Critic.* Athens: University of Georgia Press, 1961.

Payne, Edward F. *Dickens Days in Boston.* Boston and New York: Houghton Mifflin Company, 1927.

Peach, Linden. *British Influence on the Birth of American Literature.* New York: St. Martin's Press, 1982.

Peckman, Howard H. "Books and Reading on the Ohio Valley Frontier." *Mississippi Valley Historical Review* 44 (1957–58):649–63.

Pence, James Harry. *The Magazine and the Drama. An Index. Publications of Dunlap Society.* New series, no 20. New York: The Dunlop Society, 1896.

Pettigrew, Richard C. "Emerson and Milton." *American Literature* 3.1 (1931):45–59.

Pettigrew, Richard C. "Lowell's Criticism of Milton." *American Literature* 3.4 (1932):457–64.

Phelps, Henry P. *Players of a Century. A Record of the Albany Stage. Including Notices of Prominent Actors Who Have Appeared in America.* Second ed. [first appeared in 1880] New York: Benjamin Blom, Inc., 1972.

"Pioneer Impresarios: Tom Maquire, Doc Robinson, M. B. Leavitt." San Francisco Theatre Research. Edited by Lawrence Estavan. Vol. 2. First series. San Francisco 1938. MS at Harvard Theatre Collection.

Pioneer Western Playbills. Edited by Frank L. Fenton. San Francisco: Book Club of California, 1951.

Poirier, Richard. *A World Elsewhere: The Place of Style in American Literature.* New York: Oxford University Press, 1966.

Pollard, Graham. Introduction. In Isidore Brussell, *Anglo-American First Editions.*

Popular Literature in America: A Symposium in Honor of Lyon N. Richardson. Edited by James C. Austin [and] Donald A. Koch. Bowling Green, Ohio: Bowling Green University Popular Press, 1972.

Power, Julia. *Shelley in America in the Nineteenth Century; His Relations to American Crtitical Thought and His Influence. University Studies.* Lincoln, Nebr.: University of Nebraska. Vol. 40. No 2. 1940.

Pritchard, John Paul. *Literary Wise Men of Gotham: Criticism in New York, 1815–1860.* Baton Rouge: Lousiana State University Press, 1963.

Publishers for Mass Entertainment in Nineteenth Century America. Edited by Madeleine B. Stern. Boston, Mass.: G.K. Hall & Co., 1980.

Quinn, Arthur Hobson. *A History of the American Drama, from the Beginning to the Civil War.* New York: Harper & Brothers, 1923 (new edition: New York: Appleton-Century-Crofts, 1951).

Randall, David A. "Waverley in America." *The Colophon. New Series. A Quarterly for Bookmen* 1.1 (1935):39–55.

Rathbun, John W. and Harry H. Clark. *American Literary Criticism, 1800–1860.* Vol. I Boston: Twayne Publishers, 1979; 1860–1905. Vol. II. Boston: Twayne Publishers, 1979.

Reed, Henry. *Lectures on English Literature, from Chaucer to Tennyson.* Philadelphia: Claxton, Remsen & Haffelfinger, 1869.

Reed, James. *Sir Walter Scott: Landscape and Locality.* London: Athlone Press, 1980.

Rees, James. *Dramatig [sic] [The] Authors of America.* Philadelphia: G. B. Zieber & Co., 1845.

Rees, James. *Scrapbooks. Old Play Bills with Remarks. Written for the Philadelphia Sunday Mercury.* 3 vols. Philadelphia, [1874–1878]. Harvard Theatre Collection.

Regionalism in America. Edited by Merrill Jensen, with a Foreword by Felix Frankfurter. Madison, Wisc.: University of Wisconsin Press, 1951.

Rella, Ettore. "A History of Burlesque." San Francisco Theatre Research Series: A Monograph History of San Francisco Stage and Its Peoplek from 1849 to the Present Day. Edited by Lawrence Estavan. Vol. 14, first series. San Francisco 1939. MS at Harvard Theatre Collection.

Richardson, Charles F. *American Literature 1607–1885. I. The Development of American Thought. II. American Poetry of Fiction.* New York, London: G. P. Putnam's Sons, 1904.

Rievald, J. G. "The Transatlantic Reception of American Literature in Europe, 1800–1900, a Review of Research." *English Studies* 60 (1979):562–602.

Roden, Robert F. *Later American Plays, 1831–1900; Being a Compilation of the Plays by American Authors Published and Performed in American since 1831.* Publications of Dunlap Society. New Series: No. 2. New York: Dunlop Society, 1900.

Rollins, Hyder Edward and Stephen Maxfield Parrish. *Keats and the Bostonians: Amy Lowell, Louise Imogen Guiney, Louis Arthur Holman, Fred Holland Day.* Cambridge, Mass.: Harvard University Press, 1951.

Rollins, Hyder Edward. *Keats' Reputation in America to 1848.* Cambridge, Mass.: Harvard University, 1946.

Roppolo, Joseph Patrick. "Local and Topical Plays in New Orleans, 1806–1865." *Tulane Studies in English* 4 (1954):91–124.

Roselle, Daniel. *Samuel Griswold Goodrich, Creator of Peter Parley: A Study of His Life and Work.* Albany, New York: State University of New York Press, 1968.

Rourke, Constance. *American Humor: A Study of the National Character.* New York: Harcourt, Brace and Company, 1931.

Rourke, Constance. *The Roots of American Culture and other Essays.* Edited, with a preface, by Van Wyck Brooks. New York: Harcourt, Brace and Company, 1942.

Ruland, Richard. *America in Modern European Literature: From Image to Metaphor.* New York: New York University Press, 1976.

Rusk, Ralph Leslie. *The Literature of the Middle Western Frontier.* 2 vols. New York: Columbia University Press, 1925.

Ryan, Kate. *Old Boston Museum Days.* Boston: Little, Brown, and Company, 1915.

Schick, Frank L. *The Paperbound Book in America: The History of Paperbacks and Their European Background.* New York: R. R. Bowker Company, 1958.

Schick, Joseph. *The Early Theater in Eastern Iowa: Cultural Beginnings and the Rise of the Theater in Davenport and Eastern Iowa, 1836–1863.* Diss. Chicago: University of Chicago Press, 1939.

Schneider, George A. "Millions of Moral Little Books: Sunday School Books in Their Popular Context." In *New Dimensions,* 1–15.

Schwarz, Lyle A. "A Phrophetic Protagonist of the Gold Frontier: George Pauncefort." In *Theatre West: Image and Impact,* ed. Dunbar H. Ogden, with Douglas McDermott and Robert K. Sarlós. Amsterdam, Atlanta: Rodopi, 1990. Pp. 99–114.

Sensabaugh, George F. *Milton in Early America.* Princeton, N.J.: Princeton University Press, 1964.

Sensabaugh, George F. "Milton in Early American Schools." *The Huntington Library Quarterly* 19.4 (1956):353–83.

Shakespeare and Southern Writers: A Study in Influence. Edited by Philip C. Kolin with a Foreword by Lewis P. Simpson. Jackson: University Press of Mississippi, 1985.

Shakespeare in the South: Essays on Performance. Edited by Philip C. Kolin. Jackson: University Press of Mississippi, 1983.

Sherman, Robert L. *Drama Cyclopedia. A Bibliography of American Plays and Players.* Published by the Author. Chicago, 1944.

Shockley, Martin Staples. "Shakespeare's Plays in the Richmond Theatre, 1819–1838." *The Shakespeare Association Bulletin* 16.1 (1940):88–94.

Shockley, Martin Staples. *The Richmond Stage, 1784–1812.* Charlottesville: University Press of Virginia, 1977.

Sibley, Agnes Marie. *Alexander Pope's Prestige in America, 1725–1835.* New York: King's Crown Press, 1949.

Smith, Bernard. *Forces in American Criticism: A Study in the History of American Literary Thought.* New York: Harcourt, Brace and Company, 1939.

Smither, Nelle. *A History of the English Theatre at New Orleans, 1806–1842.* Philadelphia: University of Pennylvania, 1944.

Smyth, Albert H. *Philadelphia Magazines and Their Contributors, 1741–1850.* Philadelphia: R. M. Lindsay, 1892.

Sneller, Delwyn L. "The Character and Function of Popular Religious Poetry 1820–1860." In *New Dimensions,* 172–88.

Spariosu, Mihai. *Literature, Mimesis and Play: Essays in Literary Theory.* Tübingen: Gunter Narr Verlag, 1982.

Spencer, Benjamin T. "Regionalism in American Literature." In *Regionalism in America.* Edited by Merrill Jensen, with a Foreword by Felix Frankfurter. Madison, Wis.: University of Wisconsin Press, 1951. Pp. 219–60.

Spencer, Benjamin. "A National Literature, 1837–1855." *American Literature* 8.2 (1936):125–59.

Spender, Stephen. *Love-Hate Relations: English and American Sensibilities.* New York: Random House, 1974.

"Starks [The], the Bakers, the Chapmans," *San Francisco Theatre Research*. Edited by Lawrence Estavan. Vol. 3, first series. San Francisco 1938. MS at Harvard Theatre Collection.

Stern, Madeleine B. *Imprints on History. Book Publishers and American Frontiers.* Bloomington: Indiana University Press, 1956.

Tanner, Tony. "Notes for a Comparison between American and European Romanticism." *Journal of American Studies* 2.1 (1968):83–103.

Taylor, Bayard. *Life and Letters of Bayard Taylor.* Edited by Marie Hansen Taylor and Horace E. Scudder. Two vols. Boston: Houghton, Mifflin and Company, 1884.

Tebbel, John. Between Covers: *The Rise and Transformation of Book Publishing in America.* New York, Oxford: Oxford University Press, 1987.

Tebbel, John. *The American Magazine: A Compact History.* New York: Hawthorn Books, Inc. Publishers, 1969.

Tebbel, John. *The Compact History of the American Newspaper.* New York: Hawthorn Books, Inc. Publishers, 1963.

Textual Criticism and Literary Interpretation. Edited by Jerome McGann. Chicago: University of Chicago Press, 1985.

Thompson, David W. "Early Actress-Readers: Mowatt, Kemble, and Cushman." In *Performance of Literature in Historical Perspectives,* ed. David W. Thompson. Lanham: University Press of America, 1983. Pp. 629–50.

Thompson, Ralph. *American Literary Annuals and Gift Books, 1825–1865.* New York: Th. H. W. Wilson Company, 1936.

Three Centuries of English and American Plays: A Checklist. England: 1500–1800, Unites States: 1714–1830. Edited by G. William Bergquist. New York: Readex Microprint Corporation, 1963.

Tocqueville, Alexis de. *Democracy in America.* Translated by Henry Reeve, edited by Francis Bower. 2 vols. Cambridge, Mass.: Sever and Francis, 1862–64.

Tompkins, Eugene. *The History of the Boston Theatre 1854–1901.* Compiled with the assistance of Quincy Kilby. Boston and New York: Houghton Mifflin Company, 1968.

Transcendentalists [The]. A Review of Research and Criticism. Edited by Joel Myerson. New York: Modern Language Association, 1984.

Trowbridge, John Townsend. *My Own Story with Recollections of Noted Persons.* Boston and New York: Houghton, Mifflin and Company, 1903.

Tryon, W. S. "Nationalism and International Copyright: Tennyson and Longfellow in America." *American Literature* 24.3 (1952):301–09.

Turner, Victor. "Dewey, Dilthey, and Drama: An Essay on the Anthropology of Experience." In *The Anthropology of Experience.* Edited by Victor Turner and Edward M. Bruner. Urbana: University of Illinois Press, 1986.

Turner, Victor. *Dramas, Fields, and Metaphors: Symbolic Action in Human Society.* Ithaca: Cornell University Press, 1974.

Vail Motter, T. H. "Byron's Werner Re-Estimated: A Neglected Chapter in Nineteenth Century Stage History." Reprinted from *Essays in Dramatic Literature: The Parrott Presentation* Volume. Edited by Hardin Craig. Princeton, N.J.: Princeton University Press, 1935. Pp. 242–75.

Vail, R. W. G. *Random Notes on the History of the Early American Circus.* Worcester, Mass.: American Antiquarian Society, 1934.

Venable, W. H. *Beginnings of Literary Culture in the Ohio Valley. Historical and Biographical Sketches.* New York: Peter Smith, 1949 [1891].

Vicinus, Martha. "'Helpless and Unfriended': Nineteenth-Century Domestic Melodrama." *New Literary History: A Journal of Theory and Interpretation.* 13 (1981–1982):127–43.

von Frank, Albert J. *The Sacred Game: Provincialism and Frontier Consciousness in American Literature, 1630–1860.* Cambridge: Cambridge University Press, 1985.

Wade, Mason. *Francis Parkman. Heroic Historian.* New York: Viking Press, 1942.

Walker, Don D. "Reading on the Range: The Literary Habits of the American Cowboy." Arizona and the West. A Quarterly Journal of History. *The University of Arizona Press* 2 (1960): 307–18.

Walker, Franklin. *San Francisco's Literary Frontier.* New York: Alfred A. Knopf, 1939.

Walsh, Townsend. *The Career of Dion Boucicault.* New York: Dunlap Society, 1915.

Ward, Julius H. *The Life and Letters of James Gates Percival.* Boston: Ticknor and Fields, 1866.

Watson, Margaret G. *Silver Theatre: Amusements of the Mining Frontier in Early Nevada, 1850–1864.* Glendale, Calif.: The Arthur H. Clark Company, 1964.

Weigel, John A. "The Milton Tradition in the First Half of the Twentieth Century." Unpublished thesis. Department of English: Western Reserve University, 1939.

Weimann, Robert. *Structure and Society in Literary History: Studies in the History and Theory of Historical Criticism.* Charlottesville: University Press of Virginia, 1976.

Weygandt, Cornelius. *The Time of Tennyson: English Victorian Poetry As It Affected America.* New York, London: D. Appleton-Century Company, 1936.

White, Henry Adelbert. *Sir Walter Scott's Novels on the Stage.* Diss. Yale Studies in English. 76. New Haven: Yale University Press, 1927.

Wilkins, William Clyde. *Charles Dickens in America.* Compiled and edited by William Clyde Wilkins. New York: Charles Scribner's Sons, 1912.

Wilkins, William Clyde. *Dickens in Cartoons and Caricature.* Edited by B. N. Matz. Privately printed from works of The Bibliophile Society. Boston: Plimpton Press, 1927.

Wilson, Francis. *Joseph Jefferson. Reminiscences of a Fellow Player.* New York: Charles Scribner's Sons, 1906.

Wilson, Garff B. *Three Hundred Years of American Drama and Theatre. From Ye Bear and Ye Cubb to Hair.* Englewood Cliffs, N.J.: Prentice-Hall, 1973.

Wilson, Herman Arthur. *A History of the Philadelphia Theatre, 1835–1855.* Diss. Philadelphia: University of Pennsylvania Press, 1935.

Wilson, James Grant. *The Life and Letters of Fitz-Greene Halleck.* New York: D. Appleton and Company, 1869.

Wilson, James Grant. *Thackeray in the United States, 1852–3, 1855–6. Including a Record of a Variety of Thackerayana . . . with Six Score Illustrations and a Bibliography.* London: Smith, Elder, & Co., 1904.

Wilstach, Paul. "Dramatisations of Dickens." *The Bookman* 14:1 (1901–2):52–62.

Wood, Alice I. Perry. *The Stage History of Shakespeare's King Richard the Third.* New York: The Columbia University Press, 1906.

Wood, James Playsted. *Magazines in the United States.* New York: The Ronald Press , 1971.

Wood, William B. *Personal Recollections of the Stage; Embracing Notices of Actors, Authors, and Auditors, During a Period of Forty Years.* Philadelphia: Henry Carey Baird, 1855.

Wright, Louis B. *Culture on the Moving Frontier.* Bloomington, Ind.: Indiana University Press, 1955.

Wynkoop, William M. *Three Children of the Universe: Emerson's View of Shakespeare, Bacon, and Milton.* The Hague: Mouton, 1966.

Young, William C. *Documents of American Theater History. Volume 1. Famous American Playhouses 1716–1899.* Chicago: American Literary Association, 1973.

Ziff, Larzer. *Literary Democracy: The Declaration of Cultural Independence in America.* New York: Viking Press, 1981.

Zimmerman, Lester Fred. "Some Aspects of Milton's American Reputation to 1900." Unpublished thesis. University of Wisconsin, 1949.

Index